CHINA

Regaining Growth Momentum
after the Pandemic

Other titles in the China Update Book Series include:

The titles are available online at press.anu.edu.au/publications/series/china-update

CHINA

Regaining Growth Momentum
after the Pandemic

Edited by Ligang Song
and Yixiao Zhou

Australian
National
University

ANU PRESS

社会科学文献出版社
SOCIAL SCIENCES ACADEMIC PRESS (CHINA)

Australian National University

ANU PRESS

Published by ANU Press
The Australian National University
Acton ACT 2601, Australia
Email: anupress@anu.edu.au

Available to download for free at press.anu.edu.au

A catalogue record for this book is available from the National Library of Australia

ISBN (print): 9781760466770
ISBN (online): 9781760466787

WorldCat (print): 1468527997
WorldCat (online): 1468541778

DOI: 10.22459/CRGMP.2024

Cover design and layout by ANU Press

Contents

List of contributors

Qiuhui Chen
Peking University

John Edwards
Lowy Institute

Fan Gang
National Economy Research Institute

Jane Golley
The Australian National University

Bert Hofman
National University of Singapore

Siying Jia
Peking University

Kaliappa Kalirajan
The Australian National University

Raghuvir Kelkar
National Tsinghua University

Sherry Tao Kong
Peking University

Aili Li
National Economy Research Institute

Tunye Qiu
The Australian National University

Chérie Simpson
The Australian National University

Yu Sheng
The Australian National University

Xinjie Shi
Zhejiang University

Ligang Song
The Australian National University

Ge Wang
Zhejiang University

Xiaolu Wang
National Economy Research Institute

Christine Wong
National University of Singapore

Xu Xiang
Peking University

Kunling Zhang
Beijing Normal University

Yixiao Zhou
The Australian National University

Acknowledgements

The China Economy Program (CEP) at the Crawford School of Public Policy, The Australian National University (ANU), acknowledges the financial support provided by BHP for the China Update 2023. We thank CEP Project Manager Timothy Cronin, from the Crawford School, for his program support. We sincerely thank our chapter authors for their valuable contributions. We would also like to thank colleagues from ANU Press, notably Nathan Hollier, Elouise Ball and Teresa Prowse, for their expeditious publication of this year's book. Our copyeditor, Jan Borrie, has consistently lent her professionalism and expertise to the China Update book series throughout the years, and her meticulous work is truly appreciated by the series' contributors. Mr Tunye Qiu from the Crawford School did an excellent job in handling the communications with authors during the revision stage. Thanks also go to our Crawford School colleagues, including Professor Janine O'Flynn, director of Crawford School, Professor Paul Burke, head of Arndt-Corden Department of Economics, for their support in participating in this year's update event. We thank Ms Yun Wei and Guanghan Wu from the Social Sciences Academic Press of the Chinese Academy of Social Sciences, in Beijing, for their long-term support in translating and publishing the Chinese version of the book each year—making this important research available to a wider readership.

Abbreviations

ADB	Asian Development Bank
AI	artificial intelligence
AIIB	Asian Infrastructure Investment Bank
ASEAN	Association of Southeast Asian Nations
BEICP	Business Environment Index for China's Provinces
BIS	Bank for International Settlements
BRCs	Belt and Road countries
BRI	Belt and Road Initiative
BRICS	Brazil, Russia, India, China and South Africa
CPC	Communist Party of China
CRNIP	China Rural Nutrition Improvement Program
DD	difference-in-differences
EVs	electric vehicles
FDI	foreign direct investment
FOCAC	Forum on China–Africa Cooperation
FTA	free-trade agreement
GDP	gross domestic product
GFB	government fund budget
GFC	Global Financial Crisis
GVC	global value chain
IBO	individual business owner
IMF	International Monetary Fund
IV	instrumental variable
LFP	labour force participation
LGFV	local government financing vehicle
MNC	multinational corporation
MOF	Ministry of Finance

MSEs	micro and small enterprises
NBS	National Bureau of Statistics
NDRC	National Development and Reform Commission
NERI	National Economic Research Institute
NPC	National People's Congress
NSOE	non-state-owned enterprise
OECD	Organisation for Economic Co-operation and Development
OLS	ordinary least squares
OSOME	Online Survey of Micro-and-Small Enterprises
R&D	research and development
RCEP	Regional Comprehensive Economic Partnership
RMB	renminbi
SCB	state capital budget
SEZ	special economic zone
SME	small and medium enterprise
SMIC	Semiconductor Manufacturing International Corporation
SOE	state-owned enterprise
SPB	special purpose bond
SSF	social security fund
STEM	science, technology, engineering and mathematics
TFP	total factor productivity
TSF	total social financing
TSMC	Taiwan Semiconductor Manufacturing Company
UIBO	unregistered individual business owner
UN	United Nations
US	United States
WTO	World Trade Organization

Figures and map

Tables

1

Growth momentum in China after the pandemic: Headwinds and policy levers

Ligang Song and Yixiao Zhou

Introduction

The growth performance of the Chinese economy since the early 1980s has been historically high, with an average annual growth rate of more than 9 per cent for more than three decades. No other large economies like China's have ever expanded continuously at such rates for so long. China's miraculous growth began with productive reforms in the rural sector in the 1980s and accelerated with reforms in urban areas, including, among others, ownership reform of state-owned enterprises (SOEs) and taxation and exchange rate and trade management system reforms in the early 1990s. This was accelerated in the early 2000s by China's accession to the World Trade Organization (WTO), after which goods made in China had more open access to global markets, paving the way for China to become the largest trading nation and a global factory of manufactured products.

China's domestic reforms go hand in hand with the opening of the economy, each reinforcing the other along the way. The deepening of its integration with the global economy has brought tremendous benefits to the Chinese economy, as evidenced by rapid growth in foreign direct investment (FDI), trade and flows of technology and knowledge. These linkages with the global economy facilitated China's unprecedented levels of rural–urban migration, enabling the labour force to move from low-productivity work in the rural sector to urban employment with significant efficiency gains at higher income levels.

Growth rates have steadily declined since 2011 as China reached a stage where economic rebalancing became necessary. The GDP growth rate was 10.2 per cent per annum in the first quarter of 2011, dropping consistently to 5.8 per cent in the fourth quarter of 2019, before the Covid-19 pandemic. After the easing of pandemic-induced quarantine policies in late 2022, there was a rebound in the second quarter of 2023, with a growth rate of 6.3 per cent. It then declined again, to 4.7 per cent in the second quarter of 2024, suggesting a resumption of the slowing trend of growth post pandemic (Figure 1.1).

As the world's second-largest economy, China has been a pivotal player on the global stage, contributing to about 30 per cent of global economic growth since the Global Financial Crisis (GFC). The year 2024 marks a challenging period as the nation grapples with a confluence of issues, including a slowdown in economic growth, a real estate market downturn, weak consumption, slowing growth in foreign trade, rising debt levels and an ageing population. The Chinese Government faces the daunting task of balancing economic reforms with the need to maintain social stability and sustain growth. At the same time, external factors such as the rising geopolitical tensions associated with economic, trade and technology decoupling, for example, and global economic uncertainties about supply-chain disruptions have further complicated the way China handles the challenges it faces in the aftermath of the pandemic.

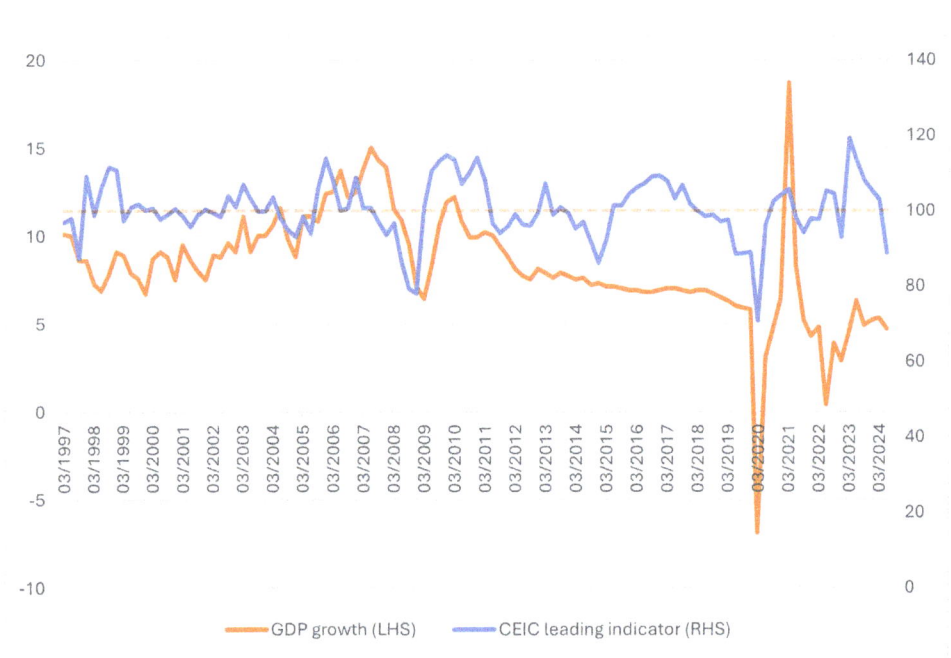

Figure 1.1 China's real GDP growth and predicted growth rate by the CEIC leading indicator

Source: CEIC Data (www.ceicdata.com/en).

The Covid-19 pandemic significantly impacted on the Chinese economy, affecting its GDP, employment, sectoral growth and exports. In 2020, China's GDP growth slowed markedly, registering a 2.2 per cent annual growth rate—the lowest in decades. The initial lockdowns caused a sharp contraction in the first quarter of that year, with GDP shrinking by 6.9 per cent. A strong recovery in the latter half of the year allowed China to be one of the few major economies to achieve positive growth by year's end. The pandemic also severely disrupted employment, particularly in sectors reliant on consumer interaction such as hospitality, retail and tourism. Millions of migrant workers were temporarily displaced due to the lockdowns and unemployment spiked early in 2020. The official unemployment rate peaked at 6.2 per cent in February 2020 but gradually declined as the economy reopened. Sectoral growth was uneven, with manufacturing industries showing resilience. China's industrial sector rebounded quickly, bolstered by global demand for medical supplies, electronics and machinery. In contrast, the services sector—particularly travel, entertainment and small business— suffered more enduring impacts, reflecting a slower recovery.

Exports initially faced disruptions due to factory shutdowns, supply-chain disruptions and reduced global demand. By mid-2020, China's exports surged as the country capitalised on its early recovery and the global demand for medical supplies, electronics and work-from-home equipment. By the end of 2020, China recorded a record trade surplus, with exports growing by 3.6 per cent.

Overall, the Covid-19 pandemic caused a short-term economic contraction in China, followed by a strong recovery driven by manufacturing and exports. However, vulnerabilities in employment and services were exposed, underscoring the uneven nature of the recovery. A subsequent downturn occurred post pandemic, partly due to shifts in consumption and saving behaviour and partly driven by challenges in businesses, especially small and medium enterprises (SMEs), and rising debt burdens, especially on the part of local governments. While this may reflect some lingering negative impacts from the pandemic, it also highlights economic structural problems that were present before the pandemic and that persist due to the unfinished tasks of reform.

In this overview, we will delve into the key macroeconomic headwinds affecting China's growth momentum in 2024 and beyond as well as accelerators that could boost that momentum, aiming to provide insights into the current and future trends in the Chinese economy.

Growth headwinds in perspective

The Chinese economy expanded 4.7 per cent in the second quarter of 2024, missing market forecasts of 5.1 per cent and slowing from 5.3 per cent growth in the first quarter of 2024. It was the weakest yearly advance since the first quarter of 2023. The China CEIC Leading Indicator, a key register of economic growth in China, suggests a possible further slowdown of the economy.[1] The latest CEIC Leading Indicator is 88.7, which is lower than the long-term average growth trend of 100, indicating a pessimistic economic growth outlook for the second half of 2024 (Figure 1.1).

This trend of weakening economic growth is also reflected in overall price levels, suggesting that the Chinese economy is facing a risk of deflation. Since October 2022, the producer price index has consistently recorded negative values, indicating weakness in investments by, and the expectations of, manufacturers. The consumer price index turned positive by a small margin in February 2024, but not enough to alleviate concerns about deflation. Deflation indicates excess supply with lack of motives for businesses to invest, which is consistent with the Purchasing Managers' Index struggling around the critical threshold of 50 since September 2022 (Figure 1.2).

The cause of deflation could be insufficient aggregate demand, which can be broken down into consumption, investment, government expenditure and net exports. By examining each component in detail, we can better understand the reasons for the observed deflationary pressure in the economy now.

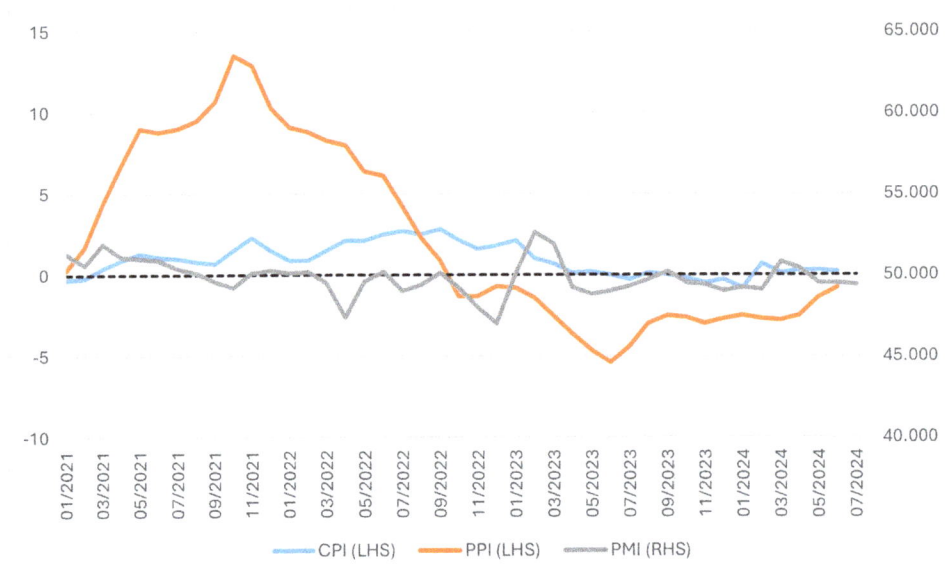

Figure 1.2 Consumer price index, producer price index and Purchasing Managers' Index for China

Source: CEIC Data (www.ceicdata.com/en).

---

1   The China CEIC Leading Indicator is a set of widely used economic leading indicators, including money supply, the Purchasing Managers' Index, foreign exchange rates, interest rates and China-specific indicators such as the floor space of commercial housing sold. The China CEIC Leading Indicator is a composite index designed to predict turning points in China's economic cycles. Historical data show that the CEIC Leading Indicator can successfully predict turning points in economic cycles two to three quarters in advance.

Demand side: Consumption

Before the pandemic, the growth rate of total retail sales of consumer goods, including catering, declined from about 20 per cent in February 2010 to 8–9 per cent in December 2019. This statistic fluctuated during the pandemic, but a significant rebound occurred after the end of quarantine policies. In April 2023, the overall total retail sales of consumer goods increased by 18.4 per cent compared with the previous year, with catering showing a 43.8 per cent increase. However, this recovery was short-lived, and the growth rate dropped to 2.5 per cent by July 2023. The highest growth rate subsequently was 10.1 per cent in November 2023, but it had fallen to just 2 per cent in June 2024. Meanwhile, catering has maintained relatively high growth, but the latest rate, of 5.4 per cent, is still much lower than pre-pandemic levels.

The flip side of consumption is saving; sluggish consumption growth implies that the extraordinary pattern of expenditure in GDP that sees half of all generated income saved and 45 per cent of it invested still prevails. Consumption has held steady, at just below 40 per cent, and the very large gaps that had developed between saving and investment before 2010, which saw the rapid build-up of foreign reserves during that period, have been mostly closed, leaving a modest current account surplus being accumulated in recent years. The period 2014–17 did see a decline in reserves as considerable private investment abroad was allowed, but this has subsequently slowed, leading to a period of relative financial closure and the return of reserve accumulation.

The tepid recovery in consumption post pandemic could be attributed to changes in household income and expectations, with two primary factors being the worsening employment environment and the real estate downturn due to the falling of so-called wealth effects.

In times of deflation, firms faced with weaker demand often attempt to reduce costs, with labour—as the most flexible variable cost in China—usually the first target. This dynamic is typically reflected in the youth unemployment rate, as it is easier to reduce new hiring than to dismiss existing employees. The youth unemployment rate, which includes individuals aged 16–24, fluctuated around 10 per cent from January 2018 to June 2019, and rose to 13.9 per cent in July 2019, coinciding with the traditional graduation month. However, the youth unemployment rate did not return to previous levels. In October 2019, when the lowest youth unemployment rates are typically expected after most graduates have secured jobs, the unemployment rate remained at 12.4 per cent, which was 2.6 percentage points higher than in October 2018. The youth unemployment rate has since increased annually, reaching a historical high of 21.3 per cent in June 2023. Subsequently, amid growing public concern, the National Bureau of Statistics of China suspended its publication of this index, resuming in December 2023 with a new statistical scope that excludes enrolled students who are actively seeking employment. Under the new standard, the youth unemployment rate dropped to 14.9 per cent in December, rose to 15.3 per cent in March 2024 and then decreased to 13.2 per cent in June 2024, but it remains much higher than the overall unemployment rate of 5 per cent (Figure 1.3).

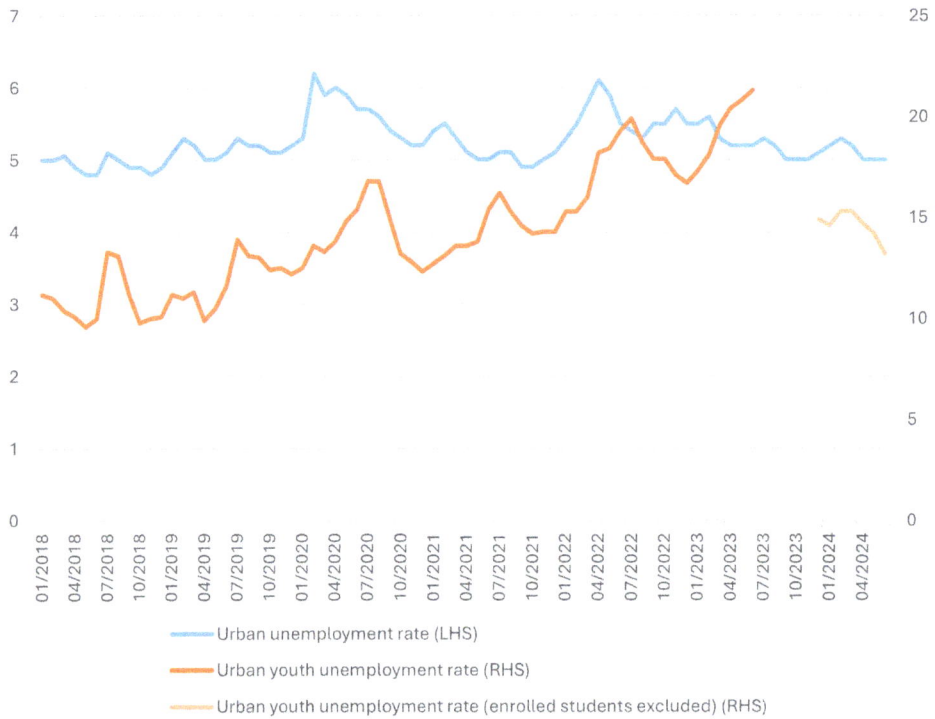

Figure 1.3 Unemployment rate (per cent)

Source: CEIC Data (www.ceicdata.com/en).

Another shift in the employment landscape is the change in employment structure. There has been a significant increase in insecure employment, notably among food delivery workers, couriers and ride-hailing drivers—often referred to in government reports as 'new employment formats'. The growth in new forms of employment may not be mainly driven by an increase in demand. Data from the ride-hailing market indicate that, while the number of ride-hailing drivers soared from 2.5 million in October 2020 to 7.1 million in June 2024—nearly a threefold increase—the number of delivery orders only rose from 630 million to 971 million. Consequently, the orders per driver plummeted from 248 per month to 136 per month. Therefore, it is likely that ride-hailing drivers, who typically own a car and belonged to at least the middle class before choosing this sort of work, have been pushed into these occupations by a weak job market to make ends meet.

The stagnation in aggregate consumption is partly attributable to the slowed growth in disposable income. From March 2014 to June 2024, the growth rate of median per capita disposable income in China showed a gradual decline. Beginning at 14 per cent in early 2014, the rate steadily decreased over the next three years, stabilising at 7–9 per cent by 2019. The onset of the Covid-19 pandemic in early 2020 led to a sharp contraction, with the growth rate turning negative in March of that year. Although a sharp recovery occurred in 2021, the declining trend resumed in subsequent years, reaching about 5.9 per cent by mid-2024. Compounding this issue, increasing income inequality could further diminish the consumption capacity of Chinese households. Data from 2013 to 2023 reveal a significant widening in the income gap between different quintiles in China, with all groups experiencing notable income growth, yet higher-income groups enjoying proportionately larger absolute gains. The lowest income quintile more than doubled from RMB4,402 to RMB9,215, while the highest quintile also doubled, from RMB47,456 to RMB95,055, effectively doubling the income disparity, from approximately RMB43,054 to RMB85,840. As lower-income families have a higher propensity to consume than higher-income families, the widening income gap is likely to be detrimental to stimulating aggregate consumption demand.

Meanwhile, China's social welfare system still plays a limited role in income redistribution. Despite notable increases over the years, social spending in China as a percentage of GDP remains significantly low compared with Organisation for Economic Co-operation and Development (OECD) countries. In 2022, China's public spending on social security and employment accounted for 16.5 per cent of its total public spending and 3.0 per cent of its GDP. This steady increase from 10.9 per cent of total public spending in 2007 and 2.0 per cent of GDP indicates a growing allocation towards social welfare as the economy grows. However, in 2022, the disparity in public social spending as a percentage of GDP between China and OECD countries was still pronounced. China allocated only 3.0 per cent of its GDP to public spending on social security and employment—substantially lower than the OECD average of 21.1 per cent. This significant difference underscores the varying fiscal priorities and extent of social welfare programs implemented by governments. The weak redistribution policies could further restrict the consumption potential of households.

The downturn in the real estate market significantly influences household income expectations, given its impact on their major financial assets. By 2015, housing assets accounted for 79 per cent of total household wealth in urban China, compared with just 27.8 per cent in the United States (Xie and Jin 2015). Consequently, a decrease in housing prices directly affects the wealth of many households. Data from CEIC reveal that September 2021 was the first time since 2015 that more than half of the 70 large cities in China saw a decrease in residential property prices. Following a brief recovery in 2023 post pandemic, this downward trend re-emerged after June 2023 and persisted until June 2024. The average housing prices in Tier 1, Tier 2 and Tier 3 cities all followed a similar declining trajectory from July 2023 through to June 2024 (Figure 1.4).

All the factors mentioned above contribute to a more conservative or precautionary spending strategy among consumers. The consumer confidence index dropped below 95 for the first time in April 2022, with its lowest and second-lowest records occurring in November 2022 and June 2024, respectively. Consequently, consumers' willingness to increase spending remains very low.

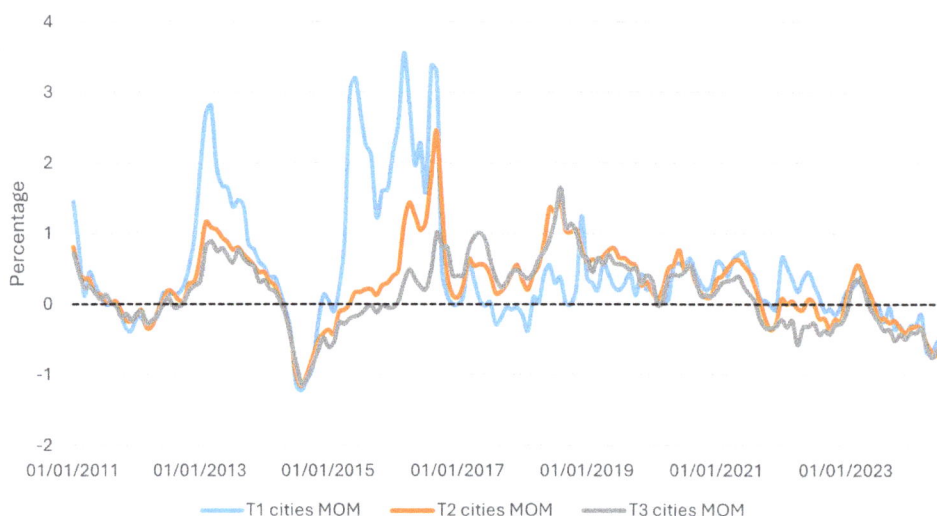

Figure 1.4 Residential property prices: Tier 1 versus Tier 2 versus Tier 3 cities (month-over-month growth rate)

Source: CEIC Data (www.ceicdata.com/en).

There is limited scope for boosting consumption through increased credit. China's household leverage ratio increased from 10.8 per cent in 2006 to 61.5 per cent in 2022. Among major economies with similar GDP per capita levels, this leverage ratio is higher than in Türkiye, Mexico, Brazil, Russia and India, and only about 5 per cent lower than in Malaysia. Therefore, the potential for further increases in the leverage ratio is constrained, suggesting a tight boundary for growth in consumer credit.

Demand side: Investment

In recent years, the composition of investment within China has undergone significant shifts. The total amount of fixed asset investment by private investors has decreased notably, dropping from RMB39.4 trillion in 2018 to RMB25.4 trillion in 2023. Concurrently, the share of private sector investment in total fixed asset investments has fallen from 61 per cent to 49.7 per cent, marking an 11.3 per cent decline over five years. This trend suggests that private sector investment is more susceptible to unfavourable economic conditions and could be particularly responsive to policy uncertainty. Compared with government and state-owned enterprises, the private sector is likely to be more sensitive to broader economic policies and changing market conditions. Addressing the challenge of boosting private sector investment becomes a crucial focus for policymakers aiming to enhance overall national investment levels as well as inject more dynamic forces into the economy.

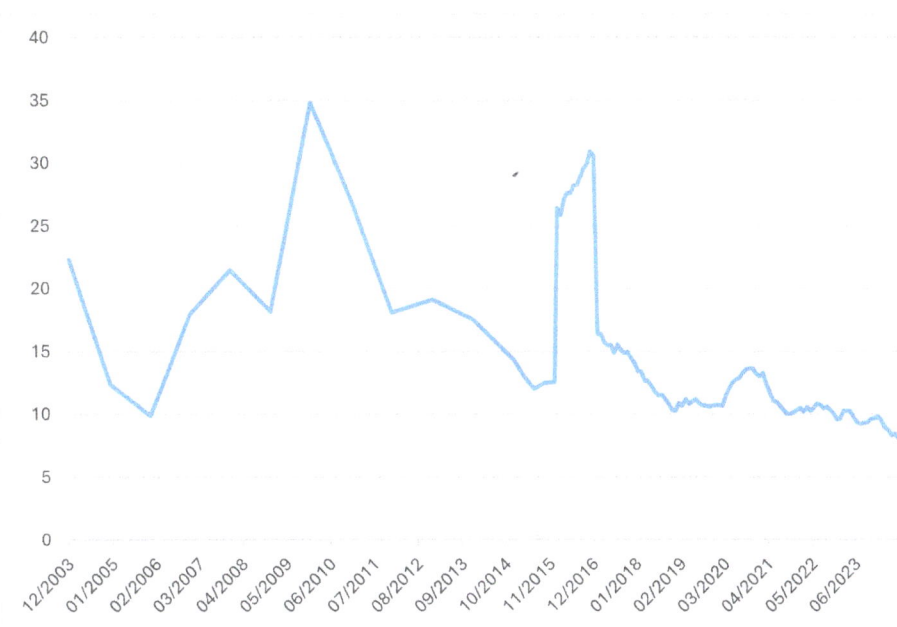

Figure 1.5 Growth rate of total social financing (year-on-year, per cent)
Source: CEIC Data (www.ceicdata.com/en).

While the growth of household consumption in China is decelerating, the growth of investment is also encountering difficulties, as evidenced by the trend in total social financing (TSF) (Figure 1.5). After robust initial growth in the early 2000s, TSF reached a peak in 2009 with a 34.8 per cent year-on-year increase. However, after 2009, the growth rates of TSF have notably moderated, with a significant decline starting in 2017. This downward trend persisted, culminating in a historical low of 8.1 per cent by June 2024.

The growth rate of medium to long-term loans has generally decreased over the years, indicating a reduced appetite for borrowing. Specifically, this rate declined to 9.2 per cent in June 2024, marking the first time it has been this low since March 2013 and highlighting a substantial slowdown in loan uptake.

However, the growth rates for savings accounts and term deposits—indicative of longer-term savings behaviour—have increased. This suggests a shift towards saving rather than spending or investing in more immediate or risky ventures. The growth rate for savings deposits has generally trended upwards, starting at 13 per cent in March 2019 and peaking at 17 per cent by December 2022, reflecting a tendency among consumers and businesses to increase their savings in response to economic uncertainty including low returns to capital investment, particularly during the pandemic. Similarly, the growth rate for term deposits initially rose to 9 per cent in March 2020, driven by a preference for securing funds in longer-term financial instruments during the initial economic shock of the pandemic. It experienced fluctuations in subsequent years, dipping to

9

3 per cent in March 2021 before rebounding to 14 per cent by September 2022, and adjusting again to 13 per cent by December 2023. Since the second quarter of 2022, the growth of savings account deposits has consistently exceeded the growth of medium to long-term loans, indicating a preference among consumers and businesses for saving over investing.

One possible cause for this is the rise in policy uncertainty. Since 2010, the policy uncertainty index in China has shown distinct periods of high volatility (Figure 1.6). The early part of the 2010s saw moderate levels of uncertainty, but this began to escalate significantly in 2015 and 2016, coinciding with domestic financial market fluctuations and regulatory changes. The index peaked sharply in 2016, suggesting a reaction to intense policy shifts and external economic pressures, including escalating trade tensions with some of China's major trading partners. This was followed by relatively elevated levels of uncertainty continuing through 2018 as China navigated its trade disputes and implemented more significant economic reforms and measures for economic opening. In 2019 and 2020, the index spiked again, notably influenced by the global impact of the pandemic and its ramifications on trade and economic policy. After 2020, the index showed signs of a gradual decrease, yet it continued to experience significant fluctuations into 2023, illustrating that policy uncertainty remains a prevalent and influential factor in China's economic environment.

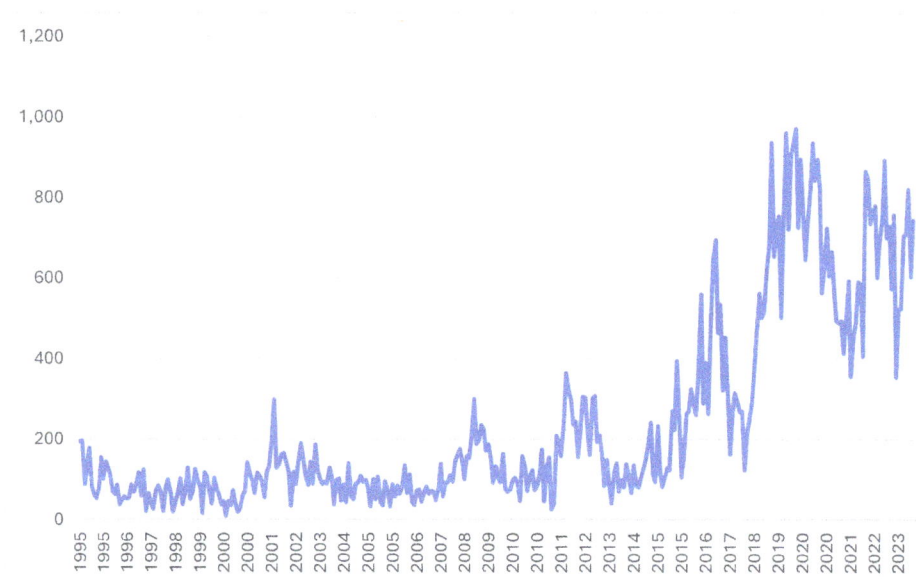

Figure 1.6 China news-based economic policy uncertainty
Source: Baker et al. (2013).

FDI in China has been consistently declining since the third quarter of 2022. Initially, the year-on-year growth rate for that quarter showed a decrease of 4 per cent. Subsequently, the rate of investment reduction slowed slightly to –2.5 per cent by the second quarter of 2023. However, the situation deteriorated further with a sharper decline of –6.5 per cent in the third quarter. Over the long run, the share of inward FDI in total investment in China has declined as well (Song and Zhou 2023).

Demand side: Government expenditure

While consumption and investment growth are slowing, the expansion in government expenses demonstrated notable fluctuations in year-on-year changes from February 2019 to June 2024. The period began with robust growth in early 2019, peaking at 15.2 per cent in April, before a decline leading to negative growth rates in 2020, bottoming out at –5.8 per cent in June. A recovery in 2021 saw a rebound to 10.5 per cent at the start of the year, tapering to lower single digits by year's end. Stable growth was maintained in 2022 and 2023, generally ranging between 5.9 per cent and 8.3 per cent. However, a downward trend emerged in 2024, starting at 6.7 per cent in February and falling to 2 per cent by June, reflecting a more restrained approach to government spending (Figure 1.7).

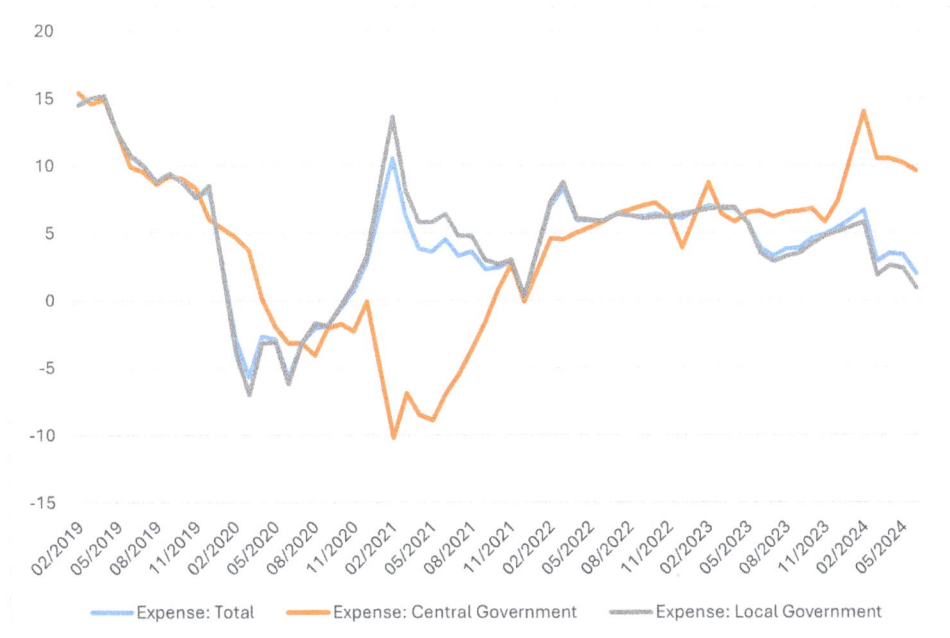

Figure 1.7 Change in government expenditure (year-on-year, per cent)

Source: CEIC Data (www.ceicdata.com/en).

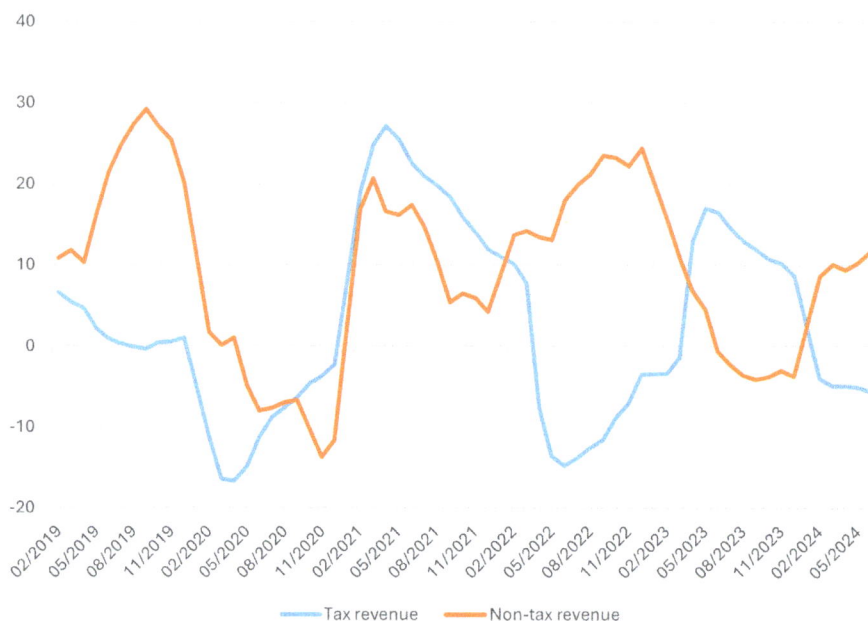

Figure 1.8 Change in fiscal revenue (per cent)
Source: CEIC Data (www.ceicdata.com/en).

This trend of stagnating fiscal expenditure is mainly seen in local governments, with a decrease from 8.8 per cent growth in March 2022 to just 0.9 per cent by June 2024, while central government expenses saw double-digit expansions from February to May 2024 compared with the previous year (Figure 1.7). This pattern aligns with the fiscal pressure from fluctuating tax revenues, which fell in 2020 and 2022, but showed rebounds in 2021 and 2023. The initial months of 2024 showed a decline in year-to-date tax income, yet during periods of reduced tax revenue, there was a significant rise in non-tax income in the form of fee collections from businesses—for example, in 2022 and 2024—suggesting attempts to find alternative revenue sources amid fixed expenses but putting more financial pressure on firms (Figure 1.8). Concurrently, government debt has been on the rise, with the debt-to-GDP ratio climbing from 53.9 per cent in the third quarter of 2017 to 83 per cent by the fourth quarter of 2023, which is 12.5 per cent lower than G20 economies but 13.5 per cent higher than in emerging market economies. The leverage ratio for the central government stood at 24.6 per cent, while for local governments it was 33.2 per cent, with the volume of outstanding local government bonds increasing from RMB34.5 trillion in July 2022 to RMB42.4 trillion in June 2024 (Figure 1.9).

An expansionary fiscal policy could potentially alleviate the stagnation of aggregate demand; however, such measures may be constrained by existing fiscal revenues and the current levels of government debt in consideration of long-term fiscal sustainability. Nevertheless, the central government retains the capacity to boost spending further to stimulate demand because of the higher revenue shares and lower shares of total expenditure compared with local governments.

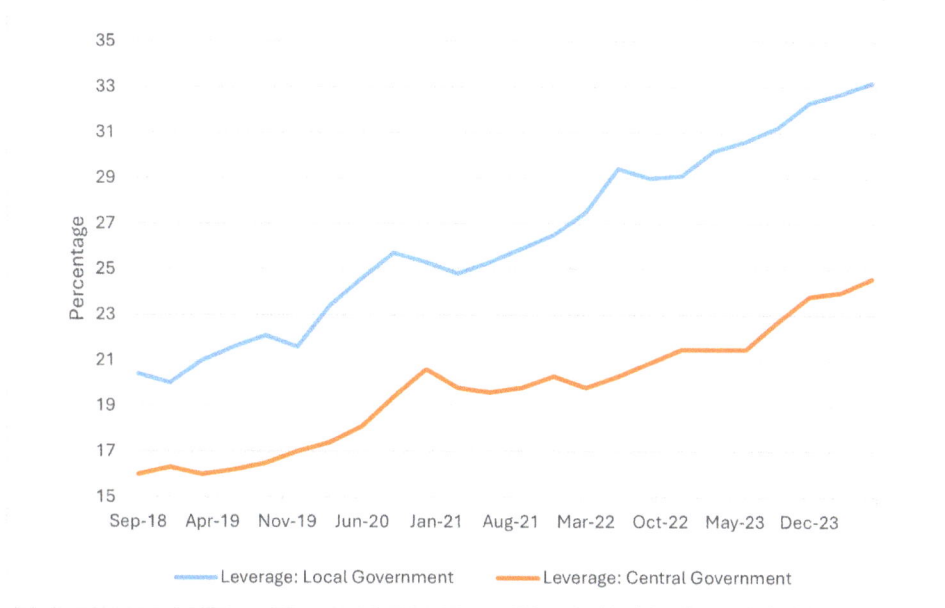

Figure 1.9 Government leverage: Local and central
Source: CEIC Data (www.ceicdata.com/en).

Demand side: Net exports

Historically, net exports have contributed significantly to economic growth in China, but their continued expansion is threatened by the trend of deglobalisation as well as rising geopolitical tensions. Since 2018, fluctuations have been notable in China's current account surplus. It started with a slight deficit of –US$2.64 billion in June 2018 but shifted to a surplus by September of the same year. Surplus levels have seen substantial variability, peaking impressively in September 2022 at almost US$151.48 billion. Following this peak, the surplus experienced a decline throughout 2023, reaching US$39.21 billion by March 2024. This trend points to a reducing surplus, influenced by changes in trade balances, economic policies or international economic pressures for rebalancing (Figure 1.10).

In 2023, exports to China's major trading partners, the United States and the European Union, saw notable reductions compared with the previous year. The value of exports to the United States fell from US$581 billion to US$506 billion, while that of exports to the European Union decreased from US$561 billion to US$504 billion. Similar reductions were observed with Japan and South Korea, the third and fourth-largest export destinations, respectively, to which combined exports diminished by US$29 billion. Although there was a US$35 billion increase in exports to Russia, it did not offset the losses experienced with other major trading partners. This downward trend persisted into 2024 and, by July, exports to the United States, the European Union, Japan and South Korea registered year-on-year changes of –1.84 per cent (Figure 1.11).

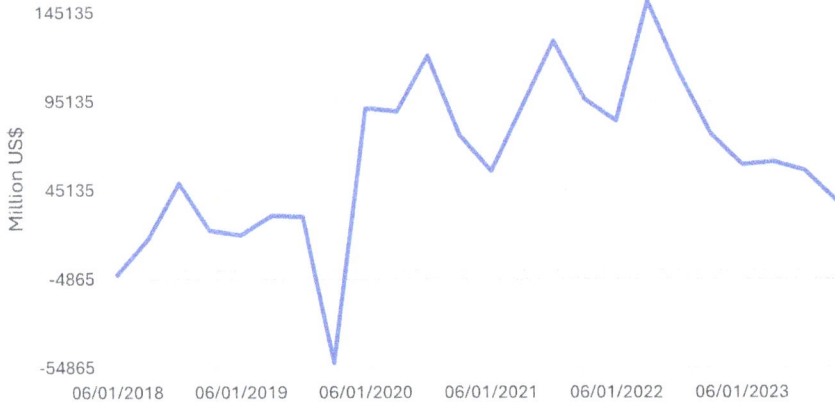

Figure 1.10 China's current account surpluses
Source: CEIC Data (www.ceicdata.com/en).

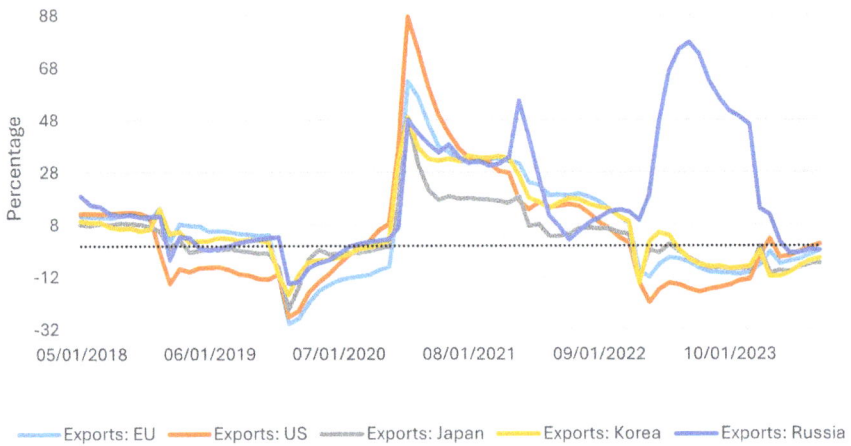

Figure 1.11 Change in exports, by country
Source: CEIC Data (www.ceicdata.com/en).

Supply-side factors

On the supply side, two main headwinds are demographic contraction (Figure 1.12) and slowing productivity growth, which together tend to lower China's potential growth rates.

In the past decade, China's demographic contraction has begun to bite (Figure 1.13a), which saw both unskilled and skilled workers become more costly. This has led to a redirection of much of China's new investment in automated technologies, with the consequence that the scarcity of skilled workers is enhanced and the level of inequality between ordinary workers' households and those with skill and capital is rising considerably. The pandemic and the policies established to control it have further restricted access to work. Considerable uncertainty has therefore hung over China's emergence from the pandemic, contributing to a stuttering recovery and declining investment returns (Figure 1.13b).

As Figure 1.14 shows, since 2010, while the trends in measured total factor productivity (TFP) in the United States, Japan and Australia have been roughly static, that in China has been downward. It is possible, of course, that this is due to the comparatively rapid expansion of China's services industries, where productivity is difficult to observe. There is no doubt that the comparative growth of sophisticated service supply is increasing quite rapidly in China (Tyers and Zhou 2024a).

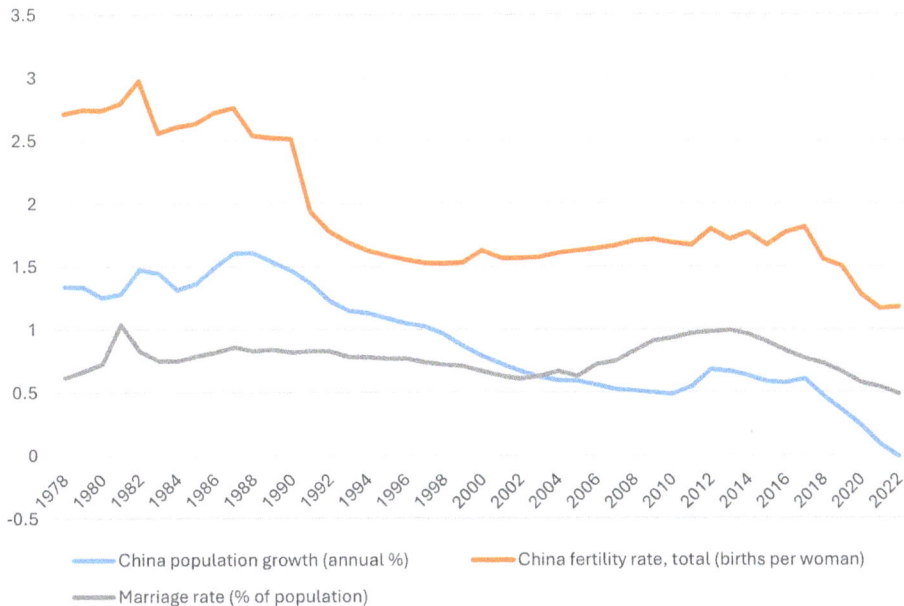

Figure 1.12 China's demographic tendency

Sources: World Bank; CEIC Data (www.ceicdata.com/en).

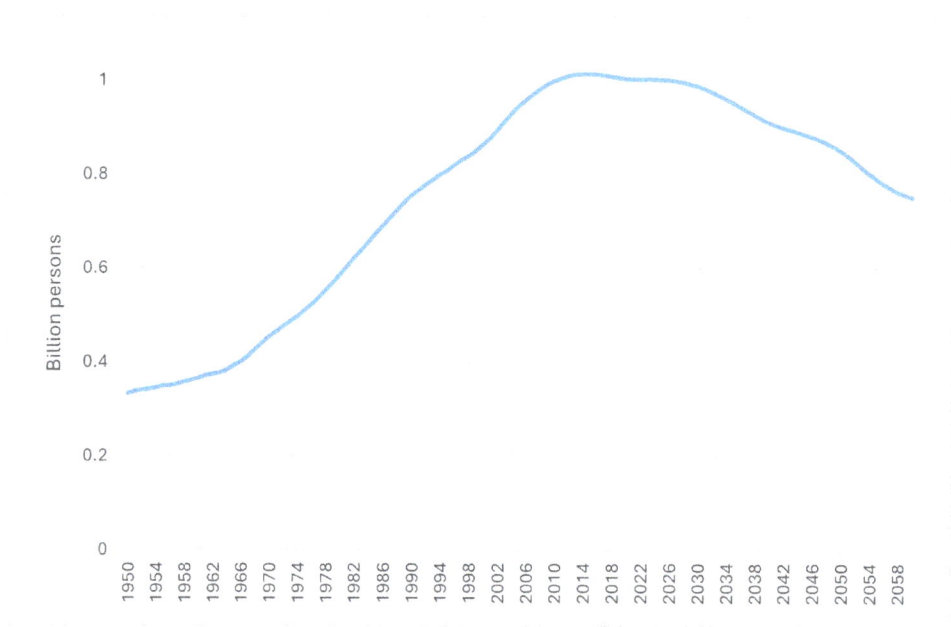

Figure 1.13a Working-age (15–65 years) population (billion persons)

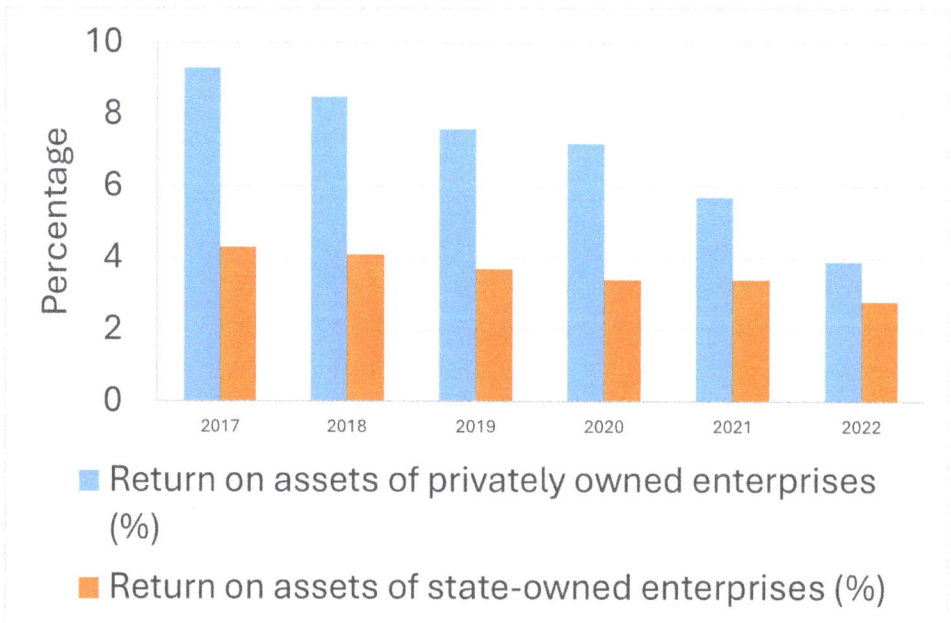

■ Return on assets of privately owned enterprises (%)

■ Return on assets of state-owned enterprises (%)

Figure 1.13b Return on assets in China, 2017–22

Sources: Data for the historical and projected working-age population (15–65 years) are obtained from OECD.Stat (www.oecd-ilibrary.org/economics/data/oecd-stat_data-00285-en). Returns on assets of SOEs and privately owned enterprises are obtained from Bruegel Datasets (www.bruegel.org/datasets).

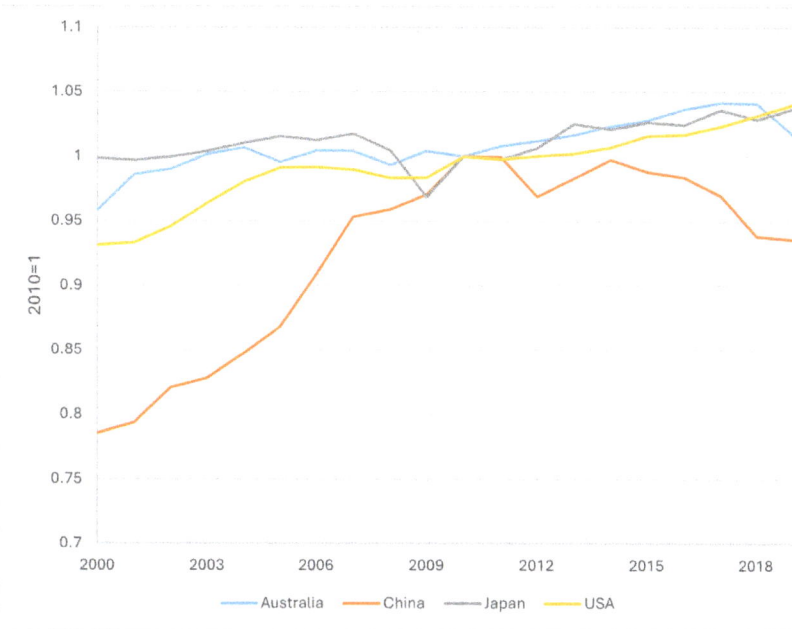

Figure 1.14 Total factor productivity of major economies

Note: The TFP values of each economy in 2010 are normalised to be 1.
Source: Authors' calculations based on data from Penn World Tables (www.rug.nl/ggdc/productivity/pwt/?lang=en).

China has the fastest rate of robot adoption in the world (Figure 1.15). This is a beneficial shock to the economy in that the marginal product of capital is increased, raising investment and capital income, notwithstanding losses accruing to low-skilled workers replaced with robots (Zhou 2020; Zhou and Tyers 2019). This trend will continue.

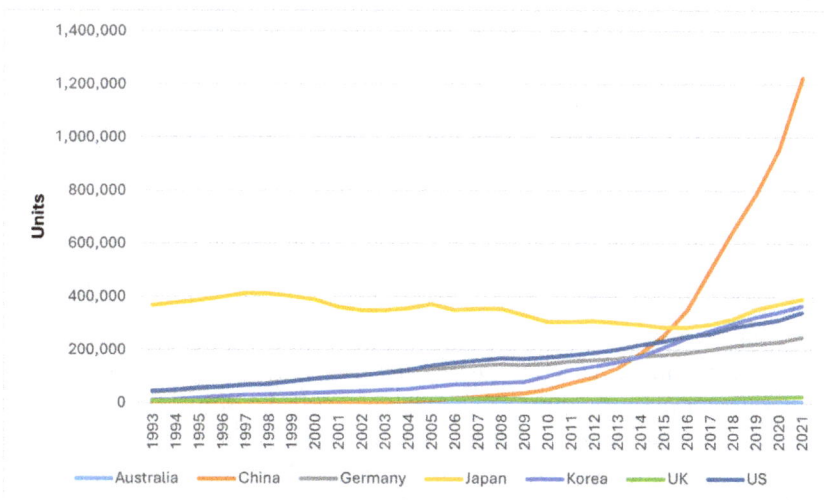

Figure 1.15 Robot stock in major economies

Source: International Federation of Robotics (ifr.org/).

Policy levers to accelerate economic growth

Against the above headwinds, there are areas of policymaking that could potentially boost the momentum of economic growth.

The first is to strengthen openness and integration with global markets (Song and Zhou 2020). Though it was widely predicted that economic globalisation—said to be already under strain—would be badly wounded by the pandemic, it survived robustly. China for a while stopped exports of surgical masks, Europe and the United States (and Australia) checked their exports of respirators and critical attention was suddenly focused on global supply chains in drug production. International travel collapsed, as did international trade. But as the pandemic eased, global trade in goods and services, global cross-border investment and global migration rebounded rapidly.

Despite the impact of the pandemic, China remains the leading trading partner of many countries. China is Australia's largest two-way trading partner, accounting for just over one-quarter (27 per cent) of Australian trade with the world. The share of Australian trade with China in Australia's global trade grew from 2.1 per cent in the second quarter of 1993 to a peak of 36.6 per cent in the fourth quarter of 2021, and then dropped to 26.4 per cent in the third quarter of 2022. During the Covid-19 pandemic, two-way trade with China grew 6.3 per cent, in 2020–21, totalling $267 billion, while Australia's global two-way trade declined 5.0 per cent during this period. In 2022, 7.5 per cent of total US exports to the world, worth US$2.1 trillion, went to China, while 16.5 per cent of total US imports, worth US$3.2 trillion, were from China. Although China was the largest source of imports to the United States in 2022, Canada and Mexico were the United States' largest two-way trading partners. In 2022, total US–China trade was worth US$691 billion, total US–Canada trade was worth US$794 billion and total US–Mexico trade was worth US$779 billion. China is now Japan's biggest two-way trade partner (23 per cent), while Japan is China's fourth-largest two-way trade partner. In 2021, bilateral trade between China and Japan rose 17.1 per cent on a yearly basis to US$371 billion—a new high. China was the European Union's second-largest trading partner in 2022 behind the United States, with total imports and exports reaching €856.3 billion, according to data from Eurostat. This accounts for 15.3 per cent of the European Union's total trade that year.

China's evolving economic conditions, including population ageing and rising labour costs, are changing its comparative advantage in trade activities. While low-end manufacturing industries may move out, higher value-added industries with longer supply chains will remain in China, benefiting from its comprehensive manufacturing system, the availability of skilled labour, well-developed infrastructure, improved business environment and supportive government services (Song and Zhou 2023). These favourable factors continue to attract foreign investment despite the ongoing challenges from rising geopolitical tensions. While the industries that have traditionally driven China's growth continue to subside proportionally, those supplying sophisticated products, such as 5G communications, electric vehicles and other green technologies such as solar panels and wind turbines, are surging. This momentum offers hope for a restoration of economy-wide productivity growth (Tyers and Zhou 2024b).

China must continue to invest in research and development activities and in human capital to enhance productivity growth (Zhou and Dahal 2024). Innovation and technological breakthroughs have the potential to significantly boost productivity through creative destruction and resource reallocation towards more efficient industries and firms. The subsequent productivity growth would be the key to sustain long-term global growth and raise living standards. The Chinese Government emphasised the importance of new technologies and high-quality labour at the Third Plenum of the Chinese Communist Party's Central Committee in 2024. The 'new quality productive forces' were one of the central growth engines identified at the plenum.

China must also enhance entrepreneurship and boost business confidence, which is much lacking. The best way of doing this is to create a more conducive business environment in which private businesses flourish through policy and institutional changes. Nurturing the spirit of entrepreneurship will play a key role in enhancing efforts to build an integrated domestic market, improving economy-wide resource allocation and changing business models for more sustainable growth and development. While being profit driven, private entrepreneurs must be conscious of both environmental imperatives and social standards in their operations, to reflect what is expected of modern entrepreneurship (Satyadini and Song 2023).

China's social security safety net must be strengthened so households will be more willing to consume and undertake risky investments in innovative activities. During the pandemic, the employment and earnings of youth, women and relatively lower-skilled workers were affected disproportionately. Therefore, spending on social programs could help limit the negative income impacts of the pandemic and lead to faster economic recovery. It should be recognised that the rise in government deficits and debt could constrain the resources available to government to fund social programs and policies.

As policymakers around the world try to identify ways to achieve sustainable post-pandemic growth, countries share common challenges that include income inequality arising from technological change, high government debt levels, risks from climate change and risks to energy and food security. China's efforts to achieve strong economic recovery post pandemic will be crucial for meeting these global challenges as well as achieving its goals of economic growth in the next phase of development.

Structure of the book

Chapter 2, titled 'China's Economy after Covid-19', by Bert Hofman provides a detailed analysis of China's economic trajectory following its exit from the zero-Covid policy. In 2023, China's growth, while recovering, was marked by a shift from property investment to manufacturing and state-driven sectors. Despite a rebound in consumption, it remains a small share of GDP due to high household savings and retained corporate earnings. The economic challenges in the second quarter of 2023 led to debates about whether China was facing a cyclical downturn or a structural slowdown. However, the third and fourth quarters saw improved growth, with GDP rising by 5.2 per cent in 2023, meeting government targets.

Key concerns include low private sector confidence, a struggling property market and foreign investor apprehension about new regulatory environments. The chapter also discusses policy measures to stimulate growth, including fiscal reforms and initiatives to re-engage the private sector. The pivot to manufacturing and the emphasis on high-quality growth, driven by innovation and emerging industries, are central to China's strategy. Looking forward, the chapter suggests that China should implement comprehensive reforms to sustain growth, including in fiscal policy, the financial sector and social safety nets.

Raghuvir Kelkar and Kaliappa Kalirajan's Chapter 3, 'Potential Efficiency in Economic Growth: A Cross-Province Perspective', examines the disparities in economic growth efficiency between China's provinces. The study focuses on the period from 2000 to 2020 and uses a stochastic frontier growth model to assess whether the central and western provinces have maximised their economic growth potential.

The authors highlight the fact that, while China's eastern provinces have experienced rapid economic development, the central and western regions have lagged. Despite initiatives like the 'Rise of Central China' and investments in renewable energy in the west, these regions have not achieved full economic efficiency. The study finds that the central provinces show the highest efficiency in economic growth, though it is still below 100 per cent. The eastern provinces, though more developed, have not fully realised their growth potential, while the western provinces exhibit the most significant gap between real and potential GDP.

The chapter concludes that, to achieve more balanced and sustainable growth, China must enhance skilled education, attract more FDI and improve infrastructure in the less-developed regions. By addressing these factors, the central and western provinces could improve their growth efficiency, contributing to more equitable economic development across the country.

Chapter 4, 'The State of Public Finance in China: Why Tax and Intergovernmental Reform Are Urgently Needed', by Christine Wong provides a critical analysis of China's current fiscal challenges. It highlights the pressing need for tax and intergovernmental reforms to address a variety of macroeconomic pressures, including managing financial risks from local government debt, dealing with an ageing population and reinvigorating economic growth after the Covid-19 pandemic.

Wong explains the complexities of China's fiscal system, which comprises four separate budgets: the general budget, the government fund budget, the state capital operating budget and the social security funds budget. These budgets interact in ways that obscure the true extent of China's fiscal deficits, which are significantly larger than the official headline figures suggest.

The chapter argues that the erosion of tax revenues, exacerbated by the economic slowdown and cuts in tax collection, has led to increasing fiscal deficits, especially at the local government level. The reliance on land revenues, which have recently declined, has further strained local government finances. Additionally, the build-up of debt, both explicit and hidden, has reached concerning levels, particularly at the local level, where fiscal consolidation is difficult due to limited revenue-raising powers.

Wong concludes that, without significant reforms, China's fiscal sustainability is at risk, which could hinder its economic growth and progress towards achieving high-income status and common prosperity.

In Chapter 5, 'Adaptive Efficiency, Institutional Change and Economic Performance: Evidence from the Chinese Economy', Chérie Simpson, Ligang Song and Yixiao Zhou provide a comprehensive examination of how adaptive efficiency contributes to economic growth, particularly in the context of China's economic transformation. The chapter introduces the adaptive efficiency framework, which integrates concepts from various economic theories to explain how institutions, market functions and innovation interact to drive long-term economic growth.

The authors apply this framework to analyse the economic growth of Chinese provinces, using an endogenous growth model that places institutions at the centre of the analysis. Their empirical study reveals that adaptive efficiency—characterised by institutional change and the creative, discovery and allocative functions of the market—positively impacts long-term economic growth. However, they also find significant regional disparities, with the eastern provinces benefiting more from these factors than the central and western regions.

The chapter highlights the importance of continuous institutional reform and decentralisation to maintain China's growth momentum, suggesting that regions lagging in development require targeted policies to enhance their adaptive efficiency. The findings underscore the need for context-specific public policy that considers regional differences to ensure balanced and sustainable economic progress across China.

Xiaolu Wang, Fan Gang and Aili Li in Chapter 6, 'Business Environment Index for China's Provinces: A Brief Version of the 2023 Report', present a summary of the 2023 Business Environment Index for China's Provinces (BEICP), which evaluates and compares the business environment across China's 31 provinces. The report is based on surveys conducted with 2,295 enterprises (primarily private) and assesses various factors affecting business operations.

The BEICP includes an overall index synthesised from eight aspect indices, which cover policy transparency, administrative efficiency, the legal environment, the tax burden, financial services, human resources, infrastructure and market conditions. The chapter highlights the fact that, while there has been general improvement in the business environment from 2006 to 2022, recent years have seen stagnation or a decline in several provinces, particularly in the western and north-eastern regions.

The chapter details the disparities in the business environment between SOEs and non-SOEs (NSOEs), with the latter consistently rating their environments lower, particularly in areas like policy transparency and financial services. The report also notes the challenges faced by small and micro-enterprises, which experience a poorer business environment compared with larger enterprises.

The chapter concludes with a call for reforms to create a more equitable business environment, particularly by addressing the challenges faced by NSOEs and smaller enterprises, to sustain economic growth across China.

Chapter 7, titled 'Vulnerability and Resilience: Understanding China's Flexible Employment through the Lens of Unregistered Individual Business Owners', by Xu Xiang, Sherry Tao Kong and Qiuhui Chen delves into the dynamics of flexible employment in China, focusing on unregistered individual business owners (UIBOs). The chapter begins by discussing the rise of flexible employment driven by structural changes and technological advancements and its increasing importance in China's labour market. Flexible employment—often informal and including UIBOs—has become a significant part of the workforce, especially during and after the Covid-19 pandemic.

Using data from the Online Survey of Micro-and-Small Enterprises (OSOME), the authors explore the characteristics, challenges and resilience of UIBOs compared with their registered counterparts. UIBOs tend to have fewer employees, lower formal business engagements and greater reliance on online platforms. They are more vulnerable to market demand fluctuations and cost pressures, with higher rates of business closure during economic downturns.

The findings in the chapter suggest that, to support UIBOs and enhance their resilience, the Chinese Government must improve the regulatory framework, provide better access to social security and promote digital transformation. This would help mitigate the vulnerabilities of UIBOs and ensure a more inclusive and resilient labour market.

Tunye Qiu's Chapter 8, 'The Trend in China's Urban Housing Affordability and Its Impact on the Total Fertility Rate', investigates the relationship between housing affordability and fertility rates in China's urban areas. The study utilises a housing affordability index based on the residual income approach and equal repayment equation, covering 70 large and medium-sized cities from 2010 to 2019. This index provides a more nuanced measure of affordability than the conventional price-to-income ratio, as it accounts for disposable income, consumption expenditure and lending rates.

The findings reveal an inverted U-shaped trend in housing affordability: it increased from 2010 to 2014, peaked in 2015–16 and then declined. The study highlights the fact that, while the superstar cities (Beijing, Shanghai, Guangzhou and Shenzhen) consistently face low affordability, other cities such as Xiamen, Tianjin and Zhuhai have also experienced significant affordability issues in recent years.

Importantly, the chapter establishes a causal relationship between housing affordability and the total fertility rate, finding that a 10 per cent increase in the affordable housing area leads to a 4.58 per cent increase in fertility. This suggests that improving housing affordability could be a key policy lever to counteract China's declining fertility rates, complementing the Three-Child Policy introduced in 2021.

In Chapter 9, 'Chinese Women in the Workforce and Free School Lunches: A "Small" Program with Big Implications', Ge Wang, Xinjie Shi and Jane Golley examine the impact of the China Rural Nutrition Improvement Program (CRNIP) on the labour force participation (LFP) of rural Chinese mothers. The CRNIP, which provides free lunches to students in impoverished counties, was found to significantly increase maternal LFP, by 4.25 percentage points. The program reduces the time mothers, particularly less-educated women, spend on child care by approximately 2.5 hours daily, enabling them to engage more in off-farm and informal work.

The study utilises a difference-in-differences approach, drawing on data from the 2010 and 2015 Chinese population censuses. The authors highlight the fact that, while the provision of free lunches does not eliminate the need for child care entirely, it significantly alleviates the time constraints faced by rural mothers, offering them greater flexibility to participate in the workforce. The chapter concludes that expanding access to similar childcare services, such as preschool and after-school care, could have substantial effects on women's LFP, contributing to addressing China's declining and ageing population.

Chapter 10, titled 'Chips, Subsidies and Commercial Competition between the United States and China', by John Edwards explores the strategic and economic implications of the ongoing semiconductor competition between the United States and China. In October 2022, the United States imposed a ban on the export of advanced semiconductors to China, aiming to curb China's progress in artificial intelligence (AI) and other advanced technologies. This move has significant consequences: if it is successful, China could fall behind in key areas like AI, manufacturing and military applications. Conversely, if China overcomes these restrictions, it could accelerate its development of an independent semiconductor industry, intensifying global competition.

The chapter highlights how this competition is emblematic of broader shifts in global trade policy, where industrial subsidies and national security considerations increasingly overlap. The US strategy combines subsidies for domestic chip production with efforts to prevent China from acquiring advanced semiconductor technologies. However, China's resilience and technological advancements suggest that the United States could struggle to maintain its lead. The chapter also discusses the broader implications for global trade norms, as the focus shifts from traditional trade agreements to state-supported technological competition, raising concerns about the marginalisation of international trade institutions like the WTO.

Kunling Zhang's Chapter 11, 'A Policy Analysis of the Belt and Road Initiative', provides a comprehensive evaluation of the Belt and Road Initiative (BRI) as it marks its tenth anniversary. The BRI, launched in 2013, aims to enhance global connectivity, promote economic cooperation and foster shared prosperity among participating countries. The chapter examines the initiative's policy framework, which includes the objectives, instruments and conditions necessary for its implementation.

Zhang utilises a three-dimensional policy analysis framework to dissect key BRI policy documents and speeches. The analysis reveals that the BRI's objectives have evolved from maintaining a global free-trade system to a more ambitious goal of promoting global modernisation and building a community with a shared future for humankind. The policy instruments, centred on the 'five connectivities' (policy coordination, infrastructure connectivity, unimpeded trade, financial integration and people-to-people ties), have remained stable but have been refined to address emerging challenges such as green development and digital innovation.

The chapter also discusses the challenges facing the BRI, including geopolitical tensions, criticisms of the initiative's impact on debt and governance and the need for China to refine its internal mechanisms to support the initiative's sustainable development. The analysis concludes that, while the BRI policy system is relatively complete, future success will depend on enhancing market mechanisms and deepening international cooperation.

Chapter 12, 'Analysing the Impact of China–Africa Agricultural Trade on Rural Transformation in Africa: An Application of the Gravity Model', by Siying Jia and Yu Sheng investigates the relationship between China–Africa agricultural trade and rural transformation in Africa. Using a gravity model, the study analyses data from 41 African countries over the period 1992–2021, focusing on the impact of Chinese demand, African production capacity and bilateral trade policies on agricultural exports and their value-added components.

The chapter highlights the fact that, while Chinese demand has significantly boosted the volume of agricultural exports from Africa, it has not correspondingly increased the value-added component of these exports. The analysis reveals that African production capacity positively influences both the gross value and the value-added proportion of exports. However, increasing Chinese demand appears to have a negative impact on value-added growth, leading to a puzzling situation in which higher exports do not translate into greater economic benefits for African countries.

The authors decompose the impact into two effects: composition and upgrading. The results show that Chinese demand tends to favour high-value products, causing a positive composition effect, but this is offset by a negative upgrading effect due to constraints in African production capacity. The study suggests that enhancing African production capacity could better align with Chinese demand, leading to more beneficial outcomes for rural transformation in Africa.

References

Baker, Scott, Nick Bloom, Steven J. Davis, and Sophie Wang. 2013. 'Economic Policy Uncertainty in China.' Unpublished working paper, January. static1.squarespace.com/static/5e2ea3a8097ed30c779bd707/t/5e3059cde0d1180621cc26b5/1580227022322/Economic+Policy+Uncertainty+in+China%2C+January+2013.pdf.

Satyadini, A., and L. Song. 2023. 'Modern Entrepreneurship and the "Doughnut": Productive or Destructive?' *Asia Pacific Economic Literature* 37, no. 2: 119–41. doi.org/10.1111/apel.12396.

Song, L., and Y. Zhou. 2020. 'The COVID-19 Pandemic and Its Impact on the Global Economy: What Does It Take to Turn Crisis into Opportunity?' *China & World Economy* 28, no. 4: 1–25. doi.org/10.1111/cwe.12349.

Song, L., and Y. Zhou. 2023. 'China Is Invaluable to Global Value Chains.' *East Asia Forum*, 24 July. eastasiaforum.org/2023/07/24/china-is-invaluable-to-global-value-chains/.

Tyers, R., and Y. Zhou. 2024a. 'A Bamboo Curtain: The Grim Australian Consequences of China Conflict.' *The Australian Economic Review* 57, no. 1: 41–60. doi.org/10.1111/1467-8462.12535.

Tyers, R., and Y. Zhou. 2024b. 'China Slowdown Shocks, the West and Australia.' *Economic Papers* 43, no. 3: 205–35. doi.org/10.1111/1759-3441.12424.

Xie, Y., and Y. Jin. 2015. 'Household Wealth in China.' *China Sociological Review* 47, no. 3: 203–29. doi.org/10.1080/21620555.2015.1032158.

Zhou, Y. 2020. 'Automation, the Future of Work and Income Inequality in the Asia-Pacific.' In *Achieving Inclusive Growth in the Asia Pacific*, edited by A. Triggs and S. Urata, 103–49. Canberra: ANU Press. doi.org/10.22459/AIGAP.2020.06.

Zhou, Y., and S. Dahal. 2024. 'Has R&D Contributed to Productivity Growth in China? The Role of Basic, Applied and Experimental R&D.' *China Economic Review* 88 (December): 102281. doi.org/10.1016/j.chieco.2024.102281.

Zhou, Y., and R. Tyers. 2019. 'Automation and Inequality in China.' *China Economic Review* 58 (December): 101202. doi.org/10.1016/j.chieco.2018.07.008.

2

China's economy after Covid-19

Bert Hofman

Introduction

After a challenging exit from its zero-Covid policy, China's growth regained momentum in 2023, and calls of 'peak China' seem premature. China's growth is now driven less by property, as investments have shifted to industry and manufacturing. Consumption has rebounded from its lows during the Covid-19 pandemic but, as a share of GDP, remains exceptionally low in international comparison, mainly because of high household savings and high retained earnings of corporations. Higher manufacturing investment and moderate domestic demand are leading to higher trade surpluses, particularly in manufacturing, which in today's climate could lead to further trade tensions. To achieve more sustainable growth, China's policy agenda should focus on cleaning up the fallout of the real estate bust and strengthening domestic demand.

Concerns about growth momentum

The Chinese economy's first year after the Covid-19 pandemic was anything but smooth riding. The disappointing economic numbers of the second quarter of 2023 triggered a widespread debate about the country's economic future. While GDP growth came in at a respectable 3.2 per cent annualised growth rate, for some analysts, lacklustre private investment in the property sector, faltering exports and declining prices were signs that China's economic model was running out of steam. 'The end of China's miracle' (Posen 2023), 'a lost decade' (Economist 2023), 'Japanification' (Wigglesworth 2023) and a 'balance sheet recession' (Koo 2023) were some of the terms used for the country's current predicament.

In contrast, some domestic observers argued that this was a necessary side effect of China's transition to President Xi Jinping's New Development Concept, in which growth would be driven by innovation, productivity and output in emerging sectors such as new energy and electric vehicles (Global Times 2023). Others noted that China's economy was doing much better than those of some advanced economies and saw a conspiracy in the negative reporting rather than problems in China's economy (Ross 2023). Some Chinese economists, though, argued that the overall trend is negative and China must take steps to address it (Wen 2023).

The improved economic numbers for the third and fourth quarters muted the 'peak China' debate in recent months. GDP growth rebounded 5.2 per cent for 2023, easily meeting the indicative growth target of 'about 5 per cent' (Table 2.1) and 2 percentage points higher than the 2022 outcome. Consumption growth contributed most to the outcome, especially through a rebound in services demand after a year of pandemic lockdowns (Figure 2.1). Investment in 2023 was still dragged down by the continuing property slump. Investment in real estate development fell by almost 10 per cent year-on-year, but investment in infrastructure (5.9 per cent growth) and manufacturing (6.5 per cent) was relatively strong. And whereas private investment overall was down by 0.4 per cent, excluding real estate, it grew by more than 9 per cent. The government supported growth by issuing an additional RMB1.5 trillion in special treasury bonds, which was announced on 25 October 2023. Local governments were also allowed to issue bonds up to an additional RMB2 trillion from their 2024 quota. This came on top of the RMB1.7 trillion of fiscal measures that were announced in August 2023.

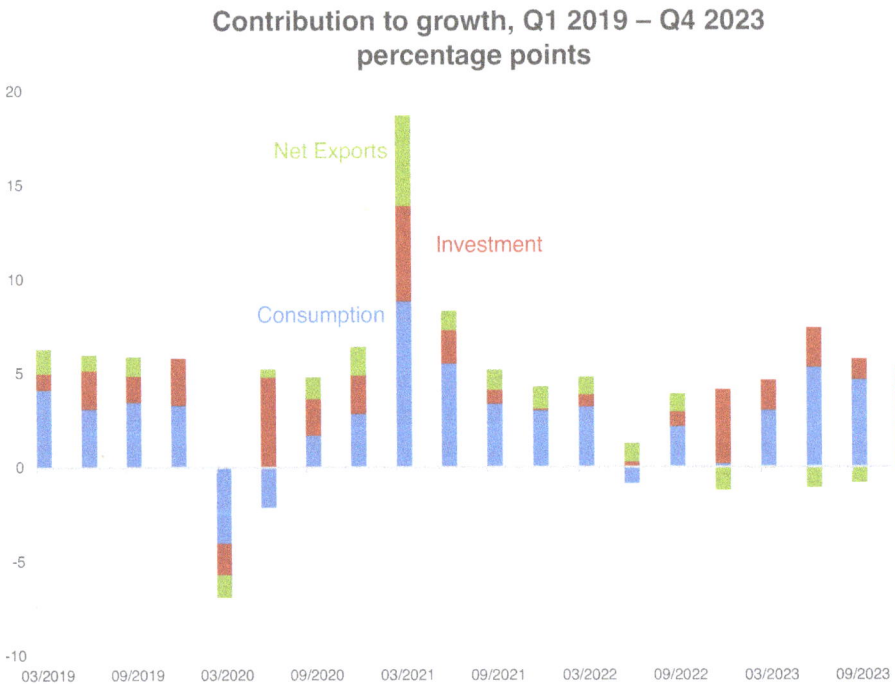

Figure 2.1 Consumption leading the post-Covid recovery

Source: NBS via CEIC Data (www.ceicdata.com/en).

Table 2.1 China: Government targets and outcomes, 2021–24

	2024 target	2023 outcome	2023 target	2022 outcome	2022 target	2021 outcome	2021 target
GDP growth (%)	~5	5.2	~5	3.0	~5.5	8.1	>6
Job creation (million)	>12	12.4	~12	12.1	>11	12.7	>11
Unemployment (%)	~5.5	5.2	<5.5	5.6	<5.5	5.1	~5.5
Budget deficit (% GDP)	3	3.8	3.0 (3.8)[a]	2.8	2.8	3.1	3.2
LG bonds (RMB trillion)	3.9	3.8	3.8	4.0	3.65	3.58	3.65
Special treasury bonds (RMB trillion)	1	1					
LG transfers	10.2	10.3	10.1 trillion	–	9.70 trillion		
Tax and fee cuts	tbd	'Additional 2.2 trillion'[b]	Measures to be extended	3.46 trillion	2.50 trillion	1.10 trillion	–
CPI inflation (%)	~3	0.2	~3	2.0	~3.00	0.9	~3
Grain output (million tonnes)	>650	695	>650	685	>650.00	681	>650
Total social financing (% growth)	In line with projected nominal GDP	9.5	In line with projected GDP	9.6	In line with projected GDP	10.3	In line with projected GDP
Balance of payments	'Basic balance'		'Basic balance'		'Basic balance'		'Basic balance'
Total debt to GDP	tbd		No target	–	Stable	–	Stable
Energy intensity decline (%)	–/-2.5	'Short of expectations'	–/-2	–	No target	–	–/-3

~ = approximate
CPI = consumer price index
LG = local government
tbd = to be determined
[a] Revised to 3.8 in October 2023.
[b] Not clear whether this is beyond the measures already implemented.
Source: Hofman (2024).

Despite the recovery after Covid, the question remains whether China can avert the 'reversal to the mean' of 2–3 per cent growth in the medium term.[1] The International Monetary Fund (IMF 2024), in its latest *World Economic Outlook*, projects a gradual decline in GDP to 3.2 per cent by 2029, ascribing the projected slowdown to a lack of structural reforms. This is important for China as well as the rest of the world; after all, China is now some 18 per cent of the world economy and was projected to deliver more than one-third of global growth in 2024, according to the IMF.

Whether China is facing a cyclical downturn or a structural slowdown is also key for economic policymakers; if it is the former, an economic stimulus would shore up growth, whereas in case of the latter, structural reforms could help rekindle growth. It is therefore important to understand the factors that drove recent growth performance. The remainder of this chapter reviews some of the drivers of growth and emerging issues that could impede growth, discusses recent policy initiatives to accelerate growth and outlines a policy agenda that could put China's growth on a more sustainable footing.

Policy triggers

Much of China's economic slowdown has been policy induced. China's zero-Covid policy was successful at first, and the economy rebounded strongly in 2021 with ultimately 8 per cent GDP growth, after the Covid-driven 2.2 per cent outcome in 2020. However, the highly infectious Omicron variant of the virus forced a growing number of lockdowns and increasingly restrictive measures on mobility slowed the economy again, to 3 per cent growth in 2022. The sudden exit from zero-Covid in December 2022 initially boosted household consumption, particularly in services (domestic tourism), but this petered out in the second quarter of 2023. The damage done to job creation has been large: according to Xing Ziqiang (2023) of CF40, a Beijing-based think tank, in the years before the pandemic, the service sector created 10 million new jobs each year, absorbing many graduates. During the pandemic, the service sector created barely more than 1 million jobs a year.

A second brake on growth came from the property sector. The sector had been a major driver of investment demand since the 2008–09 Global Financial Crisis (GFC), but property developers had also increasingly accumulated debt and, in the eyes of the authorities, had become a source of risk for financial stability. 'Housing is for living in, not for speculation' became the policy mantra often repeated by President Xi and in Communist Party documents. To contain the risk, the authorities intervened with the 'three red lines' policy in August 2020, which effectively limited bank credit to property developers. When advanced sales as substitute finance dried up during the pandemic, key developers ran into financial problems. This triggered a sharp drop in property sales, new construction starts and land transactions. In turn, this affected local

---

1   Summer and Pritchett (2014) predicted that China would soon reverse to the mean growth of developing countries.

government finances, which in recent years had relied more and more on revenues from land sales. While measures to stabilise the sector seem to have halted the decline, the recovery remains wanting and will likely drag down the economy for some years to come.

Low confidence within the private sector generates a third headwind for growth. The clampdown on internet platform companies of the past few years along with a perception that the current administration favours state-led development has shaken the confidence of the private sector. In addition, diminishing growth prospects and ample available production capacity amid sagging demand have reduced the need to invest in new capacity. As a result, private investments shrank in 2023, further slowing growth. Much of this was due to the slump in real estate, however, and the growth of private investment in manufacturing remained positive, although lagging that of state-owned enterprises (SOEs).

Foreign investors face challenges in the new era. Aside from the Covid restrictions, they must manage an environment dramatically changed by cybersecurity and data security laws, amendments to anti-espionage laws and the possible fallout of great-power competition. While total foreign direct investment (FDI) numbers held up quite well in 2022, 2023 saw a sharp decline (Figure 2.2). Moreover, the nature of FDI is changing, with more concentrated in big firms and a growing share coming from Hong Kong and Singapore (Pieke et al. 2024: Fig. 16), which indicates these funds are really Chinese firms repatriating offshore funds. Forward-looking data on announced FDI indicate that China will receive a smaller share of global FDI in future (Pieke et al. 2024: Fig. 9). The outlook for foreign investors in China has been increasingly subdued. Some have called it quits. Some 11 per cent of respondents to a survey by the European Chamber of Commerce in China (2023) said they had moved investment out of the country. A survey of members of the American Chamber of Commerce in Shanghai found most were negative about prospects in China since the beginning of the survey (Bloomberg 2023b).

Growing policy concerns

While authorities are concerned by slowing growth, they waited until the final quarter for an all-out stimulus. The July 2023 Politburo meeting on economic work in the second half of 2023 reiterated the 'proactive fiscal policy and prudent monetary policy' phrase already included in the December 2022 report of the Central Economic Work Conference (Xinhua 2023d). The slowdown was, according to the Politburo readout, due to 'new difficulties and challenges, mainly due to insufficient domestic demand, difficulties in operating some enterprises, many hidden risks in key areas, and [a] complex and severe external environment'. The solution lies, according to the Politburo, in restoring confidence, promoting domestic demand, stimulating innovation, speeding up construction of a modern industrial system and 'high-quality' growth, and focusing on emerging industries such as electric cars.

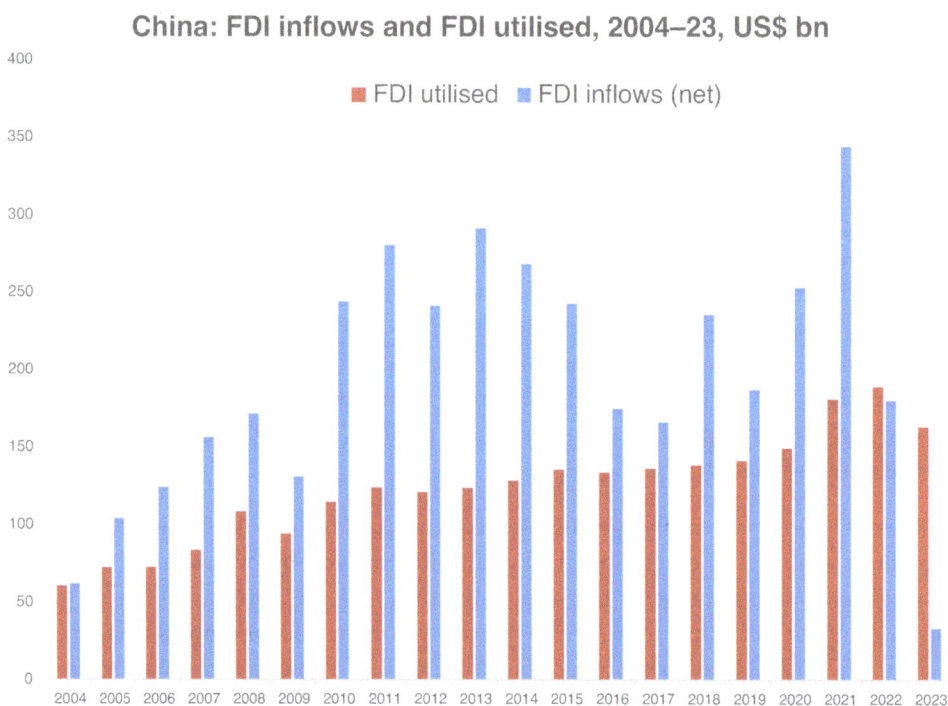

Figure 2.2 Taking the profits home

Note: Utilisation data transformed from year-to-date monthly data.
Source: Author's calculations based on People's Bank of China and Ministry of Commerce data via CEIC Data (www.ceicdata.com/en).

The sustained emphasis on high-quality growth signals that the authorities remain cautious about an all-out stimulus. 'High quality' is shorthand for growth that the economy can achieve without additional policy stimulus and is part of President Xi's New Development Concept. The concept recognises that the relentless pursuit of growth of times past has created inefficiencies and wasteful investment. It inspired measures such as the three red lines policy in real estate and fed central government reluctance to stimulate the economy. But the readout also suggests that several measures to revamp growth are in the pipeline, including: measures to address local government debt; an acceleration in the issuance of local government bonds, which would open financing for infrastructure; and measures to promote consumption, including the recent decision to extend the tax credit for electric vehicles. Much of a revival in growth, though, will have to come from the private sector.

Re-engaging the private sector

To revamp the confidence of the country's private sector, the authorities demonstrated renewed affection for the sector in recent months. Xi Jinping held a meeting with leading private sector representatives during the 'Two Sessions' in March 2023.

He assured them of his 'unwavering support' for the private sector. The 'two unwaverings' is party language for the support of both the public and the private sectors, and it was reiterated in a Central Committee/State Council document in support of the private sector. Premier Li Qiang followed suit in July by meeting tech entrepreneurs and pledging support for the 'platform economy' previously hit by the regulatory crackdown (Bloomberg 2023a). The National Development and Reform Commission promised detailed support measures for the private sector as well and set up a department for this (China Daily 2023).

The Central Committee/State Council document itself promises numerous measures to support the private sector, some old and some new. A better legal and policy environment is no doubt important for the private sector to regain confidence. At the same time, the document reiterates measures against monopolies, non-market behaviour and corruption. And it promises plenty of guidance for the private sector (the word 'guide' appears 22 times) and refers to the 'traffic light' system for private investment, which was first proffered in the context of the tech crackdown to control the 'excessive expansion of capital'. In the end, the proof of the pudding is in the eating and, over time, the government's track record will be decisive for any return of confidence within the private sector.

Another document jointly issued by the Central Committee and the State Council pledged to make the private economy 'bigger, better and stronger' with a series of policy measures designed to help private business and bolster the flagging post-pandemic recovery (Xinhua 2023c). Since the onset of reform and opening in 1978, the private sector has steadily become the mainstay of China's economy and now contributes some 50 per cent of the country's tax revenue, 60 per cent of its GDP, 70 per cent of its technological innovation and 80 per cent of its urban employment, according to government sources (Xinhua 2023a).

The Ministry of Finance extended its tax-relief program, which was supposed to expire at the end of this year, until the end of 2027. Private companies will enjoy a simpler process in gaining tax deductions for research and development and a shorter wait to receive export rebates. The People's Bank of China, China's central bank, pledged to guide more financial resources towards the private economy, including expanding debt financing tools to firms that requested broader bond-financing channels (Chen 2023).

Officially, the importance of the private sector has been recognised since former president Jiang Zemin's 'three represents' was announced in 2000 and private property was enshrined in the state constitution in 2004. Well before that, Deng Xiaoping's 'cat theory' gave the blessing to the private sector after decades of state planning. At the same time, the 'basic economic system' considers the public sector to be dominant so the private sector is acutely conscious of changes in political winds. There have been plenty of those in recent years, including the crackdown on the tech sector and the possible implications of the 'Common Prosperity' strategy and the New Development Concept launched by Xi Jinping. More broadly, the political changes in Beijing, the growing focus on national security, Xi's consolidation of power and the increasing dominance of the party over the government have created a less predictable environment for the private sector, despite the authorities' objective of 'rule by law'.

The pivot to manufacturing

Despite the economic headwinds, China's authorities seem less concerned about the economy than most observers, especially foreign observers. One reason for this is that the government is achieving one of its primary goals: a pivot to manufacturing. China's goal of high-quality growth implies a shift away from real estate and, to a lesser extent, towards manufacturing. The creation of a 'modern industrial system' is a key concern for President Xi (see, for instance, Xinhua 2023b; Zheng 2023) and became the top priority of economic work for the government in 2024 (Table 2.2). This also serves the goal of self-sufficiency in critical supply chains as embodied in the 'dual circulation' objective and underpins national security.

Table 2.2 Government priorities from the Government Work Report, 2022–24

Priority no.	2024	2023	2022
1	Striving to modernise the industrial system and developing new quality productive forces at a faster pace.	Expanding domestic demand.	Achieving stable macroeconomic performance and keeping major economic indicators within the appropriate range.
2	Invigorating China through science and education and consolidating the foundations for high-quality development.	Accelerating the modernisation of the industrial system.	Keeping the operations of market entities stable and maintaining job security by strengthening macro-policies.
3	Expanding domestic demand and promoting sound economic flows.	Unswervingly consolidating and developing the public sector and encouraging, supporting and guiding the development of the non-public sector.	Steadfastly deepening reform to strengthen market vitality and internal momentum for development.
4	Continuing to deepen reform and boosting internal momentum for development.	Intensifying efforts to attract and utilise foreign investment.	Further implementing the innovation-driven development strategy and strengthening the foundation of the real economy.
5	Pursuing higher standards of opening and promoting mutual benefits.	Effectively preventing and defusing major economic and financial risks.	Expanding domestic demand and promoting coordinated regional development and new urbanisation.
6	Ensuring both development and security and effectively preventing and defusing risks in key areas.	Stabilising grain output and advancing rural revitalisation.	Boosting agricultural production and promoting general rural revitalisation.

Priority no.	2024	2023	2022
7	Making sustained efforts to deliver on work relating to agriculture, rural areas and rural residents, and taking solid steps to advance rural revitalisation.	Continuing the transition to green development.	Pursuing higher standards of opening and promoting stable growth of foreign trade and investment.
8	Promoting integrated development between urban and rural areas, advancing coordinated development between regions and optimising regional economic layout.	Meeting people's basic living needs and developing social programs.	Continuing to improve the environment and promoting green and low-carbon development.
9	Enhancing ecological conservation and promoting green and low-carbon development.		Ensuring and improving the people's wellbeing and promoting better and new ways of conducting social governance.
10	Ensuring and improving people's wellbeing and promoting better and new ways of conducting social governance.		

Source: Hofman (2024).

This pivot is well under way. Bank credit has seen the strongest turnaround away from real estate since the 'three red lines' policy was announced, and new credit has almost completely dried up. In contrast, credit to industry, and manufacturing in particular, has seen a strong rise in the past two years (Figure 2.3). While this has put pressure on economic growth, the leadership is likely to consider it a desirable direction.

The decline in real estate investment has resulted in an overall decline in private investment. But excluding real estate, private sector investment retains positive growth and private investment in manufacturing remains particularly strong and rebounded after the Covid-19 pandemic. Since the pandemic, the fixed-asset investments of SOEs have grown faster than those of private enterprises. This has not happened for a long time, in contrast with the perception of some observers that the state was striking back much earlier (see, for example, Lardy 2019). The growth in SOE investment could reflect their traditional countercyclical role rather than a major shift in ideology, though the rhetoric of China's leadership increasing emphasises the leadership of party and state in the economy.

Waiting for a larger consumption share

Forming a second plank in the government's strategy to counter the ongoing slowdown are efforts to ramp up domestic demand, particularly consumption demand. This is hardly new and is an integral part of the 'dual circulation' approach intended to lessen China's dependence on foreign demand. That objective dates back to the days of the Hu Jintao/Wen Jiabao administration, when then premier Wen cautioned that 'the biggest problem with China's economy is that the growth is unstable, unbalanced, uncoordinated, and unsustainable' (Wen 2007).

Change in Bank Loans Outstanding,
Quarterly, Absolute Values, RMB Trillions, 2013/1-2023/6

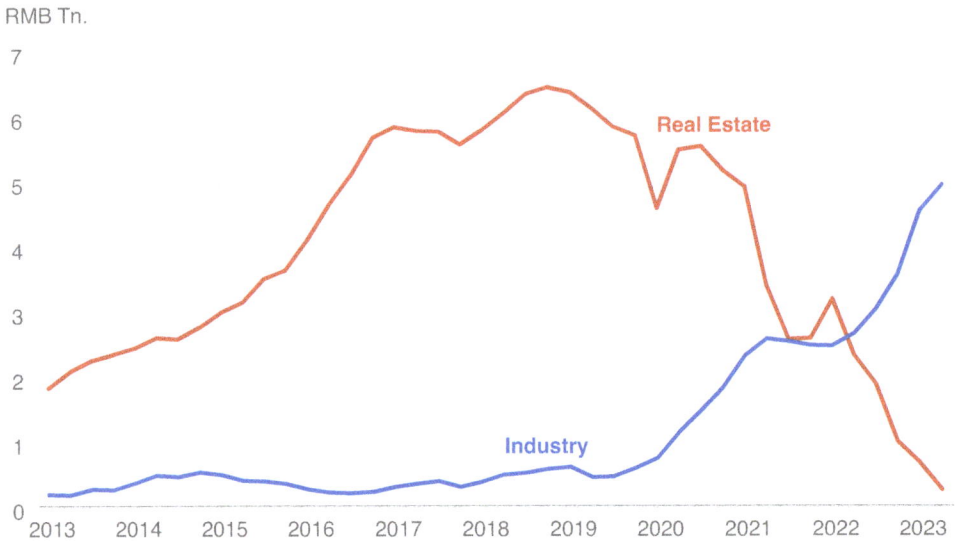

Figure 2.3 The great rotation

Source: Author's chart based on People's Bank of China Data via CEIC (www.ceicdata.com/en), after an idea from Shanghai Macro Strategist (X [Twitter] post, 9 October 2023, 7.03 pm, x.com/shanghaimacro/status/1711291278011638161?s=46&t=-my_1dLUkn-H33ualxTdgA).

China's household consumption has since increased as a share of GDP, but only slowly. The share was 35 per cent in 2008, after which it gradually increased, to 39 per cent in 2018, only to fall to 38 per cent during the pandemic. This is of significance not only for China: globally, China's consumer market is far less important than its weight in world GDP suggests. While China's GDP now approximates three-quarters of that of the United States, its household consumption is only 40 per cent of that of the United States. Nevertheless, China's consumption has been growing at a respectable rate, outpacing GDP growth for most of the past decade and a half. The question is: can consumption save growth and, if so, how?

There are two schools of thought on this point. One argues that China's household share of national income is too low—a view propagated by Peking University economist Michael Pettis (2023) and Fudan University Dean of Economics Zhang Jun, among others. The other school claims that China's households are saving too much for a variety of reasons, including a weak social safety net, high costs of education and high down payments on property. This is not a trivial difference among academics: the truth on this question will determine what policies are required to increase consumption and therefore potentially economic growth.

Table 2.3 Household income and savings, 2019 (percentage of GDP)

	China	USA	EU	Japan	Germany	Brazil	Mexico
Wage income	52.0	53.5	47.7	51.5	61.3	43.6	26.8
Gross income (gross balance of primary income)	61.3	80.8	68.5	65.9	85.8	68.6	73.3
Disposable income	60.2	76.6	59.9	59.3	68.9	71.5	73.4
Household savings	20.9	11.3	7.5	5.9	13.0	7.8	15.7
Household savings rate	34.8	14.8	12.6	9.9	18.9	10.9	21.4
Consumption	39.2	65.3	53.4	53.3	58.0	63.2	63.7

Source: OECD National Accounts data, 2019 or closest year (www.oecd-ilibrary.org/economics/data/oecd-national-accounts-statistics_na-data-en).

Compared with the United States (and some Latin American middle-income countries like Brazil and Mexico), China's household *disposable* income as a share of GDP is low: 60 per cent versus 77 per cent, according to Organisation for Economic Co-operation and Development (OECD n.d.) data for 2019—the most recent available for China (Table 2.3). However, this share is not too different from that of the European Union (also 60 per cent) and Japan (59 per cent). The big difference between China and the United States is in entrepreneurial income accruing to households, which is high in the United States due to a friendly tax treatment of such income. Another difference is that China's households receive hardly any dividends from enterprises (0.4 per cent of GDP)—less than one-tenth of that for the European Union and the United States. Finally, China's statistical bureau underestimates imputed rents—the amount of (implicit) income an owner-occupier receives from not having to pay rent. This could account for as much as 4 percentage points of GDP in disposable income and, by definition, the same amount of consumption.

Irrespective, the big differences in consumption share of GDP result from China's high household savings rates. China's households put some 35 per cent of their disposable income aside in savings—much more than the United States (15 per cent), the European Union (13 per cent) and Japan (10 per cent). This means China's households save some 21 per cent of GDP compared with 11 per cent for those in the United States, 8 per cent for the European Union and 6 per cent for the no longer frugal Japanese.

In terms of policy, this means that addressing the underlying causes of such high savings would have greater—and more immediate—results than increasing the income share of China's households. Strengthening the country's social safety net, shoring up the pension system, broadening unemployment insurance and deepening health insurance would all help in reducing the incentives for China's households to save, as would reducing the down payments needed to buy real estate, though this could conflict with government policies for that sector. Finally, China could over time increase the household share in the economy. This will happen as wage increases outpace GDP growth but could also be policy driven. Notably, the paltry dividends that SOEs pay to the government could be increased.

A balance sheet recession? China versus Japan's experience

High debt, demographic headwinds, declining real estate prices and signs of deflation have triggered a debate about whether China is experiencing a 'balance sheet recession' (International Economy 2023). The term was coined at the end of the 1990s by Richard Koo, then chief economist for investment bank Nomura, to describe Japan after the bursting of the financial bubble in the early 1990s. Because of the massive decline in asset prices, Koo argued, households, the corporate sector and banks all focused on repairing their balance sheets. Consequently, demand plunged and Japan went into a decade-long recession. To get out of it, he argued, Japan should embark on massive public spending. Today, China might be entering a balance sheet recession, according to Koo.

There are some similarities between Japan then and China now, but a balance sheet recession for China still seems far off. The blow to Japan's balance sheets at the time was staggering: the Nikkei Stock Index fell from 39,000 at its peak to 13,000 by the end of the decade, commercial real estate lost 80 per cent of its value and residential land prices fell by two-thirds between 1991 and 2005 according to Bank for International Settlements (BIS) data. The collapse happened at a time when Japan was already an aged society and urbanisation, at some 77 per cent in 1990, had started slowing.

China is in a different situation today. Though the property sector is seriously affected by the current downturn, the adjustment has thus far been largely in terms of volume of sales and construction, not prices. Thus, at least for now, the perceived wealth of China's households, which have some two-thirds of their wealth in real estate (China Economic Net 2019), has barely been affected. The balance sheets of the sector itself have been adjusting, but on both sides; deleveraging was the policy objective that triggered the problems in the first place. According to Gavekal-Dragonomics, the balance sheet of the sector has shrunk by some RMB1.7 trillion (about US$230 billion or 1.4 per cent of GDP).

On the other side of the balance sheet, this was matched by a decline in the sector's equity of RMB401 billion (0.4 per cent of GDP) and a reduction in debt of RMB1.3 trillion (1.1 per cent of GDP), out of a total of some RMB19 trillion in loans outstanding to developers. This is only a minor adjustment thus far, not the major shock Japan experienced in the early 1990s or even the decline in asset values the United States experienced in the GFC. According to former Bank of Japan governor Masaaki Shirakawa (2023), the decline in the combined value of Japanese property and stocks amounted to about 230 per cent of GDP, and in the United States the decline in assets values after the GFC was 100 per cent of GDP. For now, the decline in property values in China is nowhere near this and losses are largely contained to the property sector itself. China's corporate sector is far less leveraged than Japan's in the 1980s: the debt-to-equity ratio is about 1.25 in China today and has been coming down in recent years. In Japan, it was three times as high at the peak of the bubble.

Koo's analysis is on the mark in flagging that China's economy has become less and less responsive to monetary policy. Indeed, the (modest) reductions in interest rates have barely had an effect. The reason is clear: companies face uncertain growth prospects, have abundant capacity and remain uncertain about what the new policy environment means for them. Moreover, they have been deleveraging for several years now, in line with government policy. Households face uncertainty about future property prices or completion of any property they buy. Furthermore, many have seen their children, or the children of their neighbours, struggle to find jobs. These are not conducive conditions for major consumer spending growth.

All that debt

Efforts to stimulate the economy are constrained by the high levels of debt, particularly of local governments and households. According to the BIS, total debt-to-GDP reached 311 per cent at the end of Q3 2023—a level that exceeds that of most advanced economies and all emerging market economies, and more than double that before the GFC. Of that debt, household debt-to-GDP stands at about 60 per cent, which equals the household income share of GDP. Government debt is now 75 per cent of GDP, but when including the debt incurred by local government financing vehicles (LGFVs), it is more than 100 per cent.

There were more modest increases in the debt of non-financial corporations in the past 15 years, if corrected for the debt of LGFVs, which in China is included in the statistics for corporations. Without such LGFV debt, corporate debt as a share of GDP is more comparable with that of other emerging market economies (Figure 2.4). The leverage of corporations has increased since the onset of the GFC, but it has been far more modest than the raw numbers suggest—from 84 per cent of GDP to 115 per cent of GDP, rather than 165 per cent of GDP in Q3 2022. Thus, a rebalancing of bank credit to industry and manufacturing would not necessarily result in unsustainable debts in corporations, at least for now.

The situation is different for local government debt, including the debt of the LGFVs, either implicit or explicit. Many local governments have seen their revenue base eroded because of two factors: 1) the halving of revenues from land lease sales; and 2) the fallout of tax reductions granted by the central government to support the economy through Covid-19 (Figure 2.5). In contrast, the central government has abundant capacity to take on additional debt. Strains are starting to show in many local governments. The central government has kept its deficit at a conservative level of about 3 per cent— like the now discarded eurozone criteria—and total central government debt to GDP is below 25 per cent, which is very modest in international comparison. It would, therefore, make sense that the central government, rather than local governments, takes on additional debt to finance a more proactive fiscal policy. Because the central government hardly spends on its own books, the proceeds of debt issuance would best be transferred to local governments, either to assist in the work out of debt or simply for keeping spending at reasonable levels (Wong 2024).

Debt decomposition, end-2022, percentage of GDP

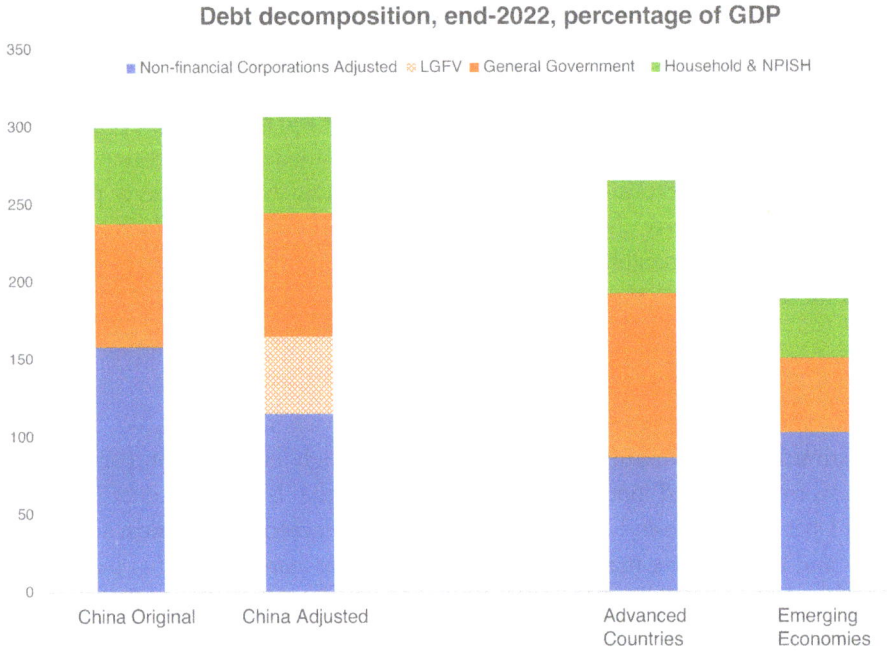

Figure 2.4 Deep in debt, but less than it appears for corporations

NPISH = non-profit institutions serving households
Source: Author based on BIS and IMF data.

Total government revenues, 2010–23, percentage of GDP

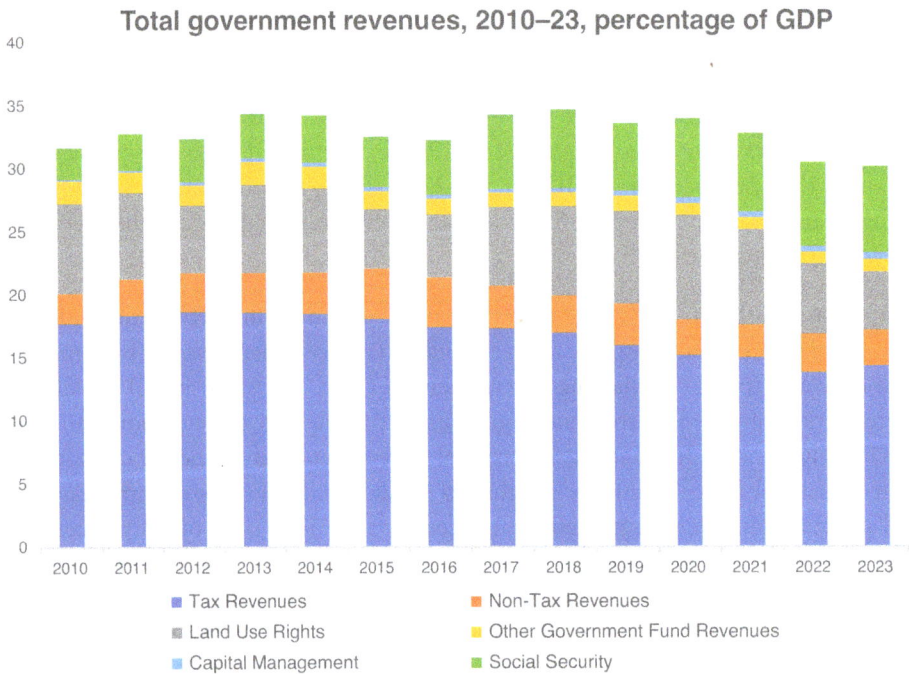

Figure 2.5 Total government revenues in decline

Source: Hofman (forthcoming).

**Trade balance as share of China's GDP and global GDP
percentage, Q1 2000 – Q3 2023**

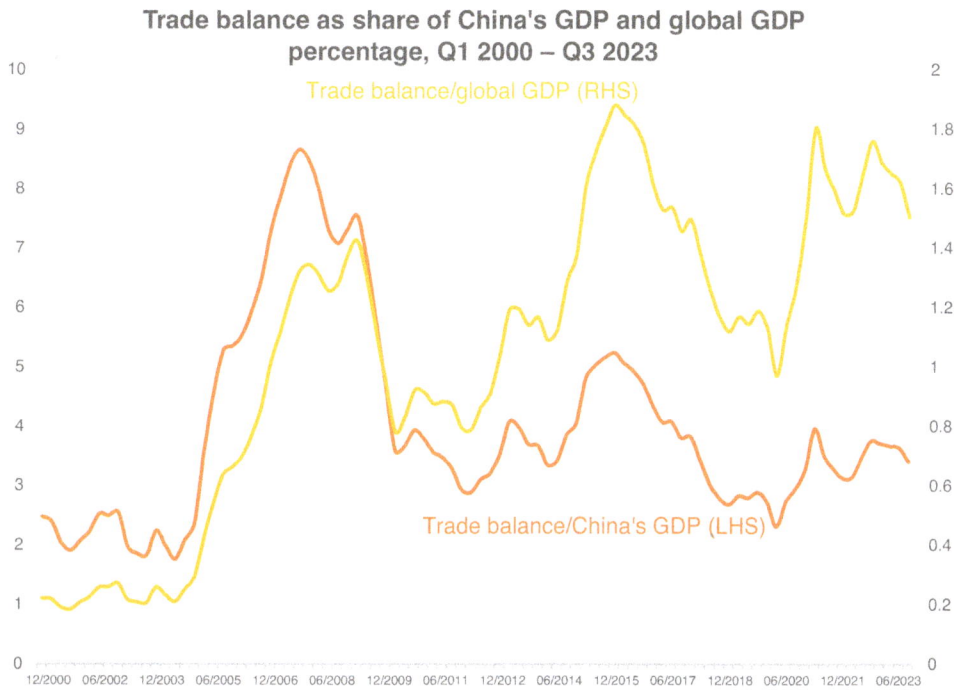

Figure 2.6 More trade tensions to come

Note: Quarterly global GDP constructed from annual GDP by linear interpolation. Credit to Adam Wolfe of Absolute Strategy Research for the original idea for the chart published in a client note. Source: Author based on Ministry of Commerce of China and IMF via CEIC Data (www.ceicdata.com/en).

External circulation to the rescue?

With the pivot from real estate to manufacturing and lacklustre domestic demand, external demand has come to the rescue, of sorts. Even though exports have recently not been growing, neither have imports, and external surpluses have again been on the rise. As a share of China's GDP, surpluses remained modest at 0.6 per cent by mid-2023. But as a share of *global* GDP, China's surpluses are now larger than they were before the GFC (Figure 2.6) and little different from the surpluses recorded in 2015—a year in which China experienced considerable financial market turbulence.

These trade surpluses are increasingly less with the United States and more with the European Union, as well as with Association of Southeast Asian Nations (ASEAN) countries. In 2023, China ran a trade surplus with 173 economies whereas it ran a deficit with 50, according to Chinese customs data, most of them natural resource producers, and Taiwan and South Korea due to semiconductors. Chinese companies have been redirecting trade given the Trump administration's tariffs and have been exporting more intermediary goods to ASEAN countries, which in turn export to the United States. Also, new markets along the Belt and Road, in Central Asia and the Middle East are also noteworthy. The growing surpluses with the European Union, in particular in manufacturing, could result in a backlash against China's exports in the near future. The European Union announced an investigation into subsidies for electric vehicles (EVs) in October 2023, and results were expected in June. The United States plans to quadruple already high tariffs on EVs and other new-energy supplies (New York Times 2024).

Towards more sustainable growth

Despite several major challenges, China's economy has emerged from the Covid-19 pandemic at reasonable growth rates and with a healthier pattern of growth that relies less on unsustainable investments in real estate and infrastructure and more on the manufacturing industry. China's past industrial policies have come through and industries such as the 'three new' (EVs, batteries and solar) and other advanced manufacturing are booming. At the same time, the fallout from the real estate bust is yet to be fully dealt with. The real estate industry will require major restructuring and downsizing, while the fallout on the banking system and local government finance, as well as consumer confidence, is yet to become fully clear.

In the medium term, a comprehensive set of reforms will be needed to ensure that China can continue to grow in a sustainable manner. This should include a range of reforms to support domestic demand.

The complexity and interconnectedness of these reforms would make a Central Committee plenum the appropriate forum at which to discuss such changes. In the readout of the Politburo meeting at the end of April 2024, the long-awaited Third Plenum of the Twentieth Central Committee was announced for July 2024. While signs are that the focus will again be on the supply side of the economy, some of the critical reforms needed for more balanced growth could yet be addressed. These include the following.[2]

Fiscal reforms

At the core of the misallocation of capital in infrastructure and real estate are the problems with the fiscal system. A growing demand for public services at the local level has not been met with more resources. Moreover, incentives for local government officials remain biased towards growth. Major fiscal reforms are needed, including expansion of the tax base, a better revenue base for local governments, revisiting the economic functions of local government and the intergovernmental fiscal system. A carbon tax, a property tax and broader application of the personal income tax are concrete options that would restore China's revenue.

Financial sector reforms

China's abundance of savings is likely to decline in the coming decades, more so in the absence of reforms to improve productivity. Lower savings implies that the *allocation* of those savings would need to improve to keep growth at acceptable levels. Financial

---

2   This section relies on Hofman (2023).

sector reforms are key to this and the reorganisation of the financial sector supervisor is a start. The thousands of local banks that have emerged are little more than development banks for local governments and should be centrally, rather than locally, supervised. Moreover, the sector is likely to see a consolidation in the coming years, to weed out the weak banks (most likely by mergers with strong banks, if the past is any guide). In addition, cleaning up the debts of local financing vehicles is critical in the short term, but longer-term reforms to diversify the financial sector and increase returns on investment will require deeper reforms as well.

Retirement age and pension reforms

The decline in the labour force, which has been occurring for a decade, could be slowed by implementing reforms to the retirement age. If China's workers were to retire at the same age as the Japanese, an additional 40–50 million workers would be in the labour force by 2035. Reforms to the pension system could encourage people to work longer and at the same time improve the financial sustainability of the system and enable its expansion to migrants and rural areas (the urban and rural resident system).

Household registration reforms

Urbanisation has been a major driver of growth in the past but has slowed in recent years. The urban population is now 65 per cent of the population, but almost 20 percentage points of this are migrant workers. Moreover, some 25 per cent of the labour force is still employed in agriculture, compared with an average of 3 per cent among OECD countries. Further reforms of the household registration system are critical for increased mobility and labour productivity growth. In parallel with these reforms, a change to the rights over rural construction land must be implemented so that those who permanently move to the city retain their rights in rural areas.

Social safety net reforms

Providing rural citizens and migrant labour with the same social protection as urban workers would help support consumer confidence and consumption growth, as well as strengthen countercyclical policies and wean government off infrastructure investment as the only tool to stabilise the economy. This will not break the bank, at least not yet; most of the programs, such as pensions and unemployment insurance, are contribution based and would therefore in principle be self-financing. The issue is that the existing systems themselves may not be financially sustainable and that, over time, all the premiums must go up or a larger share of general revenues must be dedicated to those programs.

State enterprise reforms

Even though China will continue to maintain a large SOE sector, there is broad agreement among Chinese policymakers that the sector should perform better. The third plenum of the Eighteenth Central Committee in 2013 had already decided that better 'state capital management' should be a priority. Increasing dividend payments from SOEs would be a good start—and these could be dedicated to social security funds to avoid a looming deficit there. Divesting non-core activities from SOEs, such as real estate development and tourism, would allow the sector to perform better at its core tasks and also allow local governments to pay off some of their excess debts with the assets they own. Reorganising SOEs into non-commercial and commercial, and managing the latter through state investment companies, would further increase the returns that the state (and the Chinese people) would receive from its property.

It has been more than a decade since the Central Committee held an economic plenum. The third plenum of the Nineteenth Central Committee was used to discuss proposals for constitutional change that would abolish term limits for the president and vice-president. Moreover, numerous reforms that were announced at the third plenum of the eighteenth party congress were only partially implemented or were reversed after policy priorities changed. The upcoming third plenum will provide more clarity about what China's medium-term economic trajectory will look like.

References

Bloomberg. 2023a. 'China Premier Meets Major Tech Companies, Vows More Support.' *Straits Times*, [Singapore], 13 July. www.straitstimes.com/business/china-premier-meets-major-tech-companies-vows-more-support.

Bloomberg. 2023b. 'Western Firms in China Are Historically Glum about Outlook.' *Bloomberg News*, 19 September. www.bloomberg.com/news/articles/2023-09-19/us-companies-are-the-gloomiest-in-decades-about-china-outlook?utm_source=google&utm_medium=bd&cmpId=google#xj4y7vzkg.

Chen, Meredith. 2023. 'China's Private-Sector Crisis: Everything You Need to Know about the Mess and What Beijing Is Doing to Clean It Up.' *South China Morning Post*, [Hong Kong], 13 August. www.scmp.com/economy/china-economy/article/3230781/chinas-private-sector-crisis-everything-you-need-know-about-mess-and-what-beijing-doing-clean-it.

China Daily. 2023. 'Private Firms on Tap for More Govt Assistance.' 21 July. Beijing: State Council of the People's Republic of China. english.www.gov.cn/policies/policywatch/202307/21/content_WS64b9d9dec6d0868f4e8ddfeb.html.

China Economic Net. 2019. 'China Household Wealth Survey Report: The Proportion of Real Estate Remains High.' *China Economic Net*, 30 October. www.ce.cn/cysc/fdc/fc/201910/30/t20191030_33470849.shtml.

Economist. 2023. 'Does China Face a Lost Decade?' *The Economist*, [London], 10 September. www.economist.com/finance-and-economics/2023/09/10/does-china-face-a-lost-decade?gclid=Cj0KCQjwx5qoBhDyARIsAPbMagDiJlVh0kDEkZFp2nORQSEhVFLjsnvGsai61hD01ZFXqCSxPM9kW-YaAlGoEALw_wcB&gclsrc=aw.ds.

European Chamber of Commerce in China. 2023. *Business Confidence Survey 2023*. Beijing: European Chamber of Commerce in China. www.europeanchamber.com.cn/en/publications-archive/1124/Business_Confidence_Survey_2023.

Global Times. 2023. 'Riding on New Cycle of Tech Innovation, China's Economy is Entering a "Golden Age".' *Global Times*, [Beijing], 29 March. www.globaltimes.cn/page/202303/1288183.shtml.

Hofman, Bert. 2023. *China's Economy Ahead of the Third Plenum: The End of the 'China Miracle'?* October. New York, NY: Asia Society Policy Institute. asiasociety.org/policy-institute/chinas-economy-ahead-third-plenum-end-china-miracle.

Hofman, Bert. 2024. 'China's Government Work Report: First Impressions.' *EAI Commentary*, No. 75, 8 March. Singapore: East Asian Institute, National University of Singapore. research.nus.edu.sg/eai/wp-content/uploads/sites/2/2024/03/EAIC-75-20240308-1.pdf.

Hofman, Bert. Forthcoming. *How Much Revenues Can China Raise?*

International Economy. 2023. 'Could China Become Like Japan in the Early 1990s?' *The International Economy* (Winter), [Washington, DC]. www.international-economy.com/TIE_W23_ChinaLikeJapanSymp.pdf.

International Monetary Fund (IMF). 2024. *World Economic Outlook Database*. April 2024 edn. Washington, DC: IMF. www.imf.org/en/Publications/WEO/weo-database/2024/April.

Koo, Richard. 2023. 'China Is Likely to Face a "Balance Sheet Recession", Economist Says.' *CNBC International TV*, 6 June. www.youtube.com/watch?v=HTabysmCpDo.

Lardy, Nicholas. 2019. *The State Strikes Back*. Washington, DC: Peterson Institute of International Economics.

New York Times. 2024. 'U.S. to Announce New Tariffs on Chinese Electric Vehicles.' *New York Times*, 10 May.

Organisation for Economic Co-operation and Development (OECD). n.d. *OECD Data Explorer*. Paris: OECD. stats.oecd.org/index.aspx?lang=en.

Pettis, Michael. 2023. 'China Must Slow Down Investment if It Wants to Rebalance Its Debt-Laden Economy.' *South China Morning Post*, [Hong Kong], 12 September. www.scmp.com/comment/opinion/article/3233610/china-must-slow-down-investment-if-it-wants-rebalance-its-debt-laden-economy.

Pieke, Frank N., Bert Hofman, with Rumi Aoyama, Emma Burgers, Ryan Ho, Kong Tuan Yuen, Tan Chia How, and Eric Siyi Zhang. 2024. *Dealing with Decoupling from China: Business Strategies in a Changing World*. February. Leiden, Netherlands: China Knowledge Network, Leiden Asia Centre and East Asian Institute, National University of Singapore. leidenasiacentre.nl/wp-content/uploads/2024/03/Dealing-with-Decoupling-Business-Strategies-in-a-Changing-World-3.pdf.

Posen, Adam S. 2023. 'The End of China's Economic Miracle: How Beijing's Struggles Could Be an Opportunity for Washington.' *Foreign Affairs*, September/October. www.foreignaffairs.com/china/end-china-economic-miracle-beijing-washington.

Ross, John 2023. 'The News Is Full of Headlines about "China's Economic Collapse"—Ignore Them.' *Morning Star Online*, [London], 24 August. morningstaronline.co.uk/article/f/the-news-is-full-of-headlines-about-china-economic-collapse-ignore-them.

Shirakawa, Masaaki. 2023. 'China Can Avoid "Japanification" with Prompt Action.' *Nikkei Asia*, [Tokyo], 25 August. asia.nikkei.com/Opinion/China-can-avoid-Japanification-with-prompt-action.

Summers, Lawrence H., and Lant Pritchett. 2014. *Asiaphoria Meets Regression to the Mean*. M-RCBG Faculty Working Paper Series 2014-04. Cambridge, MA: Mossavar-Rahmani Center for Business & Government, Harvard Kennedy School. www.hks.harvard.edu/sites/default/files/centers/mrcbg/files/mrcbg_fwp_2014-4_Summers_Asiaphoria.pdf.

Wang, Wen. 2023. 'Rekindling the Passion for China's Rise.' *Aisixiang*, 27 August. www.aisixiang.com/data/145695.html.

Wen, Jiabao. 2007. 'Premier Wen Jiabao's Press Conference.' 17 March. Beijing: National People's Congress. jm.china-embassy.gov.cn/eng/news/202209/t20220902_10761130.htm.

Wigglesworth, Robin. 2023. 'China's Japanification.' *Financial Times*, [London], 18 August. www.ft.com/content/52c805d5-c759-46cc-a0fe-2de2f2d71850.

Wong, Christine. 2024. 'Cracking the Code: Deciphering China's Fiscal Trends in the 2024 Budget.' *East Asia Institute Commentary*, no. 77 (25 April). Singapore: East Asian Institute, National University of Singapore. research.nus.edu.sg/eai/wp-content/uploads/sites/2/2024/04/EAIC-77-20240425-2.pdf.

Xing, Ziqiang. 2023. 'Stronger Policies are Needed to Bolster Recovery.' *China Finance 40 Forum*, 22 May. www.cf40.org.cn/en/news_detail/13332.html.

Xinhua. 2023a. 'China's Private Entrepreneurs Confident in Achieving High-Quality Development.' *Xinhua*, 6 May. english.news.cn/20230506/e287015d961946a187726 cf60e3a056c/c.html#:~:text=*%20The%20private%20sector%20contributes%20 approximately,percent%20of%20its%20urban%20employment.

Xinhua. 2023b. 'Xi Focus: Xi Urges Modernization of Industrial System, High-Quality Population Development.' *Xinhua*, 6 May. english.news.cn/20230506/d0c1737e54624a 2ab3d898115f7296bd/c.html.

Xinhua. 2023c. 'Opinions of the Central Committee of the Communist Party of China and the State Council on Promoting the Development and Growth of the Private Economy.' *Xinhua*, 19 July. www.news.cn/politics/2023-07/19/c_1129758014.htm.

Xinhua. 2023d. 'CPC Leadership Holds Meeting to Analyse Economic Situation, Make Arrangements for Work in the Second Half of the Year.' *Xinhua*, 25 July. english.news. cn/20230725/80b63f5a077c448d80d870c84908c53d/c.html.

Zhang, Jun. 2023. *Chinese Families Have Long Faced the Problem of Low Wages, and Wages Are Not Linked to Nominal GDP Growth*. Report, 26 June. Hangzhou, China: NetEase Financial Intelligence Center. mp.weixin.qq.com/s/YtwmtMC_DB6Af5Mu80ygyQ.

Zheng, Shanjie. 2023. 'Accelerating the Development of a Modern Industrial System Underpinned by the Real Economy.' *Qiushi Journal*, no. 13 (September). en.qstheory. cn/2023-09/13/c_918853.htm.

3

Potential efficiency in economic growth: A cross-province perspective

Raghuvir Kelkar and Kaliappa Kalirajan

Introduction

After the economic reforms of 1978, China opened to the world with a positive environment for foreign direct investment, concentrated on skilled education, encouraged privatisation and made its SOEs competitive. In recent years, China's economic growth has been a concern for its policymakers. Most of the growth and development are concentrated in the eastern coastal provinces, while the western and central provinces have not yet experienced the expected economic growth. China initiated plans like the 'Rise of Central China' and set up renewable energy projects in the west of the country. This chapter addresses the following research questions: Have central and western provinces achieved the potential efficiency in their economic growth? Have China's provinces used their resources to their fullest in implementing economic development strategies? Applying the stochastic frontier GDP model to a panel dataset covering the period 2000–20, this study concludes that the central provinces show the highest rate of efficiency in economic growth, although not 100 per cent, followed by eastern and western provinces. By increasing and improving skilled educational institutions and intensifying supply chain opportunities through FDI, achieving 100 per cent growth efficiency in the central provinces cannot be ruled out.

Growth performance in regional perspective

The Chinese economy has developed rapidly since the country's entry into the World Trade Organization (WTO) in 2001. China successfully reduced its poverty levels from 75.5 per cent in the 1970s to virtually zero in 2020 (World Bank 2020). The Chinese socialist market-driven economy became the cradle of academic economic research. Cities like Shenzhen and Shanghai became competitive as global financial centres thanks to their powerful stock exchanges. Exports to the world grew and, by 2021, China was the largest trading partner of more than 120 countries, with free-trade agreements (FTAs) such as the Regional Comprehensive Economic Partnership (RCEP) and China–ASEAN FTA, and a willingness to join the Digital Economy Partnership Agreement and build an efficient 24-hour port system (Suvannaphakdy 2021). China should become the largest economy in the world by 2028 (Hamidi 2021). It is a prominent player in collaboration with the BRICS countries (Brazil, Russia, India, China and South Africa), a dominant player in the Asian Development Bank (ADB) and the Asian Infrastructure Investment Bank (AIIB) and is taking on the ambitious Belt and Road Initiative (BRI).

Most of the country's economic development, however, has been concentrated in its eastern provinces, including Beijing, Shanghai, Jiangsu and Shenzhen. The inequality of economic development between the eastern and western provinces is evident, with that of inner western regions such as Ningxia, Qinghai, Tibet and Hainan relatively backward. Steps are being taken to develop the western regions, such as infrastructure upgrades and incentives for private industry; one of the landmark achievements in this regard has been the building of an elevated rail route connecting the Tibet Autonomous Region with Qinghai Province, which has slashed the average travel time on this route by about 80 per cent and connects 34 major cities (Gao and Li 2022). Even with these interventions, the western provinces are nowhere near as developed as those in the east. Meanwhile, recognising the importance of the central provinces as the geographical and economic link between the eastern and western regions, the Chinese Government in 2004 announced a plan to accelerate their economic development. Furthermore, in the Thirteenth Five-Year-Plan of 2016, greater emphasis was placed on economically strengthening the central provinces (Yuan 2019).

The main objective of this chapter is to measure the efficiency of the economic growth process in 31 Chinese provinces and identify the factors that are important at the provincial level in achieving their potential growth. The next section reviews the literature and determines the indicators for the economic growth of provinces. The methodology is explained within a theoretical framework in the third section. The fourth section discusses the results of the empirical model used to measure the efficiency of the economic growth process for the 31 provinces of China. The fifth section concludes this study by identifying economic policies that must be initiated for the provinces to reach their potential growth levels.

Literature review

According to the United Nations, the warning level for social and economic inequality for any country begins with a Gini index of 40; China's Gini index was 46.6 in 2021 (Textor 2024). This indicates that there is economic inequality in China. Nationally, China's financial performance is excellent, but this result is concentrated in the eastern coastal cities.

Ang (2018) studied the capital and industrial investments taking place in the poorer central and western provinces starting in the early 2000s. Most of these investments were by SOEs in Anhui, Henan, Jiangxi, Hunan and Hubei provinces and by collective enterprises through the central government, which began concentrating on the development of the inner provinces. Ang (2018) explains these investments through the flying-geese model of V-shaped economic growth. He applied the model to a cross-section of China's regions. He admits there was a delay in the policies taken by the government for the inner provinces. Most technologically oriented and labour-intensive industries were concentrated in the coastal cities. In 2004, then premier Wen Jiabao inaugurated the 'Rise of Central China' campaign to reduce the income disparities between the central and eastern provinces (Lai 2007: 121). Many state industries invested in these regions, generating local employment and increasing GDP. Along with investment, various initiatives for upgrading infrastructure were provided: roads were improved, bridges and railway links were extended, water and sanitation facilities were rebuilt and high-speed railway links were planned to connect the east and west. Provincial investments became a significant source of regional economic growth in the inner provinces.

Cheung (2010) examined the effects of technology on Chinese domestic industries and their innovation performance. Cheung argues that the provincial state-owned and private firms benefited from technology spillovers from foreign firms. Technology-led exports by local industries increased, thereby increasing the value added of GDP. Due to increased competition, many private firms made efforts through research and development (R&D) to produce international-quality innovative products to survive and profit in the domestic market. Employment was provided through private investments, as evident in Cheung's panel dataset for 1995–2006, which improved living standards. Due to increased demand, private and state investments ensured that industrial total factor productivity (TFP) increased to its fullest potential. Cheung's examination of TFP and innovation performance used the fixed-effects and random-effects models through empirical results. The author concluded that, with the increased R&D and technological advancements, domestic and private enterprises could spur the development of homegrown technology and innovation. This will improve the GDP of individual provinces and, subsequently, of China.

As the importance of the role of SOEs in China's political and economic development increased, Yu (2014) investigated their growth and the consequences on GDP growth. The central SOEs have been the pillar of China's economic growth, employment and the 'Going Out' strategy that followed the 1978 reform and opening policies. The central SOEs have become globally and domestically competitive. Many provinces in the western and eastern coastal areas try to attract some of this SOE investment to generate employment. In a World Bank report authored by Zhang (2019), it is estimated that SOEs enjoy a 23–28 per cent share of China's total GDP. The reforms of 1978 allowed the SOEs greater autonomy in their organisational and functional structures, and they began to operate according to market forces of demand and supply. Generally, the state-run enterprises of developing nations are loss-making and on the verge of shutdown, but in China, the opposite is the case. Yu (2014) shows that Chinese SOEs are profit-making and many private and foreign firms try to conduct joint businesses with them. Morck et al. (2008) maintain that SOE profits are reinvested to improve and expand the business and for public welfare. Brodsgaard (2012) mentions that SOE CEOs, although appointed by the Communist Party of China (CPC) and the State-Owned Assets Supervision and Administration Commission (SASAC), function in an autonomous market-oriented way and many also hold top posts as governors or vice-premiers, or hold secretarial and ministerial positions in government. The CEOs of China Eastern, Sinopec, China Telecom and Haier hold important roles in the CPC and related ministries. This means SOEs know the regional requirements and tend to invest more in western regions to focus on an equal development strategy for the provinces. Yu (2014) holds some reservations about the level of incentives and subsidies provided to SOEs that could result in unfair treatment for private companies. On the other hand, this could prompt the private sector to become more competitive and speed up their upgrading. As of 2022, the overall industrial profits of SOEs grew by 8 per cent, while private profits decreased by 7.1 per cent (Huang and Lardy 2022). SOEs should invest more in China's backward regions to lessen regional economic inequalities.

FDI is crucial for developing countries. China's is the best example of an FDI-led growth economy. As of 2022, China had received US$189.13 billion in FDI inflows (Xinhua 2023). Recognising the importance of FDI for regional development, Tuan and Ng (2004) reviewed China's FDI and the related economic growth at the provincial level. They collected data from 29 Chinese provinces and performed a two-stage system of equations test with ordinary least squares (OLS) estimates to provide empirical results. Their study looked at the beneficiaries of FDI and the distribution of FDI inflows into China's provinces. The authors concluded that China's FDI inflows went to the areas with stronger economic growth—specifically, the coastal areas and special economic zones (SEZs). The authors also argue that higher educational attainment is one of the main factors persuading investors to invest in certain provinces. The study also demonstrated that the higher level of infrastructural developments in central and eastern areas encourages regional investment and attracts more companies to create more jobs. Educational attainment is essential as most companies use high-end technology that requires highly skilled workers. The coastal provinces that have produced skilled labour through higher education have been the primary beneficiaries of China's inward FDI flows. Local and provincial governments should draft policies that incentivise FDI flows into the eastern provinces, while the central and regional governments should try to increase the output levels of this FDI. Higher FDI flows into the regions will increase enrolment in higher education and provincial GDP will grow.

Wei and Liefner (2012) scrutinise the impact of FDI based on geographical location. The authors believe that most FDI inflows come from profit-oriented multinational corporations (MNCs). Location-related factors like land and labour availability, port access, education rates and infrastructure determine investors' decision-making.

Wei and Liefner (2012) acknowledge that FDI is distributed unevenly. Though land and labour are more costly in the developed coastal cities of Shanghai and Shenzhen, 80–85 per cent of the total FDI in China flows into these regions. Companies are finding new locations, but these are never beyond the Pearl River and Yangtze River deltas and Beijing's industrial corridor with Tianjin. Investments are taking place in the inner areas of China, but local adaptability, home–host relationships, infrastructure and government policies must improve. The regional dynamics related to investment procedures are often made according to location-specific aspects of geography, settlement, population needs and social welfare, but such policies can hamper profit-oriented investments in coastal China, which is more metropolitan and has higher living standards.

Chen and Zheng (2008) argue that the regional programs for development launched in 2003 and 2004 have substantially benefited the inner regions of China so that the central and western provinces are now comparable with eastern coastal areas, especially in terms of land prices and availability. Labour is relatively cheaper in the inner regions. The authors claim the internal areas of China offer vast potential for foreign and private investors in terms of land availability. However, the government cannot redistribute incoming FDI because its direction is decided by the market-driven forces of supply and demand. Xu et al. (2013) observe setbacks in the government's implementation of regional policies due to a lack of skilled labour and educational enrolment and investors' high confidence in coastal areas and SEZs. This has raised income disparities in China—something that can be reduced only by developing the inner regions through institutional reform, professional education and proper implementation of investment policies (Zhou and Song 2016).

After the country's reform in 1979, there was a wave of privatisation and many private enterprises emerged in telecommunications, electronics, aviation and ports. Private investment in China's industrial and service sectors grew significantly. The share of the private sector in China's industrial sphere was 42.8 per cent in 2022 (Huang and Véron 2023). Li et al. (2012a) studied the effect of private business entrepreneurship on China's economic growth, compiling a cross-sectional dataset of 29 Chinese provinces and using the generalised method of moments regression technique to obtain empirical results. Their study concluded that private enterprises played a significant, positive role in the economic growth of Chinese provinces. Private industries are generally profit-oriented. Promotions and appointments in these sectors are based purely on merit and performance records. These industries try to maximise their output value by using the minimum input value, thereby increasing the productivity of labour employed. Greater output enables the private sector to compete in global industrial markets. Proper incentives given to private industry can motivate it to invest in the inner and eastern Chinese provinces. The capital–output ratio and trade within Chinese provincial markets appeal to the investment portfolios in the region (Ma et al. 2017). Increased domestic trade value attracts private investors as these players already have a robust local market in which to sell their output. Private investment in Chinese provinces will help the economic growth of those regions.

Taking a different approach, Cai (2020) considers the demographic dividend as a driver of economic growth in China and its provinces. China gained a lot through its young population after the reform period. SOEs and private and foreign industries had access to plentiful young, cheap and skilled labour. China's population growth was so high that, in 1980, the government imposed the One-Child Policy on families. However, with an ageing population and a substantial increase in FDI inflows, the government lifted that policy in 2016. As the working-age population ages, labour performance tends to decrease, and productivity seems to be slowing with the declining TFP. Industrial gross output has been decreasing. Cai (2010) also predicted that China had reached the Lewis turning point in the demographic dividend it enjoyed and its advantage of a young population would end in 2013. By 2020, the average age in China was 37.4 years and it is predicted to reach 40 in 2025 and 50 in 2050, which is a dangerous sign for economic growth, especially in rural areas (Textor 2023). The government should provide incentives to increase the birthrate to maintain FDI flows and increase private and SOE investments. The population factor is a golden opportunity for China's eastern provinces since, due to the high cost of living in eastern coastal areas, the birthrate is slowly increasing in places like Shanghai and Shenzhen. Investments can be diversified and raised in eastern provinces because they enjoy a demographic dividend in comparative terms domestically.

Based on the existing literature, when measuring the economic progress of a province, GDP at current prices is an acceptable indicator of economic growth. GDP is also affected by population, the value of SOEs, the value of private enterprises, the value of FDI, higher educational enrolment and domestic trade value. Notably, the above literature has been measuring the value of GDP determinants using empirical models of how those determinants affect GDP growth. In this chapter, we try to fill in the gap in the literature by measuring the efficiency of the economic growth process in Chinese provinces.

Methodology and framework

The size of any economy is typically measured by the total production of goods and services, which is generally referred to as gross domestic product. In other words, GDP is the total value added to the goods and services produced within an economy. How does the concept of efficiency enter the economic growth process? The efficiency of economic growth reveals the quality of production potential, which is the peak level of performance using the least number of inputs and existing technology to achieve the highest output. Hence, GDP efficiency indicates whether an economy can achieve its maximum production potential by utilising its resources and production capacity.

The theory of the stochastic frontier production function popularised by Aigner et al. (1977) and Meeusen and van den Broeck (1977) facilitates the measurement of GDP efficiency. Drawing on this, the above-cited studies demonstrated how to measure the average production efficiency of a group of firms. However, what would be interesting is to measure the firm-specific production efficiency of a group of firms. Jondrow et al. (1982) and Kalirajan and Flinn (1983) each developed a method to measure this along with the average efficiency of a group of firms. Individual province-specific GDP efficiency is measured by dividing real GDP by the potential GDP of each province for each year. The weighted average gives the efficiency rate of the province in its GDP performance.

Drawing on the time-decaying varying stochastic frontier production function model suggested by Battese and Coelli (1992), the theoretical framework followed in this chapter is shown in Equation 3.1.

Equation 3.1

$$\ln \mathrm{GDP}_{ct} = \ln f\,(Y_{ct}) + v_t - u_t$$

In Equation 3.1, 'ln' is the natural logarithm; GDP is real gross domestic product of province c at time t; and $f\,(Y_{ct})$ is the function of Y_{ct} in natural logarithm, wherein Y_{ct} is the determining or independent variable of province c that affects GDP_{ct} in the tth period.

In Equation 3.1, v_t is the statistical error term that has a normal distribution with an average mean of zero and constant variance, σ_v.

The non-negative error term, u, indicates that real GDP has not reached its potential due to many province-specific constraining factors. It is distributed as a truncated normal distribution at zero with a mean (μ) and constant variance, σ_u.

When the province-specific non-negative error term, u, is equal to zero, it implies that the real GDP is equal to the potential GDP of the province. Therefore, the GDP efficiency (θ) is defined as the ratio of real GDP to the estimated potential GDP and it varies between 0 and 1 (Equation 3.2).

Equation 3.2

$$\theta = \frac{\ln f\,(Yct) + vt - ut}{\ln f\,(Yct) + vt}$$

Table 3.1 presents all the variables used in the model. Additionally, the stochastic frontier gravity model has some assumptions that must be considered:

1. The provinces have not achieved their potential GDP growth and real GDP is below the potential.
2. Some domestic factors are hindering the Chinese provinces from achieving their potential growth rate.

The empirical model is given in Equation 3.3.

Equation 3.3

$$\ln \mathrm{GDP}_{it} = \Omega_0 + \Omega_1 \ln \text{population}_{it} + \Omega_2 \ln \text{SO Evalue}_{it} + \Omega_3 \ln \text{private value}_{it} \\ + \Omega_4 \ln \text{FDI value}_{it} + \Omega_5 \ln \text{higher education enrolment}_{it} + \Omega_6 \ln \\ \text{domestic trade value}_{it} + v_t - u_t$$

Table 3.1 Variable descriptions

Variable	Definition	Measurement unit	Expected value
GDP	Total GDP of the Chinese province in the given period.	Per million RMB at nominal prices	Positive
Population	Total population of the Chinese province in the given year.	Per 10,000 people	Positive
SOE value	Total gross output value of the SOE in the given year in Chinese provinces.	Per million RMB at nominal prices	Positive
Private value	Total gross output value of private enterprises in the given year in Chinese provinces.	Per million RMB at nominal prices	Positive or negative
FDI value	Total gross output value of FDI companies in Chinese provinces in the given year.	Per million RMB at nominal prices	Positive or negative
Domestic trade value	Total value and stock of domestic trade in Chinese provinces in the given year.	Per million RMB at nominal prices	Positive

Source: National Bureau of Statistics of China (2023).

Empirical results and discussions

Table 3.2 shows the results for the whole country. A statistically significant eta (η), which is built into the estimation software (Stata), with a positive value means that the constraints on real GDP reaching potential GDP declined over the period of analysis. If η is significant and negative, it implies that the constraints have been increasing over time. If the estimate of eta is not statistically significant, it indicates that GDP efficiency is stagnant and has neither increased nor decreased over time.

Table 3.2 reveals that the estimates of γ, μ and η are statistically significant at the 1 per cent level, while the significance of γ denotes that the stochastic frontier gravity model best suits the panel dataset used in this chapter. It also indicates that the gap between the Chinese provinces' real and potential GDP is quite large. The positive value of μ confirms that the assumption of the truncated normal distribution for the province-specific random error, u, is valid for this dataset. η is positive, which means that, during 2000–20, the gap between provinces' real and potential GDP was narrowing, proving that China was paying substantial attention to the development of its eastern and central regions.

The population estimate is significantly positive and favourably impacting GDP. This proves that increasing China's population would increase GDP, confirming the demographic dividend that China would enjoy. In this context, it is worth noting that China's economic rivals, India and Vietnam, were enjoying the demographic dividend of a very young median age—of 32.4 and 31.6 years, respectively—in 2020 (O'Neill 2024a, 2024b). Chinese policymakers should ensure that China does not become the new Japan, which cannot cope with its vast ageing population. There is a possibility that some manufacturing industries will shift to India and Vietnam instead of diversifying into the eastern and western provinces of China.

Table 3.2 Results of the estimation of the stochastic frontier growth model

Variable name	Estimated coefficients
Constant	14.0086*** (1.147826)
Population	0.4050445*** (0.0481231)
SOE value	0.1409822*** (0.0226459)
Private value	0.0528022*** (0.0099891)
FDI value	0.0406848*** (0.0123765)
Higher education enrolment	0.1807266*** (0.0296402)
Domestic trade value	0.0775788*** (0.0138949)
Gamma (γ)	0.6713298*** (0.0688914)
Mu (μ)	3.236942*** (0.8669325)
Eta (η)	0.0169996*** (0.004119)
Total number of observations	651

*** significant at 1 per cent
** significant at 5 per cent
* significant at 10 per cent
Note: Standard errors in parentheses.
Source: Authors' estimates.

SOEs have a positive and statistically significant impact on a province's GDP. SOEs have contributed to provincial employment and economic development since the founding of the People's Republic of China. Chinese SOEs are merging with private, foreign and small and medium enterprises (SMEs) and increasing their output value. They are competing at both the provincial and the national levels, and globally. The profits of these provincial SOEs are used for the development of the respective province as well as for reinvestment to grow the SOE, just like the Eastern Development Program's success in developing eastern provinces (Jia et al. 2020). China's SOEs are also among the most critical job providers in many regions.

Private companies are profit centric. Since Chinese SOEs receive preferential treatment and subsidies, private enterprises must fight hard to survive and make a profit, which is done using technology and innovation. In this process, they fully utilise their labour, which increases labour productivity and TFP. Such enterprises employ skilled labour, which raises the demand for educated youth and increases the government's attention to raising the standards of education, health and social welfare in a province. If the demand for skilled employment is increased, wages will increase, thereby increasing the standard of living. Private enterprises would make full use of labour, increasing labour output and efficiency (Li et al. 2012). In this process, the output value of private enterprises rises, increasing the respective province's GDP.

The estimated values of FDI are statistically significant. Delis and Kyrkilis (2017) have concluded, using the spatial distribution and analysis of variance (ANOVA), that China's FDI is concentrated in SEZs and coastal cities since these are close to the seaports facilitating international trade. FDI is being diversified properly in the Chinese regions. Since FDI inflows into China—most of which are related to the product assembly process—are vital for international business, they are also crucial to provincial GDP development.

Many private investors and SOEs are moving towards increased technology use, innovation and high-end quality products. Especially since its accession to the WTO in 2001, its FTA with ASEAN and its entry into the RCEP, China has significantly liberalised its service sectors such as finance, banking and information technology; and there are now many public–private partnerships in technology and R&D (Jones and Bloomfield 2020). These sectors must be diversified in the Chinese provinces. R&D and related enterprises require highly skilled and educated labour to handle machinery, data analysis, policy initiation and digitalised financial transactions. Higher educational enrolment includes vocational and undergraduate education in 31 Chinese provinces. When a province is recognised for the high performance of its education sector, more and more industries will look to invest there, creating employment that will contribute to the province's GDP.

A solid domestic trade value in a province indicates a high standard of living and high purchasing power of the population. Each sector and industry like to invest in an area with a robust domestic market, which is one of the virtues that China's economy has maintained and that helped it survive the 2008 GFC and the Covid-19 pandemic while maintaining a strong economic growth rate (Gunay et al. 2021). Domestic trade value increases with domestic market transactions. A strong domestic market value for any province increases economic activity, which fuels the province's economic growth.

Most indicators identified as the determinants of an increasing GDP growth rate in 31 Chinese provinces have shown statistically significant empirical results, but the real value of GDP has not reached its potential. Table 3.3 shows the efficiency of economic growth (θ) defined in Equation 3.2 of 31 Chinese provinces as a ratio of the average real GDP value to the average potential GDP value for the period 2000–20.

Table 3.3 Results of the estimates of provincial GDP growth efficiency

Province	Average real GDP in natural logarithm figures	Average potential GDP in natural logarithm figures	Average potential efficiency
Beijing	27.778	31.376	0.885
Tianjin	27.297	31.051	0.879
Hebei	28.161	31.940	0.881
Shanxi	27.289	31.357	0.870
Inner Mongolia	27.380	31.001	0.883
Liaoning	27.944	31.788	0.879
Jilin	27.241	31.263	0.871
Heilongjiang	27.503	31.394	0.876
Shanghai	28.027	31.547	0.888
Jiangsu	28.886	32.359	0.892
Zhejiang	28.484	31.936	0.891
Anhui	27.744	31.770	0.873
Fujian	27.934	31.508	0.886
Jiangxi	27.424	31.449	0.872
Shandong	28.809	32.415	0.888
Henan	28.303	32.164	0.879
Hubei	28.006	31.916	0.877
Hunan	27.954	31.786	0.879
Guangdong	28.980	32.457	0.892
Guangxi	27.485	31.428	0.874
Hainan	25.935	29.793	0.870
Chongqing	27.264	31.251	0.872
Sichuan	28.053	31.954	0.877
Guizhou	26.818	31.029	0.864
Yunnan	27.265	31.370	0.869
Tibet	24.634	28.411	0.867
Shaanxi	27.421	31.430	0.872
Gansu	26.592	30.895	0.860
Qinghai	25.440	29.480	0.862
Ningxia	25.587	29.756	0.859
Xinjiang	26.910	30.844	0.872

Source: Authors' calculations.

However, the country-level analysis may not effectively reflect the heterogeneous growth pattern that exists across the provinces, which necessitates a regional analysis of growth dividing China into central, eastern and western provinces. The eastern areas are near the coast and are more developed. Map 3.1 shows the provinces of China.

Map 3.1 Eastern, central and western provinces of China
Source: NWCCW et al. (2018).

With China's regions classified into three groups, we extend the stochastic frontier growth modelling to the three groups and their respective provinces. Table 3.4 provides the estimates of the stochastic frontier growth model for the three regions of China.

The results of the in-built estimators of *gamma* are statistically significant for all the estimations for western, eastern and central provinces (Table 3.4). A statistically significant *gamma* indicates that the constructed panel dataset best suits the stochastic frontier gravity model analytical framework, and that the model is best suited for the constructed panel dataset. The μ and η are not statistically significant for western and eastern provinces. There is a need for rigorous primary research in the field to gather more appropriate data on the constraints preventing GDP in the western and eastern provinces from reaching its maximum potential. However, the μ and η for the central provinces are significant, which is evidence that during the period 2000–20, the gap between real and potential GDP closed significantly.

After differentiating the provinces into three groups, the modelling produces the empirical results (Table 3.4) that further explain the GDP growth of the eastern, western and central provinces. Tables 3.5, 3.6 and 3.7 show the efficiencies of the western, central and eastern provinces, respectively.

Table 3.4 Results of the estimation of the regional stochastic frontier growth model

Variables	Western provinces	Central provinces	Eastern provinces
Constant	18.525*** (4.608)	5.533*** (1.993)	10.892*** (2.215)
Population	0.238*** (0.081)	1.001*** (0.118)	0.599*** (0.045)
SOE value	0.154*** (0.039)	0.144*** (0.039)	0.102*** (0.030)
Private value	0.079*** (0.015)	0.079*** (0.019)	−0.018 (0.017)
FDI value	0.026* (0.015)	−0.026 (0.034)	0.121*** (0.030)
Higher education enrolment	0.268*** (0.051)	0.057 (0.052)	0.123*** (0.041)
Domestic trade value	0.044* (0.023)	0.025 (0.021)	0.128*** (0.022)
Gamma (γ)	0.582*** (0.120)	0.507*** (0.191)	0.260** (0.118)
Mu (μ)	6.090 (4.512)	1.502*** (0.361)	3.125 (2.200)
Eta (η)	0.009 (0.006)	0.037*** (0.007)	0.016 (0.010)
Observations	252	175	231

*** significant at 1 per cent
** significant at 5 per cent
* significant at 10 per cent
Note: Standard errors in parentheses.
Source: Authors' estimates.

Table 3.5 Results of the estimates of western provinces' GDP growth efficiency

Province	Average real GDP in natural logarithm figures	Average potential GDP in natural logarithm figures	Average potential efficiency	Rounded off to the nearest two decimal points (% terms)
Inner Mongolia	27.38090803	33.69537	0.812601495	81.26
Guangxi	27.48545183	34.05266286	0.807145448	80.71
Chongqing	27.2641338	33.93747429	0.803363667	80.34
Sichuan	28.05360523	34.55621381	0.811825201	81.18
Guizhou	26.81802392	33.67433952	0.796393465	79.64
Yunnan	27.26549082	33.96066714	0.802854982	80.29
Tibet	24.63413284	31.23322762	0.788715567	78.87
Shanxi	27.42131166	34.14829857	0.803006674	80.30
Gansu	26.59230097	33.59862571	0.791469901	79.15
Qinghai	25.44050166	32.27206333	0.788313452	78.83
Ningxia	25.5871334	32.57627333	0.785453055	78.55
Xinjiang	26.91046518	33.51726524	0.802883678	80.29

Source: Authors' estimates.

Table 3.6 Results of the estimates of central provinces' GDP growth efficiency

Province	Average real GDP in natural logarithm figures	Average potential GDP in natural logarithm figures	Average potential efficiency	Rounded off to the nearest two decimal points (% terms)
Heilongjiang	27.503	29.565	0.930	93.03
Jilin	27.241	29.232	0.931	93.19
Anhui	27.744	30.170	0.919	91.96
Jiangxi	27.424	29.722	0.922	92.27
Henan	28.303	30.758	0.920	92.02
Hubei	28.006	30.192	0.927	92.76
Hunan	27.954	30.258	0.923	92.39
Shanxi	27.289	29.551	0.923	92.35

Source: Authors' estimates.

Table 3.7 Results of the estimates of eastern provinces' GDP growth efficiency

Province	Average real GDP in natural logarithm figures	Average potential GDP in natural logarithm figures	Average potential efficiency	Rounded off to the nearest two decimal points (% terms)
Beijing	27.778	31.468	0.882	88.27
Tianjin	27.297	30.967	0.881	88.15
Hebei	28.161	31.937	0.881	88.18
Liaoning	27.944	31.790	0.879	87.90
Shanghai	28.027	31.647	0.885	88.56
Jiangsu	28.886	32.522	0.888	88.82
Zhejiang	28.484	32.022	0.889	88.95
Fujian	27.934	31.602	0.883	88.39
Shandong	28.809	32.505	0.886	88.63
Guangdong	28.980	32.743	0.885	88.51
Hainan	25.935	30.310	0.855	85.57

Source: Authors' estimates.

The western, central and eastern provinces show average GDP growth efficiencies of 79.95 per cent, 92.49 per cent and 88.18 per cent, respectively. These growth efficiencies are in line with the real economic developments taking place in China across the different regions. These efficiency rates are healthy but should be more properly maintained to achieve the fullest potential. These efficiency rates are evidence of the fact that the resources needed for economic development are being diversified and used in a well-organised manner, resulting in sustainable growth patterns. McDowall et al. (2017) argued that, although China is a developing country, it is efficiently achieving its aim of becoming a circular economy and its performance is better than European countries.

The central Chinese provinces have shown the highest rate of GDP efficiency of the three regions. This shows that the 2004 plan for the 'Rise of Central China' has been successfully implemented, the central provinces have been adequately looked after by the central government and there is proper coordination between the central, provincial and county levels in policy implementation (Yuan 2019). The Thirteenth Five-Year-Plan for 2016–20 also outlined the central government's policy focus on the economic development of the central provinces (NDRC 2015). The average efficiency of the central provinces has been above 90 per cent, indicating that implementation of the policies outlined in the 2004 and 2016 plans has been successful. Although the central provinces are in transition, their growth efficiency performance has become a leading example of China's model of provincial economic growth efficiency for other transitional economies around the world.

It is important to note that FDI value, higher educational enrolment and domestic trade have not yielded significant results on GDP growth for central China. From the empirical results, it can be understood that most FDI has been invested in the eastern and western provinces, with the latter winning renewable energy investments due to the availability of land and high altitude. Zhu et al. (2019), in their study of financial inclusion in Chinese regions due to FDI, used the Hotelling model and concluded that there were negative spatial spillover effects on the central Chinese provinces. Educational enrolment has unexpectedly shown statistically insignificant estimates. This could be an indication of the lack of higher educational institutions in the central provinces. Zhu et al. (2018) carried out a study on the panel data of six central provinces' economic growth determinants and concluded that the contribution of education was less than 5 per cent and yielded insignificant effects on the educational quality level in the central provinces. Due to better opportunities in eastern China and the concentration of significant FDI industrial growth in the coastal regions, many educated youth could be migrating to SEZs in the east for better career opportunities (Xia et al. 2022).

Hence, there is a direct causal relationship between FDI and education combined on economic growth at the provincial level. There are investments by domestic private enterprises in central China due to the incentives provided by the central and provincial governments in the 2004 policy and the Thirteenth Five-Year-Plan. Domestic trade in central China must be improved through the establishment of efficient provincial supply chains that would help the forces of supply and demand function more effectively. Liu et al. (2020) suggested that enhanced supply chain responsibilities through diversification and incorporation would impact positively on community development, especially in rural areas of the central Chinese provinces.

Conclusions and policy implications

This study has conducted a productivity survey of China's 31 provinces by measuring their GDP growth efficiencies. The empirical results have indicated that the Chinese Government has been improving economic development across all regions. The study also concludes that the gap between potential and real GDP growth has been narrowing over time at the national level, which means that the efficiency of GDP growth increased yearly from 2000 to 2018. However, the performance of GDP growth efficiency at the regional level shows a different picture. Supported by empirical evidence, this chapter provides policy recommendations for improving the GDP growth and efficiency of economic growth for all 31 provinces of China.

Nationally, China's future growth should be concentrated on improving the growth efficiency of its 31 provinces. Economic development should be diversified across all provinces and GDP growth made more efficient. As the empirical model suggests, none of the Chinese provinces has achieved 100 per cent growth efficiency. The growth efficiency figures estimated by the model are heterogeneous and vary across the provinces. Though the eastern provinces are the most developed, with SEZs and ports, they have greater potential than the central provinces to increase their GDP growth efficiency. The eastern provinces exhibited 85–88 per cent efficiency, while the central provinces showed 90–92 per cent efficiency. By increasing and improving skilled educational institutions and intensifying supply chain opportunities through FDI, it is possible for the central provinces to achieve 100 per cent growth efficiency.

The western provinces have the highest potential to increase their GDP growth efficiency, and policies discussed in our recommendations should be implemented to achieve that growth potential. It is important to observe that the central provinces, which are in transition, have effectively closed the gap between their real and potential GDP over time. This is evident from the positive and significant μ and η. However, the growth efficiency performances of the eastern provinces, which form the most developed region, and the western provinces, which have been underdeveloped, were stagnant as μ and η were not significant during the period of analysis. This warrants further analysis, which is beyond the scope of this chapter due to the lack of proper data.

References

Aigner, D., C.A.K. Lovell, and P. Schmidt. 1977. 'Formulation and Estimation of Stochastic Frontier Production Function Models.' *Journal of Econometrics* 6, no. 1: 21–37. doi.org/10.1016/0304-4076(77)90052-5.

Ang, Y.Y. 2018. 'Domestic Flying Geese: Industrial Transfer and Delayed Policy Diffusion in China.' *The China Quarterly* 234: 420–43. doi.org/10.1017/S0305741018000516.

Battese, G.E., and T.J. Coelli. 1992. 'Frontier Production Functions, Technical Efficiency and Panel Data: With Application to Paddy Farmers in India.' *Journal of Productivity Analysis* 3 (June): 153–69. doi.org/10.1007/BF00158774.

Brodsgaard, K.E. 2012. 'Politics and Business Group Formation in China: The Party in Control?' *The China Quarterly* 211: 624–48. doi.org/10.1017/S0305741012000811.

Cai, F. 2010. 'Demographic Transition, Demographic Dividend, and Lewis Turning Point in China.' *China Economic Journal* 3, no. 2: 107–19. doi.org/10.1080/17538963.2010.511899.

Cai, F. 2020. 'The Second Demographic Dividend as a Driver of China's Growth.' *China & World Economy* 28, no. 5: 26–44. doi.org/10.1111/cwe.12350.

Chen, M., and Y. Zheng. 2008. 'China's Regional Disparity and Its Policy Responses.' *China and World Economy* 16, no. 4: 16–32. doi.org/10.1111/j.1749-124X.2008.00119.x.

Cheung, K.Y. 2010. 'Spill Over Effects of FDI via Exports on Innovation Performance of China's High-Technology Industries.' *Journal of Contemporary China* 19, no. 65: 541–57. doi.org/10.1080/10670561003666152.

Delis, T., and D. Kyrkilis. 2017. 'Locational Concentration of Foreign Direct Investment in China: A Cluster Factor-Based Analysis.' *Journal of the Knowledge Economy* 8, no. 4: 1115–32. doi.org/10.1007/s13132-016-0367-7.

Gao, D., and S. Li. 2022. 'Spatiotemporal Impact of Railway Network in the Qinghai–Tibet Plateau on Accessibility and Economic Linkages during 1984–2030.' *Journal of Transport Geography* 100: 103332. doi.org/10.1016/j.jtrangeo.2022.103332.

Gunay, S., G. Can, and M. Ocak. 2021. 'Forecast of China's Economic Growth during the COVID-19 Pandemic: A MIDAS Regression Analysis.' *Journal of Chinese Economic and Foreign Trade Studies* 14, no. 1: 3–17. doi.org/10.1108/JCEFTS-08-2020-0053.

Hamidi, H. 2021. 'China's Economic & Military Growth: The Effects and Consequences on the U.S.A. Since 2000 to 2019.' *International Journal of Innovative Research in the Humanities* 1, no. 4: 135–42.

Huang, T., and N. Lardy. 2022. 'China's Private Firms Are Trailing the State-Owned Sector on Several Key Indicators in 2022.' *PIIE Charts*, 1 September. Washington, DC: Peterson Institute for International Economics. www.piie.com/research/piie-charts/chinas-private-firms-are-trailing-state-owned-sector-several-key-indicators.

Huang, T., and N. Véron. 2023. 'The Private Sector's Share of China's Largest Listed Companies Continued to Decline to 43 Percent in the Second Half of 2022.' *Realtime Economics Blog*, 2 February. Washington, DC: Peterson Institute for International Economics. www.piie.com/blogs/realtime-economics/private-sectors-share-chinas-largest-listed-companies-continued-decline-43.

Jia, J., C. Qin, G. Ma, and L. Wang. 2020. 'Place-Based Policies, State-Led Industrialisation, and Regional Development: Evidence from China's Great Western Development Programme.' *European Economic Review* 123, no. 4: 103398. dx.doi.org/10.1016/j.euroecorev.2020.103398.

Jondrow, J., C.A.K. Lovell, I.S. Materov, and P. Schmidt. 1982. 'On the Estimation of Technical Inefficiency in the Stochastic Frontier Production Function Model.' *Journal of Econometrics* 19, nos 2–3: 233–38. doi.org/10.1016/0304-4076(82)90004-5.

Jones, L., and M. Bloomfield. 2020. 'PPPs in China: Does the Growth in Chinese PPPs Signal a Liberalising Economy?' *New Political Economy* 25, no. 5: 829–47. doi.org/10.1080/13563467.2020.1721451.

Kalirajan, K.P., and J.C. Flinn. 1983. 'The Measurement of Farm [Firm] Specific Technical Efficiency.' *Pakistan Journal of Applied Economics* 2, no. 2: 167–80.

Lai, H. 2007. 'Developing Central China: A New Regional Programme.' *China: An International Journal* 5, no. 1: 109–28. doi.org/10.1353/chn.2007.0002.

Li, H., L. Li, B. Wu, and Y. Xiong. 2012a. 'The End of Cheap Chinese Labour.' *Journal of Economic Perspectives* 26, no. 4: 57–74. doi.org/10.1257/jep.26.4.57.

Liu, L., H. Ross, and A. Ariyawardana. 2020. 'Community Development through Supply Chain Responsibility: A Case Study of Rice Supply Chains and Connected Rural Communities in Central China.' *Sustainability* 12, no. 3: 2–19. dx.doi.org/10.3390/su12030927.

Ma, G., I. Roberts, and G. Kelly. 2017. 'Rebalancing China's Economy: Domestic and International Implications.' *China & World Economy* 25, no. 1: 1–31. doi.org/10.1111/cwe.12184.

McDowall, W., Y. Geng, B. Huang, E. Bartekova, R. Bleischwitz, S. Turkeli, R. Kemp, and T. Domenech. 2017. 'Circular Economy Policies in China and Europe.' *Journal of Industrial Ecology* 21, no. 3: 651–61. doi.org/10.1111/jiec.12597.

Meeusen, W., and J. van den Broeck. 1977. 'Technical Efficiency and Dimension of the Firm: Some Results on the Use of Frontier Production Functions.' *Empirical Economics* 2, no. 2: 109–22. doi.org/10.1007/BF01767476.

Morck, R., B. Yeung, and M. Zhao. 2008. 'Perspectives on China's Outward Foreign Direct Investment.' *Journal of International Business Studies* 39, no. 3: 337–50. doi.org/10.1057/palgrave.jibs.8400366.

National Bureau of Statistics (NBS). 2023. *Statistical Database*. Beijing: National Bureau of Statistics of the People's Republic of China. data.stats.gov.cn/english/.

National Development and Reform Commission (NDRC). 2015. *The 13th Five Year Plan for Economic and Social Development of the People's Republic of China (2016–2020)*. Beijing: Central Compilation & Translation Press. en.ndrc.gov.cn/policies/202105/P020210527785800103339.pdf.

National Working Committee on Children and Women (NWCCW), National Bureau of Statistics of China, and United Nations Children's Fund. 2023. 'Figure 1.1 Geographic Regions of China.' In *Children in China: An Atlas of Social Indicators 2018*, 15. Beijing: UNICEF China. www.unicef.cn/sites/unicef.org.china/files/2019-06/01EN-Population%20demographics%20Atlas%202018.pdf.

O'Neill, A. 2024a. 'India: Average Age of the Population from 1950 to 2100 (Median Age in Years).' *Statista Database*. www.statista.com/statistics/254469/median-age-of-the-population-in-india/.

O'Neill, A. 2024b. 'Vietnam: Average Age of the Population from 1950 to 2100 (Median Age in Years).' *Statista Database*. www.statista.com/statistics/444584/average-age-of-the-population-in-vietnam/#:~:text=The%20median%20age%20in%20Vietnam,to%2047.4%20years%20by%202100.

Suvannaphakdy, S. 2021. 'Assessing the Impact of the Regional Comprehensive Economic Partnership on ASEAN Trade.' *Journal of Southeast Asian Economies* 22, no. 1: 133–54. doi.org/10.1355/ae38-1f.

Textor, C. 2023. 'Population Distribution in China in 2021, by Five-Year Age Group.' *Statista Database*, 11 December. www.statista.com/statistics/1101677/population-distribution-by-detailed-age-group-in-china/#:~:text=Population%20distribution%20 by%20five%2Dyear%20age%20group%20in%20China%202021&text=As%20of%20 2021%2C%20the%20bulk,than%20half%20of%20the%20population.

Textor, C. 2024. 'Inequality of Income Distribution Based on the Gini Coefficient in China from 2012 to 2022.' *Statista Database*, 22 May. www.statista.com/statistics/250400/ inequality-of-income-distribution-in-china-based-on-the-gini-index/.

Tuan, C., and Linda F.Y. Ng. 2004. 'Manufacturing Agglomeration as Incentives to Asian FDI in China after WTO.' *Journal of Asian Economics* 15, no. 4: 673–93. doi.org/10.1016/j. asieco.2004.05.014.

Wei, Y.H.D., and I. Liefner. 2012. 'Globalization, Industrial Restructuring, and Regional Development in China.' *Applied Geography* 32, no. 1: 102–5. doi.org/10.1016/j. apgeog.2011.02.005.

World Bank. 2019. 'Ease of Doing Business Rank (1 = Most Business-Friendly Regulations): China.' World Bank Doing Business Project. Washington, DC: World Bank Group. data. worldbank.org/indicator/IC.BUS.EASE.XQ?locations=CN.

World Bank. 2020. 'Poverty Headcount Ratio at National Poverty Lines (% of Population): China.' *World Bank Poverty and Inequality Platform*. Washington, DC: World Bank Group. data.worldbank.org/indicator/SI.POV.NAHC?locations=CN.

Xia, H., L. Qingchun, and E.A. Baptista. 2022. 'Spatial Heterogeneity of Internal Migration in China: The Role of Economic, Social and Environmental Characteristics.' *PLoS ONE* 17, no. 11: e0276992. doi.org/10.1371/journal.pone.0276992.

Xinhua. 2023. 'China's FDI Inflow up 6.3% in 2022.' 18 January. Beijing: State Council Information Office of the People's Republic of China. english.scio.gov.cn/ pressroom/2023-01/18/content_85065705.htm.

Xu, X., X. Wang, and Y. Gao. 2013. 'The Political Economy of Regional Development in China.' In *China's Regional Development: Review and Prospect*, edited by M. Lu, Z. Chen, Z. Xiwei, and X. Xiangxiang, 41–90. London: Routledge.

Yu, Hong. 2014. 'The Ascendency of State-Owned Enterprises in China: Development, Controversy and Problems.' *Journal of Contemporary China* 23, no. 85: 161–82. doi.org/10. 1080/10670564.2013.809990.

Yuan, Y. 2019. 'The Central Boom: Six Provinces in Central China Gear Up for More Robust Development.' *Beijing Review*, 13 June. www.bjreview.com/China/201906/ t20190610_800170314.html.

Zhang, C. 2019. *How Much Do State-Owned Enterprises Contribute to China's GDP and Employment?* Working Paper, 15 July. Washington, DC: World Bank Group. documents1. worldbank.org/curated/en/449701565248091726/pdf/How-Much-Do-State-Owned-Enterprises-Contribute-to-China-s-GDP-and-Employment.pdf. doi.org/10.1596/32306.

Zhou, Y., and L. Song. 2016. 'Income Inequality in China: Causes and Policy Responses.' *China Economic Journal* 9, no. 2: 186–208. doi.org/10.1080/17538963.2016.1168203.

Zhu, B., J. He, and S. Zhai. 2019. 'Does Financial Inclusion Create a Spatial Spill Over Effect between Regions? Evidence from China.' *Emerging Markets Finance and Trade* 55, no. 5: 980–97. doi.org/10.1080/1540496X.2018.1518779.

Zhu, T.T., H.R. Peng, and Y.J. Zhang. 2018. 'The Influence of Higher Education Development on Economic Growth: Evidence from Central China.' *Higher Education Policy* 31, nos 5–6: 139–57. doi.org/10.1057/s41307-017-0047-7.

4

The state of public finance in China: Why tax and intergovernmental reform are urgently needed

Christine Wong

Introduction

China is facing a multitude of macroeconomic pressures, among them how to reinvigorate growth after several years of the Covid-19 pandemic and a slimmed down real estate sector going forward, how to manage financial risks from the looming local government debt crisis and how to meet the challenges of a rapidly ageing population and declining labour force.[1] All these require a strong fiscal response. Over the past few years, getting a clear read on China's fiscal policy direction has been difficult.

Through the pandemic, fiscal policy responses often appeared weak and inconsistent. In 2020, at the onset of Covid-19, the government announced a headline deficit of RMB3.76 trillion, equal to just 3.6 per cent of projected GDP. This was far smaller than that of other major economies, many of which vowed to do 'whatever it takes'.[2] Since then, even while economic growth has remained below past levels, the government kept official deficit targets hovering around 3 per cent of GDP each year. The 3 per cent headline deficit announced at the National People's Congress (NPC) in March 2024 was especially surprising, and widely seen as inadequate support for achieving the 5 per cent growth target given the growing geopolitical tensions and deepening gloom over the Chinese economy (MOF 2024b).

---

1   Refer to some other chapters in this volume.
2   France, Germany, Italy and Japan were among those with stimulus programs of 20 per cent or more of GDP. See, for example, Kaneko and Kajimoto (2020).

Of course, the official headline deficit is not the whole story. In fact, the 2024 budget projects general revenue of RMB22.4 trillion and expenditure of RMB28.5 trillion. The projected deficit of RMB4.1 trillion—the headline figure of 3 per cent of GDP— is produced by bringing in RMB2.1 trillion from the government funds budget (GFB) and the state capital budget (SCB), along with carryovers and reserves to offset a part of the RMB6.1-trillion gap in the general budget.[3] There are additional deficits in the GFB and social security funds (SSFs) accounts as well. Ahead of the NPC, Finance Minister Lan Fo'an explained that the budget deficit will be only one of three policy instruments used for stimulus. The other two are tax and fee cuts to support businesses, and RMB3.9 trillion in special purpose bonds (SPBs) and a RMB1-trillion super-long treasury bond to support investment in infrastructure (Wang and Qu 2024). In China's budget accounting, while the deficit and the effects of tax cuts are reflected in the general budget, the effects of the SPBs and special treasury bond are reflected in the GFB and not included in the reported deficit. To see the full effects of the stimulus measures cited by the finance minister requires looking at all four fiscal accounts reported annually to the NPC.

This chapter examines the state of China's public finances and argues that tax and intergovernmental reform are urgently needed. Part one explains the four budgets and how they interact. Part two examines the trends in each of the three main budgets over the past decade to show that they are all moving in an unsustainable direction, and to expose deficits that are bigger than the headline deficit but are largely hidden from scrutiny. Part three concludes by noting the urgency for reform.

The four budgets and their interactions

The Chinese budget has become more complicated and opaque since accounting changes were introduced under the new budget law in 2015, which called for the government to present four budget accounts in its annual report to the NPC. These accounts represent all the fiscal resources of government but are controlled and managed by different authorities. The Ministry of Finance (MOF) controls the main account, the general budget, which draws revenues from taxes and administrative fees to fund the day-to-day operations of government and public services. The government-managed funds budget (GFB) contains two dozen or so 'funds', such as the Civil Aviation Development Fund, the Railway Construction Fund and lottery funds, which are separately collected and controlled by the recipient agencies. Since 2007, when they were first designated as a government fund, land lease revenues have constituted by far the largest part of the GFB and are controlled by local governments by derivation. The state capital budget is small and comprises profit remittances from the state-owned enterprises under the purview of the State-Owned Assets Supervision and Administration Commission.

---

3   There is a small discrepancy due to rounding.

The social security funds comprise the revenues and expenditures of the seven social insurance schemes and are managed by the Ministry of Human Resources and Social Security and the National Healthcare Security Administration.

Under the revised budget law, the MOF has gradually extended greater control over the GFB and the SCB. Since 2015, several government-managed funds have been abolished and their revenue streams moved into the general budget.[4] Sunset clauses have been placed on the remaining funds, with 'expired' balances swept into the general budget. These changes introduced a clearer delineation of scope that moved recurrent expenditures to the general budget, leaving the GFB more clearly focused on capital expenditures. The budget law also expanded the scope of and set new rules for profit remittances from SOEs into the SCB. The share of the SCB transferred to the general budget has been incrementally raised to 30 per cent since 2020, for use in social expenditures (see MOF 2019).

Since 2015, the funds brought in from other budgets, along with carryovers and a small amount of reserves from the budget stabilisation fund (BSF), have been used to offset a significant portion of the general budget deficit each year and allowed the headline deficit to be kept at or below 3 per cent of GDP—long considered a sacred red line by China's top leaders (Table 4.1 and Figure 4.1).

Table 4.1 General budget deficits, headline deficits and inter-budget transfers (RMB billion)

Year	General budget deficit	Transfers from carryovers, BSF and other budgets	Official ('headline') deficit	Share of deficit financed by transfers (%)
2015	2,361	824	1,620	35
2016	2,815	723	2,180	26
2017	3,049	1,004	2,380	33
2018	3,755	1,477	2,380	39
2019	4,847	2,220	2,760	46
2020	6,277	2,630	3,767	42
2021	4,312	1,112	3,570	26
2022	5,690	2,474	3,370	43
2023	5,779	1,684	3,880	29
2024p	6,154	2,094	4,060	34

Note: Figures for the deficit and transfers are from final accounts except for 2024.
Source: Author's calculations based on budget reports to the NPC, 2016–24, and CEIC Data (www.ceicdata.com/en).

---

4   The number of funds in the GFB has been cut from more than 50 to about 20, and revenue streams such as the rural and urban education surcharges were reclassified and absorbed in the general budget. See MOF (2017).

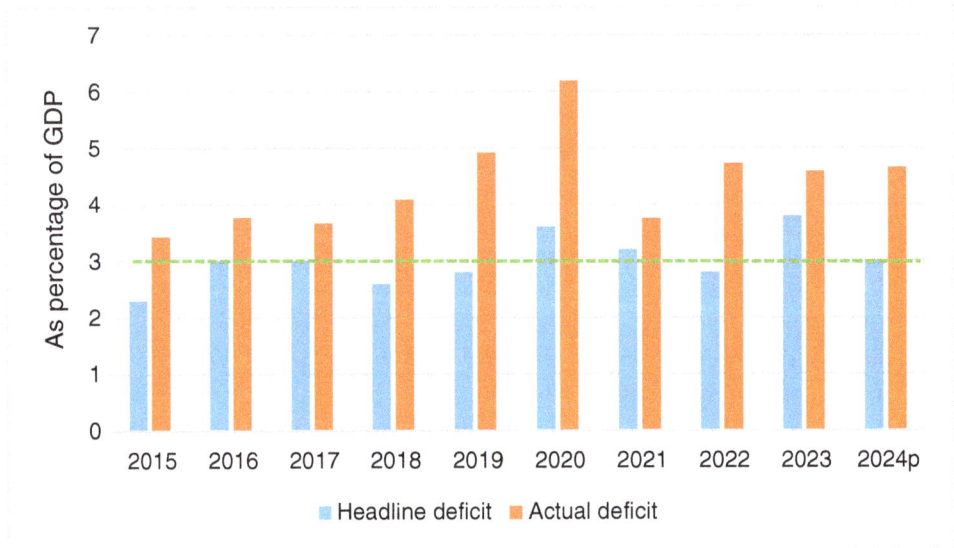

Figure 4.1 Headline deficits versus projected real deficits in the general budget
Sources: Table 4.1; CEIC Data (www.ceicdata.com/en).

The introduction of local government debt and its treatment in 2015 have added to the complexity of reading the budget. When the new budget law permitted local governments to borrow directly for capital spending, two types of local government debt were created, and they are differentiated by use and budgeting treatment. General bonds are designated for use in financing public infrastructure projects with no revenue generation (for example, schools and village roads) and to cover local government deficits that are approved by the NPC. The debt is included as a deficit in the national budget to be repaid from local government general revenues. Special purpose bonds (专项债) are to be used for financing public infrastructure that has revenue streams (for example, toll roads and urban water systems). They are to be repaid from the local GFB, with project revenues and other incomes. Because the GFB is not formally part of the budget, special purpose debt—while recognised and counted as government debt—is not included in the budget deficit.

From their inception, the use of SPBs has grown rapidly, with a quota approved by the NPC peaking at 3.7 per cent of GDP in 2020 when a large stimulus was applied in response to the Covid-19 pandemic. The approved quotas have since remained at the level of nearly 3 per cent of GDP per annum (Figure 4.2).

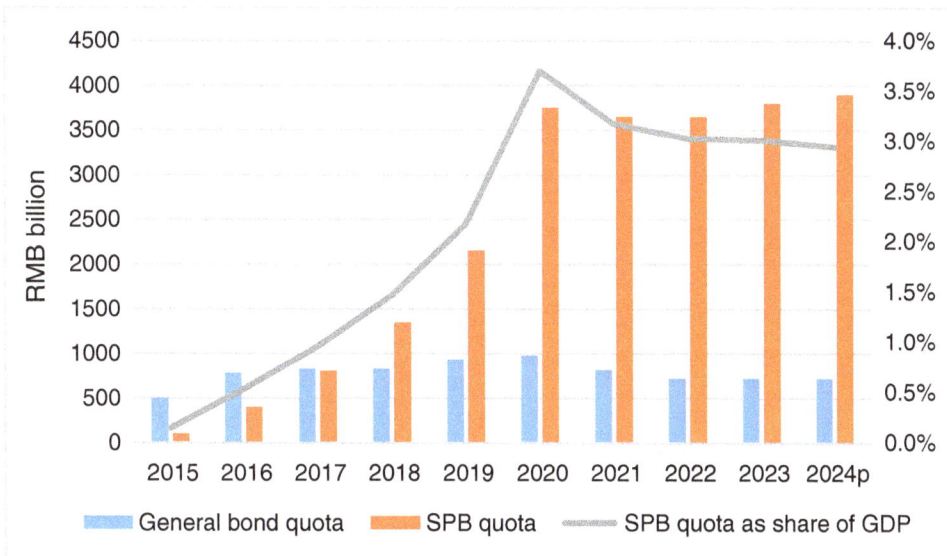

Figure 4.2 Annual quotas of general and special purpose bonds for local governments

Source: Author's calculations based on budget reports and CEIC Data (www.ceicdata.com/en).

Putting SPBs in the GFB opened the door to a second source of fiscal deficits that is, notably, not broken out and reported explicitly to the NPC, and has attracted little notice. Before 2015, as a composite of legally mandated fees earmarked for specific uses—such as the Civil Aviation Development Fund levied on air travel—the GFB had surpluses each year, rather than deficits, since each fund was required to be balanced from year to year.[5] Land revenues are legally, though loosely, restricted to uses including land preparation and development, farmland improvement, urban infrastructure and contributions to rural education, etcetera.

With the growing use of SPBs for stimulus spending especially through the pandemic, the GFB turned from surplus to deficit in 2016, and the deficit grew, to 2.7 per cent and 2.4 per cent of GDP in 2022 and 2023, respectively. In 2024 it will reach 3.7 per cent with the addition of RMB3.9 trillion in SPBs and the RMB1-trillion super-long treasury bond that will also be placed in the GFB.[6]

---

5   Aggregate data for the government funds have been available since 2010 and showed surpluses for every year before 2016. See MOF final accounts—for example, for 2010, see MOF (2011).

6   This deficit is based on projected land revenues roughly at the same level as 2023. If land revenues continue to decline, the fund deficit will be even larger.

Trends in the three main budgets

The general budget

As economic growth slowed from 2010, tax revenues plateaued from 2012 and then began a long decline in 2015, when a cascading series of tax and fee cuts was introduced that reduced tax collection. From 2015 to 2023, general revenues fell by almost 5 per cent of GDP (see Wong 2021). If revenues reach the budget target of RMB22.4 trillion this year, they will be equal to 16.9 per cent of projected GDP, returning to the level of collection last reached in 2005 (Figure 4.3). Since 2005, though, many big social spending programs have been introduced to provide basic universal social welfare such as free basic education, medical insurance and pensions, which were the main forces pushing aggregate spending up by almost 8 per cent of GDP to 2015.

The erosion of revenues has forced a significant cut in expenditures and increased the deficit. Aggregate data show the general budget expenditure shrinking from 25.5 per cent of GDP in 2015 to 21.8 per cent in 2023, with across-the-board cuts in the main categories (Table 4.2).

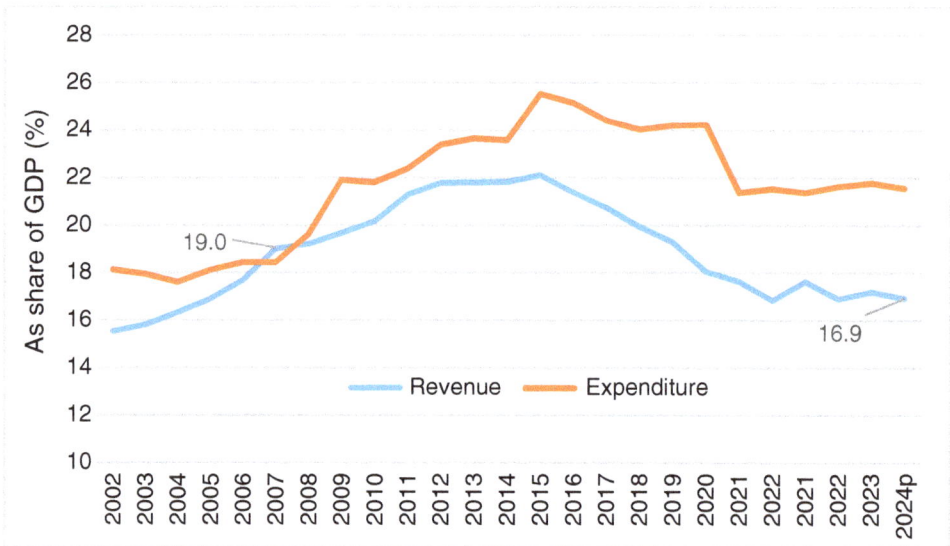

Figure 4.3 Trends in general budget revenues and expenditures

Source: Author's calculations based on budget reports and CEIC Data (www.ceicdata.com/en).

Table 4.2 General budget expenditures, main categories (percentage of GDP)

	2015	2017	2019	2021	2022	2023
General budget expenditure	25.5	24.4	24.2	21.4	21.5	21.8
Education	3.8	3.6	3.5	3.3	3.3	3.3
Health	1.7	1.7	1.7	1.7	1.9	1.8
Environmental protection	0.7	0.7	0.7	0.5	0.4	0.4
Urban and rural community affairs	2.3	2.5	2.5	1.7	1.6	1.6
Agriculture, forestry and water conservation	2.5	2.3	2.3	1.9	1.9	1.9
Transport and shipping	1.8	1.3	1.2	1.0	1.0	1.0
Subtotal of listed categories	**12.9**	**12.1**	**12.0**	**10.0**	**10.0**	**10.0**

Note: The major category of social security and employment is omitted because its scope was changed in 2018 to include expenditures on public employee pensions that were previously reported elsewhere, and the data are not comparable across the period covered in this table.
Sources: Budget reports for 2020–24; MOF (2024a).

Behind the numbers, the cutback in spending spread pain throughout the intergovernmental fiscal system and created funding crises in many localities.[7] Anecdotal reports of local financing problems have grown in frequency and severity. They include widespread complaints of wage arrears, cancelled bonuses and performance pay to public employees, excess fines and fees levied on businesses and residents, curtailed bus services and even central heating being cut off in northern cities during the harsh winter months. In their review of the 2022 budget implementation, the Finance and Economics Committee of the NPC noted the 'relatively prominent' funding gap at the grassroots level and their difficulty in meeting the 'three guarantees' of payroll, government operations and basic services (MOF 2023). A recent Chinese Academy of Fiscal Sciences survey of 521 counties and cities found most local governments admitting to 'leaving a considerable portion of policy mandates unmet' due to funding shortages (Cheng 2023).

This also drove local governments to become more dependent on land revenues. In China's highly decentralised but asymmetrical fiscal system, local governments provide almost all public services and account for more than 85 per cent of national budget spending but collect only 55 per cent of revenues. They depend on central government transfers to fill the gap. Aggregate data show that the combination of local revenues and central transfers has fallen short of fully funding local expenditures since 2015 (Figure 4.4).

---

7   See Wong (2021, 2023) for discussion of problems of local finance.

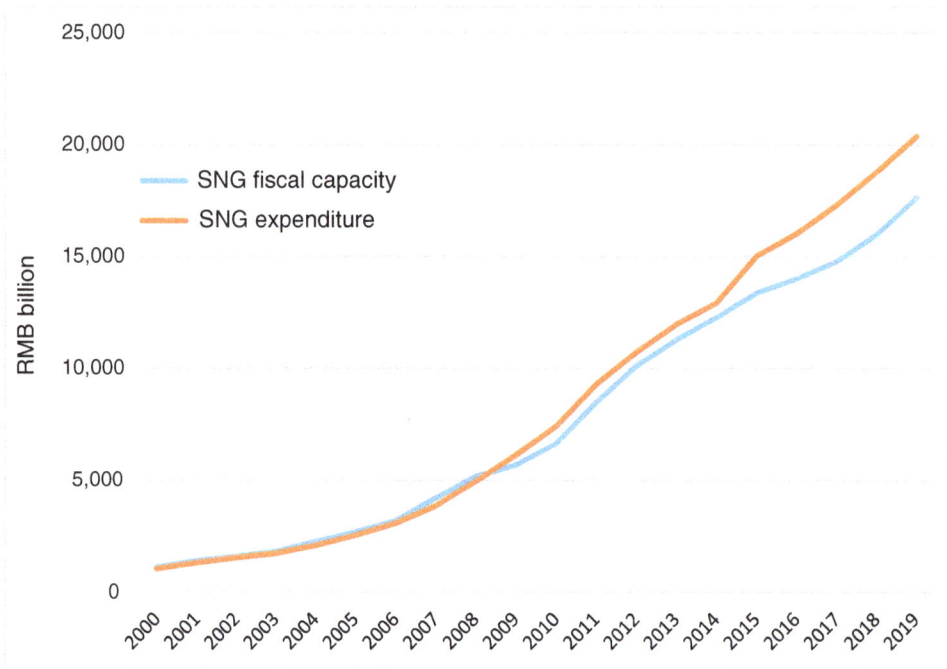

Figure 4.4 The local government funding gap

Note: Local government fiscal capacity is defined as local government general revenue plus gross transfers.
Source: Author's calculations based on budget reports and CEIC data (www.ceicdata.com/en).

With the new budget law opening the door to tapping other budgets, inter-budget transfers and carryovers grew quickly, to peak at RMB1.9 trillion in 2019, which is equal to 9.3 per cent of local budget expenditures (Figure 4.5). Since the state capital operating budget is very small and the social security budget is earmarked for pension and health expenditures, the GFB is the primary source of these transfers, of which land revenues constituted 85–90 per cent (and more than 90 per cent of local government funds). With the collapse of land sales in recent years, these transfers have shrunk. In 2023 they were RMB899 billion and funded just 3.8 per cent of local budget expenditures.

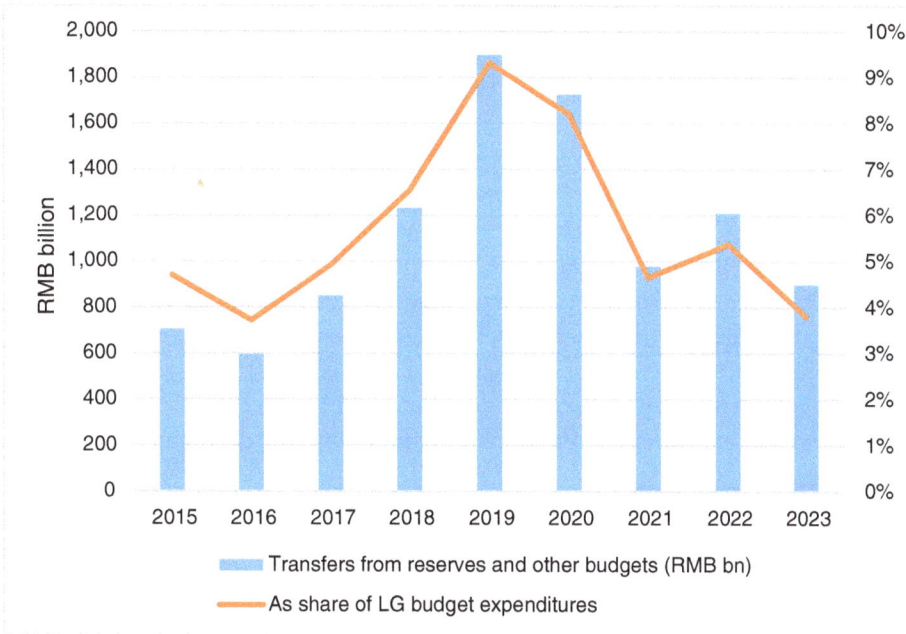

Figure 4.5 Gap-filling transfers from other budgets
Sources: MOF budget reports to the NPC, 2015–23; NBS data.

Nor is the central government spared. During the pandemic, with local governments under growing fiscal stress, the central government had to step up transfers. Since 2020, in every year except 2021, transfers to local governments have taken 100 per cent or more of central government general budget revenues, leaving it also dependent on drawing from other budgets and dipping into deficit finance (Figure 4.6).

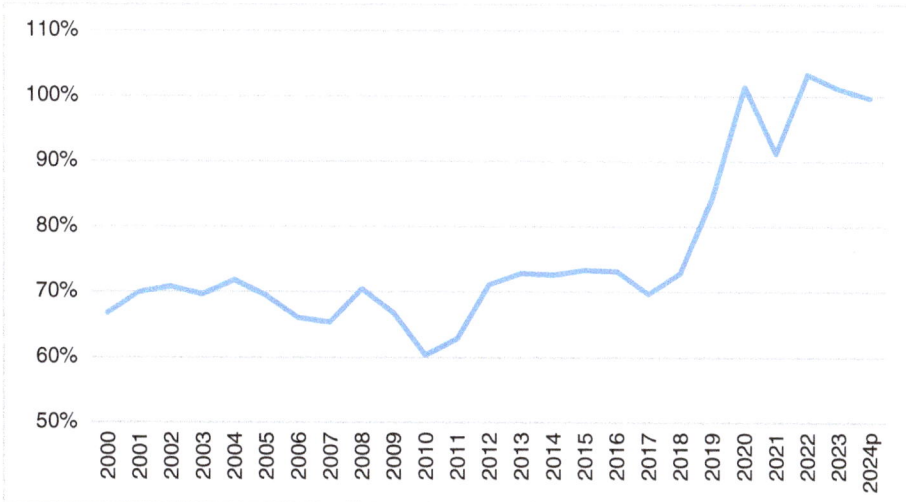

Figure 4.6 Transfers as a share of central government revenues*
* Transfers include tax rebates.
Source: Author's calculations based on budget reports and CEIC Data (www.ceicdata.com/en).

The government fund budget

Since the new budget law in 2015 cut the number of funds and reclassified some revenues, growth in government fund revenue has come solely from land. Under increasing pressure on their general budget, local governments intensified efforts to develop land revenues. With land revenues growing from 4.7 per cent of GDP in 2015 to 8.3 per cent in 2020, government fund revenues grew from 6.1 per cent to 9.2 per cent, and the share from land climbed to 90 per cent of government fund revenues at the peak (Figure 4.7). This ramp-up was cut short by the retrenchment of the real estate sector that began in July 2021, and land revenues declined from 2022.[8] With government fund revenues falling to 5.6 per cent of GDP in 2023 and projected to fall further, to 5.3 per cent in 2024. Even with the increased issuance of SPBs and treasury bonds propping up expenditures, the GFB is trending towards declining capacity and growing deficit.

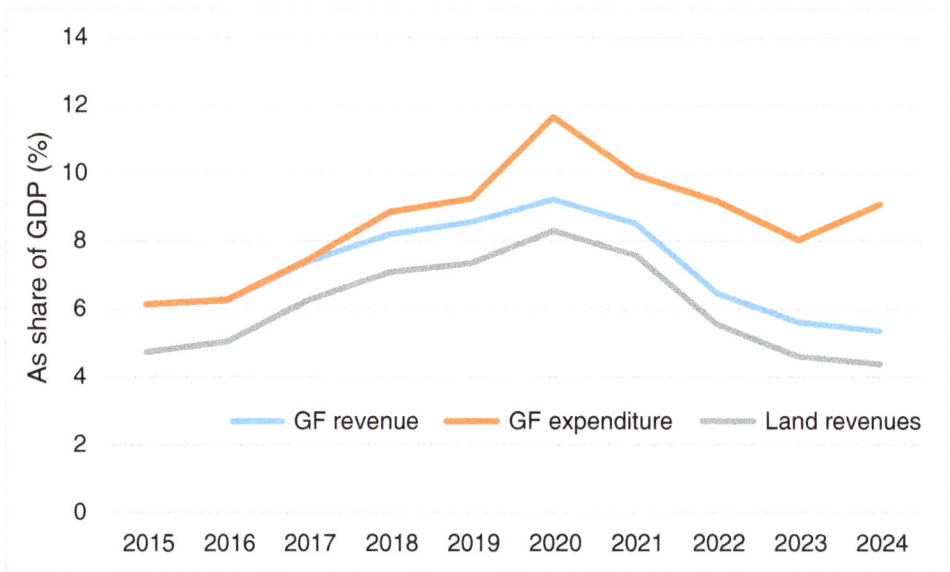

Figure 4.7 The rise and fall of revenues and expenditures in the GFB
Source: Author's calculations based on budget reports and CEIC Data (www.ceicdata.com/en).

The decline of land revenues has been devastating to local government finances. Not only had land become an important supplementary source of finance for recurrent expenditures, it is even more important as the principal source of financing for investing in infrastructure and debt servicing.

---

8   Land revenue receipts typically lag auction sales by 6–12 months or more, so the decline in land sales from the second half of 2021 showed up only in 2022.

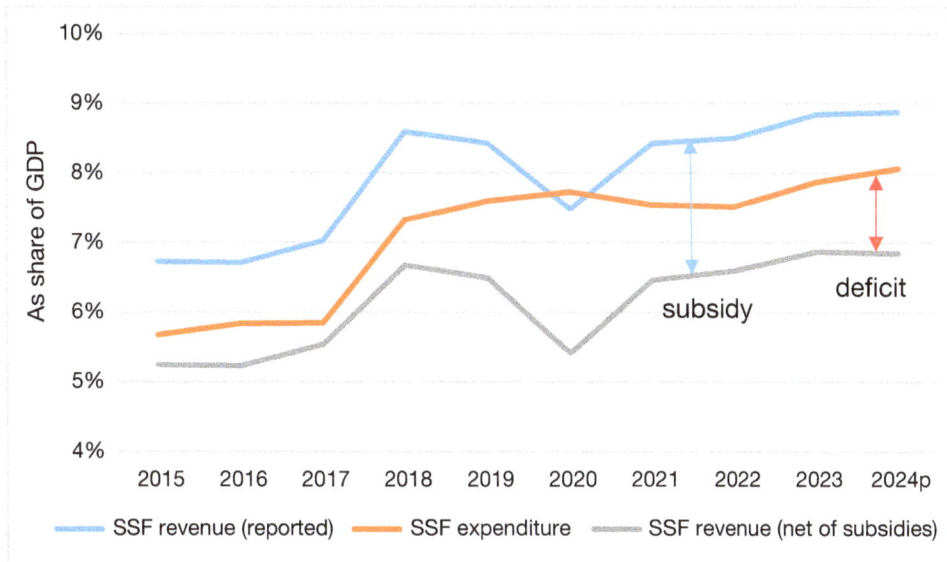

Figure 4.8 Trends in the SSF budget

Source: Author's calculations based on budget reports, final accounts and CEIC Data (www. ceicdata.com/en).

The social security funds budget

The SSF comprises seven social insurance programs: three pension schemes, two medical insurance schemes, workplace disability insurance and unemployment insurance. Each one has three sources of revenue: insurance premiums/contributions, interests and dividends, and fiscal subsidy. In contrast to the general budget and GFB, SSF revenues are growing as a share of GDP, from 6.7 per cent in 2015 to 8.8 per cent in 2023. In the annual reports to the NPC, the SSF budget has shown a surplus each year except 2020 (when the government waived pension and unemployment insurance contributions during the Covid-19 pandemic).

Net of fiscal subsidies, which make up 22–23 per cent of revenues, the SSF budget turns from surplus to a small deficit of just more than 1 per cent of GDP (Figure 4.8). With China's ageing population pushing up both health and pension expenditures, this deficit is expected to grow over the next decade and will require growing fiscal subsidies unless rules are changed to increase contribution rates, reduce benefit levels or raise the retirement age. The urgency for action is underscored by the size and rapid growth of these subsidies, which are projected to take up nearly one-tenth of general budget expenditures in 2024 (Figure 4.9).

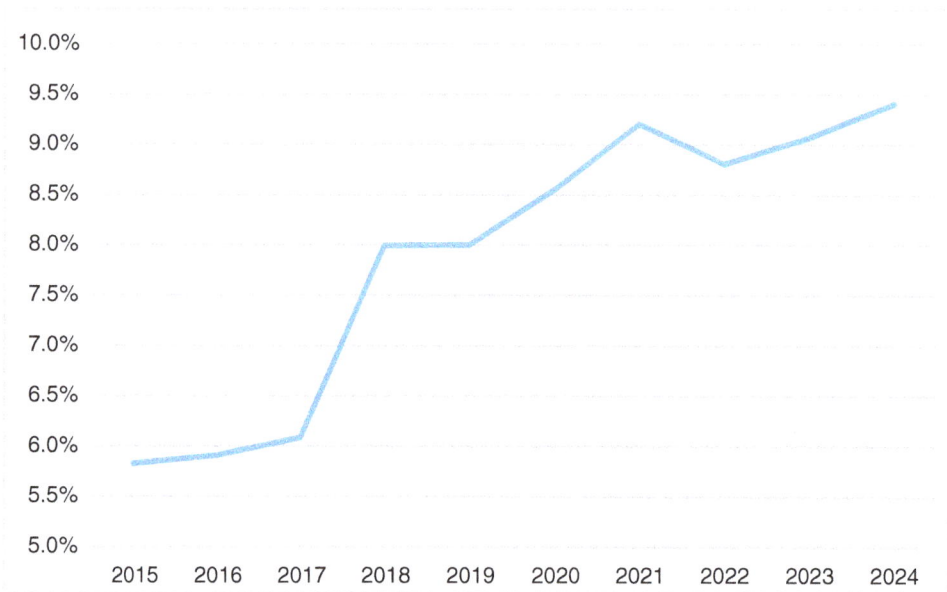

Figure 4.9 Fiscal subsidies to the SSF as share of general budget expenditures

Source: Author's calculations based on budget reports, final accounts and CEIC Data (www. ceicdata.com/en).

The whole picture

Adding together the balances across the four budgets requires correcting for the accounting of subsidies for social insurance expenditures, which are reported both in the general budget, under 'social security and employment expenditures', and in the expenditures of the SSF budget. This is presented in Table 4.3, in which the figures for general budget expenditures and SSF revenues differ from the official data reported separately for each budget.

Together, the four budgets produced a consolidated deficit of RMB7.3 trillion, or 5.8 per cent of GDP in 2023—1.5 times the headline deficit of 3.8 per cent. Likewise, the consolidated deficit for 2020 was 8.6 per cent of GDP—2.4 times the current year headline deficit—and 8.2 per cent in 2022. These were all sizeable in providing support to the economy and significantly larger than portrayed by the headline deficits.

What is concerning is that the deficits are large compared with fiscal capacity. The 2023 consolidated deficit was almost 40 per cent as large as the tax revenues of RMB18.1 trillion for the year. In 2024, the projected deficit will be smaller; at RMB5.9 trillion, it will be equal to one-third of the projected tax revenues of RMB18.8 trillion.[9] However, these deficits have grown steeply through the decade, from 2.3 per cent of GDP in 2015 to 5.8 per cent in 2023, and they have come at the expense of shrinking expenditures on public services, as shown in Table 4.2.

---

9   Author's calculations and CEIC data (www.ceicdata.com/en).

Table 4.3 The four government budgets (percentage of GDP)

	2015	2016	2017	2018	2019	2020	2021	2022	2023
General budget									
Revenue	22.1	21.4	20.7	19.9	19.3	18.0	17.6	16.9	17.2
Expenditure	24.0	23.7	22.9	22.1	22.3	22.2	19.4	19.7	19.8
General budget balance	*–1.9*	*–2.3*	*–2.2*	*–2.2*	*–3.0*	*–4.1*	*–1.8*	*–2.8*	*–2.6*
Government fund budget									
Revenue	6.1	6.2	7.4	8.2	8.6	9.2	8.5	6.5	5.6
Expenditure	6.1	6.3	7.4	8.9	9.3	11.6	10.0	9.2	8.0
Government fund budget balance	*0.0*	*0.0*	*–0.1*	*–0.7*	*–0.7*	*–2.4*	*–1.4*	*–2.7*	*–2.4*
State capital operating budget									
Revenue	0.4	0.3	0.3	0.3	0.4	0.5	0.5	0.5	0.5
Expenditure	0.3	0.3	0.2	0.2	0.2	0.3	0.2	0.3	0.3
State capital operating budget balance	*0.1*	*0.1*	*0.1*	*0.1*	*0.2*	*0.2*	*0.2*	*0.2*	*0.3*
Social security budget									
Revenue (net of fiscal subsidy)	5.2	5.2	5.5	6.7	6.5	5.4	6.5	6.6	6.9
Expenditure	5.7	5.8	5.8	7.3	7.6	7.7	7.5	7.5	7.9
Social security budget balance	*–0.4*	*–0.6*	*–0.3*	*–0.7*	*–1.1*	*–2.3*	*–1.1*	*–0.9*	*–1.0*
Consolidated budget									
Revenue	33.9	33.2	34.0	35.1	34.8	33.2	33.1	30.4	30.2
Expenditure	36.2	36.1	36.5	38.5	39.4	41.8	37.2	36.7	36.0
Consolidated fiscal balance	*–2.3*	*–2.9*	*–2.5*	*–3.4*	*–4.6*	*–8.6*	*–4.1*	*–6.3*	*–5.8*
As a multiple of the headline deficit	*1.0*	*1.0*	*0.8*	*1.3*	*1.6*	*2.4*	*1.3*	*2.2*	*1.5*
Consolidated fiscal balance (RMB billion)	*–1,590*	*–2,142*	*–2,059*	*–3.126*	*–4,548*	*–8,762*	*–4,696*	*–7,546*	*–7,281*

Source: Author's calculations based on budget reports and CEIC data (www.ceicdata.com/en).

The build-up of debt

The persistent and growing deficits translate into a build-up of government debt that accelerated during the pandemic. Since 2015, central government debt has nearly tripled, from RMB10.7 trillion to RMB30 trillion in 2023, growing from 15.5 per cent of GDP to 23.8 per cent. Of this, RMB9.1 trillion was added in the three years since 2020. Local government debt grew from RMB14.8 trillion to RMB40.7 trillion during 2015–23, with RMB15 trillion added since 2020. In 2024 total debt could reach RMB79 trillion, or 60 per cent of GDP (Figure 4.10).

While this level of debt is not high by international standards, it has grown rapidly. More concerning is that 57 per cent of it is on local government balance sheets and, in China's fiscal system, local governments have little autonomy for raising revenues or cutting expenditures—the conventional means for fiscal consolidation.

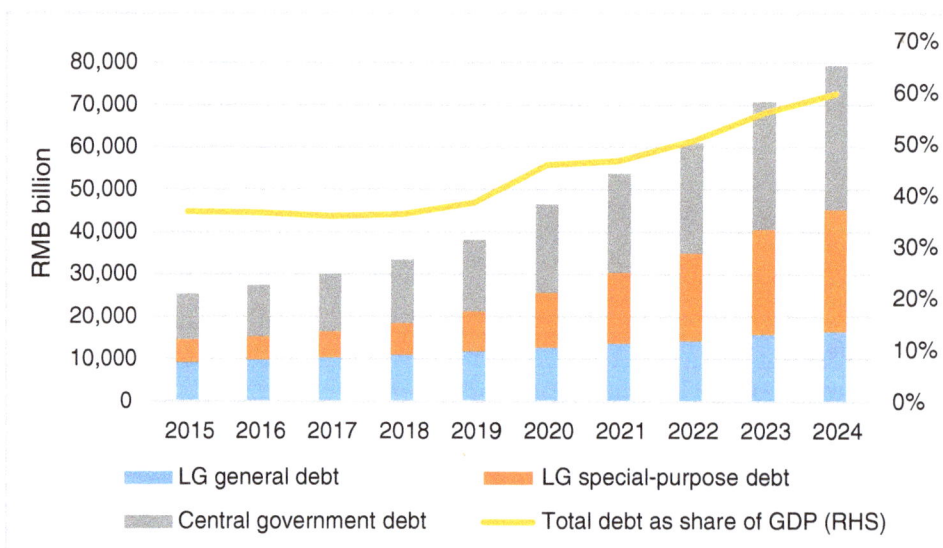

Figure 4.10 The growth of government debt

Source: Author's calculations based on budget reports and CEIC Data (www.ceicdata.com/en).

In addition to the official, explicit debt, there is a large hidden local government debt that is estimated to be as high as RMB60–70 trillion by the IMF, Chinese think tanks and other analysts, adding another 45–50 per cent of GDP in contingent liabilities to local government balance sheets. When this 'hidden debt'—largely raised by local government financial vehicles—is included, local government debt could be as much as 80 per cent of GDP in 2023, or about four times local government fiscal capacity.[10]

---

10 Local government fiscal capacity is the sum of local governments' own revenues, local government fund revenues and transfers.

The urgent need for reform

The current system of fiscal reporting obscures critical information on fiscal balances by scattering them in separate budgets, using transfers from the GFB and SCB to disguise deficits on the general budget and not reporting on deficits in the GFB and SSF. This is a paradoxical outcome since the intent of reforms embedded in the 2015 revision of the budget law was to promote transparency and more effective oversight of fiscal resources. By putting together and scrutinising information on the four budgets, we have uncovered more fully the parlous state of China's public finances.

The government faces two urgent problems. The erosion of tax collection over the past decade has created an aggregate fiscal gap, where the government is not collecting enough revenue to meet expenditure needs, leaving a chronic primary deficit. For a time, these deficits were partly ameliorated by the resort to tapping land revenues. Since 2022 sharp cuts have been implemented to tamp down deficits, but many local governments now struggle to meet basic operating requirements and service provision. There are no empirical studies to track the effect of fiscal erosion on the quality and distribution of public services. The experience of fiscal decline in the 1990s suggests that regional inequalities will widen (see Wong 2021).

Fiscal problems also spill over to affect economic growth, most notably via growing payments arrears to suppliers, which create liquidity problems especially affecting small and micro enterprises (Wong 2024). Stories abound about cash-starved local governments upping fees and fines on citizens and businesses alike. More recently they include reports of 'profit-seeking law enforcement actions' and 'offshore fishing expeditions' in which government agencies launch investigations into private enterprises—especially deep-pocketed, non-local enterprises—to look for infractions to justify levying fines and penalties (Huang and Ma 2024; Bai 2024).

The second problem is local government debt, which dominated headlines throughout 2023 as one of the key risks facing the Chinese economy. Land revenues are the primary source of funds for servicing debt at the local level and their recent collapse has been devastating, exacerbating fiscal stress and precipitating a debt crisis. Adding to the near-term challenge was the approach of a peak repayment period, with an estimated RMB9 trillion coming due in 2023–24. To avert the rising default risks, in late July 2023 the government launched a massive program to refinance and restructure the maturing debt from the most at-risk local government financing vehicles (Caixin Global 2023). While the steps succeeded in defusing the near-term debt risks, they were only stopgap measures. The Central Economic Work Conference held in late October and presided over by President Xi Jinping called for a long-term mechanism for local government debt resolution (Xinhua 2023).

Given this backdrop, the budget presented in March 2024 was surprisingly silent on these large and urgent issues. There was no hint of a fiscal consolidation plan involving either tax increases or expenditure cuts, and there was barely a mention of local government debt. Instead, the budget presented a sizeable stimulus using the old playbook of deficit spending, tax cuts and infrastructure investments. We can only hope that, behind the scenes, the government is hard at work on 'actively planning a new round of fiscal and taxation reform to build a modern fiscal system that is compatible with Chinese modernization, that effectively prevents fiscal risks, and enhances fiscal sustainability', as Minister Lan told participants at the China Development Forum held in April (China Development Forum 2024). Otherwise, the fiscal drag will continue to worsen, hindering China's progress to high-income status and common prosperity.

References

Bai, Chongen. 2024. 'Bai Chongen: Local Government Debt Urgently Needs to Be Resolved: Interview with CPPCC Members.' *Economic Transformation Research*, 19 March. url. au.m.mimecastprotect.com/s/H0WkCjZroMFjOVo7rUW1d84?domain=mp.weixin.qq.com.

Caixin Global. 2023. 'Local Debt Pressures Remain Unabated: Why Are Bank Debt Conversions and Incremental Financing Falling Short of Expectations?' *Caixin Global*, [Beijing], 23 December. www.caixinglobal.com/2023-12-23/weekly-aheadwhy-havent-local-debt-pressures-eased-substantially-and-why-are-bank-debt-reduction-and-incremental-financing-falling-short-of-expectations-102149262.html.

Cheng, Siwei. 2023. 'What Are the Risks of Local Fiscal Operations? Research and Calculation by the Academy of Fiscal Sciences.' *Caixin*, [Beijing], 28 February. economy.caixin.com/2023-02-28/102002952.html.

China Development Forum. 2024. 'How Does Finance Support High-Quality Development? Lan Fuan Introduces Five Key Tasks.' *Xinhua*, 25 March. mp.weixin.qq.com/s/EEF1P1KsD2O1Lk9b79Jb2Q.

Huang, Yuxin, and Ma Xueying. 2024. 'How to Solve "Offshore Fishing" Cases? Scholars Call for the Fines and Confiscations to Be Returned to the Central Government.' *Caixin*, [Beijing], 15 March. china.caixin.com/m/2024-03-15/102175639.html.

Kaneko, Kaori, and Tetsushi Kajimoto. 2020. 'Japan Eyes Another Stimulus Package as Pandemic Crushes Economy.' *Reuters*, 8 May. www.reuters.com/article/us-health-coronavirus-japan-stimulus/japan-eyes-another-stimulus-package-as-pandemic-crushes-economy-idUSKBN22K0AM.

Ministry of Finance (MOF). 2011. *2010 National Government Fund Revenue Final Statement*. 20 July. Beijing: Ministry of Finance of the People's Republic of China. yss.mof.gov.cn/2010juesuan/201107/t20110720_578413.htm.

Ministry of Finance (MOF). 2017. *National Government Fund Directory List*. 20 June. Beijing: Ministry of Finance of the People's Republic of China. szs.mof.gov.cn/zt/mlqd_8464/mlqd/zyzfxjjmlqd/201706/t20170620_2626929.htm.

Ministry of Finance (MOF). 2019. *A Description of Central Government's State Capital Operations in 2018*. 18 July. Beijing: Ministry of Finance of the People's Republic of China. yss.mof.gov.cn/2018czjs/201907/t20190718_3303400.htm.

Ministry of Finance (MOF). 2020. *Report on the Implementation of the Central and Local Budgets in 2019 and the Draft Central and Local Budgets for 2020 (Abstract)*. 23 May. Beijing: Ministry of Finance of the People's Republic of China. www.mof.gov.cn/zhengwuxinxi/caizhengxinwen/202005/t20200523_3518993.htm.

Ministry of Finance (MOF). 2023. *Report of the Financial and Economic Committee of the 14th National People's Congress on the Review of the Implementation of the Central and Local Budgets in 2022 and the Draft Central and Local Budgets for 2023*. 9 March. Beijing: Ministry of Finance of the People's Republic of China. www.mof.gov.cn/zhengwuxinxi/caizhengxinwen/202303/t20230309_3871498.htm.

Ministry of Finance (MOF). 2024a. *Fiscal Revenue and Expenditure in 2023*. 1 February. Beijing: Ministry of Finance of the People's Republic of China. gks.mof.gov.cn/tongjishuju/202402/t20240201_3928009.htm.

Ministry of Finance (MOF). 2024b. *Report on the Implementation of the Central and Local Budgets for 2023 and the Draft Central and Local Budgets for 2024*. 14 March. Beijing: Ministry of Finance of the People's Republic of China. www.mof.gov.cn/zhengwuxinxi/caizhengxinwen/202403/t20240314_3930581.htm.

Wang, Guan, and Qu Zhehan. 2024. 'Strengthen Policy Support and Financial Guarantee to Promote Smooth Circulation of National Economy: Q&A with Lan Fuan, Party Secretary and Minister of the Ministry of Finance, on the Current Economic and Fiscal Situation.' *People's Daily*, 4 January. paper.people.com.cn/rmrb/html/2024-01/04/nw.D110000renmrb_20240104_2-02.htm.

Wong, Christine. 2021. 'Plus ça Change: Three Decades of Fiscal Policy and Central–Local Relations in China.' *China: An International Journal* 19, no. 4: 1–31. muse.jhu.edu/article/839228. doi.org/10.1353/chn.2021.0039.

Wong, Christine. 2023. 'Why There Is No Fiscal Stimulus in 2023.' *EAI Commentary* No. 66, 30 August. Singapore: East Asian Institute, National University of Singapore. research.nus.edu.sg/eai/wp-content/uploads/sites/2/2023/08/EAIC-66-20230830.pdf.

Wong, Kandy. 2024. 'China's "Financially Unhealthy" Small Firms Have a Serious Cash-Flow Problem that Threatens to Topple More Dominoes, Survey Finds.' *South China Morning Post*, [Hong Kong], 2 February. www.scmp.com/economy/china-economy/article/3250618/chinas-financially-unhealthy-small-firms-have-serious-cash-flow-problem-threatens-topple-more.

Xinhua. 2023. 'Central Financial Work Conference Is Held.' 2 November. Beijing: State Council of the People's Republic of China. english.www.gov.cn/news/202311/02/content_WS65430bb8c6d0868f4e8e0e33.html.

5

Adaptive efficiency, institutional change and economic performance: Evidence from the Chinese economy

Chérie Simpson, Ligang Song and Yixiao Zhou

Introduction

We are yet to comprehensively explain the dynamic mechanisms behind the evolution of some countries (China, for example), which, despite relatively low-quality market-compatible institutions, relatively low levels of human capital and relatively low levels of intangible capital stock, have achieved remarkable rates of growth (La Porta et al. 2004; Yang et al. 2018). We know that human capital, technology, institutions and institutional change play a fundamental role in determining long-run economic growth (Acemoglu et al. 2005; Jones and Romer 2010; North 1990; Romer 1990), but we have much to learn about why some emerging, developing and transitioning countries are among the fastest-growing while others are some of the slowest-growing nations in the world and why some countries have escaped the poverty trap while others languish.

This chapter offers a novel perspective to understand the drivers of economic growth by applying the adaptive efficiency framework. The adaptive efficiency framework, as introduced by Song and Simpson (2018), draws on and encompasses the concepts and models of North (1990, 2005), Hayek (1978), Buchanan and Vanberg (1991), Solow–Swan (Solow 1956; Swan 1956), Schumpeter (1947), Coase (1937, 1960), Williamson (2007), Greif (2006), Acemoglu et al. (2005), and Jones and Romer (2010). In so doing, this framework is compatible with, and extends, existing theories of growth by providing an alternative understanding of the complex, interdependent relationship between the institutional framework, the functions of the market and economic growth.

In this context, we present a study of how the environment created by the institutional framework of a society can facilitate the operation of the creative, discovery and allocative functions of the market, leading to higher economic growth and good economic performance over time. Formally defined as 'adaptive efficiency', this ongoing process of innovation and modification allows an economy to flexibly adapt to changing conditions and shocks (North 2005).

For this chapter, we restrict our analysis to the core elements of the adaptive efficiency framework to test it using real economic growth experience. An empirical case study of provincial economies in China is presented and we draw implications for reform and public policy for the betterment of society from the results. More specifically, our empirical case study seeks to understand how the core elements of the adaptive efficiency framework affect the short-term and long-term economic growth of China and its regional economies.

The rest of the chapter is organised into five parts. Section two introduces the adaptive efficiency framework. Section three presents an empirical case study. Using an endogenous growth model that places institutions at the heart of economic growth, we examine the dynamic effect of adaptive efficiency on economic growth based on evidence from Chinese provinces. Section four presents the regression results and the fifth section outlines implications for reform, public policy and regional development policy. Concluding remarks and suggestions for future research follow.

Adaptive efficiency: A novel framework for understanding economic growth

The adaptive efficiency framework proposed by Song and Simpson (2018) links North's concept of adaptive efficiency to Buchanan and Vanberg's (1991) and Hayek's (1978) three market functions. We adopt the extended definition of adaptive efficiency that redefined adaptive efficiency as:

> an ongoing condition of innovation and modification in which the market, through the allocative, discovery and creative functions, responds to the incentive structures that confront choice-makers, utilises localised information, and exploits the creative potential of man to provide solutions to problems and novel situations as they arise. (Song and Simpson 2018: 547)

In this context, adaptive efficiency is expected to be most effective when all three market functions operate freely within a robust, yet flexible institutional environment that promotes a pursuit of profits that is bounded by social norms and morality and empowers entrepreneurs and firms through the decentralisation of the decision-making process and freer competition.

Quantifying the impact of adaptive efficiency using econometric methods remains a challenge. What we intend to do in this chapter is incorporate the proxied core elements of the adaptive efficiency framework into the more conventional neoclassical economic growth models that are often used for estimating the growth impact of factors of production as well as total factor productivity.[1] This chapter is the first empirical attempt to explain and test the core factors of the adaptive efficiency framework (as shown in Figure 5.1).

As indicated in Figure 5.1, the focus of this chapter's theoretical and empirical analyses are the core elements of the adaptive efficiency framework—namely: institutional change, the creative function, the discovery function and the allocative function. These elements are discussed in more detail in the following subsection.

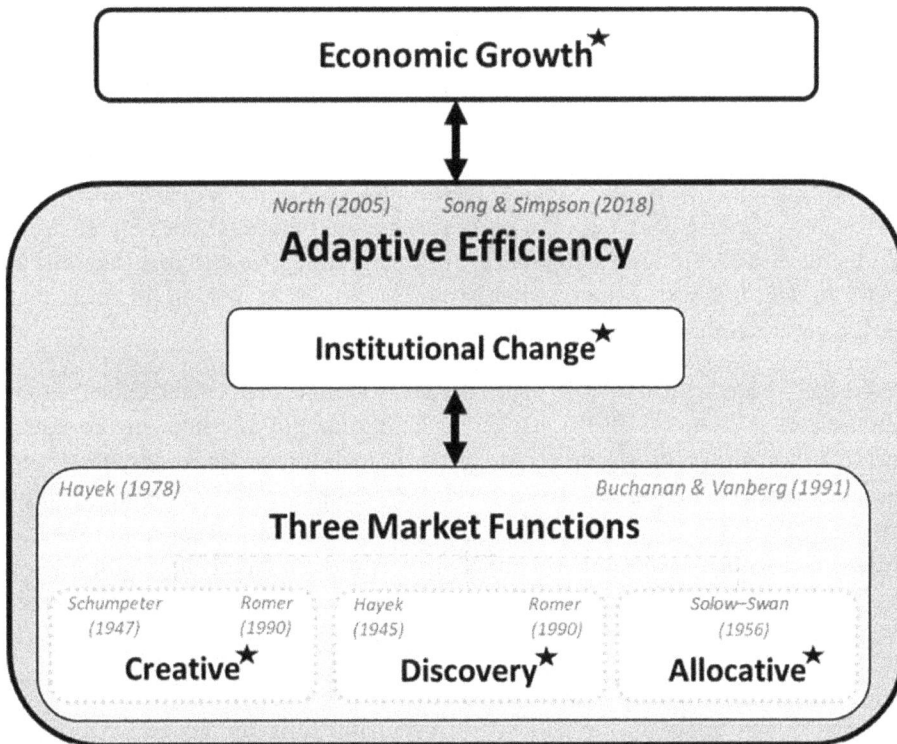

Figure 5.1 Core elements of the adaptive efficiency framework

Note: A bold star indicates the core elements of the framework that are captured in the empirical specification in section three of this chapter. The names of authors that appear in the flowchart indicate the seminal works from which the adaptive efficiency framework draws and that it encompasses.

Source: Authors' own.

---

1   The framework could be further developed in several dimensions. For example, the broader adaptive efficiency framework can be developed to address more comprehensively the key elements of the global economy such as social progress, sectoral change, demographics, infrastructure, climate change and globalisation.

Institutions, adaptive efficiency and endogenous change in institutions

Institutions are the formal rules, informal constraints and enforcement mechanisms that provide order and mitigate conflict, facilitate the mutual gains of exchange and reduce the uncertainties and transaction costs associated with interactions in the social, political and economic spheres (North 1990; Commons 1932; Williamson 2007). Over time, the needs and values of a society evolve, domestic and global conditions change and both endogenous and exogenous shocks disrupt economies. This dynamic process unfolds in an unpredictable and uncertain way.

The responsiveness of an economy to this dynamic environment is captured by Douglass C. North's (2005: 169) concept of adaptive efficiency, which he defined as 'an ongoing condition in which the society continues to modify or create new institutions' as problems evolve and bottlenecks arise. At the core of adaptive efficiency is understanding how a society's institutions influence the direction of learning and the willingness of individuals to acquire new knowledge and skills, provide the incentives and environment conducive to entrepreneurial activity, and shape the direction and performance of an economy over time (North 2005). In other words, adaptive efficiency is concerned with how a society creates an institutional framework that will flexibly adapt in the face of change and creates an environment that not only nurtures and guides the creative spirit of entrepreneurs towards productive activities that lead to economic growth, but also shapes the behaviours and decision-making processes that will lead to good economic performance and social progress.

As preferences, societal demands or the path of economic performance change, so, too, do behaviours (Greif 2006). Changes in behaviour put pressure on prevailing institutional structures. Institutional change tends to be slow; however, changes in the demands that a society makes of its state (for example, concerns about equality, the environment, climate change and artificial intelligence) can occur more quickly, particularly in reaction to crises, and prevailing institutions can rapidly become outdated and disconnected. If these changes in behaviour undermine an institution to the extent that it must be modified or a new institution created, we can say that the institutional framework has undergone a process of endogenous change.

Institutional change goes hand in hand with sustainable long-run economic growth. In fact, Acemoglu et al. (2005) identify economic institutions as a fundamental cause of long-run economic growth.[2] Over time and at different stages of development, the requirements and needs of a society change, as does the complexity of the marketplace in terms of its size and the goods and services that are exchanged. Furthermore, the formal and informal institutions and enforcement mechanisms that induce or promote economic growth at one point in time may be detrimental or inimical at

---

2   The central role of institutions in determining economic growth and development is also evidenced by the works of Dollar et al. (2005), Knack and Keefer (1995), Lin et al. (2010), Rodrik (2007) and Rodrik et al. (2004).

another. It is in this context that the adaptive efficiency framework emphasises the importance of institutional change. As a society evolves, institutions must change and, as an economy progresses through the different stages of development, institutions must change. Failure to change can stall, prevent or even reverse economic growth and social progress.

The three functions of the market

Institutions are human-made constructs that evolve over time in response to social, economic and political interactions. These informal and formal institutions make up the institutional framework that creates the environment in which the three market functions (creative, discovery and allocative) operate. It is in this context that we study the dynamics of the economic system in terms of the effects of 'the market as an allocative process, responding to the structure of incentives that confront choice-makers; the market as a discovery process, utilising localised information; [and] the market as a creative process that exploits man's creative potential' (Buchanan and Vanberg 1991: 184).

The creative function of the market relates to the innovation of new products and processes. Through experimentation and R&D activities, entrepreneurs expand the production possibilities frontier. The role of the state, through public policy, is to harness the creative potential of entrepreneurs by creating an environment that encourages society to undertake the risky and often very costly activities that lead to technological progress (Buchanan and Vanberg 1991; North 1992). Paul Romer's (1990) theory of endogenous technological change places the search for new ideas by entrepreneurs and researchers at the heart of economic growth and Schumpeter (1947) emphasised that economic evolution is shaped by the creative activity of entrepreneurs who create the alternatives that replace the status quo (a process known as creative destruction). Of foremost importance to the incentives faced by entrepreneurs are the predictability and certainty provided by robust legal institutions, accessible and secure financial markets, reliable infrastructure and the completeness and openness of the market (North 1990).

The discovery function relates to the use of local knowledge to adjust, refine and improve existing alternatives—providing local solutions to local problems (Buchanan and Vanberg 1991). When problems arise that are specific to a particular place and time, those who are best equipped to provide solutions are those who possess localised knowledge (Hayek 1945). This type of information and knowledge is not easily or readily available to the state or central planner. Given the diversity and complexity of the elements that make up an economy, the role of the state is better suited to guiding the overall direction of the economy and providing an environment that encourages flexibility and adaptability at the local level. It is more efficient to decentralise decision-making processes and provide greater autonomy to entrepreneurs, firms and lower levels of government to give them greater freedom to choose (Sen 1999) how to allocate their scarce resources and determine the most appropriate course of action.

The allocative function relates to the efficient allocation of scarce resources through the market price mechanism and the coordination of dispersed knowledge. Knowledge exists 'as the dispersed bits of incomplete and frequently contradictory knowledge which all separate individuals possess' (Hayek 1945: 519). It is for this reason that the allocative function depends not only on the price mechanism to convey the necessary information to efficiently allocate scarce resources, but also on the ability of the society to disseminate and aggregate knowledge (Hayek 1945). The allocative function of the market can be improved through market-oriented institutional changes that reduce distortions in allocating resources and enhance competition. The experience of market reform in China provides a test case to illustrate how the progress of marketisation enhances more efficient resource allocation even though market distortions remain, especially relating to markets for factors of production.

What is the place of the adaptive efficiency framework in the economic growth literature?

The adaptive efficiency framework complements existing growth theories in that at its core lie North's (1990) theory of institutions, endogenous institutional change (Greif 2006), endogenous growth (Romer 1990), allocative efficiency in terms of resources (Solow 1956; Swan 1956) and the dissemination of incomplete knowledge (Hayek 1945), the exploitation of localised knowledge (Buchanan and Vanberg 1991) and the creative capacity of entrepreneurs that leads to the discovery of new knowledge (Hayek 1978), ideas (Romer 1990) and creative destruction (Schumpeter 1947).

Additionally, the adaptive efficiency framework enhances the explanatory power of existing theories and perspectives by introducing a novel approach in which the complementary and interrelated nature of the key pathways and determinants of growth in the existing literature are considered from an institutional perspective that centres on the incentives, limitations and pursuits of the individual in the context of the allocative, discovery and creative functions of the market. Important insights are discovered when these theories and perspectives are brought together under a single, unique framework known as the adaptive efficiency framework (Song and Simpson 2018). Most important is that the structure of the adaptive efficiency framework permits the production of a comprehensive historical narrative that captures the effects of economic and social progress from the individual to the institutional level to explain the key determinants of an economy's growth and is empirically testable.

The framework is not limited by assumptions of rationality, utility maximisation, certainty or perfect information. Rather, the adaptive efficiency framework acknowledges the unknown and the complexity and uncertainty of the world in which we live and the limitations that are imposed by the scarcity of physical resources and the cognitive limits of the human mind. We cannot predict future innovations or know what characteristics drive the behaviour of competitors. But we can learn from experience and, through the lens of the adaptive efficiency framework, study the factors that have resulted in the widely divergent economic and social outcomes within and across developing, transitioning and developed economies.

Underpinning the adaptive efficiency framework is the interrelated nature of the institutional framework and the three market functions, the endogenous nature of growth and change and the importance of social progress alongside economic growth. The mechanisms of economic growth are approached from an institutional perspective. The allocative, discovery and creative functions of the market operate within institutional frameworks (local, national and international), and the functions of the market are the direct result of the decisions and actions of individuals who, via government means, promulgate and modify the institutional framework to better align with the needs and demands of society. What makes the adaptive efficiency framework different from existing theories is that adaptive efficiency is primarily concerned with the study of how the institutional framework, the three functions of the market and the organisations and individuals of an economy can interact, adapt and evolve over time to achieve sustainable, long-run economic growth alongside equitable social progress.

An empirical case study: Evidence from Chinese provinces

The economic transformation that has taken place in China over the past 40 years is a testimony to institutional change in transition economies (Lin and Shen 2018; Perkins 2013). Such market-oriented transformation provides a good opportunity to test the adaptive efficiency framework because, throughout the reform period, the development of the market system helped guide resource allocation towards more productive uses, improving its allocative efficiency. The process of decentralisation makes it possible for locals (local governments, firms and individuals) to discover where business opportunities are and to incentivise those who act on them. The processes of privatisation and liberalisation (opening trade and investment) and enhanced market competition (level playing fields) allow private entrepreneurial activities to flourish, enhancing innovation and discovery.

Institutional changes in transition economies are complex processes requiring a multitude of different forces (including political, economic, social and cultural) to interact to guide and determine outcomes. The adaptive efficiency framework is a unique approach to dealing with and understanding such complexity in a simplified manner.

China presents a special case of economic growth in that it is the most contemporary example of spectacular growth and is also a transition economy. Economic growth has not been equal across China and there is great regional disparity in terms of the levels and rates of growth (Chen 2010; Crane et al. 2018). In the context of the adaptive efficiency framework, these characteristics provide an opportunity for us in this chapter to understand how effectively the core elements of the framework contribute to economic growth at the country level and at different stages of economic development (proxied by China's western, central and eastern regions).

This section presents the first empirical application of the adaptive efficiency framework using the latest panel error-correction techniques to analyse the key drivers of economic growth in terms of the core elements of the adaptive efficiency framework using provincial-level data from China. The results of the estimation form the basis of an empirical explanation of the insignificant or seemingly contradictory effects of the institutional environment and the market functions at different time horizons and across different geographical regions.

China's transition to a market economy

When China embarked on its transition to a market economy in 1978 it was one of the poorest countries in the world. Only 40 years later, China has become an upper-middle-income country, reaching GDP per capita in 2018 of US$9,770, which is more than 62 times greater than it was in 1978 (US$156). Reflecting this remarkable achievement, more than 700 million people have been lifted out of poverty. Various institutional changes underpinned this remarkable achievement, including, for example, reform of rural land tenure (household production responsibility and long-term leasing of rural land), ownership reform in the cities and fundamental changes to its trading system and trade policy following the rules of the General Agreement on Tariffs and Trade (GATT)/WTO. This extraordinary growth, however, has come at a significant cost: widening income and wealth inequality, regional inequality, environmental degradation and corruption. Addressing these key challenges, while maintaining economic growth momentum to become a high-income country, has become a central policy objective for the Chinese Government.

In addition to these key challenges, there remains ample capacity and opportunity to improve the quality of the institutional environment, the relatively low levels of human capital and relatively low levels of intangible capital stock (La Porta et al. 2004; Yang et al. 2018). The fact that the quality of the institutional environment has ample capacity to improve provides promise that continued economic growth and increasing prosperity for all can be achieved as long as institutional reform continues.

It is also important to note that economic growth and development have not been equal across regions or provinces. Wide variations in levels of development can in part be attributed to geographical differences and a development strategy that initially focused on rapidly opening and reforming coastal provinces. Another source of variation relates to the decentralisation of the Chinese economy and the four levels of government that together provide greater scope for local governments to experiment and implement central government mandates in a manner that is better suited to local circumstances (Shen and Tsai 2016). The capacity and willingness of local governments and the workforce also play a significant role in development and economic growth at the local level. For example, a study of the nationally promulgated research and development tax deduction policy found that the varying degrees in which provinces implemented the policy had significant impacts on the innovation output of local firms (Sun et al. 2018).

Transitioning from a planned economy that lacked many of the basic market-compatible institutions (for example, a modern legal system) to accession to the World Trade Organization in 2001 illustrates the wide-ranging domestic reform that China underwent to better align with international standards and expectations. Since accession to the WTO, China's economy has, in general and until recently, become more outward-oriented and marketised and the labour force more urbanised. There was no blueprint for economic reform and institution-building; instead, China embarked on a pragmatic path of experimentation and incremental change or, as leaders in China described it, 'crossing the river while feeling the stones' (Xu 2011). For China to achieve sustainable, long-run economic growth driven by innovation, continued institutional reform will be essential.

In this context, the focus of this chapter is to understand the extent to which the core elements of the adaptive efficiency framework affect short-run and long-run economic growth. Using evidence from Chinese provinces, this chapter adopts proxy measures of the institutional environment and the three market functions to provide empirical evidence of how each of these elements affects growth dynamics.

The empirical specification for testing the adaptive efficiency framework in China's case

The empirical specification of this study is in line with the current literature that places endogenous technological change and the institutional environment as the key determinants of economic growth. The measures used in this chapter are not perfect, but they are the best available proxies for the institutional environment and the three market functions. We may be limited by the reliability of provincial-level GDP statistics provided to the National Bureau of Statistics (NBS), which have been the subject of suspicions of overstatement by several studies (Chen et al. 2019; Rawski 2001). However, the data corrections proposed by various studies are diverse and there is yet no consensus on how to reach the most reliable statistics. Therefore, rather than using a particular adjustment approach or introducing a subjective calculation of a 'fudge factor' to the analysis, we have used the provincial-level data as reported to the NBS and acknowledge that the results should not be interpreted as conclusive. However, the results will illustrate the direction and magnitude of the adaptability of the institutional environment and the creative, discovery and allocative functions of the market on economic growth.

The Cobb–Douglas production function is widely used in the economic growth literature for its convenient analytical form. This study adopts the Cobb–Douglas function as in Equation 5.1.

Equation 5.1

$$y_{it} = A_{it} k_{it}^{\alpha} hk_{it}^{\beta}$$

In Equation 5.1, y_{it} is real GDP per capita adjusted to 1999 prices of province i in year t; k_{it} represents net capital stock per capita of province i in year t; hk_{it} is the human capital stock per capita of province i in year t; α and β are the output elasticities of net capital stock per capita and human capital stock per capita, respectively. A_{it} captures total factor productivity (TFP), which comes from the institutional environment and the creative, discovery and allocative functions. The proxy measures that are used to capture the main sources of TFP are: R&D expenditure, the proportion of non-state firms and the National Economic Research Institute (NERI) Index of Marketisation. Therefore, this study defines TFP as in Equation 5.2.

Equation 5.2

$$A_{it} = Ae^{\left(\delta lnRnDexp_{it} + \theta lnNSF_{it} + \rho NERIIndex_{it} + \lambda_i + \varepsilon_{it}\right)}$$

In Equation 5.2, $lnRnDexp_{it}$ represents the amount of R&D expenditure of province i in year t in logarithmic form; $lnNSF$ is the proportion of non-state firms of province i in year t in logarithmic form; $NERIIndex_{it}$ is the NERI Index of Marketisation of province i in year t; and δ, θ and ρ are the output elasticities of R&D expenditure, the proportion of non-state firms and the NERI index, respectively. Province-specific effects that do not vary over time are captured by λ_i, and ε_{it} is the random disturbance term.

Substituting A_{it} in Equation 5.2 into Equation 5.1 and taking logarithms of both sides, we obtain Equation 5.3.

Equation 5.3

$$lny_{it} = lnA + \alpha lnk_{it} + \beta lnhk_{it} + \delta lnRnDexp_{it} + \theta lnnsf_{it} + \rho NERIIndex_{it} + \lambda_i + \varepsilon_{it}$$

Data and variables

The balanced panel dataset used in this study consists of 30 Chinese provinces over the period 1999–2012. Tibet was excluded from the study due to data availability. GDP statistics have been adjusted to the 1999 price and are sourced from the NBS, as were the R&D expenditure, firm ownership, employment figures and net capital stock data. The underlying datasets of the five fields of the NERI were sourced from reports made available by the institute (Fan et al. 2018). The measure of the human capital stock comes from the China Center for Human Capital and Labor Market Research's 2015 human capital report.

The dependent variable is real GDP per capita adjusted to 1999 prices and is denoted by *lnGDPpc1999*. The 'per capita'[3] measure used in this chapter is in terms of the labour force, not the population. Consistent with the common approach of using the Cobb–Douglas production function for the empirical study of economic growth, the measures of the net capital stock per capita (*lnKWpc*) and the human capital stock per capita (*lnHKpc*) are included in the model (Lucas 1988). The *net* capital stock or *wealth* capital stock is the surviving stock of assets from past periods adjusted for depreciation. The human capital stock variable is the China Human Capital Index for each province. Parameters used in the calculation of the China Human Capital Index include age distribution, survival rate, enrolment rate, years of schooling, education level attained, employment rate, years of work experience, household income, hours worked and hourly compensation. The index estimates China's human capital stock using a modified Jorgenson–Fraumeni lifetime income approach with data from the period 1985–2012 (Li et al. 2013). The effects of the GFC are captured by a dummy variable that is equal to 1 for periods after 2007, and 0 otherwise.

The purpose of this study is to understand empirically the dynamic effects of the core elements of the adaptive efficiency framework on economic growth. This requires that we use the best available proxy measures, as shown in Table 5.1, for the institutional environment and the creative, discovery and allocative functions of the markets.

Table 5.1 Proxy measures for the core elements of the adaptive efficiency framework

Core element		Proxy measure
Institutional change	→	NERI index
Creative function	→	R&D expenditure
Discovery function	→	Proportion of non-state-owned firms
Allocative function	→	NERI index

Source: Authors' own.

The NERI index (Fan et al. 2018) is used as a proxy measure for the institutional environment and the allocative function and is denoted by *NERIIndex*. The NERI index is a provincial-level assessment system that uses a comparative method to measure each province's relative progress in marketisation. In essence, it is a measure of

---

3   The employment measure has been used to capture the Lucas-defined measure of human capital and the effectiveness of the labour force (Lucas 1988). Using the labour force measure also avoids issues related to local population measures that are used to calculate provincial GDP per capita. In the past, household status (*hukou*) was used to calculate provincial GDP on a per capita basis. The problem with this method is that provincial GDP per capita will be understated for migrant-sender provinces and overstated for migrant-receiver provinces. It was not until about 2005 that the largest migrant-sender and receiver provinces switched to using residence status as the basis for per capita statistics, and it took until 2009 for all provinces to adopt the new approach.

market-oriented reform and progress. The current index covers the period 1997–2014 and comprises five[4] fields and 24 basic indicators (see Appendix 5.1 for a detailed list of the indicators).

In terms of the adaptive efficiency framework, it could be argued that the five fields and the 24 indicators of the NERI index capture the effects of the institutional environment and the three market functions, so there is no need to include any other explicit measures in the model. This is not the case for several reasons. First, when we look at each of the fields and indicators individually, we find that the institutional environment and the allocative functions are represented to a far greater extent than the creative and discovery functions (see Appendix 5.1). Specifically, the institutional environment is captured by fields one and five and across 10 of the basic indicators. The allocative function is captured by fields three and four and across nine basic indicators. The discovery function is captured only by field two and two basic indicators, and the creative function is captured across only three basic indicators.

Second, the adaptive efficiency framework implies that the institutional environment and the three market functions have an interdependent relationship. The correlation among the five fields and the basic indicators means that it would be impossible to disentangle the effects of the market functions and the institutional environment if we only used some of the five fields of the index. For these reasons, the aggregate NERI index is used in this model as a proxy for the institutional environment and the allocative function, and an additional two proxy measures are introduced to the model to account for the creative and discovery functions.

The proxy measure for the creative function is R&D expenditure. This is a widely used measure of innovation in the literature (Grossman and Helpman 1994; Segerstrom 1990; Stokey 1995) and was therefore seen as an appropriate measure for this study.

The proxy measure for the discovery function is the proportion of non-state-owned firms in the economy. These firms have greater autonomy over their everyday operations and internal investment decisions although we acknowledge that World Bank surveys have revealed that some private sector manufacturing firms do report state intervention in investment-making decisions, with some firms reporting only between 0 and 19 per cent autonomy over these decisions (World Bank 2005, 2011–13). The greater the share of non-state-owned firms in the economy, the more decisions are made by those who possess localised knowledge and are driven by the pursuit of positive profit rather than social objectives or policy goals. Furthermore, increasing levels of privatisation and the decentralisation of decision-making are equivalent to increasing competition among firms. In other words, as the proportion of privately owned firms with greater autonomy over their investment decisions increases, the discovery function will

---

4   The five fields of the NERI Index of Marketisation are: 1) evaluation of the relationship between the state and the market; 2) development of the non-state (private) sector; 3) degree of development of product markets; 4) degree of development of factor markets; and 5) degree of development of market intermediaries and the legal environment.

operate more effectively because decision-making processes will become increasingly decentralised, and those with local knowledge are empowered to choose how to best allocate and invest their time, effort and resources.

Descriptive statistics for all variables are shown at the country and regional levels to draw attention to the significant differences in the level of development within China (see Table 5.2). Reflecting widening income and wealth inequality, the GDP per capita and human capital stock per capita in the eastern provinces are, on average, approximately 28 per cent and 15 per cent higher, respectively, than in the western provinces. Similarly, R&D expenditure, the share of non-state-owned firms and net capital stock are all, on average, 21 per cent and 20 per cent higher, respectively, in the eastern than in the western provinces. Of note is how far the western provinces lag in terms of market-oriented reform, with an average NERI index score of 4.471— well below the average of 7.728 in the eastern provinces. The central region performs better than the western provinces and, in general, closely reflects the mean values at the country (30 provinces) level.

Table 5.2 Descriptive statistics

Variable	Mean	Median	Std dev.	Min.	Max.
			30 provinces		
lnGDP1999pc	3.292	3.290	0.683	1.605	5.030
lnRnDexp	8.619	8.705	1.626	4.420	12.015
lnNSF	−0.289	−0.175	0.310	−1.838	−0.011
NSOFs	0.780	0.839	0.187	0.159	0.989
NERIIndex	5.879	5.715	1.884	1.720	11.710
lnKWpc	3.346	3.319	0.851	1.434	5.364
lnHKpc	5.670	5.596	0.604	4.472	7.745
			Eastern region		
lnGDP1999pc	3.701	3.721	0.623	2.072	5.030
lnRnDexp	9.335	9.590	1.688	4.420	12.015
lnNSF	−0.200	−0.107	0.244	−1.344	−0.011
NSOFs	0.839	0.899	0.161	0.261	0.989
NERIIndex	7.278	7.230	1.736	3.930	11.710
lnKWpc	3.728	3.740	0.804	1.661	5.364
lnHKpc	6.070	5.908	0.659	4.865	7.745
			Central region		
lnGDP1999pc	3.151	3.142	0.557	2.161	4.335
lnRnDexp	8.588	8.616	1.156	5.224	10.841
lnNSF	−0.284	−0.155	0.291	−1.457	−0.038
NSOFs	0.780	0.856	0.183	0.233	0.963
NERIIndex	5.422	5.490	1.084	3.320	7.730

Variable	Mean	Median	Std dev.	Min.	Max.
lnKWpc	3.114	3.047	0.797	1.454	5.187
lnHKpc	5.539	5.534	0.353	4.756	6.198
Western region					
lnGDP1999pc	2.887	2.907	0.568	1.605	4.087
lnRnDexp	7.696	7.728	1.471	4.426	10.713
lnNSF	−0.412	−0.279	0.364	−1.838	−0.070
NSOFs	0.699	0.757	0.194	0.159	0.933
NERIIndex	4.471	4.365	1.363	1.720	8.100
lnKWpc	3.068	3.093	0.776	1.434	4.900
lnHKpc	5.269	5.262	0.352	4.472	5.951

Notes: *lnGDPpc1999* is real GDP per capita adjusted to 1999 prices in logarithmic form; *lnRnDexp* is R&D expenditure in logarithmic form; *lnNSF* is the proportion of non-state-owned firms in logarithmic form; *NSOFs* is the proportion of non-state-owned firms as a percentage; *NERIIndex* is the NERI Index of Marketisation score; *lnKWpc* is the net capital stock in logarithmic form; *lnHKpc* is the human capital stock in logarithmic form.
Source: Authors' own calculation.

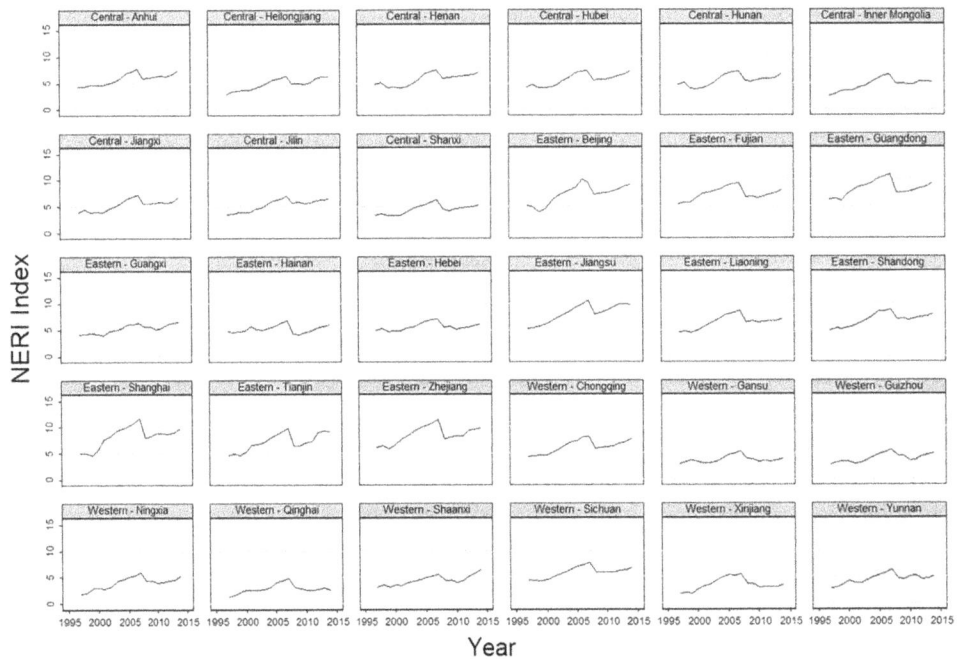

Figure 5.2 Overall NERI Index of Marketisation
Source: Authors' own.

The overall NERI Index of Marketisation score is provided at the provincial level for the period 1997–2014 in Figure 5.2 to illustrate the progress that each province has made in marketisation.

We note that, in general, the western provinces report a lower score against the index relative to the eastern and central provinces. We also note that, in general, there appears to be an upward trend towards greater marketisation except for the period of the GFC, which saw setbacks in progress for all provinces.

The empirical strategy: The vector error-correction model, pooled mean group method

To identify the correct empirical method for our provincial-level dataset, we conducted several tests on the data. Here we report key test results. Further information about the tests conducted on the data can be made available on request from the authors.

First, we undertook a cross-sectional dependency test because the dataset has many cross-sectional units (provinces) and few time-series observations. Testing for these interdependencies shows strong evidence of cross-sectional dependence across all variables at the 1 per cent level of significance.

Second, we tested to determine whether the variables are stationary or non-stationary and found that all variables, across various lags, are I(1) at the 1 per cent level of significance. Next, we applied cointegration analysis to determine whether there is a long-run relationship between the variables. From the results, we conclude that all the variables are cointegrated—that is, there is a linear, stable, long-run relationship between all the variables.

From the above test results, we have established that the panel dataset used in this study is characterised by cross-sectional dependence and that all the variables are cointegrated and stationary after first differencing. Given this, the most appropriate method to empirically measure the dynamic effects of adaptive efficiency on economic growth is a vector error-correction model.

The advantages of this model are that it adjusts to short-run changes in variables and changes in equilibrium, and it allows us to analyse the dynamic effects of adaptive efficiency at the provincial and regional levels rather than just at the country level. This is important given the wide variations we observe within China in terms of geographical factors as well as economic, political and social outcomes.

Three error-correction methods can be applied to evaluate the short-term and long-term variables: the mean group (Pesaran et al. 1996), dynamic fixed effects and the pooled mean group (PMG) methods (Pesaran et al. 1999). All methods are computed by maximum likelihood.

The PMG is the preferred method for this dataset because it involves both pooling and averaging and allows the short-run coefficients and error variances to vary across each group (province). Further, the PMG is the only method that can allow for cross-sectional dependency. Provided the cross-sectional dimension is sufficiently large, consistent estimates of the mean of the short-run coefficients across provinces are generated by taking the average of individual province coefficients. A limitation of the PMG is that it restricts the long-run coefficients for all the provinces to be the same. We have attempted to address this limitation by running the regression at not only the country level, but also the three regional levels.

The vector error-correction form of Equation 5.4 was adopted.

Equation 5.4

$$
\begin{aligned}
\Delta lny_{it} = \phi_i[lny_{i,t-1} &- (\beta_0^i + \beta_1^i lnRnDexp_{it} + \beta_2^i lnNSF_{it} + \beta_3^i NERIIndex_{it} \\
&+ \beta_4^i lnKWpc_{it} + \beta_5^i lnHKpc_{it})] + \gamma_{it}\Delta y_{i,t-1} + \delta_1^i \Delta lnRnDexp_{it} + \delta_2^i \Delta lnnsf_{it} \\
&+ \delta_3^i \Delta NERIIndex_{it} + \delta_4^i \Delta lnKWpc_{it} + \delta_5^i \Delta lnHKpc_{it} + GFC_i + \mu_i + \varepsilon_{it}
\end{aligned}
$$

In Equation 5.4, lny_{it} is real GDP per capita adjusted to 1999 prices of province i in year t in logarithmic form; $lny_{i,t-1}$ is the lagged dependent variable in logarithmic form; $lnRnDexp_{it}$ represents the amount of R&D expenditure of province i in year t in logarithmic form; $lnNSF_{it}$ is the proportion of non-state-owned firms of province i in year t in logarithmic form; $NERIIndex_{it}$ is the NERI Index of Marketisation score of province i in year t; $lnKWpc_{it}$ is the net capital stock of province i in year t in logarithmic form; $lnHKpc_{it}$ is the human capital stock of province i in year t in logarithmic form; GFC_i is a dummy variable that captures the ongoing effects of the GFC set equal to 1 for years after 2007 and 0 otherwise; ϕ_i is the coefficient of the speed of adjustment to long-run equilibrium (the error-correction term); γ_i is the short-run coefficient of the lagged dependent variable; β_i are the long-run coefficients (output elasticities) of the level variables; δ_i are the short-run coefficients (output elasticities) of the first differenced variables; μ_i controls for unobserved province-specific effects that do not vary over time; and ε_{it} is the random disturbance term.

Empirical findings

Limitations in the data and the short period of our panel mean that we are restricted in the number of control variables and lags that can be included in the empirical specification. For this reason, we were unable to include variables to account for infrastructure (for example, road and railway length or mobile phone penetration), openness of the economy (for example, foreign direct investment) or migration (for example, urbanisation). Further, the lag structure was imposed due to data limitations; we could not extend the lag length beyond 1 because we would run into problems of a lack of degrees of freedom. As a result of these limitations, our results should not be interpreted as conclusive findings. Instead, we propose the empirical results be interpreted as identifying the direction of the effect on economic growth by the sign of the coefficient and the magnitude of the coefficient be used to order the variables in terms of greatest effect.

Estimation results

The empirical results show that, *ceteris paribus*, at the country level and for the eastern region of China, the quality of the institutional environment and the creative, discovery and allocative functions have a positive and significant effect on long-run economic growth. For the central region, the creative function has a negative effect on economic growth, while for the western region, the linear, stable, long-run (cointegrated) relationship between all the variables no longer holds. Overall, these findings are consistent with the framework, in that the adaptive efficiency of an economy is expected to be most effective when the three market functions can freely operate within a robust yet flexible environment that promotes the bounded pursuit of positive profits through a decentralised decision-making process.

Earlier we established the following proxies for the key elements of adaptive efficiency: R&D expenditure is the proxy measure for the creative function (*lnRnDexp*); the proportion of non-state-owned firms proxies the discovery function (*lnNSF*); and the NERI Index of Marketisation is a proxy measure that captures both the allocative function and the institutional environment (*NERIIndex*). Table 5.3 reports the PMG regression and Hausman-type specification test results. Columns (1) and (2) report the country-level results; columns (3)–(5) report the regional-level regression results; the GFC dummy is not included in these specifications due to data limitations.

Table 5.3 Pooled mean group regression results

	(1) All provinces GFC	(2) All provinces No GFC	(3) Eastern region No GFC	(4) Central region No GFC	(5) Western region No GFC
Long-run estimates					
lnRnDexp	0.051*** (0.004)	−0.045*** (0.013)	0.077*** (0.014)	−0.042*** (0.016)	0.504*** (0.236)
lnNSF	0.164*** (0.006)	0.145*** (0.019)	0.263*** (0.040)	0.148*** (0.036)	0.011*** (0.051)
NERIIndex	0.019*** (0.001)	0.032*** (0.002)	0.020*** (0.002)	0.031*** (0.004)	−0.028*** (0.034)
lnKWpc	0.442*** (0.005)	0.507*** (0.017)	0.486*** (0.026)	0.504*** (0.023)	0.854*** (0.223)
lnHKpc	0.371*** (0.008)	0.374*** (0.022)	0.291*** (0.029)	0.351*** (0.031)	−0.415*** (0.517)
Short-run estimates					
ec	−0.262*** (0.073)	−0.221*** (0.045)	−0.263*** (0.094)	−0.270*** (0.108)	−0.001*** (0.026)
lnRnDexp	0.004*** (0.007)	0.004*** (0.006)	0.024** (0.016)	0.002*** (0.010)	−0.024*** (0.015)
lnNSF	0.051*** (0.044)	−0.080*** (0.048)	0.274*** (0.080)	0.048*** (0.039)	0.046*** (0.042)
NERIIndex	−0.002*** (0.002)	−0.003*** (0.002)	−0.001*** (0.002)	−0.005*** (0.004)	0.004*** (0.003)

	(1) **All provinces** *GFC*	(2) **All provinces** *No GFC*	(3) **Eastern region** *No GFC*	(4) **Central region** *No GFC*	(5) **Western region** *No GFC*
lnKWpc	0.676***	0.737***	0.532***	0.733***	0.663****
	(0.090)	(0.070)	(0.085)	(0.133)	(0.298)
lnHKpc	−0.062***	−0.074***	0.030***	−0.091***	−0.008*****
	(0.018)	(0.023)	(0.029)	(0.046)	(0.047)
GFC	−0.005***				
	(0.006)				
_cons	−0.205***	−0.066***	−0.184**	−0.056***	0.011***
	(0.059)	(0.014)	(0.075)	(0.026)	(0.032)
Obs.	390	390	156	117	117
Obs. per group	13	13	13	13	13
No. of groups	30	30	12	9	9
Log likelihood	1,544.581	1,430.885	578.5389	468.3492	430.298
Hausman[a] PMG|MG	0.00	0.16	0.13	1.02	1.36
Hausman[b] MG|DFE	0.00	0.00	0.00	0.00	0.00

*** significant at 1 per cent
** significant at 5 per cent
* significant at 10 per cent
MG = mean group
DFE = dynamic fixed effects
Notes: Standard errors in parentheses. Estimations were done using the *xtpmg* command in Stata (Blackburne and Frank 2007). Hausman tests: a) H_0: PMG is the efficient estimator; b) H_0: MG is the efficient estimator. The lag structure is ARDL (1, 1, 1, 1, 1, 1) and the variables are: *lnRnDexp* is R&D expenditure in logarithmic form; *lnNSF* is the proportion of non-state-owned firms in logarithmic form; *NERIIndex* is the NERI Index of Marketisation; *lnKWpc* is the net capital stock in logarithmic form; *lnHKpc* is the human capital stock in logarithmic form; ec is the error-correction term; and *GFCi* is a dummy variable that captures the ongoing effects of the GFC set equal to 1 for years after 2007 and 0 otherwise. Source: Authors' own estimations.

The results in column (1) show that, at the country level, all variables positively and significantly affect long-run economic growth. The error-correction term is negative and highly statistically significant and falls within the dynamically stable range, confirming that there is a stable, long-run relationship between all the variables. The coefficient of the error-correction term tells us that a deviation from long-run equilibrium is corrected at a speed of 26.2 per cent per annum. Consistent with growth theory, net capital stock and human capital stock are the most significant contributors to economic growth.

In terms of the adaptive efficiency framework, we find that the proxy measures for the creative, discovery and allocative functions and the institutional environment are positively and significantly linked to the measure of GDP growth in the long run. The discovery function has the greatest effect, followed by the creative function, the institutional environment and the allocative function. This ordering could be reflective of the state's innovation-led growth strategy, the role of decentralisation and the continued progress of SOE reform over the tested period.

Of interest are the negative short-run dynamics of human capital stock. A possible explanation is that, in the short run, increasing human capital stock requires individuals to undertake further study and/or training, removing or reducing their engagement in the labour force. This is particularly the case in times of rapid technological change or crises, which can lead to a mismatch in the capacity and capability of the labour force, requiring workers to acquire new knowledge and skills or risk becoming redundant.

In the short run, the effect of the creative function is not statistically significant. This could be due to a number of reasons: first, experimentation and R&D are costly and risky exercises; second, there can be a long lag between the creation of a new product or process, commercialisation and profitability; third, R&D activities can be wasteful or unproductive in that there can be too much innovation or the innovation does not positively contribute to economic growth; and last, innovation is a process of creation and destruction (Schumpeter 1947) that can be quite costly in the short term as the economy and the society adjust to these changes.

The effects of the proportion of non-state-owned firms and the NERI index are also not significant in the short run. Like the case for creative function, the changes to the ownership structure of a firm or the institutions of a society require old behaviours, knowledge, rules and processes to be replaced. So, we have a transition period in which, on the one hand, short-run adjustment to new technologies, ownership structures and governance mechanisms can be disruptive and burdensome as the status quo is destroyed. On the other hand, long-run economic growth is positively and significantly affected by welfare-enhancing and productivity-improving innovation (creative destruction), the bounded pursuit of profit by non-state-owned firms (decentralisation) and market-oriented reform (institutional adaptation and resource allocation).

The results also show that failing to control for the GFC underestimates the effects of R&D and the proportion of non-state-owned firms in the economy and overestimates the effects of net capital stock, human capital stock, the institutional environment and the allocative function. This suggests that the government's stimulus measures in response to the crisis and adjustment mechanisms put in place to stimulate the economy had a significant, positive effect on economic growth. This is of great importance to public policy because it indicates that caution must be taken as stimulus measures are unwound and positions are deleveraged. Areas of the economy where this is particularly relevant are the reduction of subsidies that are supporting 'zombie' SOEs and winding back the massive scale of infrastructure investments that could have significant consequences for regional areas and the country if not done pragmatically.

Columns (3)–(5) reveal how regional disparities and differences impact the effectiveness of the market functions and the institutional environment to facilitate long-run economic growth. As we saw in the descriptive statistics presented in Table 5.2, the eastern provinces have achieved, on average, higher levels of development across most economic measures. The eastern region also enjoys the geographical advantages of a coastline, smaller size and denser population. The initial development strategy of rapidly opening and reforming the coastal provinces led to the eastern region being more open to global trade, more attractive to FDI and more suitable for the agglomeration of industry. All variables have a positive and significant effect on long-run economic growth, and the error-correction term indicates that the speed of adjustment back to equilibrium is 26.3 per cent per annum. The negative sign and high statistical significance of the error-correction term confirm the cointegrated relationship of the variables in the long run. The long-run coefficients of the three market functions and the institutional environment are all greater than the country level. These results indicate a positive relationship between the quality of the institutional environment and the level of economic development on the effectiveness of the three market functions and, ultimately, long-run economic growth.

We are more cautious in our interpretation of the results for the central and western regions, presented in columns (4) and (5), respectively. The central region is midway in terms of economic development, while the western region lags furthest behind for most economic indicators and is the most geographically isolated. These regions are characterised by a higher concentration of SOEs, greater reliance on the agricultural sector and less reliance on foreign trade and FDI. Impediments to the functioning of the markets and economic growth are borne out in the empirical results and are most clearly illustrated in terms of the adaptive efficiency framework.

First, we note that the results for the central region (column [4]) show that, while there is still a linear, stable, long-run relationship between all the variables, and the speed of adjustment back to the equilibrium is 27 per cent per annum, the creative function has a significant and negative effect on economic growth. Second, the results for the western region (column [5]) show that the cointegrated relationship between the variables no longer holds (the error-correction term is negative but not statistically significant). Taken together, these results indicate that, *ceteris paribus*, long-run economic growth depends not only on the efficient operation of the market functions but also on the quality of the institutional framework and environment.

To summarise, the results in columns (3)–(5) reflect the key concepts of the adaptive efficiency framework. In situations where the institutional environment does not provide the necessary levels of stability, legal protections and autonomy of decision-making, the allocative, discovery and creative functions do not operate as effectively. When institutional foundations are lacking, firms and entrepreneurs are less likely to engage in risky long-term investments such as R&D; the economy is less open to trade and less attractive to FDI, which means that firms and entrepreneurs have less exposure to new ideas and technology and less access to alternative streams of finance; and the labour force is more likely to migrate to urban areas where there are more opportunities and higher returns to labour. By way of contrast, higher-quality institutions create an environment of adaptability and flexibility that nurtures the entrepreneurial spirit, facilitates the bounded pursuit of positive profit and is responsive to changing conditions and shocks to the economy. In this environment, the allocative, discovery and creative functions of the market can operate more efficiently and, through the processes of endogenous technological and institutional change, can lead to positive long-run economic growth alongside equitable social progress.

Implications for reform and public policy

The adaptive efficiency framework incorporates and complements the main theories of economic growth and presents a narrative that centres on how the institutional framework of a society interacts with the decisions and actions of individuals as they allocate, discover and create the economic, social, political and environmental realities in which they live. In the Chinese context, the role of the institutional framework is to guide as well as provide an adaptive and flexible environment that enables entrepreneurs, firms and lower levels of government to experiment, innovate and pursue profits in a manner that is consistent with sustainable long-run growth and, ultimately, good economic performance.

The findings in this chapter have clear implications for reform and public policy at the country level: adaptive efficiency, through the three market functions and the institutional environment, has a significant, positive impact on economic growth. Improving the quality of institutions, encouraging purposive experimentation and research, reforming ownership structures and further decentralising decision-making processes will lead to higher economic growth and, in turn, better economic performance in the long run.

There are also clear policy implications at the regional level: public policy must consider the wide variations that exist within a country when promulgating nationwide reforms, policies and growth strategies. To put it simply, public policy must be context specific. As we saw in this study, the progress of improving governance structures at the provincial level can vary widely. This has significant implications for economic growth because poor governance structures generally result in high institutional transaction costs, which can significantly impede the functioning of markets; and, as we have shown in this study, lower-quality institutions are associated with lower development and growth outcomes.

This chapter also provides evidence that the adaptive efficiency of the Chinese economy at the regional level is, *ceteris paribus*, significantly affected by the level of economic development and degree of market-oriented reform that have been undertaken at the provincial level. So much so that, for the western region, the long-run relationship between economic growth and the three market functions, the institutional environment and net capital and human capital stock breaks down. While it is important that the state allows local governments to have greater autonomy and the freedom to experiment with policy implementation, it also has a role in guiding the development path of the overall economy and a responsibility to ensure that regions and provinces are not left behind in its process of modernisation. The future prosperity of all China's people depends on it.

It is important to note that this empirical case study is reflective of a period (1999–2012) of relatively outward and expansionary policies and captures the responsive measures to the GFC. The period considered was before the Covid-19 pandemic (which revealed fragilities in health and financial systems as well as supply chains), heightened geopolitical tensions, the rise of friend-shoring and protectionist policies, and an increasing awareness of the need to respond to the risks of climate change. Taking this into consideration, our results suggest that increased marketisation, openness and integration combined with continued progressive institutional reform would place China in a favourable position to realise sustainable long-term economic growth alongside equitable social progress and prosperity for all.

Expanding this consideration to the global context reinforces the need to resist geopolitical fragmentation, to pursue the benefits of free trade and global governance structures, to embrace experimentation and innovation, to continue progressive economic, social and institutional reform and encourage cooperation and collaboration across governments and multilateral forums to address common challenges.

Conclusion

The incremental and experimental approach to reform adopted by China on its path of transition exhibits many elements of the adaptive efficiency framework. Decentralisation empowered entrepreneurs, firms and local and provincial governments with greater autonomy over investment decisions and the ability to experiment with nationally promulgated policies and reforms. Marketisation exposed the economy to the competitive forces of the market. Institutional reforms created an environment more conducive to the pursuit of profit and undertaking the inherently risky and costly activities of R&D, and the policy of opening the economy to the outside world expanded the extent of the market, deepened the divisions of labour and specialisation and increased the knowledge transfer of ideas and sophisticated technologies.

While China's growth miracle has lifted hundreds of millions of people out of poverty, it has also come at the significant cost of widening inequality, environmental degradation and corruption. Addressing these key challenges, while maintaining the necessary growth momentum to become a high-income economy, will be fundamental to achieving sustainable, high-quality economic performance and equitable social progress and prosperity for all.

Using provincial-level data from 1999 to 2012, this chapter has sought to understand the extent to which the core elements of the adaptive efficiency framework affect economic growth in a transition economy. At the country level, the empirical findings of this study indicate that, *ceteris paribus*, improving the quality of the institutional environment and the effectiveness of the creative, discovery and allocative functions of the market will lead to higher economic growth. At the regional level, this study reveals not only significant variation in the effectiveness and impact of these factors, but also, for the less-developed and more geographically isolated western region, the long-run relationship between economic growth and elements of the adaptive efficiency framework, human capital and net capital stock broken down over the period under study. The empirical results have shown that the interdependent nature of economic growth and the core elements of the adaptive efficiency framework have important implications for reform and public policy. Specifically, development strategies, domestic reform and responses to shocks and crises must consider the significant intra-country variations to minimise waste and increase the likelihood of success.

This chapter sets a benchmark and provides initial evidence to support the validity of the adaptive efficiency framework. Future research will fill the gaps of this chapter by further refining the model, improving proxy measures and incorporating measures such as the openness of the economy, hard infrastructure and migration.

References

Acemoglu, D., S. Johnson, and J.A. Robinson. 2005. 'Institutions as the Fundamental Cause of Long-Run Economic Growth.' In *Handbook of Economic Growth. Volume 1. Part A*, edited by P. Aghion and S. Durlauf, 385–472. Amsterdam: North Holland. doi.org/10.1016/S1574-0684(05)01006-3.

Blackburne, III, E.F., and M.W. Frank. 2007. 'XTPMG: Stata Module for Estimation of Nonstationary Heterogeneous Panels.' *Statistical Software Components S456868*. Boston, MA: Boston College Department of Economics. doi.org/10.1177/1536867X0700700204.

Buchanan, J.M., and V.J. Vanberg. 1991. 'The Market as a Creative Process.' *Economics and Philosophy* 7, no. 2: 167–86. doi.org/10.1017/S0266267100001383.

Chen, A. 2010. 'Reducing China's Regional Disparities: Is There a Growth Cost?' *China Economic Review* 21, no. 1: 2–13. doi.org/10.1016/j.chieco.2009.11.005.

Chen, W., X. Chen, C.T. Hsieh, and Z. Song. 2019. *A Forensic Examination of China's National Accounts*. Brookings Papers on Economic Activity, Spring. Washington, DC: Brookings Institution. doi.org/10.1353/eca.2019.0001.

China Center for Human Capital and Labor Market Research. 2015. *Human Capital in China 2015*. Beijing: Central University of Finance and Economics.

Coase, R.H. 1937. 'The Nature of the Firm.' *Economica* [NS], no. 4: 386–405. doi.org/10.1111/j.1468-0335.1937.tb00002.x.

Coase, R.H. 1960. 'The Problem of Social Cost.' *The Journal of Law and Economics* 3: 1–44. doi.org/10.1086/466560.

Commons, J.R. 1932. 'The Problem of Correlating Law, Economics, and Ethics.' *Wisconsin Law Review* 8: 3–26.

Crane, B., C. Albrecht, K. McKay Duffin, and C. Albrecht. 2018. 'China's Special Economic Zones: An Analysis of Policy to Reduce Regional Disparities.' *Regional Studies, Regional Science* 5, no. 1: 98–107. doi.org/10.1080/21681376.2018.1430612.

Dollar, D., M. Hallward-Driemeier, and T. Mengistae. 2005. 'Investment Climate and Firm Performance in Developing Economies.' *Economic Development and Cultural Change* 54, no. 1: 1–31. doi.org/10.1086/431262.

Fan, G., G. Ma, and X. Wang. 2018. 'Marketisation in China from 1997–2014: Achievements and Contribution to Growth.' In *China's 40 Years of Reform and Development: 1978–2018*, edited by R. Garnaut, L. Song, and C. Fang, 257–69. Canberra: ANU Press. doi.org/10.22459/CYRD.07.2018.14.

Greif, A. 2006. *Institutions and the Path to the Modern Economy: Lessons from Medieval Trade.* New York, NY: Cambridge University Press. doi.org/10.1017/CBO9780511791307.

Grossman, G.M., and E. Helpman. 1994. 'Endogenous Innovation in the Theory of Growth.' *Journal of Economic Perspectives* 8, no. 1: 23–44. doi.org/10.1257/jep.8.1.23.

Hayek, F.A. 1945. 'The Use of Knowledge in Society.' *The American Economic Review* 35, no. 4: 519–30.

Hayek, F.A. 1978. 'Competition as a Discovery Procedure.' In *New Studies in Philosophy, Politics, Economics and the History of Ideas*, edited by F.A. Hayek, 179–90. Chicago, IL: University of Chicago Press. doi.org/10.7208/chicago/9780226321288.001.0001.

Jones, C.I., and P.M. Romer. 2010. 'The New Kaldor Facts: Ideas, Institutions, Population, and Human Capital.' *American Economic Journal: Macroeconomics* 2, no. 1: 224–45. doi.org/10.1257/mac.2.1.224.

Knack, S., and P. Keefer. 1995. 'Institutions and Economic Performance: Cross-Country Tests Using Alternative Institutional Measures.' *Economics and Politics* 7, no. 3: 207–27. doi.org/10.1111/j.1468-0343.1995.tb00111.x.

La Porta, R., F. López de Silanes, C. Pop-Eleches, and A. Shleifer. 2004. 'Judicial Checks and Balances.' *Journal of Political Economy* 112: 445–70. doi.org/10.1086/381480.

Li, H., N. Jia, X. Zhang, and B. Fraumeni. 2013. 'Regional Distribution and Development of Human Capital in China.' *Economic Research Journal* 7: 49–62.

Lin, C., P. Lin, and F. Song. 2010. 'Property Rights Protection and Corporate R&D: Evidence from China.' *Journal of Development Economics* 93: 49–62. doi.org/10.1016/j.jdeveco.2009.04.006.

Lin, J., and Z. Shen. 2018. 'Reform and Development Strategy.' In *China's 40 Years of Reform and Development: 1978–2018*, edited by R. Garnaut, L. Song, and C. Fang, 117–34. Canberra: ANU Press. doi.org/10.22459/CYRD.07.2018.07.

Lucas, R.E. 1988. 'On the Mechanics of Economic Development.' *Journal of Monetary Economics* 22: 3–42. doi.org/10.1016/0304-3932(88)90168-7.

North, D.C. 1990. *Institutions, Institutional Change, and Economic Performance*. New York, NY: Cambridge University Press. doi.org/10.1017/CBO9780511808678.

North, D.C. 1992. *Transaction Costs, Institutions, and Economic Performance*. San Francisco, CA: ICS Press.

North, D.C. 2005. *Understanding the Process of Institutional Change*. Princeton, NJ: Princeton University Press.

Perkins, D.H. 2013. 'New Institutions for a New Development Model.' In *China: A New Model for Growth and Development*, edited by R. Garnaut, C. Fang, and L. Song, 17–33. Canberra: ANU Press. doi.org/10.22459/CNMGD.07.2013.02.

Pesaran, H., Y. Shin, and R. Smith. 1999. 'Pooled Mean Group Estimation of Dynamic Heterogeneous Panels.' *Journal of the American Statistical Association* 94: 621–34. doi.org/1 0.1080/01621459.1999.10474156.

Pesaran, M.H., R.P. Smith, and K. Im. 1996. 'Dynamic Linear Models for Heterogenous Panels.' In *The Econometrics of Panel Data: A Handbook of the Theory with Applications*, edited by L. Matyas and P. Sevestre, 145–95. Berlin: Springer. doi.org/10.1007/978-94-009-0137-7_8.

Rawski, T.G. 2001. 'What is Happening to China's GDP Statistics?' *China Economic Review* 12: 347–54. doi.org/10.1016/S1043-951X(01)00062-1.

Rodrik, D. 2007. *One Economics, Many Recipes: Globalization, Institutions and Economic Growth*. Princeton, NJ: Princeton University Press. doi.org/10.1515/9781400829354.

Rodrik, D., A. Subramanian, and F. Trebbi. 2004. 'Institutions Rule: The Primacy of Institutions Over Geography and Integration in Economic Development.' *Journal of Economic Growth* 9, no. 2: 131–65. doi.org/10.1023/B:JOEG.0000031425.72248.85.

Romer, P.M. 1990. 'Endogenous Technological Change.' *Journal of Political Economy* 98, nos S71–S102. doi.org/10.1086/261725.

Schumpeter, J.A. 1947. 'The Creative Response in Economic History.' *The Journal of Economic History* 7, no. 2: 149–59. doi.org/10.1017/S0022050700054279.

Segerstrom, P.S. 1990. 'Innovation, Imitation and Economic Growth.' *Journal of Political Economy* 99, no. 4: 807–27. doi.org/10.1086/261779.

Sen, A. 1999. *Development as Freedom*. New York, NY: Alfred A. Knopf.

Shen, X., and K. Tsai. 2016. 'Institutional Adaptability in China: Local Developmental Models Under Changing Economic Conditions.' *World Development* 87: 107–27. doi.org/10.1016/j. worlddev.2016.06.010.

Song, L., and C. Simpson. 2018. 'Linking "Adaptive Efficiency" with the Basic Market Functions: A New Analytical Perspective for Institution and Policy Analysis.' *Asia and the Pacific Policy Studies* 5, no. 3: 544–57. doi.org/10.1002/app5.249.

Solow, R.M. 1956. 'A Contribution to the Theory of Economic Growth.' *The Quarterly Journal of Economics* 70, no. 1: 65–94.

Stokey, N.L. 1995. 'R&D and Economic Growth.' *Review of Economic Studies* 62: 469–89. doi.org/10.2307/2298038.

Sun, Z., Z. Lei, and Z. Yin. 2018. 'Innovation Policy in China: Nationally Promulgated but Locally Implemented.' *Applied Economics Letters* 25, no. 21: 1481–86. doi.org/10.1080/13 504851.2018.1430315.

Swan, T.W. 1956. 'Economic Growth and Capital Accumulation.' *Economic Record* 32, no. 2: 334–61.

Williamson, O.E. 2007. *Transaction Cost Economics: An Introduction*. Economics Discussion Papers, No. 2007-3, 1 March. Kiel, Germany: Kiel Institute for the World Economy. www.economics-ejournal.org/economics/discussionpapers/2007-3. doi.org/10.2139/ ssrn.1691869.

World Bank. 2005. *China: Investment Climate Survey 2005*. Washington, DC: World Bank Group. microdata.worldbank.org/index.php/catalog/602. doi.org/10.48529/fre1-ex83.

World Bank. 2011–13. *China Enterprise Survey 2012*. Washington, DC: World Bank Group. microdata.worldbank.org/index.php/catalog/1559. doi.org/10.48529/kc2d-0x45.

World Bank. 2013. *Doing Business 2013: Smarter Regulations for Small and Medium-Size Enterprises*. 2 vols. Washington, DC: World Bank Group. documents.worldbank.org/en/ publication/documents-reports/documentdetail/399811468157505743/doing-business-2013-smarter-regulations-for-small-and-medium-size-enterprises. doi.org/10.1596/978-0-8213-9615-5.

Xu, C. 2011. 'The Fundamental Institutions of China's Reforms and Development.' *Journal of Economic Literature* 49, no. 4: 1076–151. doi.org/10.1257/jel.49.4.1076.

Yang, S., Y. Zhou, and L. Song. 2018. 'Determinants of Intangible Investment and Its Impacts on Firms' Productivity: Evidence from Chinese Private Manufacturing Firms.' China & World Economy 26, no. 6: 1–26. doi.org/10.1111/cwe.12259.

Appendix 5.1

Table A5.1 The five fields and 24 basic indicators of the NERI Index of Marketisation

1. Evaluation of the relationship between the state and the market	2. Development of the non-state (private) sector	3. Degree of development of product markets	4. Degree of development factor markets	5. Degree of development of market intermediaries and legal environment
1a. Share of resource allocation in the market	2a. Proportion of industrial sales income	3a. Extent of price market determination	4a. Marketisation of financial market	5a. Development of intermediaries—legal
1b. Reduction of tax/fees burden on farmers	2b. Proportion of fixed asset investment	3b. Reduction of local protection over commodities/products	4a1. Competition for financial industry	5a1. Market for lawyers and accountants
1c. Reduction of government interference in enterprises	2c. Proportion of total urban employment		4a2. Marketisation of credit capital allocation	5a2. Degree to which industrial associations help enterprises
1d. Reduction of tax and fees burden on enterprises			4b. Degree of attracting foreign investment	5b. Legal protection of producers' rights
1e. Reduction of the size of government			4c. Mobility of labour force	5c. Protection of intellectual property rights
			4d. Marketisation/ commercialisation of technology innovation	5c1. Patent application divided by total science, research and technology workers
				5c2. Approval of patents divided by number of science and technology workers
				5d. Protection of consumer rights

Notes: Light-grey cells relate to the institutional environment; dark-grey cells relate to the allocative function; white cells relate to the discovery function; and the black cells relate to the creative function.
Source: NERI Index of Marketisation.

6

Business Environment Index for China's provinces: A brief version of the 2023 report

Xiaolu Wang, Fan Gang and Aili Li

Introduction

Starting in 2006, China's National Economic Research Institute (NERI) has conducted enterprise surveys and research on the business environment across China's 31 provinces, autonomous regions and municipalities directly under the control of the central government (hereinafter referred to as provinces for simplicity). Since 2011, we have published a series of reports on the Business Environment Index for China's Provinces (BEICP), releasing a new report approximately every three years (Wang et al. 2012, 2013, 2017, 2020, 2024). The aim is to quantitatively evaluate and compare aspects of the business environment in each province of China and to track changes over time. This chapter is a summary of the BEICP 2023 report (Wang et al. 2024). The complete report in Chinese was published by the Social Sciences Academic Press in Beijing. The BEICP was previously called the Enterprise Operating Environment Index for China's Provinces. The original title of this series of reports was the *Enterprise Operating Environment Index for China's Provinces*, but from 2023, this has been changed to the *Business Environment Index for China's Provinces*. These changes were made to better align with common usage, while maintaining the purpose of the report. The basic composition of the index is largely unchanged, with only minor adjustments.

This series of reports is based on enterprise sample surveys conducted nationwide. All information comes from survey questionnaires filled out by the responsible persons of sampled enterprises in various regions. Most of the surveys for the 2023 report were conducted in 2022, with a small number extending into the first quarter of 2023. To maintain consistency, in this report, we refer to the data obtained from this survey as the 2022 data.

This survey covered 2,295 valid sample enterprises. Among them, most were private enterprises (89.4 per cent); 6.2 per cent were wholly state-owned or state-controlled enterprises; 2.6 per cent were foreign-funded enterprises and those funded by Hong Kong, Macau and Taiwan; and 1.9 per cent were other types of uncategorised enterprises. Classified by enterprise size, large enterprises accounted for 7.0 per cent of the sample, while 30.8 per cent were medium-sized, 40.6 per cent were small and 21.6 per cent were micro-enterprises. Classified by industry, industrial enterprises accounted for 29.2 per cent; enterprises in trade, accommodation and catering, and residential services accounted for 14.9 per cent; enterprises in agriculture, forestry, animal husbandry, fisheries, construction and transportation accounted for 20.6 per cent; enterprises in information technology, scientific research and technical services accounted for 16.7 per cent; enterprises in finance, real estate, leasing and business services accounted for 13.9 per cent; and other service industries and uncategorised enterprises accounted for 4.7 per cent.

The geographical distribution of sampled enterprises covered all 31 mainland provinces, autonomous regions and municipalities directly under the control of the central government (excluding Hong Kong, Macau and Taiwan). The number of valid sample enterprises in most provinces was between 50 and 100, while the less-developed western provinces each had no less than 35 valid sample enterprises.

The current BEICP system includes an overall index, eight aspect indices and 26 sub-item indices. The overall index is synthesised from the eight aspect indices, each of which is synthesised from several sub-item indices. All indices use a one–five-point scoring standard. A higher score indicates a better business environment.

This chapter extracts the most important content from the *Business Environment Index for China's Provinces: 2023 Report* (Wang et al. 2024). More detailed information can be found in the report. The first section of this chapter reports the new developments in the business environment of each province in 2022, showing the changes in the business environment scores and rankings of each province since 2012, as well as the changes nationwide. The second section reports on the changes in the national business environment across eight different aspects, analyses those conventional factors that have a significant impact on business operations and discusses the impact of the Covid-19 pandemic on business operations in 2022. The third section compares and analyses the differences in the business environment between SOEs and non-SOEs (mostly private enterprises) and between large, medium, small and micro-enterprises. Appendix 6.1 lists the complete structure of the BEICP system and explains the calculation method.

Progress and provincial rankings of the national business environment

The Business Environment Index indicates that, from 2006 to 2022, there was a general improvement in the business environment in China. However, there have also been several setbacks over the years. Stagnation and decline were observed during the periods 2008–12 and 2019–22. Figure 6.1 illustrates the overall changes in the business environment from 2006 to 2022.

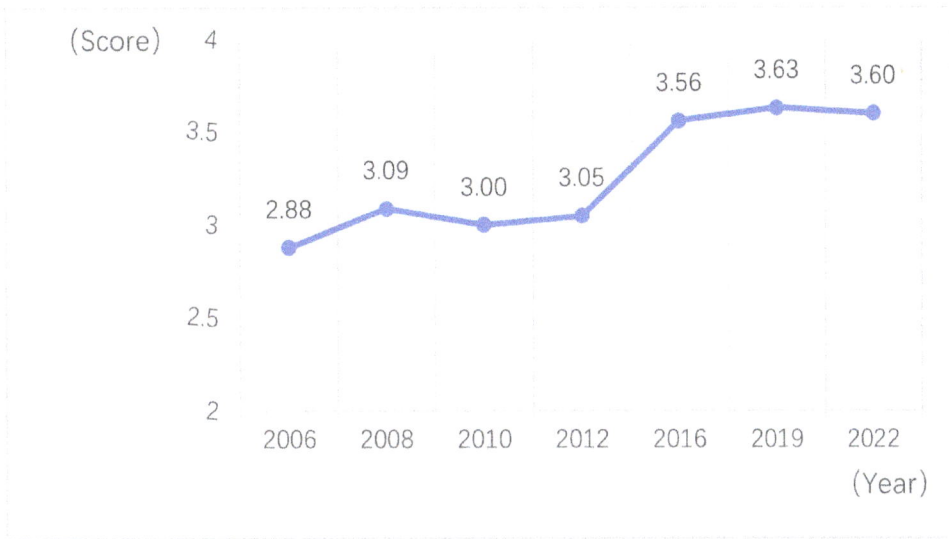

Figure 6.1 Nationwide changes in the overall Business Environment Index, 2006–22
Source: From the survey.

As analysed in previous reports, the deterioration of the business environment during the period 2008–12 was directly related to the large monetary stimulus and extensive government investments at that time. These came with a decrease in the transparency, fairness and justice of policies, an increase in excessive government intervention in enterprises, an increase in official corruption and a decrease in the degree of legal governance. The decline in the business environment scores from 2019 to 2022 was mainly attributed to a decrease in the transparency, fairness and justice of policies, worsening human resource supply conditions, sluggish market demand and excessive competition among enterprises due to industrial overcapacity.

Table 6.1 provides the historical Business Environment Index scores and their changes for each province. It can be observed that most provinces experienced significant improvements in the business environment during the period 2012–16, with a significant slowdown in improvement after 2016. From 2019 to 2022, 17 provinces experienced a decline in overall Business Environment Index scores, with an average decrease of 0.11 points, while 12 provinces saw an average increase of 0.07 points, and two provinces had no change in scores. In terms of both the number of provinces and the magnitude of scores, the provinces with declining scores outnumbered those with increasing scores. Some eastern and central provinces continued to see improvements in scores, with significant overall improvements observed in the central provinces. However, most western provinces, the three north-eastern provinces and four municipalities directly under the control of the central government experienced declines in scores. With increases and decreases offsetting each other, the national index decreased by 0.03 points.

Table 6.1 Overall scores and changes in BEICP in each province, 2006–22 (points)

Region	2006	2008	2012	2016	2019	2022	Score change (2019–22)
Beijing	2.99	3.25	3.17	3.72	3.70	3.59	−0.11
Tianjin	3.06	3.24	3.44	3.71	3.64	3.62	−0.02
Hebei	2.92	3.12	2.97	3.54	3.59	3.67	0.08
Shanxi	2.82	2.93	2.94	3.33	3.53	3.40	−0.13
Inner Mongolia	2.83	3.06	3.01	3.38	3.49	3.45	−0.04
Liaoning	2.98	3.13	3.05	3.55	3.66	3.42	−0.24
Jilin	2.87	3.11	3.11	3.58	3.56	3.49	−0.07
Heilongjiang	2.85	3.11	3.11	3.60	3.57	3.45	−0.12
Shanghai	3.16	3.34	3.25	3.92	3.88	3.79	−0.09
Jiangsu	3.08	3.27	3.14	3.66	3.87	3.86	−0.01
Zhejiang	3.13	3.26	3.15	3.84	3.79	3.90	0.11
Anhui	2.96	3.13	3.04	3.61	3.67	3.79	0.12
Fujian	2.99	3.16	3.06	3.71	3.80	3.85	0.05
Jiangxi	2.77	3.02	2.94	3.59	3.70	3.79	0.09
Shandong	3.00	3.13	3.07	3.63	3.75	3.75	0.00
Henan	2.86	3.08	3.05	3.49	3.63	3.67	0.04
Hubei	2.83	3.06	3.01	3.67	3.71	3.79	0.08
Hunan	2.75	2.97	2.98	3.57	3.60	3.70	0.10
Guangdong	2.99	3.12	3.07	3.64	3.83	3.87	0.04
Guangxi	2.80	3.07	3.09	3.68	3.69	3.69	0.00
Hainan	2.81	2.95	3.01	3.47	3.47	3.42	−0.05
Chongqing	2.82	3.07	3.12	3.74	3.75	3.57	−0.18
Sichuan	2.89	3.07	3.05	3.44	3.70	3.72	0.02
Guizhou	2.75	3.02	2.99	3.49	3.57	3.53	−0.04
Yunnan	2.83	2.98	2.86	3.38	3.63	3.64	0.01
Tibet				3.42	3.17	3.43	0.26
Shaanxi	2.75	3.02	3.01	3.53	3.61	3.57	−0.04
Gansu	2.64	2.97	2.84	3.39	3.56	3.18	−0.38
Qinghai	2.81	2.95		3.32	3.42	3.30	−0.12
Ningxia	2.66	3.06	2.98	3.48	3.54	3.51	−0.03
Xinjiang	2.84	2.97	2.80	3.32	3.45	3.27	−0.18
Average	**2.88**	**3.09**	**3.05**	**3.56**	**3.63**	**3.60**	**−0.03**

Notes: The numbers represent the scores for each province on the Business Environment Index, with values ranging from one to five points. Higher scores indicate a better business environment. The last column indicates the magnitude of change in score from 2019 to 2022, with positive values indicating an increase (improvement in business environment) and negative values indicating a decrease. Empty cells in the table indicate no data.
Source: From the surveys.

Based on the BEICP scores, Table 6.2 presents the rankings of each province in China from 2006 to 2022, as well as the changes in rankings of each province from 2019 to 2022. The order of provinces in the table is based on their index scores in 2022, arranged from best to worst.

Table 6.2 Overall rankings and changes of BEICP across provinces in China, 2006–22

Region	2006	2008	2010	2012	2016	2019	2022	Ranking change (2019–22)
Zhejiang	2	3	4	4	2	5	1	4
Guangdong	6	10	8	11	10	3	2	1
Jiangsu	3	2	2	5	9	2	3	–1
Fujian	7	6	9	12	6	4	4	0
Hubei	19	18	14	19	8	8	5	3
Jiangxi	25	23	16	25	14	10	6	4
Shanghai	1	1	1	2	1	1	7	–6
Anhui	10	7	6	16	12	13	8	5
Shandong	5	9	10	10	11	7	9	–2
Sichuan	12	16	13	15	24	11	10	1
Hunan	28	27	21	22	16	19	11	8
Guangxi	24	15	25	9	7	12	12	0
Henan	14	14	7	14	20	16	13	3
Hebei	11	11	18	24	18	20	14	6
Yunnan	18	24	15	27	28	17	15	2
Tianjin	4	5	3	1	5	15	16	–1
Beijing	8	4	5	3	4	9	17	–8
Chongqing	20	17	11	6	3	6	18	–12
Shaanxi	26	21	27	20	19	18	19	–1
Guizhou	27	22	28	21	21	21	20	1
Ningxia	29	20	26	23	22	25	21	4
Jilin	13	12	19	8	15	23	22	1
Heilongjiang	15	13	20	7	13	22	23	–1
Inner Mongolia	17	19	22	17	27	27	24	3
Tibet					25	31	25	6
Hainan	22	28	23	18	23	28	26	2
Liaoning	9	8	12	13	17	14	27	–13
Shanxi	21	30	17	26	29	26	28	–2
Qinghai	23	29			30	30	29	1
Xinjiang	16	26	29	29	31	29	30	–1
Gansu	30	25	24	28	26	24	31	–7

Notes: Empty cells indicate no data. The last column indicates changes in ranking in 2022 compared with 2019, with positive values indicating an increase in ranking and negative values indicating a decrease.
Source: From the surveys.

In Table 6.2, the top four provinces in the national business environment rankings for 2022 are Zhejiang, Guangdong, Jiangsu and Fujian—all of which are eastern coastal provinces. Most saw an increase in their scores. Several central provinces—including Hubei (ranked fifth), Jiangxi (sixth), Anhui (eighth) and Hunan (eleventh)—showed significant improvements in both scores and rankings compared with 2019, indicating noticeable enhancements. Most western provinces and the three north-eastern provinces still had relatively low rankings, with many experiencing a decrease in scores. However, Tibet saw a significant increase in both score and ranking. The scores and rankings of the four municipalities directly under the central government all declined significantly.

Changes in eight aspects of the business environment

The index for China's provinces evaluates the business environment based on eight aspects:

1. policy transparency and fairness
2. administrative intervention and efficiency
3. legal environment for business operation
4. tax and fee burden on enterprises
5. financial services and financing costs
6. supply of human resources
7. infrastructure conditions
8. market environment and intermediary services.

Each of these comprises several sub-item (or basic) indices.

Table 6.3 provides nationwide scores for the eight aspects of the BEICP from 2006 to 2022. Among these, most showed slight improvements from 2006 to 2012, with a few insignificant changes or declines. From 2012 to 2016, all eight aspect indices saw significant improvements. From 2016 to 2019, most aspect indices improved, while a few declined. From 2019 to 2022, three aspect indices showed significant improvements—namely: 'administrative intervention and efficiency', 'tax and fee burden on enterprises' and 'infrastructure conditions'. However, three aspect indices experienced notable declines: 'policy transparency and fairness', 'supply of human resources' and 'market supply and demand and intermediary services'. This led to a decrease in the overall index. Two indices showed only minimal changes: 'legal environment for enterprise operations' and 'financial services and financing costs'.

The following provides descriptions of nationwide changes in each aspect index and its subindices.

Table 6.3 Nationwide changes in the Business Environment Index across eight aspects in China

Year	2006	2008	2010	2012	2016	2019	2022
Overall index	2.88	3.09	3.00	3.05	3.56	3.63	3.60
1. Policy transparency and fairness	2.94	3.09	2.95	2.96	3.64	3.52	3.40
2. Administrative intervention and efficiency	2.99	3.17	3.23	3.23	3.53	3.69	4.01
3. Legal environment for business operation	2.99	3.24	3.10	3.21	3.83	3.87	3.88
4. Tax and fee burden on enterprises				2.79	3.62	3.43	3.64
5. Financial services and financing costs	2.41	2.90	2.82	3.07	3.31	3.60	3.63
6. Supply of human resources	2.48	2.74	2.68	2.79	3.37	3.62	3.11
7. Infrastructure conditions	3.54	3.57	3.19	3.29	3.93	3.90	4.04
8. Market environment and intermediary services	2.83	2.96	3.01	2.98	3.26	3.41	3.11

Source: From the surveys.

Policy transparency and fairness

This aspect index decreased by 0.12 points in 2022 compared with 2019 and by 0.24 points compared with 2016. Among the three subindices, 'policy transparency' remained the same in 2022 as in 2019. 'Fair competition for various enterprises' decreased by 0.05 points in 2022 compared with 2019, while 'unfair local protection' (data from cases where sample enterprises encountered unfair local protection when selling products or engaging in other business activities in various provinces) decreased by 0.10 points in the same period. Lower scores indicate higher levels of unfair local protection. A similar situation applies to some of the following indices.

This indicates the urgent need to improve the fairness of market competition. Governments at all levels should treat private and state-owned enterprises, as well as large, medium and small enterprises, fairly and without discrimination. Local governments should also refrain from adopting protective or discriminatory policies against enterprises from other regions.

Administrative intervention and efficiency

This aspect index significantly increased in 2022 compared with 2019 and 2016. Among the three subindices, 'excessive government intervention' increased by 0.09 points in 2022 compared with 2019; 'proportion of time (enterprise executives spend) dealing with government' (hereinafter 'time proportion') decreased significantly, leading to a substantial increase of 0.67 points in the score. However, this change is due to special circumstances related to the significant reduction in direct interactions between government agencies and enterprises during the Covid-19 pandemic. 'Convenient and efficient approval procedures' increased by 0.29 points in 2022 compared with 2019, indicating that administrative approval procedures have been simplified and streamlined.

Legal environment for business operation

This aspect index showed no significant change in 2022 compared with 2019. Among the four subindices, 'judicial protection of enterprises' legal rights' remained basically unchanged in 2022 compared with 2019; 'official integrity' increased by 0.16 points; and 'normal performance of enterprise contracts' decreased by 0.03 points. This does not solely reflect cases of noncompliance with contracts between enterprises. According to some enterprise executives, the failure of local governments to fulfil contracts with enterprises or to honour commitments has become relatively common. 'Intellectual property protection' increased by 0.12 points in 2022 compared with 2019.

Tax and fee burden on enterprises

This aspect index increased by 0.21 points in 2022 compared with 2019. Among the four subindices, 'appropriateness of statutory tax burden' decreased by 0.24 points in 2022 compared with 2019. Some (mostly small) enterprises reported that, under the current value-added-tax collection rules, they cannot fully deduct input costs, which is one of the reasons for their heavy tax burden. 'Lawful tax collection' increased by 0.27 points over the period, indicating that the preferential tax measures implemented in 2022 have had practical effects. The 'social security payment burden' decreased by 0.12 points in 2022 compared with 2019, reflecting the current heavy burden of these payments for enterprises, possibly due in part to the expansion of social security coverage. The score for 'other payment burdens' increased significantly, by 0.91 points, indicating a significant reduction in extra tax charges in various regions.

Table 6.4 shows that, in 2022, more than 19 per cent of sampled enterprises had social security contributions accounting for more than 5 per cent of their sales revenue, 31 per cent had contributions accounting for 1–5 per cent of sales revenue and 23 per cent had contributions accounting for 0.1–1.0 per cent of sales revenue. The remaining approximately one-quarter of enterprises contributed less than 0.1 per cent of sales revenue or did not contribute at all. Compared with 2019, the numbers of enterprises with contributions between 1 and 5 per cent of sales revenue and exceeding 5 per cent increased significantly. The number of enterprises with no contributions also increased significantly, likely due to the policy of deferred payments during the pandemic. However, looking at the sampled enterprises, the coverage of this preferential policy was not large. Given that the profit margin of most enterprises is low, social security contributions accounting for 5 per cent of enterprise sales revenue may be quite burdensome.

Table 6.4 Proportion of enterprise sales revenue used for social security contributions (per cent)

Proportion (%)	2019	2022
>5	5.3	19.4
1–5	24.5	31.4
0.1–1.0	47.9	23.3
<0.1	19.9	9.3
No. of contributions	2.3	16.6
Total	100.0	100.0
No. of sampled enterprises	1,817	2,168

Source: From the surveys.

Financial services and financing costs

In 2022, the overall index score for this aspect increased slightly, by 0.03 points, compared with 2019. Looking at the subindices, scores for both 'bank loan interest rates' and 'other financing interest rates' saw a significant increase, indicating reductions in enterprises' financing costs. However, 'bank loan accessibility' decreased by 0.26 points in 2022 compared with 2019, and there was a greater decrease in the 'other financing accessibility', indicating that while financing costs decreased, some bottlenecks for enterprises in terms of loan accessibility and financing difficulty remained unresolved, and the problems have worsened compared with previous years. Those facing difficulty in obtaining loans are mainly private enterprises. Among the sampled enterprises, non-state-owned enterprises (NSOEs) that found it 'difficult' or 'very difficult' to obtain a bank loan accounted for 29.6 per cent of the total number of sampled NSOEs, while SOEs facing the same difficulty accounted for only 11.3 per cent of the total sampled SOEs. Furthermore, there was a significant difference in the average loan interest rates between these two types of enterprises, with NSOEs having an average loan rate of 5.01 per cent compared with 4.59 per cent for SOEs. These findings indicate that the treatment of private enterprises and SOEs in bank lending remains unfair and must be urgently addressed.

Supply of human resources

The overall index score for this aspect decreased significantly, by 0.51 points, in 2022 compared with 2019. The scores for the three subindices, 'supply of technical personnel', 'supply of management personnel' and 'supply of skilled workers', decreased by 0.49 points, 0.56 points and 0.46 points, respectively. Among these, the score for 'supply of technical personnel' was the lowest and the score for 'supply of management personnel' had the largest decrease. This is directly related to the Covid-19 pandemic in 2022 and the prevention measures restricting personal mobility, which had a significantly adverse impact on the supply of human resources for enterprises.

An important phenomenon to note is the simultaneous deterioration in the supply of human resources and a significant increase in the national urban unemployment rate. In 2022, the average urban unemployment rate reached 5.6 per cent and the unemployment rate for workers aged 16–24 nationwide increased to an average of 17.6 per cent (by the end of 2023, the unemployment rate for the 16–24-year-old labour force excluding students in urban areas nationwide remained as high as 14.9 per cent). This is related not only to the pandemic and its prevention measures but also to the structural mismatch between the supply of and demand for human resources. In recent years, nearly 10 million college graduates have entered the job market annually, but the employment situation is not ideal. One important reason is the mismatch between what they have learned and the skills enterprises need, which means enterprises find it difficult to recruit the talent they need. This reflects the problem of formal education in China being disconnected from social needs, suggesting reforms are necessary in the education system.

Infrastructure conditions

The overall index score for this aspect increased by 0.14 points in 2022 compared with 2019, maintaining the highest score among the eight aspect indices. Both subindices, 'electricity, water, gas and network supply' and 'railway and road transport', saw score improvements.

Market environment and intermediary services

The overall index score for this aspect decreased significantly, by 0.30 points, in 2022 compared with 2019. Among the eight aspect indices, this had the lowest score, alongside 'supply of human resources'. The subindex 'market demand intensity' decreased by 0.24 points compared with 2019. 'Pressure from excessive competition' saw a substantial decrease of 0.61 points, dropping to 2.60 points, indicating a negative evaluation. The 'conditions of intermediary services' also decreased, by 0.15 points, compared with 2019.

The phenomenon of excessive competition among enterprises is mainly related to widespread overcapacity, in the context of which enterprises are forced to engage in fierce price competition, even below costs, to avoid greater losses. This situation is caused by previous overinvestment and is also related to weak market demand.

Among the factors affecting the business environment mentioned above, surveyed enterprises were invited in the questionnaire to state which factors had a significant impact on their business operations. We categorised the 26 influencing factors into nine groups—that is, categories based on the eight aspect indices but with the 'market environment and intermediary services' aspect split into 'market environment' and 'intermediary services'—and calculated the total occurrence rates of each group of factors. The top five categories with the highest occurrence rates are:[1]

- human resources supply: 22.3 per cent
- financial services and financing costs: 19.6 per cent

---

1   Expressed as a percentage of the total number of valid sample enterprises. The occurrence rate is calculated by summing the frequencies of occurrences, with instances of the same enterprise being counted twice if it is affected by two factors simultaneously.

- market environment: 18.3 per cent
- tax and fee burden: 15.3 per cent
- policy transparency and fairness: 12.4 per cent.

These factors are important influences on the business environment. In addition, in 2022, special factors had a significant impact on business operations. In the survey, we collected information on the impact on business operations of the Covid-19 pandemic and the preventive measures put in place at that time. These were not conventional factors and were not included in the eight aspects of the business environment; however, we found that, in the circumstances, these became the primary influence on business operations (see Tables 6.5 and 6.6 for related details).

Table 6.5 Operational status of sample enterprises during the survey period (single choice)

	Sample size	Proportion (%)
Rapid business development	194	8.5
Basic normal development	768	33.7
Maintain the status quo	617	27.1
Business difficulties	469	20.6
Hard to maintain	229	10.1
Total	**2,277**	**100.0**

Notes: The 'proportion' is based on a total of 2,277 enterprises that answered this question. As it is a single-choice question, there is no overlap between the options.
Source: From the surveys.

Table 6.6 Reasons for operational challenges faced by enterprises (multiple choice)

	Sample size	Proportion (%)
Impact of pandemic and related prevention measures	510	26.6
Financial constraints	327	14.4
Influence of institutional and policy factors	279	12.3
Pressure from excessive competition	261	11.5
Weak domestic demand	176	7.7
Worsening foreign trade situation	95	4.2
Enterprise decision-making errors	48	2.1
Other reasons	61	2.7

Notes: The total number of enterprises that responded to the relevant question is set as 100 per cent. This is a multiple-choice question. Enterprises facing challenges could choose more than one reason, so the total does not add up to 100 per cent.
Source: From the surveys.

Table 6.5 shows that, according to the sample enterprise leaders, during the survey period in 2022, only slightly more than 8 per cent of enterprises were experiencing rapid growth, while close to 34 per cent were operating under normal conditions. The combined total of these two categories barely exceeded 42 per cent. Some 27 per cent of enterprises could only maintain their current status and nearly 31 per cent were facing operational difficulties; among them, more than 10 per cent of enterprises felt it was hard to maintain their status. The reasons for the operational difficulties include several conventional factors in the business environment, as well as certain temporary factors.

As shown in Table 6.6, the most prominent influencing factor was the impact of the Covid-19 pandemic and related preventive measures, with more than one-quarter (26.6 per cent) of effective sample enterprises facing difficulties due to this reason, ranking first among all influencing factors. Other significant factors contributing to enterprise difficulties included financial constraints, affecting 14.4 per cent of enterprises; the influence of institutional and policy factors, affecting 12.3 per cent; the impact of excessive competition, 11.5 per cent; and weak domestic demand, 7.7 per cent.

Analysis of the questionnaire responses reveals that enterprise leaders' descriptions of the difficulties they faced were quite restrained. In fact, many more enterprises were affected but did not indicate they were facing difficulties. Among the 1,915 companies that answered questions about the pandemic, 1,612 (84.2 per cent) reported being affected—far exceeding the number of companies that indicated facing difficulties (26.6 per cent). Only 303 companies (15.8 per cent) reported no impact. The impacts on enterprises included decreased operating rates or reduced business hours, reduced workforce, anticipated decline in annual operating income and anticipated decline in profits or increasing losses. This is detailed in Table 6.7.

Table 6.7 Specific impact of the pandemic and related prevention measures on enterprises during the survey period

	Number of occurrences	Proportion (%)
Reduction in business operating hours	1,339	69.9
Decrease in number of employees	1,397	73.0
Anticipated decrease in annual revenue	1,297	67.7
Anticipated decrease in annual profit	1,319	68.9
Anticipated annual profit/loss		
Anticipated making a profit	345	18.0
Anticipated breaking even	391	20.4
Anticipated an annual loss	875	45.7

Note: The proportions are calculated taking the 1,915 enterprises that responded to the question as 100 per cent.
Source: From the surveys.

Table 6.8 Changes in business environment of SOEs and NSOEs, 2012–22

Enterprise type	2012	2016	2019	2022	Change from 2019 to 2022
SOE	3.13	3.83	3.76	3.85	0.09
NSOE	3.08	3.59	3.71	3.61	−0.10
Difference	0.05	0.24	0.05	0.24	

Notes: The 'difference' row indicates the difference between the business environment scores of SOEs and NSOEs in the same year. Positive values indicate scores for SOEs are higher than for NSOEs.
Source: From the surveys.

Differences in business environment among different types of enterprises

This section compares and analyses the differences in the business environment between SOEs (including state-controlled enterprises) and NSOEs (mostly private enterprises). It also examines the differences in the business environment among large, medium, small and micro-enterprises.

Table 6.8 presents the changes in the overall Business Environment Index for SOEs and NSOEs since 2012, showing that both types of enterprises experienced varying degrees of improvement from 2012 to 2019. However, the fact that the business environment for NSOEs lagged that for SOEs remained unchanged. From 2019 to 2022, while the business environment score for SOEs increased, the score for NSOEs decreased significantly. The difference between the two widened from 0.05 to 0.24, indicating that there were changes in the business environment during this period that were unfavourable to NSOEs.

Table 6.9 presents a comparison of the business environment scores between SOEs and NSOEs across different aspects in 2022. It shows that in NSOEs, seven of the eight aspect indices significantly lagged those of SOEs. Among them, the most significant differences were observed in the aspects of 'policy transparency and fairness', 'legal environment for business operations' and 'financial services and financing costs', with differences ranging from 0.37 to 0.40 points. Moreover, of the 25 sub-item indices, 23 showed significant disparities between NSOEs and SOEs.

The only aspect index for which NSOEs scored higher than SOEs was 'administrative intervention and efficiency'. From the sub-item indices in the table, it is evident that this is because the time spent by NSOE leaders dealing with the government is significantly lower than that for leaders of SOEs. This is understandable since SOEs are government-affiliated and naturally have more interactions with the government. Additionally, SOEs are mostly large or medium in size, while NSOEs include many small and micro-enterprises. It is impractical for government agencies and officials to interact extensively and frequently with so many small and micro-enterprises.

Especially due to control measures during the Covid-19 pandemic in 2022, the time spent by enterprise leaders dealing with the government significantly decreased. This is a specific reason for a particular period. Additionally, the other two sub-item indices of this aspect, 'excessive government intervention' and 'convenient and efficient approval procedures', still scored lower for NSOEs than for SOEs.

Table 6.9 Comparison of business environment between SOEs and NSOEs, by aspect, 2022

	SOEs	NSOEs	Difference
Overall index	3.85	3.61	0.24
Aspect 1: Policy transparency and fairness	4.04	3.64	0.40
Policy transparency	4.17	3.81	0.36
Fair competition for various enterprises	3.91	3.46	0.45
Unfair local protection	-	-	-
Aspect 2: Administrative intervention and efficiency	3.98	4.02	−0.04
Excessive government intervention	3.99	3.74	0.25
Time proportion	3.88	4.39	−0.51
Convenient and efficient approval procedures	4.04	3.98	0.06
Aspect 3: Legal environment for business operation	4.27	3.88	0.39
Judicial protection	4.30	3.86	0.44
Official integrity	4.23	3.95	0.28
Normal performance of enterprise contracts	4.21	3.72	0.49
Intellectual property protection	4.32	3.99	0.33
Aspect 4: Tax and fee burden on enterprises	3.74	3.64	0.10
Appropriateness of statutory tax burden	3.84	3.71	0.13
Lawful tax collection	4.38	4.34	0.04
Social security payment burden	2.68	2.73	−0.05
Other payment burdens	3.88	3.70	0.18
Aspect 5: Financial services and financing costs	3.71	3.34	0.37
Bank loan accessibility	3.74	3.23	0.51
Other financing accessibility	3.41	2.91	0.50
Loan rates	4.63	4.41	0.22
Other financing interest rates	4.95	4.03	0.92
Aspect 6: Supply of human resources	3.36	3.16	0.20
Supply of technical personnel	3.29	3.06	0.23
Supply of management personnel	3.35	3.13	0.22
Supply of skilled workers	3.44	3.28	0.16
Aspect 7: Infrastructure conditions	4.29	4.08	0.21
Electricity, water, gas and network supply	4.35	4.18	0.17
Railway and road transport	4.23	3.99	0.24

	SOEs	NSOEs	Difference
Aspect 8: Market environment and intermediary services	3.39	3.12	0.27
Market demand intensity	3.51	3.20	0.31
Pressure from excessive competition	2.86	2.62	0.24
Conditions of intermediary services	3.81	3.54	0.27

Notes: The positive values in the 'difference' column indicate that the business environment score of SOEs is higher than that of NSOEs, while negative values indicate that the score of SOEs is lower than that of NSOEs. The scoring method for the 'unfair local protection' subindex is different from the other subindices, making it impossible to distinguish between SOEs and NSOEs using the same method, so it is not included in the table.
Source: From the surveys.

From the above observations, it is evident that the business environment for private enterprises is indeed inferior to that for SOEs, indicating some degree of unequal competition between the two. This is a prominent issue that must be addressed urgently.

Table 6.10 presents a comparison of the overall business environment indices for enterprises of different scale. In 2022, the overall business environment score for large enterprises was 3.81, for medium enterprises 3.67, 3.59 for small and 3.58 for micro-enterprises. It is very clear that the larger the enterprise the better the business environment evaluation, and that, conversely, the business environment is relatively poor for small and micro-enterprises. This is consistent with the situation in previous years.

From 2012 to 2019, the overall business environment indices for all enterprises of different scale improved to varying degrees. However, from 2019 to 2022, the overall index scores for enterprises of different scale all declined, indicating that their business environments have deteriorated to some extent. Among them, large enterprises experienced a decrease of only 0.03 points, while medium, small and micro-enterprises saw decreases of 0.10, 0.09 and 0.07 points, respectively. Consequently, the disparity in the business environment between large and smaller enterprises has widened. In 2022, the scores for small and micro-enterprises were 0.22 and 0.23 points lower, respectively, than those for large enterprises, while medium-sized enterprises were 0.14 points lower than large enterprises.

Table 6.10 Changes in business environment for enterprises of different size, 2012–22

Enterprise scale	2012	2016	2019	2022	Change from 2019 to 2022
Large	3.20	3.80	3.84	3.81	–0.03
Medium	3.09	3.64	3.77	3.67	–0.10
Small	3.07	3.54	3.68	3.59	–0.09
Micro	2.98	3.40	3.65	3.58	–0.07

Table 6.11 Business Environment Index scores for enterprises of different size, 2022

	Large	Medium	Small	Micro
Overall index	3.81	3.67	3.59	3.58
1. Policy transparency and fairness	3.92	3.73	3.62	3.55
2. Administrative intervention and efficiency	3.97	4.02	3.98	4.09
3. Legal environment for business operation	4.14	3.95	3.87	3.83
4. Tax and fee burden on enterprises	3.73	3.69	3.58	3.65
5. Financial services and financing costs	3.86	3.49	3.30	3.14
6. Supply of human resources	3.21	3.13	3.17	3.20
7. Infrastructure conditions	4.28	4.08	4.06	4.13
8. Market environment and intermediary services	3.40	3.22	3.09	3.02

Table 6.11 presents the scores for different aspects for large, medium, small and micro-enterprises. Among the eight aspect indices, except for 'administrative intervention and efficiency', the remaining seven aspect indices indicate that the business environment for large enterprises was better than that for medium, small and micro-enterprises. The difference was most significant in 'financial services and financing costs', with a notable gap of 0.71 points between micro-enterprises and large enterprises. Additionally, the disparities in 'market environment and intermediary services', 'policy transparency and fairness' and 'legal environment for business operation' are also significant, with gaps of 0.38, 0.37 and 0.31 points, respectively.

Policy implications

These findings indicate that the Chinese Government's preferential treatment of large enterprises is widespread. It must urgently provide equal treatment to all enterprises and establish a fair and competitive business environment. Improving the business environment for small and micro-enterprises, especially the latter, is particularly urgent in the current macroeconomic setting in which China must boost investments from the private sector to regain the growth momentum of the economy.

References

Wang, Xiaolu, Fan Gang, and Li Aili. 2024. *Business Environment Index for China's Provinces: 2023 Report*. Beijing: Social Sciences Academic Press.

Wang, Xiaolu, Fan Gang, and Li Feiyue. 2012. *Enterprise Operating Environment Index for China's Provinces: 2011 Report*. Beijing: CITIC Press.

Wang, Xiaolu, Fan Gang, and Ma Guangrong. 2017. *Enterprise Operating Environment Index for China's Provinces: 2017 Report*. Beijing: Social Sciences Academic Press.

Wang, Xiaolu, Fan Gang, and Hu Lipeng. 2020. *Enterprise Operating Environment Index for China's Provinces: 2020 Report*. Beijing: Social Sciences Academic Press.

Wang, Xiaolu, Yu Jingwen, and Fan Gang. 2013. *Enterprise Operating Environment Index for China's Provinces: 2013 Report*. Beijing: CITIC Press.

Appendix 6.1: Construction and calculation method of the Business Environment Index for China's Provinces (BEICP)

Table A6.1 outlines the composition of the BEICP system, including the names of the overall index, all aspect indices and subindices (for 2022). All indices are scored on a scale of one to five, where a higher score indicates a better business environment.

Table A6.1 Composition of provincial Business Environment Index, 2022

Index name	Index category
Business Environment Index for China's Provinces (BEICP)	Overall index
1. Policy transparency and fairness	Aspect index
1.1 Policy transparency	Subindex
1.2 Fair competition for various enterprises	Subindex
1.3 Unfair local protection	Subindex
2. Administrative intervention and efficiency	Aspect index
2.1 Excessive government intervention	Subindex
2.2 Proportion of time spent dealing with government	Subindex
2.3 Convenient and efficient approval procedures	Subindex
3. Legal environment for business operation	Aspect index
3.1 Judicial protection of enterprises' legal rights	Subindex
3.2 Official integrity	Subindex
3.3 Normal performance of enterprise contracts	Subindex
3.4 Intellectual property protection	Subindex
4. Tax and fee burden on enterprises	Aspect index
4.1 Appropriateness of statutory tax burden	Subindex
4.2 Lawful tax collection	Subindex
4.3 Social security payment burden	Subindex
4.4 Other payment burdens	Subindex
5. Financial services and financing costs	Aspect index
5.1 Bank loan accessibility	Subindex
5.2 Other financing accessibility	Subindex
5.3 Bank loan interest rates	Subindex
5.4 Other financing interest rates	Subindex
6. Supply of human resources	Aspect index
6.1 Supply of technical personnel	Subindex
6.2 Supply of management personnel	Subindex
6.3 Supply of skilled workers	Subindex
7. Infrastructure conditions	Aspect index
7.1 Supply of electricity, water, gas and networks	Subindex
7.2 Railway and road transport	Subindex

Index name	Index category
8. Market environment and intermediary services	Aspect index
8.1 Market demand intensity	Subindex
8.2 Pressure from excessive competition	Subindex
8.3 Conditions of intermediary services	Subindex

All the raw data for the BEICP are derived from surveys of enterprises across the country. Each subindex comes from a specific question in the enterprise questionnaire, for which the responsible person of the sampled enterprise (usually the chairperson, president or CEO) evaluates or provides information on the business environment in their area. Each evaluation is rated on a scale of one to five, with three indicating a neutral evaluation and four or five indicating a relatively positive evaluation, while one or two indicates a relatively negative evaluation. Some individual subindices use quantity indicators provided by respondents, categorised into five intervals according to questionnaire design, and assigned values from one to five accordingly.

The subindex scores for each province are derived from the arithmetic mean of the corresponding indicator scores of valid sample enterprises within the province. The aspect indices of each province are formed by the arithmetic mean of their respective subindex scores. The overall index of each province is formed by the arithmetic mean of the eight aspect indices. The scores of each subindex at the national level are the arithmetic averages of the corresponding subindex scores of each province, and so forth.

7

Vulnerability and resilience: Understanding China's flexible employment through the lens of unregistered individual business owners

Xu Xiang, Sherry Tao Kong and Qiuhui Chen

Introduction

Driven by structural adjustments and rapid technological advancements, China's economic landscape has witnessed considerable transformations in recent years. These changes have given rise to flexible employment (灵活就业), which is now an integral part of China's labour market. Gaining a comprehensive understanding of the characteristics of and issues with flexible employment is of great importance given its significant implications for China's labour market dynamics, economic prosperity and social welfare. A defining feature of flexible employment is its diverse forms, ranging from part-time work, freelancing and temporary employment to remote work. However, the broad spectrum of flexible employment modalities also poses unique challenges in terms of both defining and measuring it.

The notion of flexible employment is closely linked to the conventional term 'informal employment', which commonly denotes a form of employment in which merchants conduct their business operations outside the formal state registration system and thereby play a complementary role in emerging economies (ILO 2018). In the context of the Chinese labour market, informal employment is primarily characterised by unregistered individual business owners (UIBOs; *feizhuce getihu* 非注册个体户) as opposed to those whose business is registered with the authorities and who are thus regarded as formal market operators. As UIBOs exhibit typical characteristics of adaptability through their diverse business forms and flexible work arrangements, they are increasingly being categorised as part of the 'flexible employment' system. In recent years, particularly during the Covid-19 pandemic, the term 'flexible employment' has gained significant traction in official media. It has been used extensively to refer to those who are 'self-employed', 'employed part-time' or engaging in 'new forms of employment', such as jobs enabled by digital platforms (Office of the State Council 2020).

The stringent 'dynamic clearing' policies imposed during the pandemic caused significant disruption across all business types. However, on their swift phasing out in December 2022, and contrary to expectations of a robust post-pandemic economic rebound, China's macro-economy exhibited structural difficulties despite some signs of recovery. This raises several questions: Did UIBOs suffer greater impacts than other businesses during the pandemic and did they experience slower recovery in the aftermath? What are the root causes of their vulnerability? What viable solutions exist? These questions remain largely unexplored and unresolved.

Despite its apparent importance and the vast number of people engaged in flexible employment, this employment type has received limited in-depth analysis using microlevel data, apart from anecdotal evidence. This chapter aims to address these gaps by leveraging a unique and richly granular dataset from the Online Survey of Micro-and-Small Enterprises (OSOME) conducted by Peking University (GSM 2023). Our study endeavours to provide new perspectives and nuanced data analysis to enhance our understanding of the state of flexible employment, both during and after the pandemic. By focusing on UIBOs, the present study offers a unique opportunity to gain insights into the nature and dynamics of flexible employment in China.

The rest of this chapter is organised as follows. The next section introduces the data source on which this research is primarily based, the survey design, sample characteristics as well as key findings of OSOME for the period 2020–23. Section three zooms in and depicts the UIBOs in China from various perspectives. First, we contrast the UIBOs with their registered counterparts to highlight the sectoral differences and possible reasons for registration choices. Second, we illustrate the flexibility attributes of the UIBOs in terms of their scale, working hours and level of digitisation. Last, we take advantage of the rich information collected in OSOME to examine the degree of vulnerability and resilience of this group by discussing market entry, fragility, consumption and expectation as well as the effectiveness of policies intended to provide relief and assistance to small businesses. Section four concludes by placing China's flexible employment sector in the wider cross-country context. We highlight the rising global trend of flexible employment and its underlying drivers before discussing desirable policy measures for improving China's flexible employment.

Online Survey of Micro-and-Small Enterprises (OSOME): Design and key findings

Micro and small enterprises (MSEs) are considered the capillaries of China's economy. These businesses not only serve as reservoirs of employment, but also play a crucial role in driving the high-quality development that the Chinese economy aspires to achieve. However, nuanced data on MSEs are scarce. To gain a better understanding of the status of China's MSEs, particularly the many unregistered individual businesses, two academic organisations, the Centre for Enterprise Research and the Institute of Social Science Survey of Peking University, in collaboration with the Ant Group Research Institute and MYbank,[1] which is the Ant Group's internet bank, initiated an online survey in the third quarter of 2020. This survey aimed to gather information from active MSE operators[2] on a quarterly basis. Utilising the expansive reach of big-tech platforms such as Alipay and MYbank, the survey distributes questionnaires to their users who meet the criteria of MSEs. The OSOME collects a wide array of information, including on business performance, costings, government policy coverage, the needs for, access to and costs of financing, as well as confidence and outlook for the subsequent quarter. Each quarterly survey receives 8,000 to 12,000 responses and, over 14 quarters (from Q3 2020 to Q4 2023), 192,214 valid responses were collected. The basic structure of the OSOME questionnaire is outlined in Figure 7.1.

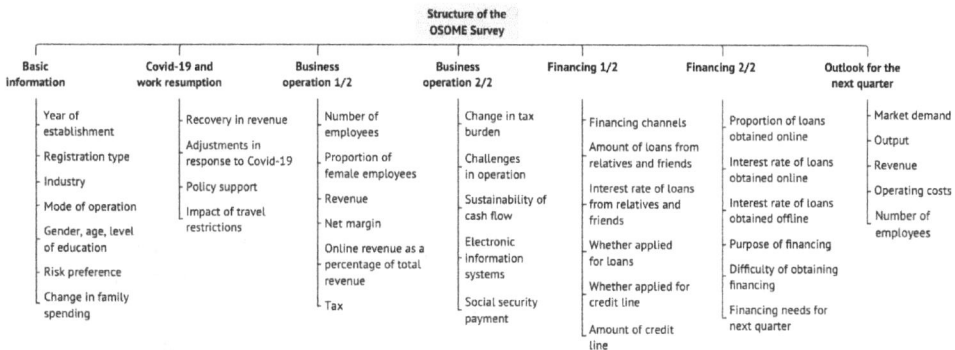

Figure 7.1 Structure of the OSOME
Source: GSM (2023).

---

1 For a detailed description of MyBank, see: www.mybank.cn.
2 Active micro and small operators are defined as those with transaction records for at least three of the past 12 months, a total number of transactions greater than 90 and total transaction flow value of more than RMB2,000. The term 'micro-and-small business operators' encompasses a range of individuals involved in business operations. This includes those who are self-employed, as well as business owners, company directors, shopkeepers, managers, shareholders and family members participating in a business who are knowledgeable about its operations.

While the OSOME is a repeated cross-sectional rather than longitudinal survey, meaning that respondents are predominantly one-off participants, the key characteristics of the sample remain remarkably stable over time. Small and micro-business operators in the OSOME sample exhibit a high degree of stability in the distribution of key characteristics such as age, gender, education and region. Furthermore, their distribution across important indicators such as industry sector, company size and operational duration closely approximates that of the data for the statistically representative offline Enterprise Survey for Innovation and Entrepreneurship in China. This suggests that, although the sample of the OSOME by no means claims statistical representativeness, it is a valuable source from which to gain meaningful insights about the MSE operator community in China. There are several key characteristics of the Chinese MSEs that emerged from the data for the 14 quarters of the OSOME (Q3 2020 – Q4 2023):

- MSEs registered as corporations constitute approximately 10 per cent of the total survey sample, while the remaining 90 per cent are individual business owners (IBOs), with roughly equal shares between registered and unregistered businesses.

- The median quarterly revenue for small and micro-operators is approximately RMB25,000, meaning most are living at a subsistence level, barely making ends meet.

- More than 80 per cent are in tertiary industries, primarily providing services to accommodate the needs of local households.

- Most are in the eastern and central regions.

- Approximately 70 per cent belong to the post-1980s and post-1990s generations, with nearly 80 per cent having obtained at least a high school education.

- Self-employment and small business are the primary forms of labour engagement, with about 80 per cent employing zero to four individuals.

- In line with the fact that MSEs serve mainly their local community, offline rather than online is the main form of business operation.

OSOME data for 14 consecutive quarters (Q3 2020 – Q4 2023) revealed several key insights into the operations of Chinese MSEs. First, in terms of business performance, the average quarterly revenue for MSEs ranged between RMB100,000 and RMB140,000. Notably, 40–50 per cent of MSEs reported quarterly revenues below RMB25,000. The net profit margin for these businesses generally fell between 3 per cent and 6 per cent, except for Q4 2022, when it dropped to 0.2 per cent due to the impact of the pandemic. MSEs typically face short cash-flow sustainability, with an average duration of two to three months (Figure 7.2). Second, regarding sources of operational pressure, weak market demand and rising operational costs were consistently identified as the top two pain points throughout the 14 quarters. Some 40–50 per cent of MSEs reported feeling pressured by operational costs, while 40–60 per cent cited weak market demand as a main challenge facing their business.

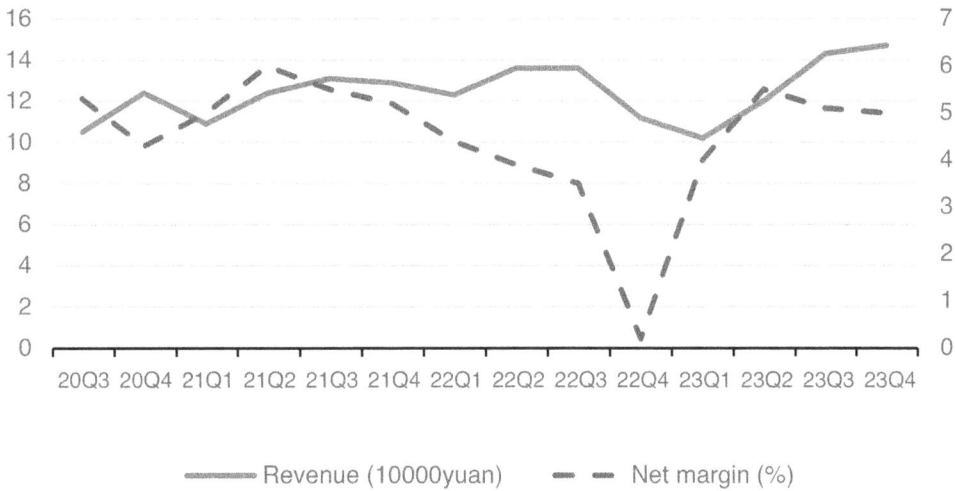

Figure 7.2 Revenue and net profit margins of Chinese MSEs
Source: GSM (2023).

Third, regarding access to financing, unlike medium and large enterprises, MSEs rely more heavily on online financing channels, revealing significantly higher adoption rates of digital financing than access to loans via offline channels. Even though online loans typically have higher interest rates than offline loans, their uncomplicated application processes, timeliness, flexibility of arrangements and short repayment cycles (such as 'borrow and repay as needed') often make them more appealing to MSEs. Fourth, after the onset of the Covid-19 pandemic in 2020, various levels of government in China introduced a wide range of policies to assist business recovery and support MSEs, including measures for pandemic control, financial and fiscal support, employment assistance and cost reduction. However, OSOME data indicate that the uptake of these policies by MSEs was relatively low, with overall policy coverage ranging from 40 to 50 per cent. Among the various policies, universal tax reductions had the broadest coverage (19–24 per cent), followed by financial support policies (14–17 per cent), cost reduction measures (8–18 per cent) and employment stabilisation policies (4–9 per cent).

Fifth, MSEs are accelerating their digital transformation to cope with changing markets and economic conditions. The OSOME shows that 70–80 per cent of MSEs are engaged in some form of online sales and about 50 per cent use electronic information systems. During the pandemic, the adoption of digital systems helped MSEs enhance their economic resilience against negative shocks. Last, OSOME data (Figure 7.3) demonstrate that the confidence index of Chinese MSEs fluctuated between 46 per cent and 53 per cent, showing a relatively stable overall trend. The sub-index for market demand expectations closely correlates with revenue expectations and exhibits strong seasonal variations. Expectations for operational costs generally remain below the 50 per cent threshold, while expectations for employee numbers hover around the threshold.

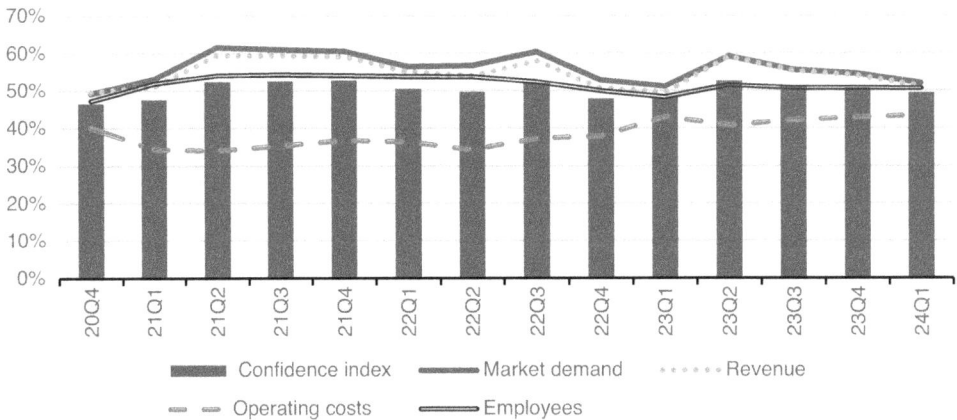

Figure 7.3 Confidence indices of MSEs by quarter
Source: GSM (2023).

Understanding the unregistered individual business owners

Why do UIBOs stay unregistered?

A registered IBO is a business entity that engages in production and commercial activities. It is recognised as a formal market entity under the owner's name. According to China's individual business registration regulations, any citizen over the age of 18 years who is capable of conducting civil behaviour is eligible to apply for IBO status. Once registered, IBOs are required to fulfil certain obligations, such as regular tax reporting (value-added tax, income tax, etcetera) and to comply with business premises requirements such as fire and health regulations. Based on official sources, by the end of 2023, 124 million IBOs were formally registered in China, accounting for two-thirds (67.4 per cent) of the total number of business entities. It is estimated that these registered IBOs have provided nearly 300 million jobs (Zhao 2024).

While the procedure for applying for IBO registration does not seem to constitute a major barrier for those who intend to do so, for a variety of reasons, IBOs may choose not to be formally registered with the prescribed authority. These could involve factors such as the industry entry requirements, registration procedures and business environment. For instance, OSOME data show that the registration rate is higher for secondary and tertiary industries than primary industries, which is likely due to the less stringent entry requirements for business licences in the service and manufacturing sectors. In addition, IBOs who participate in business solely on online platforms are less inclined to register since the e-commerce law stipulates numerous situations in which registration is not required.

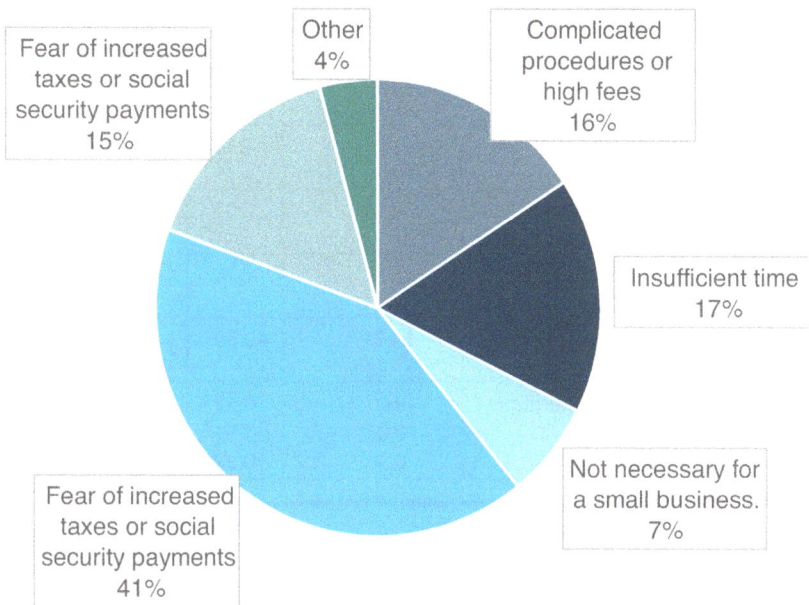

Figure 7.4 Reasons for UIBOs staying unregistered
Source: Authors' calculation based on OSOME (Q1 2021) data.

Data collected in the first quarter of 2021 by the OSOME shed light on this. When UIBOs were asked why they chose to stay unregistered, the main reasons cited were that they believed their business was too small to necessitate formal registration (41 per cent). This was followed by several other considerations, including lack of understanding of the registration procedures and fear of the cost implications from taxes and social security contributions (Figure 7.4). Indeed, OSOME data suggest that UIBOs are more prevalent in industries with lower entry thresholds and smaller average size. Overall, these findings are in line with previous literature that found that because of the thresholds required and costs of joining the formal system, informal and formal employment are commonly characterised by mutual substitutability (for example, Arias et al. 2018; Samaniego de la Parra and Fernández Bujanda 2024).

Flexibility of UIBOs: Contrast with registered IBOs

Here, we first characterise the 'flexibility' of UIBOs using the three attributes identified in the official definition of flexible employment: self-employment, part-time employment and operation on digital platforms. As indicated in Table 7.1, compared with registered IBOs, UIBOs have fewer employees and perform fewer formal business duties such as paying social security contributions and signing labour contracts. From the perspective of 'part-time employment', the average weekly operating hours of UIBOs are about 15 hours less than registered IBOs. Furthermore, UIBOs are found to rely more on online platforms to conduct their business activities and the proportion of UIBOs that operate entirely online (with no permanent offline shopfront) is much higher than that of registered IBOs (13 per cent difference).

Table 7.1 Flexibility of UIBOs: Employment characteristics

		Registered IBOs	UIBOs	Mean difference
Self-employment	Number of employees	5.04	4.08	0.97***
	Paying social security for operators	0.20	0.18	0.02***
	Paying social security for employees	0.14	0.07	0.06***
	Conclude labour contracts with employees	0.24	0.15	0.09***
Part-time employment	Average weekly operating hours	64.71	49.96	14.75***
New forms of employment	Adoption of online operation: Online only Online and offline	0.43 0.07 0.36	0.47 0.21 0.27	−0.04*** −0.13*** 0.10***

*** statistically significant at the two-tailed 1 per cent level
** statistically significant at the two-tailed 5 per cent level
* statistically significant at the two-tailed 10 per cent level
Source: Authors' calculation.

Flexibility of UIBOs: Market entry

The existing literature has indicated the connection between the diversity of entrepreneurial groups and the development of the digital economy. For example, in a traditional business environment, challenges may arise when female entrepreneurs are disadvantaged due to gender discrimination and lack of social networks. In contrast, studies show that the digital economy can provide women with more entrepreneurial opportunities and a more equal entrepreneurial environment, thus attracting more women to entrepreneurship (BRICS WBA 2023; AliResearch 2022). Similarly, a World Bank survey of e-commerce development in Indonesia during the Covid-19 pandemic revealed a significant increase in the number of female merchants on digital platforms (World Bank 2021).

In practice, as the pandemic had severe negative shocks on the labour market, becoming an IBO was evidently one of the easiest ways to generate income. Using OSOME data, we find that there has been an increase in the proportion of youth, female and better educated labour who started their business after the onset of the pandemic. This feature is particularly pronounced among the UIBOs and probably suggests that, as a key form of flexible employment, they have attracted a more diverse group of labour in the post-Covid era. In the meantime, a rise has also been observed in the proportion of those engaged in online business (including online only and combined online/offline), which is at least partly driven by new IBOs' greater reliance on online platforms for conducting business activities (Table 7.2).

Table 7.2 Flexibility of UIBOs: Market entry

		Registered IBOs		UIBOs	
		Entry before 2020	Entry after 2020	Entry before 2020	Entry after 2020
Individual characteristics	Percentage of female operators	0.18	0.21	0.16	0.22
	Years of education	12.58	12.70	12.59	12.64
	Age of operators	35.82	31.70	32.84	30.22
Form of operation	Online only	0.05	0.13	0.17	0.26
	Offline only	0.60	0.46	0.55	0.50
	Online and offline	0.34	0.41	0.29	0.24

Source: Authors' calculation.

Vulnerability of UIBOs: Fluctuation of business performance and closures

Here, vulnerability is primarily characterised by the magnitude of exposure to and speed of recovery from shocks. First, compared with the same quarter before the pandemic, during the pandemic, IBOs experienced a severe decline in business revenue (greater than 50 per cent). Among them, UIBOs were hit even harder (Figure 7.5a). Second, in terms of year-on-year changes in business revenue, the quarter-to-quarter trend for registered IBOs was more stable than that for UIBOs, especially during the worst of the pandemic (late 2022 to early 2023) (Figure 7.5b). Third, the cash flows of registered and unregistered IBOs were similar during the pandemic but the cash flows of registered IBOs rebounded by the end and in the aftermath of the pandemic, while those of UIBOs dipped deeper and experienced a much more sluggish recovery (Figure 7.5c).

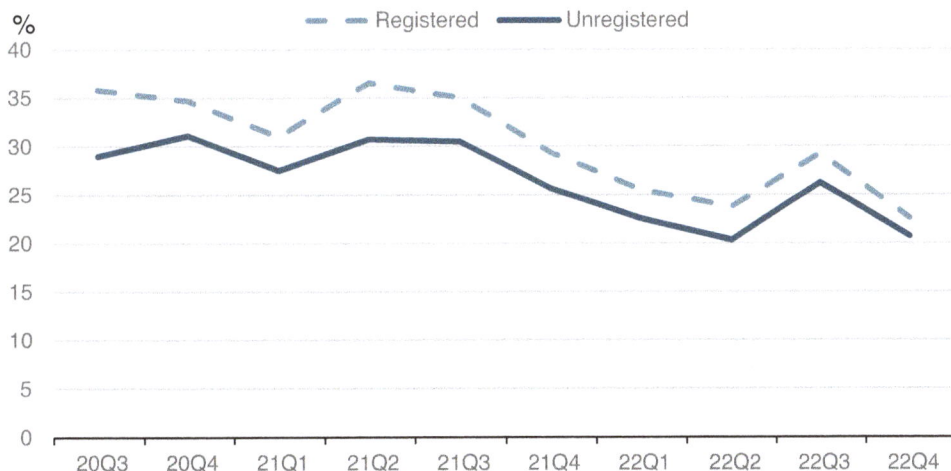

Figure 7.5a Operating income recovery of IBOs relative to 2019
Source: Authors' calculation.

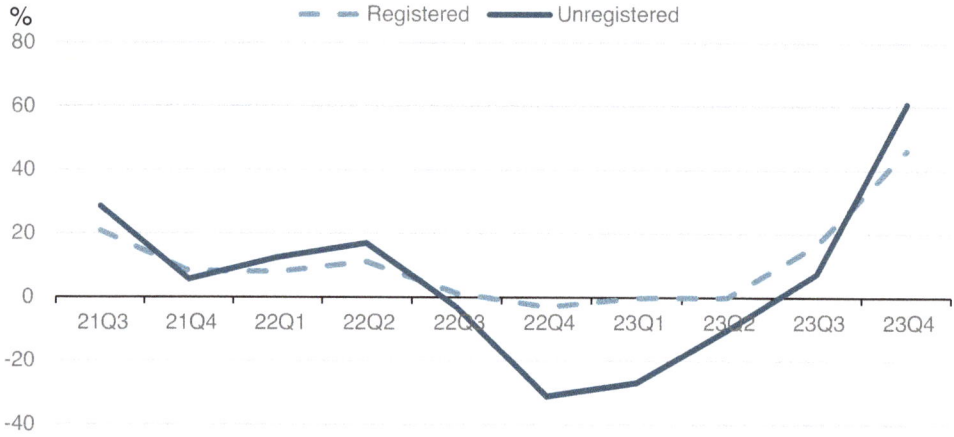

Figure 7.5b Operating income of IBOs year-on-year
Source: Authors' calculation.

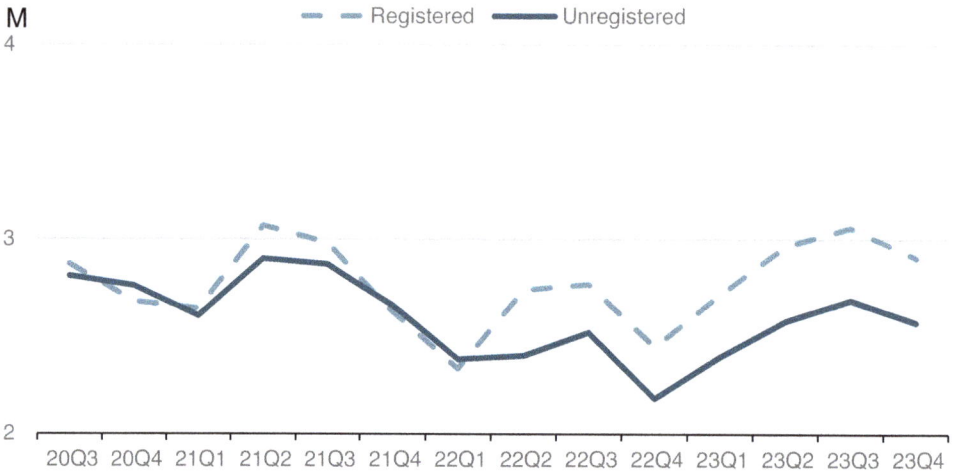

Figure 7.5c Number of months cash flow can last
Source: Authors' calculation.

Furthermore, as UIBOs often do not possess a physical shopfront and have no fixed costs such as rent, when facing greater fluctuations in business performance, they seem to be more inclined to exit the market rather than adjust their business strategies. OSOME data reveal that UIBOs were more likely to choose to shut their business during and even after the pandemic (Figure 7.6).

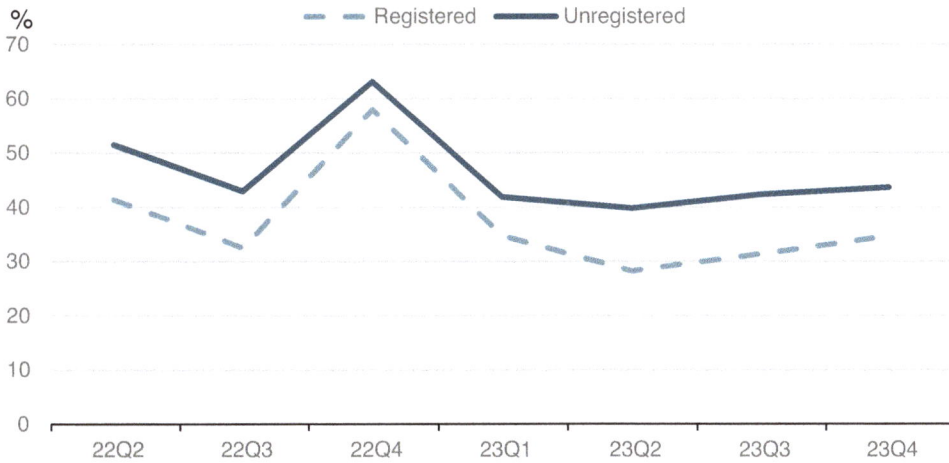

Figure 7.6 Proportion of business closures
Source: Authors' calculation.

Vulnerability of UIBOs: Pain points

To further understand the sources of their vulnerability, we examined the pain points identified by IBOs. Market demand and cost pressure have been consistently cited as the most important sources of stress for IBOs, but variation exists across registered and unregistered groups. Compared with registered IBOs, the unregistered perceive market demand more acutely than cost as a source of pressure (Figures 7.7a, 7.7b).

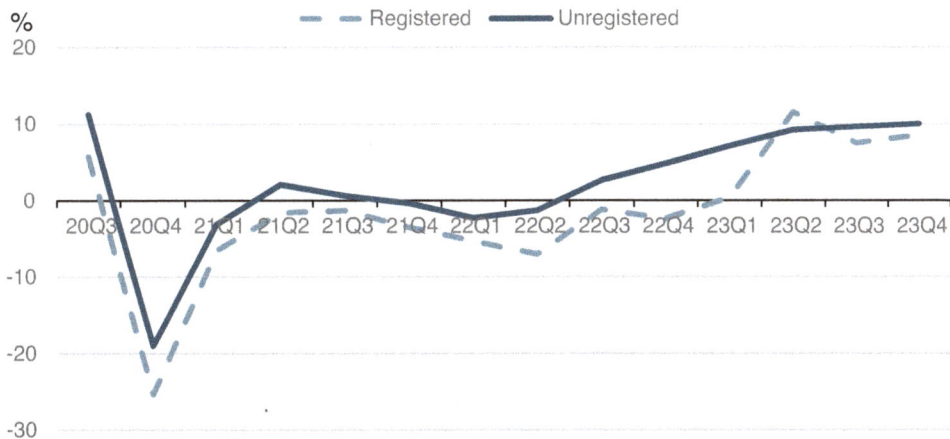

Figure 7.7a Proportion of IBOs reporting market demand as main source of pressure
Source: Authors' calculation.

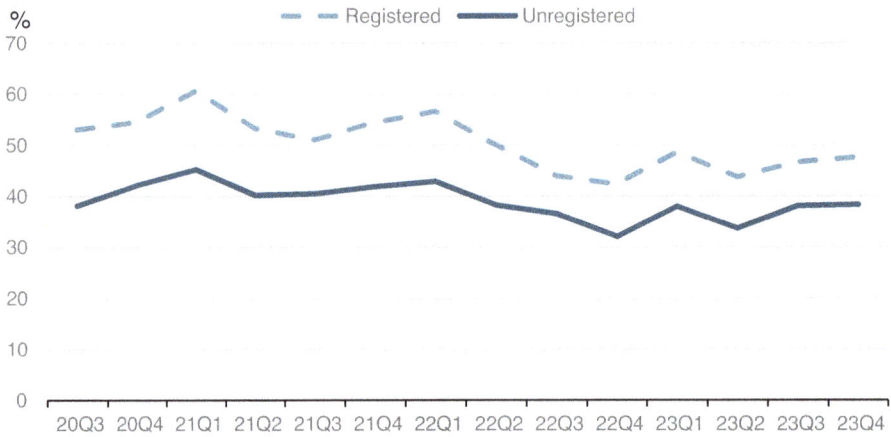

Figure 7.7b Proportion of IBOs reporting cost as main source of pressure
Source: Authors' calculation.

There are at least three reasons behind this observed difference. First, fixed costs, especially rent, are a major concern for registered IBOs as they generally operate a physical shopfront that is furnished and equipped. In contrast, UIBOs often rely on digital platforms to reduce fixed costs (such as rent). Smaller in size, UIBOs are affected more by variable costs (such as prices of raw materials and logistics), which are generally less volatile than fixed costs due to the price stabilisation mechanism (Figures 7.8a, 7.8b). Second, as mentioned, UIBOs experienced greater fluctuation in terms of business revenue and closures and a higher proportion reported market demand as the main source of pressure. Additionally, UIBOs are more flexible than registered IBOs in terms of working hours and business arrangements. In other words, UIBOs often do not have stable clientele and they were subject to external factors including weather and Covid-19 restrictions to a greater extent. As a result, market demand rather than cost is a more severe pain point for UIBOs.

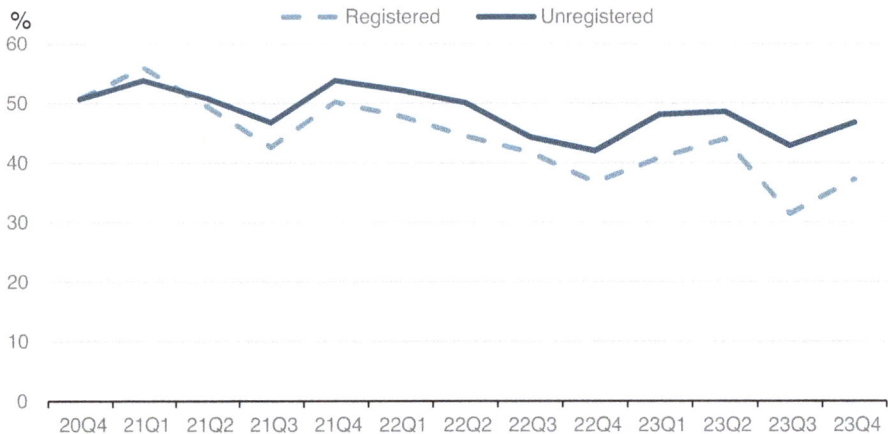

Figure 7.8a The proportion of groups reporting variable costs as a source of pressure (for example, raw materials)
Source: Authors' calculation.

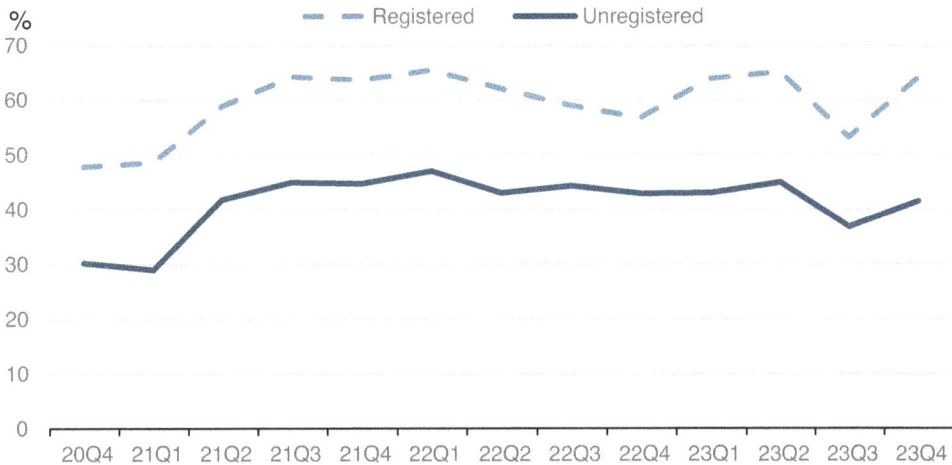

Figure 7.8b The proportion of groups reporting fixed costs as a source of pressure (for example, rent)

Source: Authors' calculation.

The relative sensitivity to market demand and costs also manifests itself in the post-pandemic period. Registered IBOs expected and experienced better market demand than UIBOs, whereas both expected and real changes in operating costs were better for UIBOs than for registered IBOs. This seems to suggest that, while UIBOs on average face lower fixed costs, registered IBOs seem able to bounce back more quickly thanks to their production facilities, business premises and customer base, which allow them to take advantage of improved external conditions.

Vulnerability of IBOs: Consumption and confidence

Next, we delve into household consumption and the evolution of confidence of IBOs. The year-on-year percentage change in household consumption reveals that household consumption of the goods or services of IBOs experienced persistently negative growth throughout the Covid-19 pandemic, extending to the end of 2023 (Figure 7.9). A more pronounced recessionary trend started at the beginning of 2022, reaching the largest dip in the fourth quarter of 2022, coinciding with the height of the pandemic shock. Although household consumption seemed to have recovered in the final quarter of 2023, the positive upturn at the end of 2023 must consider the low-base effect of the last quarter of 2022.

Comparatively speaking, the consumption patterns of registered and unregistered IBOs converged during the pandemic. However, from the third quarter of 2022, the consumption behaviour of registered IBOs has consistently outperformed that of UIBOs. This observation is consistent with the fact that UIBOs experienced slower recovery in the post-pandemic era, suggesting a greater scarring effect on the UIBOs.

143

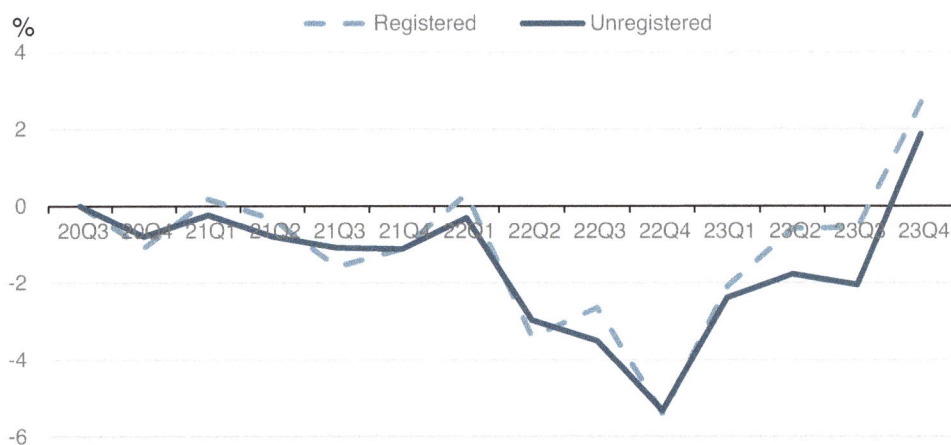

Figure 7.9 Percentage change in household consumption: Unregistered individuals fall more than registered individuals
Source: Authors' calculation.

As IBOs are at the grassroots of the social economy, their confidence levels are indicative of market sentiment and suggestive of the underlying economic recovery. To assess the patterns of business confidence of IBOs, both before and after the pandemic, we classify IBOs' confidence about the subsequent quarter's business performance into four categories: 'optimistic', 'pessimistic', 'neutral' and 'uncertain'. Our analysis reveals that during the pandemic, a larger proportion of IBOs stated clear expectations ('optimistic' or 'pessimistic'), with optimism slightly outweighing pessimism. However, after the pandemic, one can observe a notable increase among IBOs that expressed ambiguous expectations ('neutral' or 'uncertain'), alongside a slight convergence in terms of the share of optimistic and pessimistic expectations (Figure 7.10). These patterns suggest two things: one is that a narrowing of the gap between optimistic and pessimistic expectations in the post-pandemic era is indicative of a deterioration in IBOs' outlooks; and two, the surge in ambivalence among IBOs reflects heightened uncertainty—a potential explanation for subdued consumption.

Vulnerability of IBOs: Policy coverage

During the pandemic, national and local governments issued a wide range of policies particularly relevant to businesses, which can be categorised into two main types (Figures 7.11a, 7.11b): those aimed at mitigating the negative shocks inflicted by the pandemic, such as tax breaks, preferential loans, reduced costs and waived or delayed payments to social security funds; and those aiming to contain the spread of Covid-19, including mandatory measures such as quarantine, control zones, business closures and big-data surveillance. When these policies were finally phased out in December 2022, many IBOs continued to struggle with the lingering effects. Here, we discuss the effects of government policies on IBOs and focus primarily on the question of to what extent such policies achieved their intended aims of assisting businesses during the pandemic.

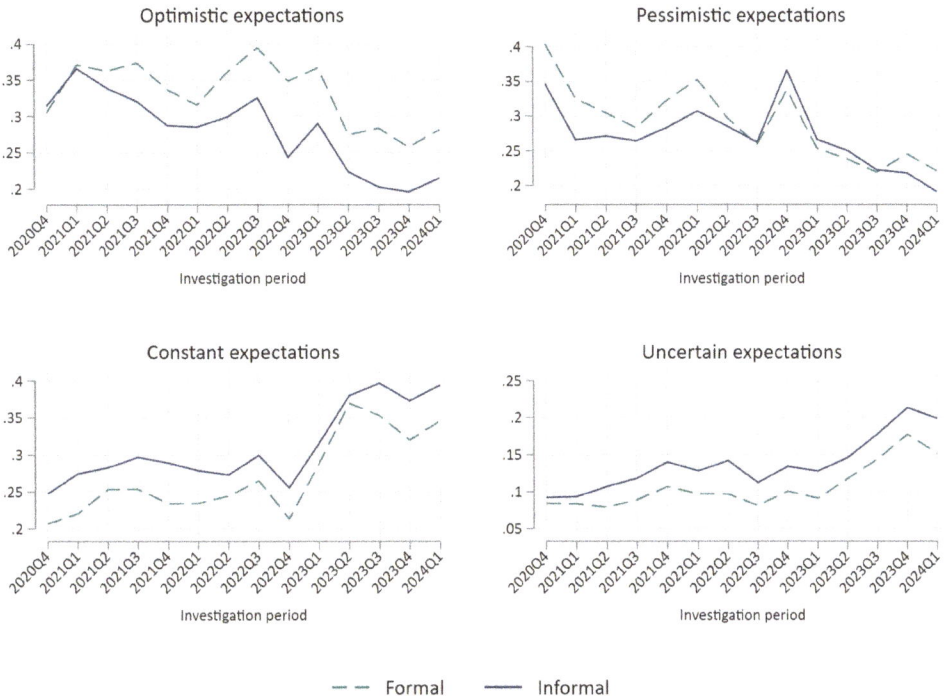

Figure 7.10 Proportion of different expectations of IBOs for business revenue in the subsequent quarter

Source: Authors' calculation.

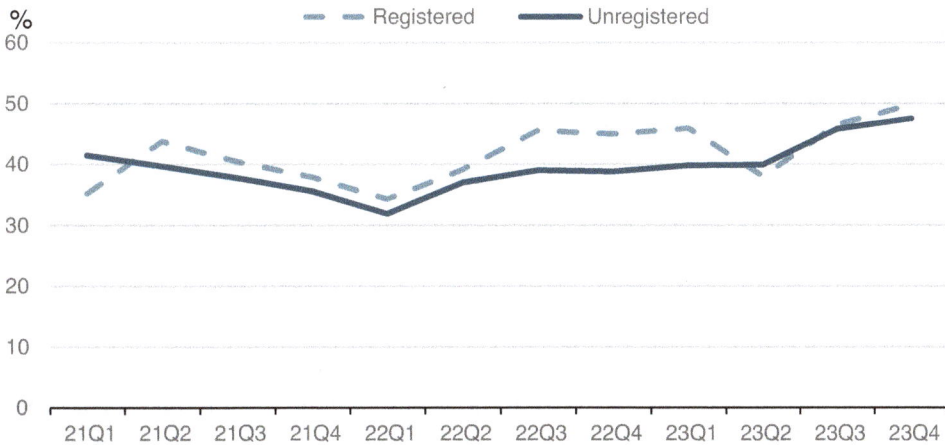

Figure 7.11a The proportion of groups reporting policy uncertainty pressure

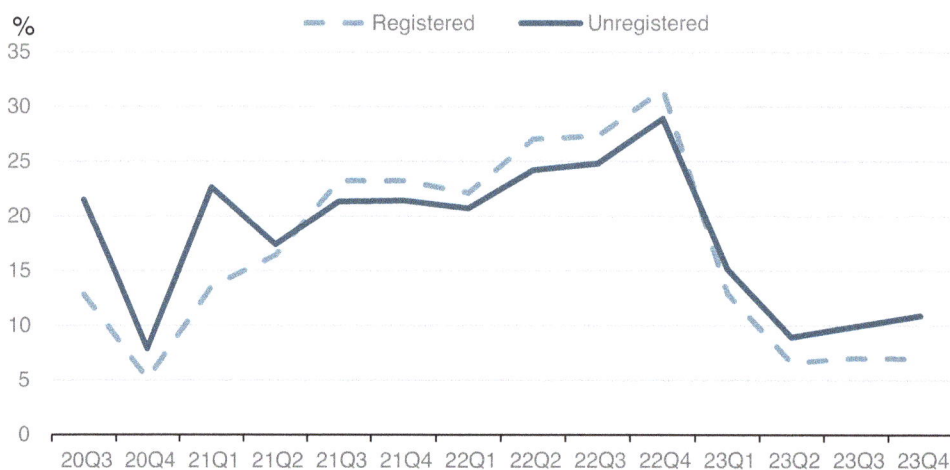

Figure 7.11b The proportion of groups reporting being a policy beneficiary
Note: This includes any one of the policies such as tax breaks, preferential loans, rent waivers, deferred payment of insurance premiums and pensions, etcetera.
Source: Authors' calculation.

First, policy uncertainty constitutes an important source of anxiety for IBOs. Our analysis indicates that stress related to policy uncertainty is comparable between registered and unregistered IBOs, with a notable decline post pandemic, suggesting a gradual dissipation of pandemic-induced policy uncertainty. Registered IBOs exhibited slightly higher policy uncertainty during the pandemic, possibly stemming from the fact that they were subject to a larger extent to Covid-19 control measures. This observation probably also reflects the fact that the fixed-cost inputs of registered IBOs rendered business closure more costly to them compared with UIBOs. However, as policies aimed at mitigating the negative shocks on business were based on business licences, with their formal status, registered IBOs reported a greater share of the benefits during the pandemic than UIBOs, which contributed to the former's greater resilience to shocks.

Government policies are thus something of a mixed blessing for IBOs. On the one hand, mobility control policies worsened the business environment and heightened policy uncertainty; on the other, preferential policies substantially aided smaller businesses in weathering adverse impacts. For registered IBOs, targeted measures like rent remission and tax breaks are imperative given the significance of fixed costs such as rent and social security contributions. For UIBOs, priority should be given to policy coverage, reducing administrative interventions and mitigating institutional friction, as well as fostering an enabling environment for sustainable operations.

Flexible employment as an international phenomenon and policy implications for China

Flexible employment has emerged as a significant trend in the global labour market. Both developed and developing countries have seen a rise in the proportion of flexible workers, particularly in recent years due to the impact of the Covid-19 pandemic. According to the International Labour Organization (ILO 2018), more than 2 billion people worldwide are engaged in informal employment, accounting for more than 61 per cent of the global workforce—underscoring the widespread nature of this kind of employment. Generally, flexible employment makes up a larger share of total employment in developing (low-income) countries, followed by emerging (middle-income) countries, with developed (high-income) countries having the lowest proportion.[3]

For instance, in Africa, informal employment constitutes a significant majority, reaching 85.8 per cent of the workforce. In Indonesia, data from the ILO and Statistics Indonesia indicate that flexible employment accounted for approximately 30–35 per cent of total employment in 2019, and this figure increased to 40–45 per cent by the end of 2021 due to various factors including the pandemic. In developed countries, the availability of formal employment opportunities is generally higher, resulting in relatively lower proportions of flexible employment. However, the rapid digital transformation and development of platform economies (through companies such as Uber, Airbnb and Freelancer) have led to an increase in flexible employment even in these countries. Based on Upwork's *Freelance Forward 2022* report, 39 per cent of the US workforce (60 million people) engaged in freelance work in 2022—a rise of 4 percentage points from pre-pandemic levels (35 per cent) (Upwork 2022). Similarly, Japan and South Korea have also seen notable increases in flexible employment in recent years. From 2000 to 2020, the proportion of part-time workers in total employment rose from 23.8 per cent to 37.6 per cent in Japan and from 11.4 per cent to 24.5 per cent in South Korea.

The growth in flexible employment globally is closely linked to rapid technological advancements, economic globalisation, increased female labour force participation and the impact of the pandemic. The rise of platform and gig economies has provided individuals with more flexible employment opportunities, enabling them to find positions easily through online platforms and apps. Globalisation and changes in supply chains have driven businesses to adopt more flexible labour practices to cope with market fluctuations. Economic structural transformations have increased the demand for flexible labour, particularly in sectors with seasonal and fluctuating needs. Additionally, higher female labour force participation has spurred the growth of flexible employment, as women often seek to balance work and family responsibilities. The pandemic has had a dual impact on flexible employment. On one hand, the decline in demand for services due to the pandemic reduced many flexible job opportunities,

---

3   Following the World Bank definition for the 2018 fiscal year, countries are grouped into developing (low-income), emerging (lower-middle and upper-middle-income) and developed (high-income).

especially in face-to-face industries such as retail, hospitality and tourism. On the other hand, the rapid growth of e-commerce and logistics during the pandemic created new flexible employment opportunities, such as delivery drivers and online customer service roles.

Flexible employment has become one of the most significant avenues for Chinese workers to achieve employment. Analysing and understanding the characteristics and trends in the development of flexible employment in China not only provides valuable insights for studying flexible employment markets in other countries but also enriches and enhances the theories and practices related to flexible employment. This, in turn, helps the international community gain a more comprehensive understanding of the characteristics and challenges of the globalisation of flexible employment, thus promoting the healthy development of the global labour market.

Although the proportion of flexible employment in China is relatively low compared with other major economies, the ILO estimated that the proportion of temporarily employed people in China was about 12 per cent of the total employed population in 2019. Moreover, during the Covid-19 pandemic, China's share of flexible employment increased rapidly. Data from the National Bureau of Statistics of China show that, by the end of 2021, the number of people engaged in flexible employment in China had reached 200 million, accounting for approximately 26 per cent of the total employed population.

The rapid development of flexible employment in China is driven by several factors that follow a global pattern, including technological advancements, economic restructuring, labour demand diversification and policy support. The development of the internet and information technology in China has enabled remote working and the platform economy, thereby fostering the gig economy[4] and creating numerous flexible job opportunities. China's flexible employment workforce includes traditional sectors such as construction, services and labour-intensive manufacturing, as well as new-economy sectors driven by the rise of live streaming, online services, ride-sharing and food delivery.

The flexible employment workforce in China is notably characterised by a younger demographic and higher average level of education. The age distribution is concentrated in the 21–30 and 31–40 age brackets, with the newer types of flexible employment skewing even younger. In terms of education, the flexible employment workforce, particularly in the new-economy sectors, tends to have higher educational attainment. According to the *China Flexible Employment Development Report* (Tengjing Research and Ant Group 2022), nearly 80 per cent of China's flexible workers have at least a high school education, with 21.73 per cent holding a bachelor's degree or higher (Figure 7.12). This trend is consistent with the OSOME's findings, which show that 80 per cent of small business operators have at least a high school education. This phenomenon may be attributed to the rapid economic development since the reform and opening period, which has improved the educational level of the workforce, especially

---

4   The 'gig economy' refers to an economic model in which individuals earn income by completing short-term, flexible tasks or projects rather than being employed long term by a single employer like traditional full-time employees. These tasks are typically matched through online platforms such as Uber, Airbnb and TaskRabbit.

younger people. Additionally, the new-economy jobs often require proficiency in the use of smartphones and software, extending the job descriptions from basic to technical roles, thereby raising the educational requirements.

From a global perspective, China shares significant similarities and commonalities with other major economies regarding flexible employment. Despite differences in the stages of economic development and labour market conditions, the forms, drivers and characteristics of flexible employment in China show remarkable consistency with international trends. Issues such as income instability, insufficient social security and labour rights protection among flexible workers are prevalent both in China and abroad.

In China, the protection of the rights and interests of flexible workers is gaining increasing attention. The Chinese Government has endeavoured to improve the regulatory framework for the protection of flexible workers. In 2021, the Ministry of Human Resources and Social Security convened administrative guidance meetings with major platform companies to enforce its *Guiding Opinions on Safeguarding the Labour and Social Security Rights and Interests of Workers Engaged in New Forms of Employment* (MOHRSS 2021). In December 2022, the Supreme People's Court issued its *Opinions on Providing Judicial Services and Guarantees for Stable Employment*, outlining considerations for the recognition of labour relations in new forms of employment. In addition, the government introduced policies to simplify individual business registration procedures and promote the inclusion of flexible workers in social security systems.

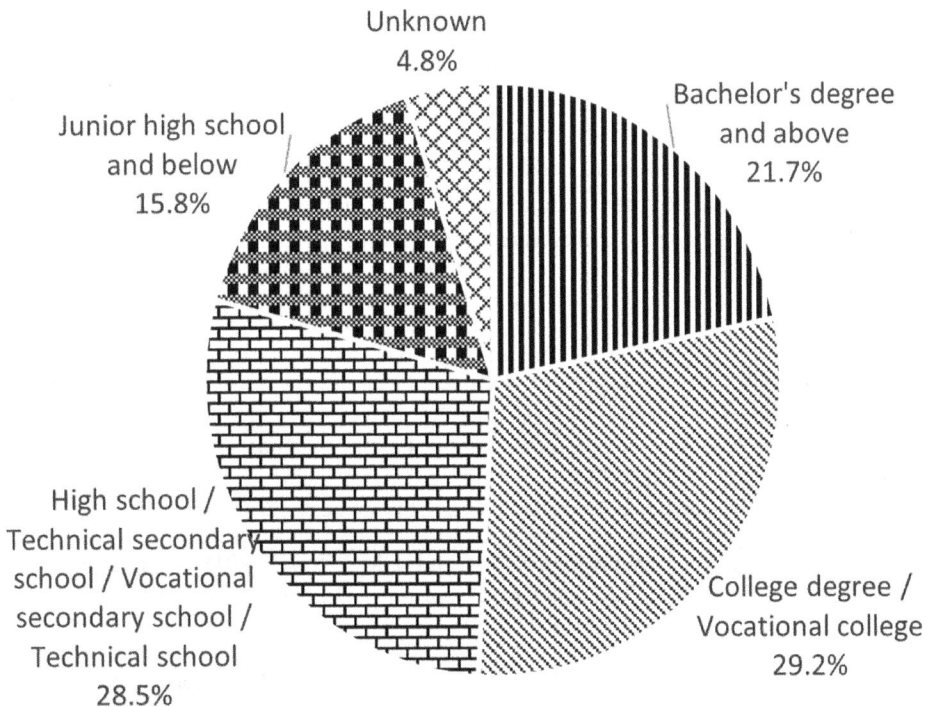

Figure 7.12 Educational distribution of China's flexible employment population
Source: Tengjing Research and Ant Group (2022).

Conclusions and implications

Despite these efforts, numerous challenges to flexible employment remain. Since the 1980s, countries like Japan, Germany, France and Italy have implemented policies to protect the rights of flexible workers, including subsidies, legal protections and improved social security. China can formulate similar measures to address issues such as social security contributions and rights protection. For instance, establishing a more flexible multitier social security system could help alleviate the burden on flexible workers, much like Japan's pension system, which comprises the national pension (fixed contributions) and employees' pension (income-based contributions). Enhancing legal protections for flexible workers is also crucial, particularly in defining the responsibilities and obligations of parties involved in new forms of flexible employment, as seen in the Netherlands' legal framework for various types of labour contracts. Furthermore, the Chinese Government could enhance its service functions for flexible employment by providing job guidance, vocational information, subsidies and tax reductions. Since 2007, the German Government has implemented tax exemptions for flexible workers and France offers a 50 per cent income tax exemption for temporary workers, effectively promoting the development of flexible employment.

Furthermore, digital transformation of MSEs not only enhances their resilience to shocks, but also creates more opportunities for flexible employment (Cong et al. 2024). The Chinese Government could continue promoting the role of digitisation in flexible employment with policy measures such as providing digital infrastructure support, encouraging digital transformation, promoting digital skills training, protecting the rights and interests of flexible workers, supporting e-commerce development, fostering innovation and entrepreneurship and enhancing international cooperation. Policies to accelerate the digitisation process hold the potential of further promoting flexible employment, enhancing the resilience and inclusiveness of the labour market and improving the competitiveness and survival chances of micro and small businesses.

References

AliResearch. 2022. *The Digital Economy and Chinese Women's Employment and Entrepreneurship.* Research Report, 7 March. Beijing: AliResearch. www.aliresearch.com/ch/information/informationdetails?articleCode=309229232767242240&type=%E6%96%B0%E9%97%BB.

Arias, Javier, Erhan Artuc, Daniel Lederman, and Diego Rojas. 2018. 'Trade, Informal Employment and Labor Adjustment Costs.' *Journal of Development Economics* 133: 396–414. doi.org/10.1016/j.jdeveco.2018.03.006.

BRICS Women's Business Alliance (WBA). 2023. *BRICS Women's Development Report 2023.* Kempton Park, South Africa: BRICS WBA. bricswomen.com/wp-content/uploads/2024/04/BRICS-Womens-Development-Report-2023-1.pdf.

Cong, Lin William, Xiaohan Yang, and Xiaobo Zhang. 2024. 'Small and Medium Enterprises amidst the Pandemic and Reopening: Digital Edge and Transformation.' *Management Science* 70, no. 7: 4167–952. doi.org/10.1287/mnsc.2023.02424.

Guanghua School of Management (GSM). 2023. *Online Survey of Micro-and-Small Enterprises (OSOME)*. Beijing: Guanghua School of Management, Peking University. cer.gsm.pku.edu.cn/survey/OSOME/report.htm.

International Labour Organization (ILO). 2018. *Women and Men in the Informal Economy: A Statistical Picture*. 3rd edn. Geneva: ILO. www.ilo.org/publications/women-and-men-informal-economy-statistical-picture-third-edition.

Ministry of Human Resources and Social Security (MOHRSS). 2021. *Guiding Opinions on Safeguarding the Labour and Social Security Rights and Interests of Workers Engaged in New Forms of Employment*. No. 56. Beijing: Ministry of Human Resources and Social Security of the People's Republic of China.

Office of the State Council. 2020. *Opinions of the General Office of the State Council on Supporting Flexible Employment through Multiple Channels*. State Council Document No. 27(2020), 31 July. Beijing: State Council of the People's Republic of China. www.gov.cn/zhengce/content/2020-07/31/content_5531613.htm.

Samaniego de la Parra, Brenda, and León Fernández Bujanda. 2024. 'Increasing the Cost of Informal Employment: Evidence from Mexico.' *American Economic Journal: Applied Economics* 16, no. 1: 377–411. doi.org/10.1257/app.20200763.

Supreme People's Court. 2022. *Opinions on Providing Judicial Services and Guarantees for Stable Employment*. No. 36. Beijing: Supreme People's Court of the People's Republic of China.

Tengjing Research and Ant Group. 2022. *China Flexible Employment Development Report*. Beijing: Beijing Tengjing Big Data Application Technology Research Institute and Ant Group Research Institute. download.caixin.com/upload/sjdlhjyqtdybg.pdf.

Upwork. 2022. *Freelance Forward 2022*. Report, 13 December. San Francisco, CA: Upwork Inc. www.upwork.com/research/freelance-forward-2022.

World Bank. 2021. *World Bank Covid-19 Digital Merchant Survey 2021*. Washington, DC: World Bank Group. thedocs.worldbank.org/en/doc/e975e535c0a25907216079e138c56307-0070012021/original/Indonesia-Shopee-World-Bank-Digital-Merchant-Survey.pdf.

Zhao, Wenjun. 2024. 'By the End of 2023, There Will be 124 Million Individual Businesses in China.' *Xinhua*, 31 January. www.gov.cn/lianbo/bumen/202401/content_6929259.htm.

8

The trend in China's urban housing affordability and its impact on the total fertility rate

Tunye Qiu

Introduction

Housing affordability is an important matter from social and economic perspectives. Socially, high housing costs force people to live in areas with poorer amenities, leading to health and public security problems due to overcrowding and financial hardship (Gabriel et al. 2005). Economically, the deterioration in housing affordability has been demonstrated to crowd out talent and possibly add downward pressure to the innovative capacity of a city (Lin et al. 2020). Meanwhile, housing affordability has been shown to be closely related to people's fertility decisions (Dettling and Kearney 2014). Based on data from the Czech Republic, Kostelecký and Vobecká (2009) find the fertility rate is lower in districts where housing prices are high in relation to local salaries and, further, worse housing affordability causes people to have children later in life.

China's total fertility rate has remained at a low level since it first implemented the One-Child Policy. To boost fertility, the Chinese Government introduced a conditional Two-Child Policy in 2013, which allowed couples to have up to two children if at least one parent was a single child, and later made this policy universal. Though the number of second babies increased in 2016 and 2017, the total fertility rate remained low as there were increasing numbers of couples deciding not to give birth at all (Liu et al. 2020). According to China's seventh national population census, the total fertility rate declined from 1.6 live births per woman in 2017 to 1.3 in 2020, raising strong concerns. The government therefore implemented a Three-Child Policy in 2021 and began to emphasise the importance of decreasing the burden of childrearing costs, especially housing affordability (Xinhua 2021). Hence, this chapter studies the trends in China's housing affordability in recent years and the impact on fertility.

In this chapter, I use the residual income approach and equal repayment equation to construct China's urban housing affordability index, which covers 70 large and medium-sized cities. The major contribution of this chapter is the identification of a causal relationship between housing affordability and the total fertility rate by creating a housing affordability index. I use the residual income approach that subtracts necessary consumption expenditure from income and apply the equal repayment equation, which is used by commercial banks to decide the amount of money someone can borrow. This approach has been adopted by many previous studies to analyse housing affordability (Cava et al. 2017; Li et al. 2015). I calculate the affordable housing area for the average household in one city in each year from 2010 to 2019. Changes in the affordable housing area across years indicate trends in housing affordability. Three key findings are based on the affordability index.

First, I find an inverted U-shaped relationship for the urban affordable housing area over time. Specifically, overall housing affordability increased from 2010 to 2014 and reached its maximum in 2015–16 before it started to decline. In particular, the four 'superstar' cities, Beijing, Shanghai, Guangzhou and Shenzhen, had low housing affordability throughout the sample period, with the affordable housing area for an average household being less than 40 square metres.[1] Xiamen, Tianjin, Zhuhai, Fuzhou and Haikou also face housing affordability problems. This suggests that the problem has spread from the superstar cities in recent years, whereas the existing literature finds the problem only exists within the 'superstar' cities.

Second, I find that the residual income approach with an equal repayment equation can be a good alternative to the conventional price-to-income ratio approach for measuring affordability. While the price-to-income ratio captures the years of income a household needs to purchase an average-sized house, housing affordability measured by the residual income approach with equal repayment equation reflects the size of house a household can afford. The latter is superior as it also captures the improvement in housing affordability from 2012 to 2015 by considering the parameters of bank lending rates, which the price-to-income ratio fails to do.

Third, and most importantly, I analyse the impact of housing affordability on the total fertility rate. By applying instrumental variable (IV) estimates, I find a causal relationship between the affordable housing area and total fertility rate; specifically, the bigger the affordable housing area, the higher is the total fertility rate. The results from IV estimates indicate that a 10 per cent increase in the affordable housing area caused a 4.58 per cent increase in the total fertility rate. I then adopted the instrument-free

---

1   In the literature, superstar cities are those that experience persistently high housing price growth (Gyourko et al. 2013). In the Chinese context, Beijing, Shanghai, Guangzhou and Shenzhen are treated as superstar cities by the existing literature.

inference approach proposed by Kiviet (2020) as a robustness test to support the IV estimates. I also adopt the tests from Nevo and Rosen (2012), Conley et al. (2012) and Kiviet (2020), which relax the assumption of instrument exogeneity—specifically, the instrumental independence assumption and exclusion restriction assumption. The estimated results validate the significance of IV estimates. This finding adds to an emerging set of the literature that documents the impact of rising housing prices on fertility in China. Moreover, compared with the existing literature, which focuses only on housing prices, the housing affordability index in this study also addresses household disposable income, consumption expenditure and lending rates, providing a more comprehensive review of housing affordability and fertility. Additionally, the causal relationship between housing affordability and the fertility rate suggests that China's government should consider policies to improve housing affordability as an effective way of boosting the fertility rate to complement the newly issued universal Three-Child Policy.

The rest of the chapter is organised as follows. In section two, I introduce the background of China's housing market and its total fertility rate. Section three provides a literature review of methods for measuring housing affordability; section four introduces the methodology and section five depicts the data and descriptive results, which are drawn from the China Real Estate Index System (CREIS), China Real Estate Information Corporation (CRIC) and China's city-level statistical yearbooks. Sections six and seven present the empirical results and robustness checks, respectively, and section eight concludes by demonstrating potential implications of the findings.

China's housing market and total fertility rate

China's housing market has undergone huge changes over the past few decades. Notably, since 1998, it has transitioned from a government-designated housing distribution and welfare-based system of housing supply to market-based supply (Lee and Zhu 2006; Chen et al. 2011). The transformation of the housing market was accomplished rapidly through the twin processes of urbanisation and government-led land conversion (Man 2011). The urbanisation process has transformed China's migrants, especially rural-to-urban migrants, into urban residents, releasing tremendous demand for newly built residential houses in urban areas.

According to the Chinese Urban Household Survey (NBS 2012), private homeownership leapt from about 20 per cent of the population in the early 1990s to 90 per cent in 2009, and the proportion of homeownership has since become the highest in the world (Huang et al. 2021). Meanwhile, housing prices have skyrocketed in response to huge demand. According to Glaeser et al. (2017) and Eftimoski and McLoughlin (2019), China's property prices increased for all cities from 2002 to 2019, except for a clear drop about 2014. Based on CEIC data, Figure 8.1 demonstrates the increasing trend in China's new residential property prices between 2011 and 2019.

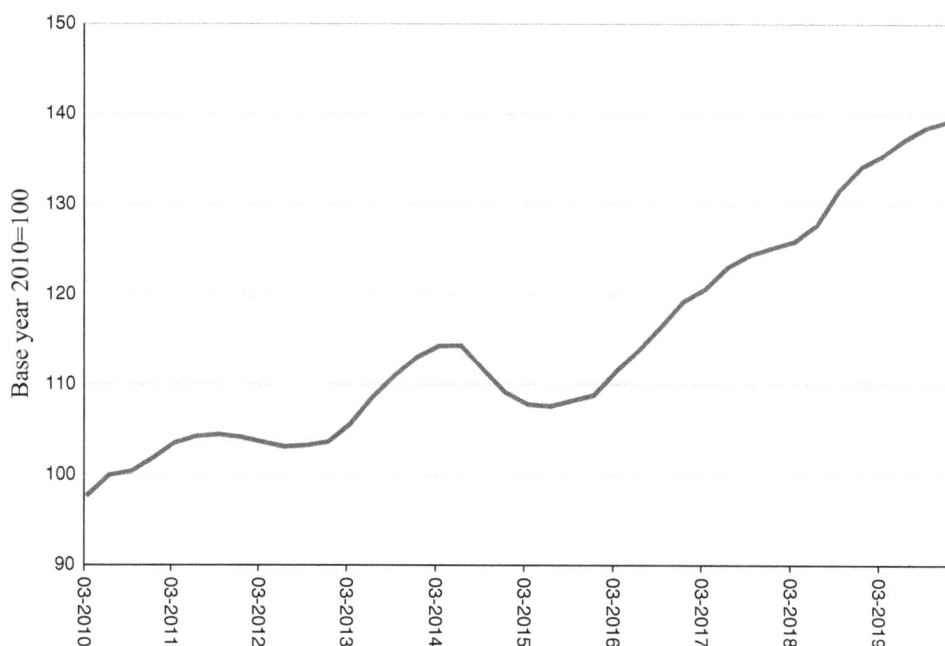

Figure 8.1 China's new residential property prices, 2011–19 (per cent)
Source: CEIC Data (www.ceicdata.com/en).

China's economic reforms have significantly increased the income levels and living standards of average households. According to China's statistical yearbooks, the Engel coefficient of Chinese households decreased from 67.7 per cent in 1978 to 28.2 per cent in 2019.[2] However, increases in living standards do not necessarily mean that rising incomes can keep pace with rising housing prices. The decrease in the Engel coefficient may also partially be caused by the huge increase in housing expenditure and deteriorating housing affordability. Fang et al. (2015) find that the price-to-income ratio for all cities in China worsened from 2003 to 2010 and then slightly improved in 2012. In 2012, the price-to-income ratio was about 8.0 for the bottom-income group and 6.2 for the middle-income group. In comparison, in the United States, the ratio was only about 3.0 even at the peak of the housing bubble in 2006.

In response to a temporary downturn in housing prices in 2014, the Chinese Government ordered a national easing of lending policies for housing purchases in March 2015 (PBC 2015). Meanwhile, previously implemented policies restricting house purchases

---

2   The Engel coefficient denotes the percentage of income spent on food. When income increases, the proportion of income spent on food would decrease so the Engel coefficient would decrease.

were removed in most cities.[3] The destocking of real estate was regarded as an important task[4] (Eftimoski and McLoughlin 2019). Housing prices have risen significantly under the stimulus of these policies. Eftimoski and McLoughlin (2019) find that residential property prices for cities of all tiers leapt sharply at the beginning of 2015 and the growth in housing prices was much faster than any previous increase.

Meanwhile, the total fertility rate in China has remained below replacement level in recent decades due to the One-Child Policy. The implementation of the Two-Child Policy in 2016 provided a brief increase in the fertility rate, although the downward trend has since continued. To boost the low fertility rate, the central government released its universal Three-Child Policy in 2021. As shown in Figure 8.2, the fertility rate in China is much lower than the global average, and even lower than many developed countries such as the United States.

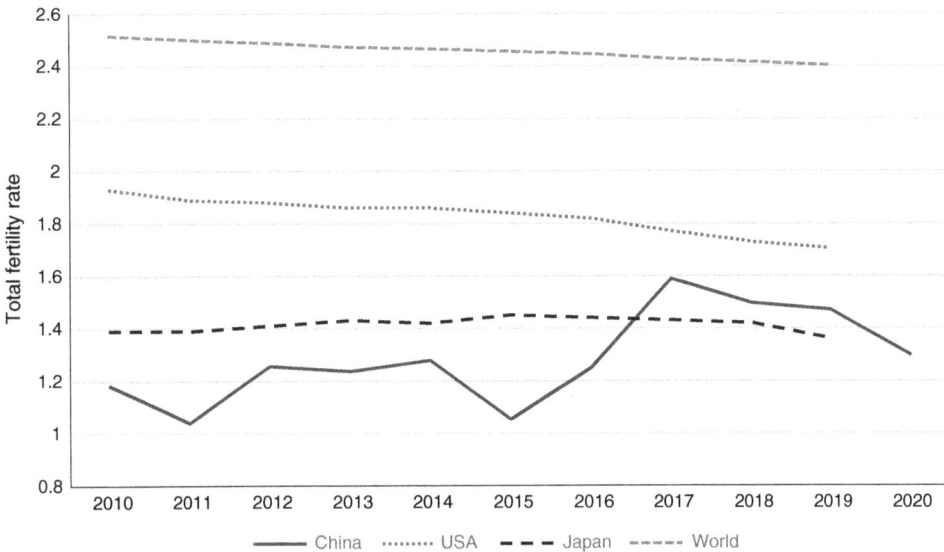

Figure 8.2 Total fertility rate, 2010–20
Sources: China's National Bureau of Statistics; World Bank data.

---

3   The housing purchase restriction policy refers to a restriction on the number of houses a household can purchase. Specifically, a household with local *hukou* ('household registration') can purchase a maximum of two houses and those with non-local *hukou* can only purchase one house in one city. The house purchase restriction policy was first implemented in Beijing in 2010 and then in 48 larger and medium-sized cities (Li et al. 2020).
4   For China's central government, the destocking of housing inventory means faster sales of commercial housing and shortened turnover to prevent overstocking of housing units (Chen et al. 2020).

Literature review

A large existing literature has examined factors in the housing sector that could influence people's decision to have children, most of which has focused on the relationship between housing prices and fertility. Changes in housing prices have two-way effects on the decision to have children. Examining data from the United States and the United Kingdom, respectively, Dettling and Kearney (2014) and Aksoy (2016) find an increase in housing prices decreases births among those who are renters but increases births among homeowners. In the Chinese context, Pan and Xu (2013) find that the provincial urban fertility rate is negatively related to housing prices; however, it is positively related to per capita housing area, based on the 2010 National Population Census. Using the same data source, Liu et al. (2020) find that a 1 per cent increase in house prices leads to a 6.4 per cent decrease in the probability of women having babies within the 12 months before the census. Those findings suggest a clear negative relationship between housing prices and the fertility rate in China.

Housing affordability can also be affected by changes in income, the mortgage lending rate and other consumption costs. So far, it appears that no study has attempted to establish a causal relationship between housing affordability and the total fertility rate. To realise this innovation, first, I must find a valid way of measuring China's housing affordability.

In the existing literature, there is no clear consensus on how to measure housing affordability. Gan and Hill (2009) indicate that there are at least three ways: purchase affordability, repayment affordability and income affordability. Purchase affordability focuses on whether a household can borrow adequate funds to purchase a house, while repayment affordability focuses on the ability of households to repay a mortgage. Income affordability simply measures the ratio of house prices to incomes.

For the empirical work of analysing housing affordability, many studies have used the price-to-income ratio (Fox and Finlay 2012; Li et al. 2018, 2020; Abeysinghe and Gu 2010; Fang et al. 2015; Ben-Shahar and Warszawski 2016). For example, Li et al. (2020) use a panel dataset of 275 Chinese prefectural cities from 2014 to 2018 to calculate the housing expenditure-to-income ratio and find the overall affordability of housing in China was stable or even improved during the sample period, except that so-called superstar cities have serious problems with housing affordability. The ratio approach can provide a clear and easy insight into housing affordability; however, simply analysing the average income over the average housing price cannot achieve a comprehensive understanding as it ignores household consumption expenditure and the burden of repaying a mortgage.

Stone (2010) argues that the residual income approach for measuring housing affordability can provide a better and more logical understanding than the conventional ratio approach. Specifically, he considers non-housing costs—for either a real individual household or an imagined 'typical' household meant to represent a particular demographic—and subtracts those from total income. What is left over, the 'residual', is how much one can afford to spend on housing without sacrificing other necessary payments. By adopting the residual income approach, Li et al. (2015) use an extended linear expenditure system to calculate residual income after deducting the consumption expenditure of urban households in Beijing to measure housing affordability. They further convert the residual income into an equal repayment equation to consider the burden of repaying a mortgage. They use cross-sectional data from 2004 and 2013 and find that housing affordability in Beijing increased during this period, while the growth of affordable housing areas for urban residents decreased. The advantage of combining the residual income approach and the equal repayment equation over the price-to-income approach lies in the consideration of more parameters when measuring affordability—for example, consumption expenditure, bank lending interest rates, down payment ratios and the length of the mortgage.

Weaknesses in the existing literature on measuring China's housing affordability include only using the ratio approach; only focusing on one city; and not including recent years, in which housing prices have rapidly increased, in the sample period. The findings of this study address all these shortcomings.

Methodology

Measuring housing affordability

The affordable housing area for the average household in each city in each year is calculated as follows. First, I calculate the affordable monthly repayment of an average household in city j in year t (Equation 8.1).

Equation 8.1

$$MAP_{j,t} = \left(Y_{j,t} - C_{j,t}\right) * \frac{1}{12}$$

In Equation 8.1, $MAP_{j,t}$ denotes the affordable monthly repayment for an average urban household in city j in year t; $Y_{j,t}$ denotes the average household disposable income in city j in year t; and $C_{j,t}$ denotes the average household consumption expenditure in city j in year t. According to China's statistical yearbooks, household consumption expenditure comprises eight items: food; clothing; shelter; household appliances and services; transport and communication; education, cultural and recreation services; health care and medical services; and miscellaneous goods and services.

The process of buying a house involves a down payment, taking a mortgage loan from a bank and then monthly repayments on the loan and interest.[5] Let D denote the down payment rate, P denote the housing price, r denote the interest rate of a mortgage loan

---

5   The equal repayment equation mainly focuses on the repayment affordability of housing. In other words, it measures the burden imposed on a household of repaying a mortgage based on the income level. The bank assumes the down payment has already been saved by borrowers before they take out the mortgage.

and n indicate the loan period. I adopt China's national bank lending interest rate and assume the loan period is 30 years. Equation 8.2 is for the equal repayment of housing loans.

Equation 8.2

$$(1 - D) * P * \left(1 + \frac{r}{12}\right)^{12n} = MAP_{j,t} * \frac{\left(1 + \frac{r}{12}\right)^{12n} - 1}{\frac{r}{12}}$$

According to Equation 8.2, this study calculates the price that an average urban household in city j in year t can afford to pay for a house (Equation 8.3).

Equation 8.3

$$P_{j,t} = MAP_{j,t} * \frac{\left(1 + \frac{r}{12}\right)^{12n} - 1}{\frac{r}{12}} * \frac{1}{(1 - D) * \left(1 + \frac{r}{12}\right)^{12n}}$$

I then calculate the affordable housing area ($AS_{j,t}$) for an urban household in city j in year t (Equation 8.4).

Equation 8.4

$$AS_{j,t} = \frac{P_{j,t}}{p_{j,t}}$$

In Equation 8.4, $p_{j,t}$ is the average housing price per square metre in city j in year t.

Housing affordability and the total fertility rate

Based on the housing affordability index, I begin to understand the relationship between the affordable housing area and total fertility rate by adopting ordinary least squares (OLS) regressions and a fixed-effects model. However, one potential threat from the OLS estimate is concern raised about the endogeneity of housing affordability and fertility. For example, spouses with different birth preferences may choose to move to cities with different housing affordability. To address the threat of endogeneity and find a causal relationship between housing affordability and fertility rates, IV estimates are used. The main estimate regression model is in the form of Equation 8.5.

Equation 8.5

$$TFR_{j,t} = \beta_0 + \beta_1 AS_{j,t} + \lambda X_{j,t} + \gamma_t + Z_j + \varepsilon_{j,t}$$

In Equation 8.5, $TFR_{j,t}$ denotes the total fertility rate in city j in year t and $AS_{j,t}$ denotes the affordable housing area in city j in year t. Therefore, β_1 captures the effect of housing affordability on the total fertility rate. Since China only publishes the total fertility rate at the city level every 10 years in the National Population Census and the 1 per cent national sample census between two population censuses, the total fertility rates I include are for 2010 and 2015.[6] $X_{j,t}$ denotes the control variables used in the regression, which have been selected based on the existing literature and economic intuition. For example, fertility in relation to female education and many economic factors has been analysed by numerous studies (Jain 1981; Bhat 2002; Panopoulou and Tsakloglou 1999; Götmark and Andersson 2020). Therefore, the control variables in this study include years of female education in city j in year t, the log of urban population density in city j in year t, the log of GDP per capita in city j in year t, the ratio of tertiary industry to GDP in city j in year t and the urban unemployment rate in city j in year t. These control variables are the major factors that impact the fertility decision so including them enhances the internal validity of the study. γ_t denotes the year fixed effects and Z_j and $\varepsilon_{j,t}$ denote the control of group fixed effects and error terms, respectively.

Why IV estimates?

In addition to the OLS and fixed-effects model, this study adopts IV estimates to address concerns about omitted variables and reverse causality. Potential risks from omitted variables and inherent reverse causality prevent me from interpreting a causal relationship between them. For example, spouses with different birth preferences may move to cities with different housing affordability, causing a potential threat from endogeneity. Additionally, according to Dettling and Kearney (2014) and Aksoy (2016), as people want more children, that desire would drive up housing prices and thus cause reverse causality. Specifically, high demand for births requires more living space for households to raise more children, which increases demand for housing and housing prices and lowers housing affordability. To address the problem of reverse causality, Dettling and Kearney (2014) and Aksoy (2016) apply IV estimates. As housing price is one of the factors used in this chapter in calculating the affordable housing index, I adopt the city-level land price as the instrumental variable of the affordable housing area to establish a causal link between housing affordability and the total fertility rate.

A valid instrument for IV estimates is needed to meet two requirements. The first is that the instrument must be strong—something the results from the F-statistic can prove. The second requirement is that the instrument must be exogenous. Furthermore, the second requirement has two conditions: 1) the instrument is independent of the error term in the structural equation, and 2) the instrument should satisfy the exclusion restriction so it can only affect the outcome variable through the endogenous variable.

In my case, a valid instrument that satisfies the exclusion restriction can only affect the total fertility rate through housing affordability. According to the previous literature, land information is frequently used as the instrument for housing information. For example, based on data from Switzerland for the period 1978–2008, Bourassa et al. (2011) use land leverage information as the instrument for housing prices. With microdata from the China Household Finance Survey between 2013 and 2017, Clark

---

6   The seventh National Population Census was finished at the end of 2020; however, it usually takes several years to publish the detailed data, so I could not use the total fertility rate at the city level in 2020.

et al. (2020) use the land price as the instrument for the housing price to investigate the impact of housing prices on household decisions to give birth. In this chapter, I adopt the city-level land price as the instrumental variable of the housing affordability index, constructed under the residual income approach with an equal repayment method.

Why is land price a good instrument in this case? In the process of housing development in China, developers bid for land rights from the local government and then build residential units—mostly apartments—on the land. An ordinary Chinese household rarely receives land information in this process. However, the land price plays an important role in determining housing prices in China. Based on data from 35 major Chinese cities between 2003 and 2011, Deng et al. (2012) indicate that housing prices appear to be driven by land prices rather than other factors such as construction costs or construction workers' wages. Hence, it is reasonable to believe that the average household in China would not consider changes in land prices when deciding whether to give birth. Meanwhile, the land price drives the housing price and affects housing affordability, which would likely affect the fertility rate.

One of the advantages of IV estimates is that they solve the omitted variable bias between the outcome variable and the treatment variable. However, the potential risk of applying IV estimates is that the chosen instrument itself correlates with the omitted variables. To address the potential threat from omitted variables, multiple control variables have been included in this study. However, a correlation may exist between the land price and the stock of urban construction land. In other words, the less land is left undeveloped for construction in a city, the higher land prices are likely to be. However, data on city-level urban construction land stock cannot be found. To address this concern, I use city-level land area as a substitute. The reason behind this is that the larger the size of a city, the higher is the amount of land that can be used for construction. I then regress the land area on the land price to include the control of variables and fixed effects. According to the results from Appendix Table A8.2, there is no statistically significant relationship between land area and land prices. Another potential omitted variable of interest is childrearing expenses. The existing literature has frequently discussed the role of childrearing costs in determining fertility rates. For example, Becker (1992) indicates that childrearing expenses depend not only on the cost of food, clothing and housing, but also on the time spent by parents on childrearing. However, it is hard to measure an accurate value of childrearing costs in the real world, so I cannot control for such expenses in this study. In the next part of this chapter, I conduct a bound estimation method, developed by Nevo and Rosen (2012), which relaxes the assumption of the independence of the instrument to the omitted variables, and the estimated results are still significant. It addresses the potential threat from other omitted variables to the instrumental variable.

Data and descriptive results

The main contribution of this study is to construct an affordable housing area index under the residual income approach with an equal repayment equation and cover the major cities of China, and then to use this index to examine the relationship between housing affordability and fertility. To achieve this goal, I have used multiple sources of data. The housing price data are collected from the China Real Estate Index System (CREIS) and China Real Estate Information Corporation (CRIC),[7] both of which have widely recognised housing databases that provide China's housing price index. Many existing studies have used these two databases in analysing China's housing market. For example, Wu (2015) uses CREIS to study the housing market cycle in Chinese cities and Kemp et al. (2020) use CRIC data to analyse the effect of Covid-19 on China's residential property sector. The data I collected from both CREIS and CRIC included the newly built residential housing price in 70 major Chinese cities from 2010 to 2019.[8] The other source of data are the statistical yearbooks of each city.

China's housing prices

According to Figure 8.3, the differences in housing prices across years between CREIS and CRIC tend to be relatively large in the early years but shrink over time. Overall, the two datasets provide similar price figures. To further facilitate accuracy, I adopt the average of the two datasets for different cities across years to prevent overestimating or underestimating from a single dataset.

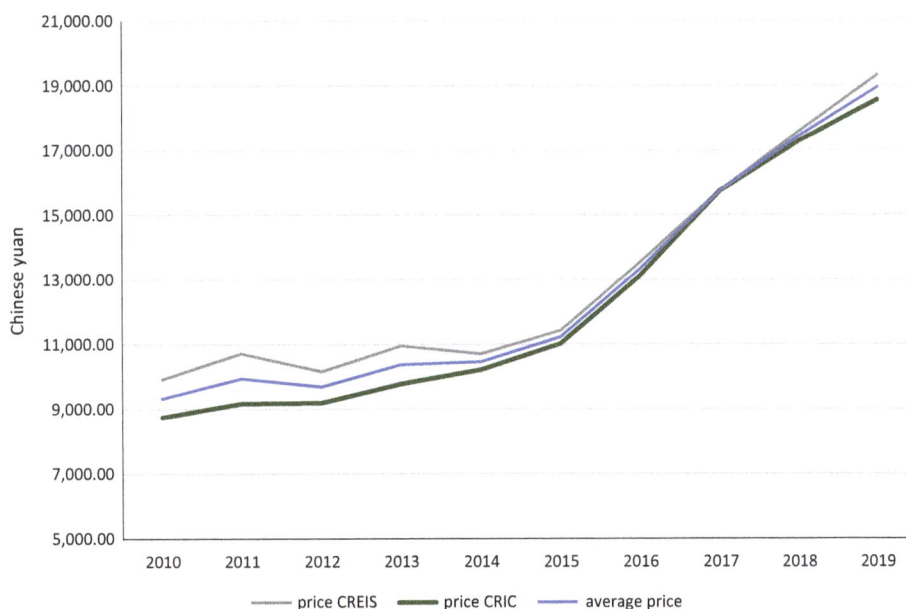

Figure 8.3 Housing prices from CREIS, CRIC and their average, 2010–19
Sources: CREIS; CRIC.

7   For CREIS, see: fdc.fang.com/creis/. For CRIC, see: www.cricchina.com/.
8   The 70 cities are Beijing, Shanghai, Guangzhou, Shenzhen, Tianjin, Shijiazhuang, Taiyuan, Hohhot, Shenyang, Dalian, Changchun, Harbin, Nanjing, Hangzhou, Ningbo, Hefei, Fuzhou, Xiamen, Nanchang, Jinan, Qingdao, Zhengzhou, Wuhan, Changsha, Nanning, Haikou, Chongqing, Chengdu, Guiyang, Kunming, Xi'an, Lanzhou, Xining, Yinchuan, Ürümqi, Tangshan, Qinhuangdao, Baotou, Dandong, Jinzhou, Jilin, Mudanjiang, Wuxi, Xuzhou, Yangzhou, Wenzhou, Jinhua, Bengbu, Anqing, Quanzhou, Jiujiang, Ganzhou, Yantai, Jining, Luoyang, Pingdingshan, Yichang, Xiangyang, Yueyang, Changde, Shaoguan, Zhanjiang, Huizhou, Guilin, Beihai, Sanya, Luzhou, Nanchong, Zunyi and Dali.

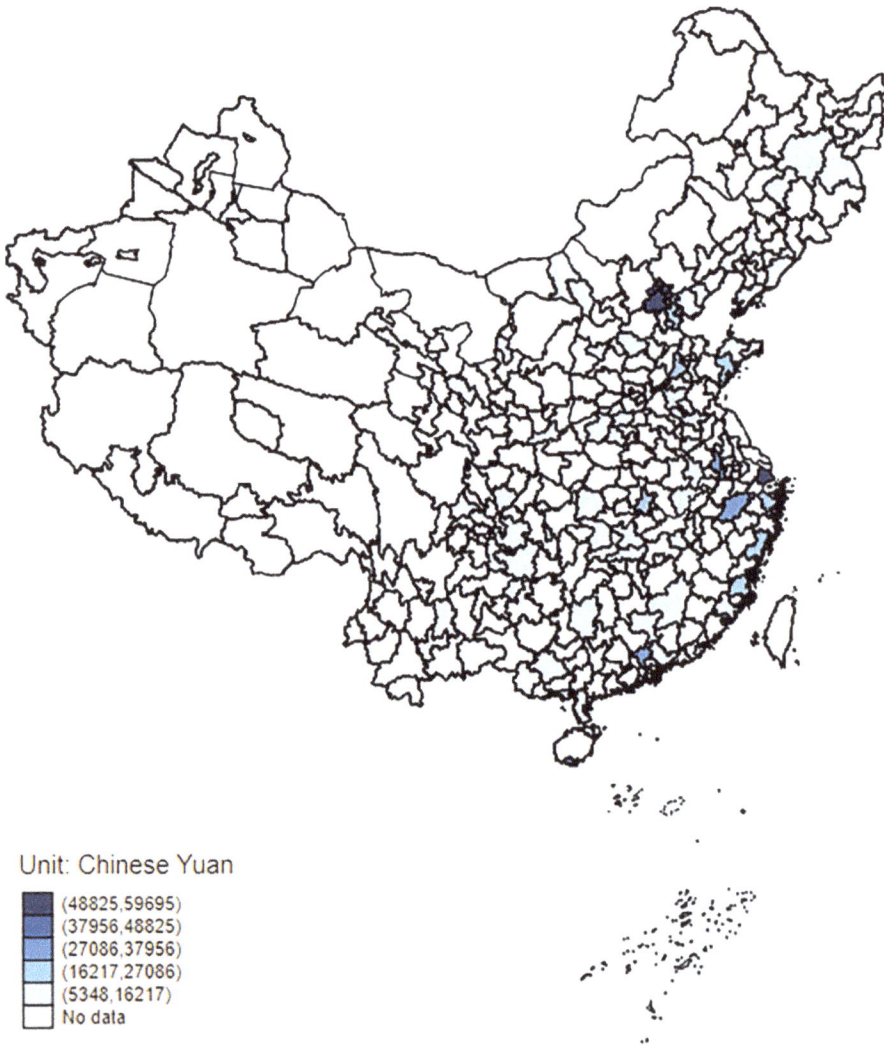

Unit: Chinese Yuan

- (48825,59695)
- (37956,48825)
- (27086,37956)
- (16217,27086)
- (5348,16217)
- No data

Figure 8.4 Sample cities' housing prices, 2019
Sources: CREIS, CRIC.

Figure 8.4 shows the sample cities' housing prices in 2019 from the dataset average. Prices in cities in coastal regions are higher than those of inland cities, and Beijing, Shanghai, Guangzhou and Shenzhen have the highest prices among all cities.

Figure 8.5 contains sample cities' housing price trends from 2010 to 2019. Before 2014, the increases in prices for cities of all tiers were largely parallel with one another. However, the growth rate of housing prices in first-tier cities becomes much higher than in second, third and fourth-tier cities after 2014. The reason for the increasing difference across tiers is that cities experienced different levels of demand shock after the People's Bank of China announced a national easing of lending policies for housing purchases (Eftimoski and McLoughlin 2019). As of 2019, housing prices in first-tier cities were already several times higher than those in other cities.

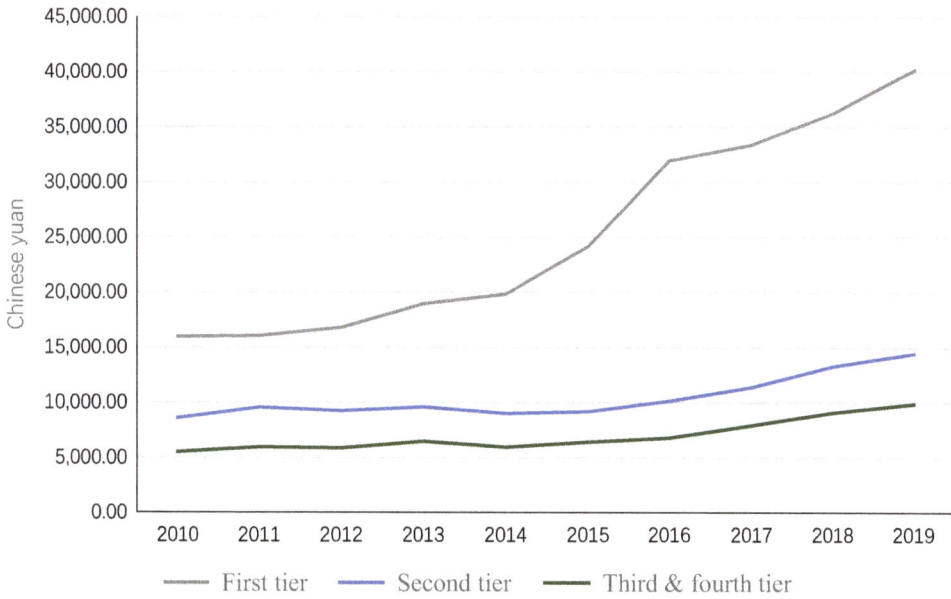

Figure 8.5 Sample cities' housing price trends, 2010–19
Sources: CREIS; CRIC.

Affordable housing area

Figure 8.6 illustrates the change in affordable housing area, calculated by the residual income approach with an equal repayment equation, from 2010 to 2019.[9] According to the blue line in the figure, the affordable housing area reached its maximum about 2015 and then started to decrease, suggesting that a series of policies to stimulate the housing market in 2015 significantly worsened housing affordability in the following years. The affordable area in the first-tier cities remains at a low level across the sample years. The affordable area of second-tier cities endures an inverse U shape, but these cities have the highest level of affordable housing of all tiers, reaching a maximum of about 90 square metres in 2015 and then decreasing to slightly less than 80 square metres in 2019. The evidence in the graph suggests that China's affordable housing area for the average household was increasing from 2010 to 2015 and then kept decreasing after that.

---

9   Appendix Table A8.1 contains summary statistics about the variables used to calculate the housing affordability index.

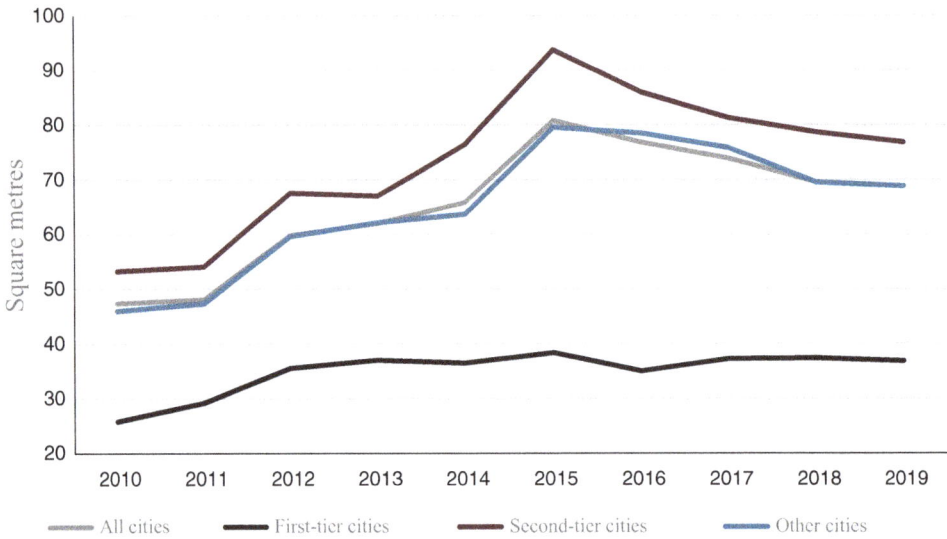

Figure 8.6 Affordable housing area under the residual income approach, 2010–19
Sources: CREIS; CRIC.

Variables in the regression model

Tables 8.1a and 8.1b show the summary statistics of variables used in analysing the relationship between housing affordability and the total fertility rate. The city-level data for the total fertility rate, years of female education and the urban dependency ratio are collected from the 2010 National Population Census and the 2015 1 per cent population sample survey. The total fertility rate in this study indicates the total number of children that would be born to each woman in her childbearing years in different cities in 2010 and 2015; in China, the childbearing age is between 15 and 49 years. According to the table, the total fertility rate is low in all cities, with most below one, which is consistent with the strict implementation of the One-Child Policy in urban areas. The mean years of female education in most cities remains 10 to 11 years.

The land price data are from CREIS; cities with better economic development have higher land prices and cities in coastal areas have higher land prices than inland cities. For example, the mean land price in Shanghai, one of the first-tier cities, is RMB8,386 per square metre—much higher than the inland city of Lanzhou's RMB887 per square metre. The remaining variables—urban population density, GDP per capita, composition of the tertiary sector to GDP and the urban unemployment rate—are collected from the statistical yearbooks of each city.

Table 8.1a Summary statistics of covariates at the city level: Analysis of total fertility rate

City	Total fertility rate		Land price (RMB per sq m)		Years of urban female education		Urban population density	
	Mean	SD	Mean	SD	Mean	SD	Mean	SD
Shanghai	0.70	0.02	8,386.39	2,480.40	11.00	0.41	3,719.50	126.57
Ürümqi	1.06	0.10	498.58	255.80	10.76	0.16	184.95	12.30
Lanzhou	0.86	0.06	886.40	0.77	11.16	0.47	1,272.55	23.22
Beijing	0.74	0.05	11,995.66	6,611.08	11.96	0.91	1,462.00	111.72
Nanjing	0.76	0.03	6,105.50	1,508.12	11.09	1.16	975.68	22.17
Nanning	1.08	0.18	1,768.46	488.52	11.27	0.41	3,005.00	574.17
Nanchang	1.01	0.03	1,961.93	229.68	10.62	0.26	8,708.50	1,658.16
Hefei	0.91	0.09	2,804.64	902.28	10.83	0.19	3,867.00	721.24
Harbin	0.67	0.10	1,020.95	255.65	11.43	0.37	11,484.50	167.58
Tianjin	0.78	0.19	3,794.07	2,745.94	10.97	0.44	3,122.00	523.26
Taiyuan	0.86	0.05	1,387.55	507.17	11.30	0.25	2,861.50	1,044.40
Guangzhou	0.78	0.02	6,124.79	2,029.18	10.90	0.29	4,100.50	2,601.45
Chengdu	0.78	0.12	1,783.94	263.01	11.70	0.17	5,844.00	384.67
Kunming	1.04	0.03	1,476.61	302.82	10.71	0.57	4,624.00	3,470.48
Hangzhou	0.85	0.04	5,710.16	2,014.11	9.90	0.91	3,391.00	192.33
Wuhan	0.94	0.07	2,612.74	1,243.82	11.26	0.34	3,383.50	1,455.93
Shenyang	0.67	0.10	1,345.51	299.13	12.20	0.08	2,330.50	1,197.13
Jinan	1.05	0.01	1,402.04	260.17	11.32	0.15	2,417.50	122.33
Haikou	1.04	0.08	1,781.43	537.37	10.23	0.56	4,029.50	1,574.73
Fuzhou	0.81	0.06	4,559.42	1,958.87	10.37	0.26	2,144.50	251.02
Xining	0.90	0.01	892.57	222.58	9.96	0.06	3,014.00	528.92
Xian	0.88	0.03	1,091.02	108.23	11.93	0.70	9,072.00	1,770.60
Guiyang	1.34	0.17	550.34	40.38	10.41	0.40	3,702.00	2,176.48
Zhengzhou	0.97	0.08	1,070.11	569.94	11.61	0.61	13,220.50	2,594.38
Chongqing	0.82	0.04	1,349.00	178.94	10.11	0.01	1,882.00	31.11
Changchun	0.63	0.06	1,967.28	591.18	11.30	0.10	7,520.00	244.66
Changsha	0.83	0.12	1,008.06	101.17	11.69	0.27	2,739.00	130.11

SD = standard deviation
Notes: The mean for each city is the average of the sample years. The table contains the descriptive results for municipalities and provincial capitals.
Sources: CREIS; CRIC.

Table 8.1b Summary statistics of covariates at the city level: Analysis of total fertility rate (continuous)

City	GDP per capita		Composition of tertiary sector to GDP (%)		Urban unemployment rate (%)	
	Mean	SD	Mean	SD	Mean	SD
Shanghai	89,935	19,602.41	62.15	7.28	4.2	0.28
Ürümqi	26,763.5	10,535.18	60.07	9.98	3.59	0.18
Foshan	95,106	20,640.45	36.64	1.68	2.1	0.28
Lanzhou	44,239	18,247.6	54.35	6.19	2.445	0.95
Beijing	90,176.5	23,080.67	79.6	2.83	1.4	0.00
Nanjing	91,722	37,404.53	54.61	3.83	2.25	0.49
Nanning	38,214.5	15,762.12	49.94	0.38	3.195	0.71
Nanchang	57,208.5	20,470.03	39.5	2.40	3.34	0.06
Hefei	63,949	12,944.3	41.96	1.12	3.115	0.45
Harbin	47,989	15,610.09	53.44	3.51	3.595	0.40
Tianjin	90,477	24,724.7	48.85	4.31	3.55	0.07
Taiyuan	54,090	10,933.29	57.65	5.44	3.405	0.01
Guangzhou	108,990	30,450.85	63.905	4.09	2.25	0.07
Chengdu	54,337	19,868.29	51.5	1.84	2.85	0.49
Kunming	46,910	18,895.31	52.155	4.45	2.55	0.64
Hangzhou	93,612	33,358.47	53.47	6.75	1.97	0.32
Wuhan	81,546.5	31,940.72	51.2	0.28	3.65	0.64
Shenyang	75,095	18,014.25	46.2	1.84	3.15	0.07
Jinan	71,933	19,779.19	54.9	3.22	2.94	1.27
Haikou	41,094	16,131.93	72.71	4.43	1.32	0.03
Fuzhou	61,883	21,934.45	48.02	1.58	2.79	0.49
Xining	38,649	14,890.25	47.32	1.9	3.33	1.18
Xian	53,124.5	21,683.43	58.65	4.55	3.8	0.57
Guiyang	44,530	26,124.77	55.67	2.11	3.16	0.08
Zhengzhou	63,489.5	19,359.88	44.69	5.59	2.2	0.85
Chongqing	39,958.5	17,483.22	47.7	0.99	3.75	0.21
Changchun	58,277.5	20,243.76	42.22	2.09	3.64	0.09
Changsha	90,943	34,648.23	43.85	2.76	2.84	0.23

SD = standard deviation
Notes: The mean for each city is the average of the sample years. The table contains the descriptive results for municipalities and provincial capitals.
Sources: CREIS; CRIC.

Empirical analysis

Comparison of the price-to-income ratio and residual income approach with equal repayment equation

In this section, I calculate the housing affordability index under the price-to-income (PTI) approach to compare with the residual income approach with equal repayment equation. The equation for calculating PTI is Equation 8.6.

Equation 8.6

$$PTI_{j,t} = \frac{ALS_t * p_{j,t}}{I_{j,t}}$$

In Equation 8.6, $PTI_{j,t}$ denotes the price-to-income ratio for an average household in city j in year t; ALS_t denotes the national average household living area; $p_{j,t}$ denotes average housing price per square metre in city j in year t; and $I_{j,t}$ denotes the disposable income for an average household in city j in year t. Therefore, the numerator represents the total expenditure on purchasing an average housing unit in city j in year t and PTI measures how many years of income a household needs to purchase an average house in one city.

Table 8.2 further illustrates the comparison across cities for housing affordability measured under the residual income approach with equal repayment equation and price-to-income ratio. These indexes are calculated by regressing the affordable housing area and price-to-income ratio on city dummies, with the baseline city as Beijing. According to the table, Shanghai, Tianjin, Shenzhen, Guangzhou and Beijing have the worst housing affordability among all sampled cities. Meanwhile, average households in Xiamen, Tianjin, Fuzhou and Haikou have similar housing affordability problems as those in superstar cities. On the other hand, Wuxi, Changsha and Nanning have the best housing affordability. The residual income approach with equal repayment equation and price-to-income ratio show similar results in measuring housing affordability across cities. For example, between 2010 and 2019, under the residual income with an equal repayment equation approach, the affordable housing area for an average household in Shenzhen was 10 square metres smaller than in Beijing, while under the price-to-income ratio, a household in Shenzhen must spend about eight more years of income than one in Beijing to purchase an average housing unit.

Table 8.2 Comparison of affordable residential area for households, by city

City	RI	PTI	City	RI	PTI
Shanghai	−6.329 (5.538)	4.634*** (0.999)	Guangzhou	4.363 (5.538)	−5.832*** (0.999)
Ürümqi	15.443*** (5.538)	−9.799*** (0.999)	Chengdu	38.340*** (5.538)	−8.826*** (0.999)
Lanzhou	21.331*** (5.538)	−8.855*** (0.999)	Kunming	46.336*** (5.538)	−8.782*** (0.999)
Nanjing	27.717*** (5.538)	−4.806*** (0.999)	Hangzhou	11.332** (5.538)	−3.933*** (0.999)
Nanning	66.388*** (5.538)	−7.833*** (0.999)	Wuhan	45.084*** (5.538)	−9.624*** (0.999)
Nanchang	34.054*** (5.538)	−8.424*** (0.999)	Shenyang	41.301*** (5.538)	−11.17*** (0.999)
Xiamen	−7.613 (5.538)	−0.605 (0.999)	Jinan	57.596*** (5.538)	−9.939*** (0.999)
Hefei	34.796*** (5.538)	−7.910*** (0.999)	Fuzhou	4.909 (5.538)	−2.265** (0.999)
Harbin	16.328*** (5.538)	−8.392*** (0.999)	Haikou	7.925 (5.538)	−5.242*** (0.999)
Tianjin	7.558 (5.538)	−5.888*** (0.999)	Changsha	67.029*** (5.538)	−12.34*** (0.999)
Taiyuan	41.231*** (5.538)	−6.646*** (0.999)	Xining	28.773*** (5.538)	−9.234*** (0.999)
Xian	52.061*** (5.538)	−9.849*** (0.999)	Guiyang	22.849*** (5.538)	−10.38*** (0.999)
Zhengzhou	25.595*** (5.538)	−7.469*** (0.999)	Chongqing	23.780*** (5.538)	−8.218*** (0.999)
Changchun	11.971** (5.538)	−9.956*** (0.999)			

RI = residual income
PTI = price-to-income
*** significant at 1 per cent
** significant at 5 per cent
* significant at 10 per cent
Notes: The dependent variable is the affordable residential area of a household at the city level. The table contains the estimated results for municipalities and provincial capitals. The baseline city is Beijing.
Sources: CREIS; CRIC.

Figure 8.7 illustrates the trend in China's housing affordability under the two methods, both of which reflect the deterioration of housing affordability after 2015. However, the price-to-income ratio does not capture the improving housing affordability from 2013 to 2015, when the affordable housing area calculated by the residual income approach increased from 60 square metres, in 2013, to 80 square metres, in 2015. The reason for this is that the calculation of affordable housing area includes the bank lending interest rate. According to Figure 8.8, China's bank lending interest rate decreased from 6.00 per cent in 2013 to 4.35 per cent in 2015, which enhanced households' ability to repay mortgages and increased the affordable housing area. Hence, compared with the price-to-income approach, the residual income approach considers the impact not only of consumption expenditure but also of interest rates on mortgage repayments. Additionally, it provides an alternative way of understanding housing affordability by measuring the affordable housing area, rather than years of income under the price-to-income ratio.

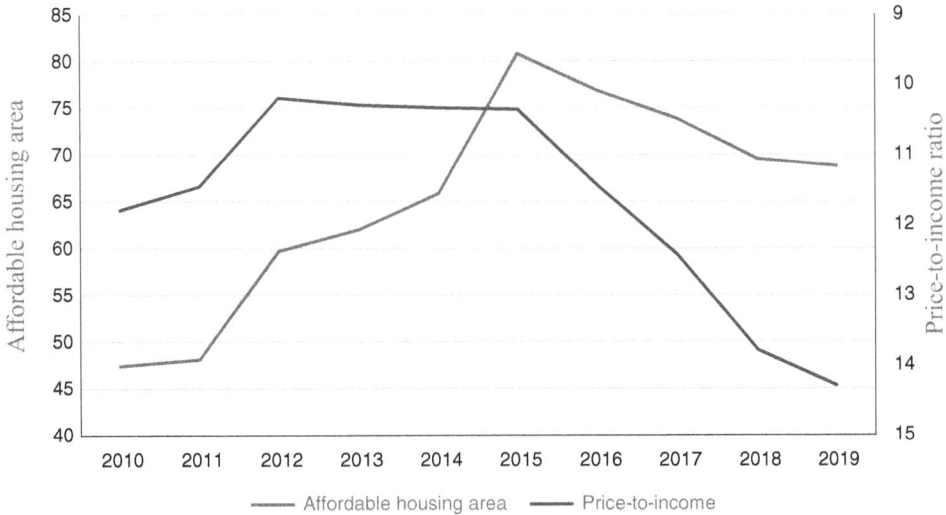

Figure 8.7 Comparison between the residual income approach and the price-to-income approach

Sources: CREIS; CRIC.

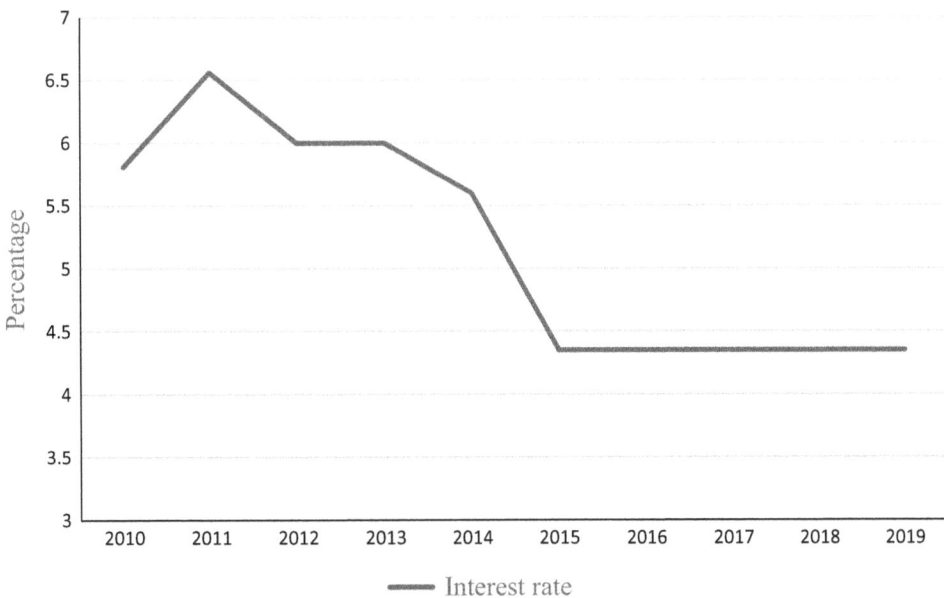

Figure 8.8 Chinese bank lending interest rates

Source: CEIC Data (www.ceicdata.com/en).

How housing affordability affects the total fertility rate

In this section, I present the results of the relationship between housing affordability and the total fertility rate.[10] Table 8.3 presents the results of estimating Equation 8.5, which further validates the positive relationship between the total fertility rate and the affordable housing area. Column (2) includes additional control variables compared with column (1); column (3) includes year fixed effects; and column (4) shows the results from the fixed-effects model and the standard errors clustered at the city level. Overall, there is no huge difference between the estimated coefficients in front of the log of affordable housing area; they vary from 0.136 to 0.338 and all are positive and statistically significant at the 1 per cent level. Hence, according to the results from Table 8.3, the affordable housing area is positively correlated with the total fertility rate.

Table 8.3 Housing affordability and total fertility rate: OLS and fixed-effects approach

	OLS		Fixed effect	
	(1)	(2)	(3)	(4)
Log of affordable housing area	0.136***	0.179***	0.194***	0.338***
	(0.045)	(0.044)	(0.058)	(0.081)
Years of female education		−0.051*	−0.051*	0.043
		(0.026)	(0.026)	(0.044)
Log of urban population density		0.016	0.017	−0.004
		(0.026)	(0.023)	(0.070)
Log of GDP per capita		−0.157***	−0.145**	0.111
		(0.046)	(0.056)	(0.193)
Composition of tertiary sector to GDP		0.004	0.004	−0.004
		(0.003)	(0.003)	(0.008)
Urban unemployment rate		−0.006	−0.005	−0.033
		(0.027)	(0.027)	(0.033)
Year fixed effect	No	No	Yes	Yes
City fixed effect	No	No	No	Yes
No. of cities				70
No.	140	140	140	140
R-squared	0.010	0.2297	0.2198	0.402
	(adjusted)	(adjusted)	(adjusted)	(within)

*** significant at 1 per cent
** significant at 5 per cent
* significant at 10 per cent
Notes: The difference between model (1) and model (2) is the inclusion of the control variables. The difference between model (2) and model (3) is the inclusion of the year fixed effects. The difference between model (3) and model (4) is the inclusion of the city fixed effects. Column 5 presents results of the fixed-effects model. The dependent variable is the total fertility rate at the city level.
Source: Author's own.

---

10   I have used the 'power' to calculate the minimum sample size I need for this study, which is 55. The sample size of my dataset is 74, which is greater than the minimum sample size required.

Table 8.4 Housing affordability and total fertility rate: IV estimates

	(1)	(2)
	First stage	**Second stage**
Log of land price	−0.488***	
	(0.094)	
Log of affordable housing area		0.458***
		(0.164)
Years of urban female education	−0.002	0.049
	(0.076)	(0.036)
Log of urban population density	0.004	0.015
	(0.109)	(0.065)
Log of GDP per capita	−0.815***	0.141
	(0.292)	(0.172)
Composition of tertiary sector to GDP	−0.004	−0.002
	(0.011)	(0.007)
Urban unemployment rate	0.013	−0.033
	(0.053)	(0.023)
F-statistic (instruments)	27.12	
Year fixed effects	Yes	Yes
City fixed effects	Yes	Yes
No.	140	140
R-squared		0.362
No. of cities	70	70

*** significant at 1 per cent
** significant at 5 per cent
* significant at 10 per cent
Notes: Column (1) presents the results of first-stage 2SLS with fixed effects. Column (2) presents the results of second-stage 2SLS with fixed effects. The dependent variable in column (1) is the log of affordable housing area at the city level. The dependent variable in column (2) is the total fertility rate at the city level.
Source: Author's own.

Despite the OLS and fixed-effects models both indicating a positive correlation between the affordable housing area and the total fertility rate, potential risks from omitted variables and inherent reverse causality prevent me from interpreting a causal relationship between them. As housing price is one of the factors used by this chapter in calculating the housing affordability index, I adopt the city-level land price as the instrumental variable of the affordable housing area to establish a causal link between housing affordability and the total fertility rate.

Table 8.4 presents the results from two-stage least-squares regression (2SLS) with control of fixed effects. Column (1) of Table 8.4 indicates the first-stage estimate of the instrument with the control of variables and fixed effects. According to column (1), the first-stage relationship between the log of land price and log of affordable housing area is negative and statistically significant at the 1 per cent level. The result follows the intuition that the higher the land price, the higher is the housing price and the worse is housing affordability. Additionally, the value of the F-statistic is 27.12, which is higher than 10, in line with Staiger and Stock's (1997) rule of thumb, indicating that land price is a strong instrument in determining the affordable housing area. A recent study, however, suggests a more conservative threshold of 104.7 (Lee et al. 2022). Even though my F-statistic is lower than 104.7, I correct the critical values and calculate 'tF 0.05 standard errors', as proposed by Lee et al. (2022). I estimate the usual 2SLS standard error and then multiply the standard error by the adjustment factor in the table provided by Lee et al. (2022) corresponding to the observed first-stage F statistic. The adjusted standard error is 0.13, which means the finding remains statistically significant at the 5 per cent level. Column (2) presents the IV estimate, which follows the OLS specification from Table 8.5. According to column (2), the log of affordable housing area has a positive effect on the log of total fertility rate and is statistically significant at the 1 per cent level. Specifically, for a 10 per cent increase in affordable housing area, the total fertility rate increases by 4.58 per cent. Overall, the IV coefficient cross-validates the results from the OLS and the fixed-effects models and the difference between the estimated coefficients is not huge.

Table 8.5 Relaxation of the instrument independent of the error term

Dependent variable: log(total fertility rate)	Lower bound (CI)	Lower bound (estimator)	Upper bound (estimator)	Upper bound (CI)
Instrumental variable: log (land price)	0.091	0.213	0.308	0.599

CI = confidence interval
Note: The upper and lower bounds on the confidence interval are estimated by using the identification assumptions of Nevo and Rosen (2012).
Source: Author's own.

Sensitivity analysis by instrument-free test

A recent study from Kiviet (2020) provides a statistical inference to test the sensitivity of IV estimates. Specifically, Kiviet (2020) introduces an instrument-free inference approach named the 'kinky least squares' (KLS) estimation, which produces a set of correlations and confidence intervals that allows researchers to compare results from IV estimates.[11] Additionally, the KLS corrects the bias of OLS, which is inconsistent when non-zero endogeneity correlations occur.

Figure 8.9 shows the KLS and 2SLS confidence intervals. First, I choose the range of endogeneity correlations by correlating the residuals from the 2SLS estimates and the endogenous variable and –0.08 is the correlation. So, I assume that housing affordability is negatively correlated with the omitted variables. To check the accuracy, I further extend the range to –0.5. Over the range from –0.5 to 0, the KLS and 2SLS confidence intervals overlap for the whole range so the results of KLS provide support for the results of the IV estimates.

---

11 I follow the Stata commands from Kripfganz and Kiviet (2021) to conduct this sensitivity analysis.

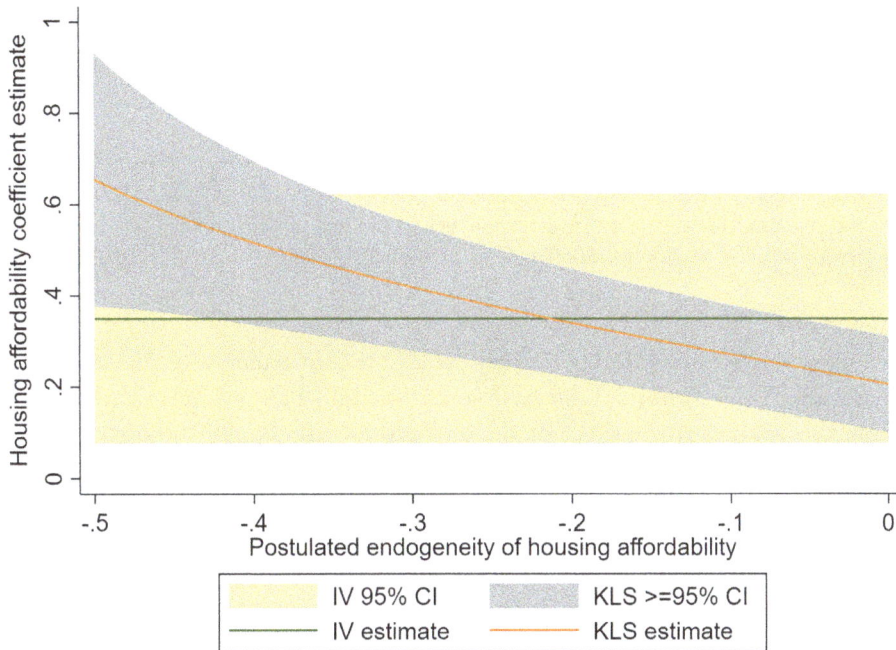

Figure 8.9 KLS and IV coefficient estimates and confidence intervals for housing affordability

Source: Author's own.

Relax the exogeneity assumption

In this subsection, I will present three more estimates that allow me to relax the instrument exogeneity assumption. Nevo and Rosen (2012) propose a method that estimates bounds by using 'imperfect instrumental variables' that relax the assumption that the instrument is exogenous to the error term. Specifically, Nevo and Rosen (2012) replace the assumption that the instrument is independent of the error term with two other assumptions: 1) the instrument is correlated less to the error than to the endogenous variable, and 2) the correlation between the endogenous variable and the error has the same sign as the correlation between the instrument and the error. To conduct this estimate, the negative sign of the correlation between the endogenous variable and the unobservable error has been assumed, which is also consistent with the above analysis. One potential omitted variable is childrearing costs and it is reasonable to think a city with good housing affordability has relatively lower childrearing costs than cities with worse housing affordability. Specifically, cities with high housing prices are generally associated with higher price levels for other goods and services. As a result, the higher price level leads to, for example, higher education costs, which generate higher childrearing expenses. Therefore, by assuming a negative correlation between housing affordability and the error, the results from Table 8.5 show that the lower and upper bounds do not include zero and include my IV estimates as well as the OLS estimates. These results validate the fact that my estimated results from IV estimates are statistically significant after relaxing the instrument independence assumption.

Table 8.6 Relaxation of the exclusion restriction

Value of g-min and g-max	Endogenous variable	Lower bound	Upper bound
g-min = −0.35, g-max = −0.09	Log of affordable housing area	0.072	0.753
g-min = −0.385, g-max = −0.099		0.065	0.751
g-min = −0.315, g-max = −0.081		0.079	0.755

Notes: The upper and lower bounds are estimated using the method from Conley et al. (2012); g-min and g-max indicate the values of the minimum and maximum of coefficients of the instrumental variable, respectively.

I then adopt the test developed by Conley et al. (2012) to explore the robustness of IV estimates after the relaxation of the exclusion restriction. This test provides the bounds of the estimated treatment effect of the endogenous variable with the relaxation of the assumption of exclusion restriction. Specifically, it allows a non-zero correlation between the instrument and the error and then tests whether the estimate of the coefficient of interest is robust to a range of these possible deviations. To perform the test, I use the union of confidence interval approach, which requires me to specify the maximum (g-max) and minimum (g-min) values that the coefficient of the instrument can take. I regress the outcome variable (total fertility rate) on the instrument and all other covariates, and the values of the g-min and g-max are the confidence intervals of the estimated coefficient of the instrument: −0.35 and −0.09. Table 8.6 presents the results of the relaxation of the exclusion restriction and suggests that my results from the IV estimates are robust, as the estimated lower bound and upper bound do not include zero and also include my IV estimates in all three cases of different values of g-min and g-max.[12]

The last test of the validity of the exclusion restriction is from Kiviet (2020). As mentioned earlier, the KLS is a robust OLS-based test and can be used to verify the exclusion restriction. The KLS produces a set of correlations and the set under which these should be rejected at a chosen significance level. Based on these two sets, the credibility of the exclusion restriction can be investigated. Figure 8.10 shows the KLS exclusion restriction test, which indicates that land price is a valid instrument. As before, I choose the range of endogeneity correlation between −0.2 and zero. Kiviet (2020) indicates that a comfortable p-value that supports the validity of the exclusion restriction must exceed 50 per cent. According to the figure, between −0.13 and −0.05, the p-values are higher than 50 per cent, so the null hypothesis that the instrument is validly excluded from the model cannot be rejected between −0.13 and −0.05. Since the correlation between the residuals and the endogenous variable is −0.08 and within the range, the results of KLS support the validity of the exclusion restriction.

---

12 I also both extend and reduce the bounds of g-min and g-max by 10 per cent to check the validity of the IV estimates.

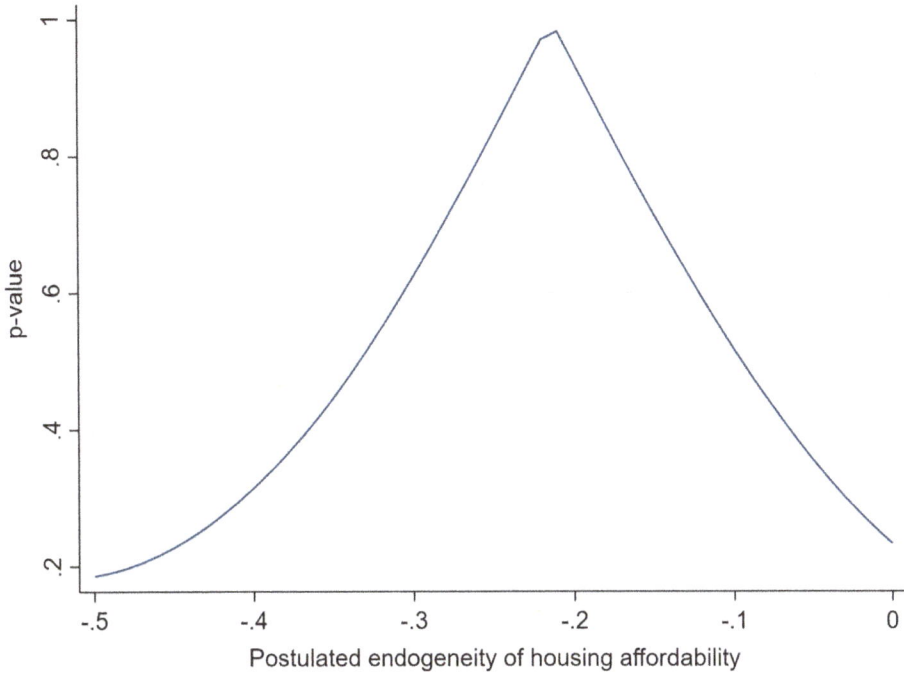

Figure 8.10 p-value for KLS exclusion restriction test
Source: Author's own.

Robustness check

Purchasing a house as first priority

The residual income approach means that households would only use the remaining proportion of their disposable income to purchase a house after paying consumption expenditure. However, the affordable housing area calculated under this assumption ignores those households with extreme saving behaviour. In other words, some households may strictly constrain their consumption expenditure so they can buy a house. Seeing the rapid growth in China's housing prices, it is rational behaviour to squeeze consumption today and save to buy a house in the hope that consumption can grow in the future.

To simulate this extreme saving behaviour, I assume the household will spend all its income on purchasing a house. In fact, China's households do limit consumption to purchase houses. Based on credit and debit card transactions in China from 2011 to 2013, Waxman et al. (2020) find that a 10 per cent increase in the housing price would decrease non-housing-related spending by 9 per cent, and point out that strong investment incentives for housing and heavy borrowing constraints are the major reasons behind this behaviour. Based on this assumption, the monthly repayment of an average household at city j in year t is as shown in Equation 8.7.

Equation 8.7

$$MAP_{j,t} = \left(Y_{j,t}\right) * \frac{1}{12}$$

I follow the equation of equal repayment to calculate the new affordable housing area and rerun the baseline models to check the relationship between affordable housing area and year. According to Table 8.7, the results in all three columns indicate that an inverse U-shaped relationship between affordable housing area and year remains after excluding consumption expenditure from consideration. I also find the turning point is 2016.

Table 8.7 No consumption expenditure

	(1)	(2)	(3)
Year	35.684***	42.972***	40.424***
	(5.677)	(8.618)	(6.733)
Year 2	−2.577***	−3.211***	−2.920***
	(0.503)	(0.690)	(0.480)
Superstar city		−68.613***	
		(18.049)	
Population		−0.038***	−0.124
		(0.012)	(0.117)
GDP growth rate		−1.736**	−1.551***
		(0.709)	(0.469)
Growth rate of value added in finance		0.239	0.165
		(0.322)	(0.199)
Residential land supply		0.003	−0.011
		(0.012)	(0.008)
City fixed effects	No	No	Yes
No.	630	630	630
R-squared	0.140 (adjusted)	0.382 (adjusted)	0.414 (within)

*** significant at 1 per cent
** significant at 5 per cent
* significant at 10 per cent
Notes: The difference between model (1) and (2) is the addition of the control variables. The difference between model (2) and model (3) is the addition of the city fixed effects. The dependent variable is the affordable residential area of households at the city level, which is calculated by excluding consumption expenditure. Robust standard errors in parentheses.
Source: Author's own.

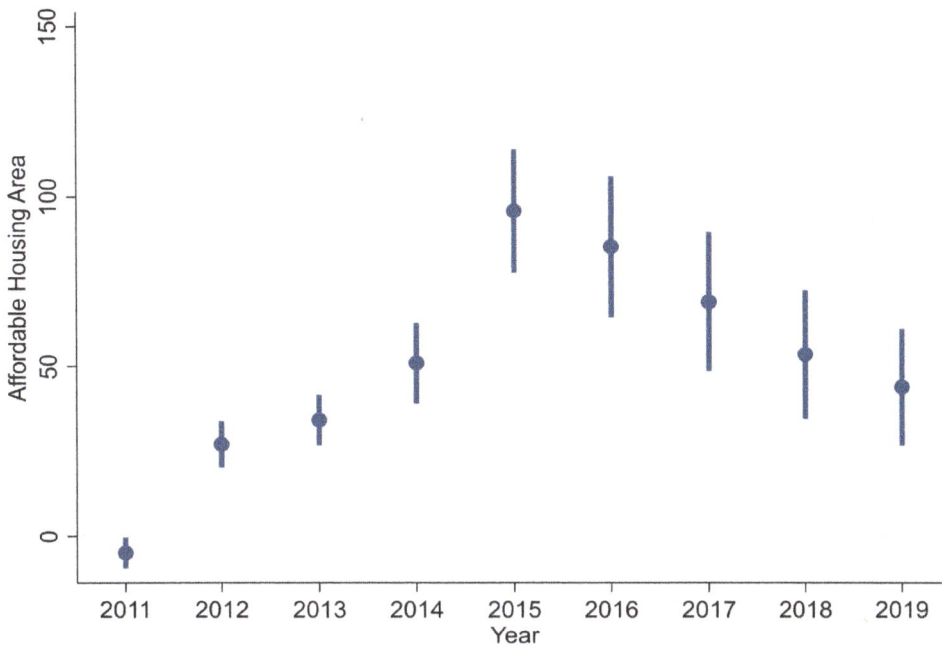

Figure 8.11 The trend of affordable housing area, excluding consumption expenditure
Source: Author's own.

I further change the year trend into a year dummy to see the trend of affordable housing area by excluding consumption expenditure. Figure 8.11 contains the coefficient plots of the year dummy with 2010 as the baseline year. According to the figure, the affordable housing area increased from 2011 to 2015, when it reached its maximum and continued to decrease in subsequent years. Overall, the result of the robustness check validates the main finding in which an inverse U-shaped relationship exists between housing affordability and year.

Housing price-to-income ratio and total fertility rate

For the main empirical results, I use the affordable housing area to depict housing affordability and the land price as the instrumental variable of the affordable housing area to find a causal relationship between affordable housing area and the total fertility rate. People may question whether the affordable housing area, which is calculated using the residual income approach with equal repayment equation, is a good measure of housing affordability and whether it can be linked to the total fertility rate. In this section, I replace the affordable housing area with the housing price-to-income ratio as the measurement of housing affordability and adopt the same estimation as Equation 8.6. I also use the land price as the instrumental variable.

The estimated results are presented in Table 8.8. According to column (1), the first-stage result indicates that the log of land price is positively correlated with the log of the housing PTI ratio and is statistically significant at the 1 per cent level. As the PTI ratio measures the years of income a household needs to buy an average house, the higher the ratio means the worse is housing affordability. Therefore, a higher land price would lead to a higher PTI ratio, resulting in worse housing affordability. The F-statistic is 34.43, which indicates that the instrumental variable is strong. According to column (2), the log of the housing PTI ratio has a negative effect on the log of the total fertility rate and is statistically significant at the 1 per cent level. For a 10 per cent increase in the housing PTI ratio, the total fertility rate decreases by 8.08 per cent. This result cross-validates the main finding that the worse is housing affordability, the lower is the total fertility rate.

Table 8.8 Housing price-to-income ratio and total fertility rate

	(1)	(2)
	First stage	**Second stage**
Log of land price	0.277***	
	(0.047)	
Log of housing price-to-income ratio		−0.808***
		(0.228)
Years of female education	0.065	0.096***
	(0.045)	(0.034)
Log of urban population density	−0.008	0.011
	(0.046)	(0.057)
Log of GDP per capita	−0.083	−0.291
	(0.169)	(0.181)
Composition of tertiary sector to GDP	−0.010	−0.012**
	(0.007)	(0.006)
Urban unemployment rate	0.071***	0.030
	(0.024)	(0.024)
F-statistic (instruments)	34.42	
Year fixed effects	Yes	Yes
City fixed effects	Yes	Yes
No.	140	140
R-squared		0.435
No. of cities	70	70

*** significant at 1 per cent
** significant at 5 per cent
* significant at 10 per cent
Notes: Column (1) presents the results of first-stage 2SLS with fixed effects. Column (2) presents the results of second-stage 2SLS with fixed effects. The dependent variable in column (1) is the log of the housing PTI ratio at the city level. The dependent variable in column (2) is the total fertility rate at the city level. Robust standard errors in parentheses.
Source: Author's own.

Conclusion and discussion

This chapter investigates housing affordability in China during the period of rapid price growth from 2010 to 2019 and explores the impact of housing affordability on the fertility rate. The main contribution of this chapter is that it links urban housing affordability and the fertility rate in causal interpretation, while existing papers only look at housing prices and fertility. According to results from IV estimates, I find that a 10 per cent increase in the affordable housing area leads to a 4.58 per cent increase in the total fertility rate, which means higher housing affordability leads to a higher total fertility rate. The robustness of my results is proven by several tests—for example, instrument-free inference and relaxation of instrument exogeneity. To accurately measure China's housing affordability, I constructed its urban housing affordability index by using the residual income approach with equal repayment equation, which covers 70 large and medium-sized cities. The index suggests that an inverse U-shaped relationship exists between housing affordability during the sample years. Specifically, affordability increased from 2010 to 2014, reached its maximum about 2015 and has since continued to decrease. This indicates a general deterioration in housing affordability following a series of housing stimulus policies after 2015. My results also suggest that first-tier cities, such as Beijing, Shanghai, Guangzhou and Shenzhen, have the most significant housing affordability problems among all the sampled cities, while households in Changsha and Wuxi experience the best affordability.

The housing affordability index developed also captures changes in affordability, which the price-to-income ratio fails to capture due to the lack of consideration of bank lending rates. This suggests that the residual income approach with equal repayment equation is a good alternative to the price-to-income ratio for measuring affordability.

One important policy implication stemming from this study relates to the decline in the fertility rate that China is confronted with. The rapid decline has pushed China's total fertility rate to well below the replacement level and is one of the lowest in the world. Meanwhile, China's population is also rapidly ageing. At the end of 2020, China had 260 million people aged over 60 years, accounting for 18.7 per cent of the total population. The issues of low fertility and ageing not only reduce the future labour supply but also pose significant challenges to China's pension system.

The findings of this chapter suggest that policies aiming to improve housing affordability would be effective in encouraging fertility. For example, in cities with high housing prices and poor housing affordability, the availability of affordable housing for young people of childbearing age is essential. Providing subsidies to first-time homebuyers can effectively reduce the barriers to ownership. Improved housing affordability would not only encourage young couples to have children earlier but also attract more young talent from other regions and boost local productivity.

References

Abeysinghe, T., and J. Gu. 2010. 'Lifetime Income and Housing Affordability in Singapore.' *Urban Studies* 48, no. 9: 1875–91. doi.org/10.1177/0042098010380956.

Aksoy, C.G. 2016. *Short-Term Effects of House Prices on Birth Rates.* EBRD Working Paper No. 192. London: European Bank for Reconstruction and Development. ssrn.com/abstract=2846173. dx.doi.org/10.2139/ssrn.2846173.

Becker, G.S. 1992. 'Fertility and the Economy.' *Population Economics* 5: 185–201. doi.org/10.1007/BF00172092.

Ben-Shahar, D., and J. Warszawski. 2016. 'Inequality in Housing Affordability: Measurement and Estimation.' *Urban Studies* 53, no. 6: 1178–202. doi.org/10.1177/0042098015572529.

Bhat, P.M. 2002. 'Returning a Favor: Reciprocity between Female Education and Fertility in India.' *World Development* 30, no. 10: 1791–803. doi.org/10.1016/S0305-750X(02)00065-7.

Bourassa, S.C., M. Hoesli, D.F. Scognamiglio, and S. Zhang. 2011. 'Land Leverage and House Prices.' *Regional Science and Urban Economics* 41, no. 2: 134–44. doi.org/10.1016/j.regsciurbeco.2010.11.002.

Cava, G.L., H. Leal, and A. Zurawski. 2017. 'Housing Accessibility for First Home Buyers.' *Bulletin*, December Quarter. Sydney: Reserve Bank of Australia. www.rba.gov.au/publications/bulletin/2017/dec/pdf/bu-1217-3-housing-accessibility-for-first-home-buyers.pdf.

Chen, J., F. Guo, and Y. Wu. 2011. 'One Decade of Urban Housing Reform in China: Urban Housing Price Dynamics and the Role of Migration and Urbanization, 1995–2005.' *Habitat International* 35: 1–8. doi.org/10.1016/j.habitatint.2010.02.003.

Chen, K., Y. Song, and G. Yang. 2020. 'Measuring Destocking Performance of the Chinese Real Estate Industry: A DEA-Malmquist Approach.' *Socio-Economic Planning Sciences* 69 (March): 100691. doi.org/10.1016/j.seps.2019.02.006.

Clark, W.A., D. Yi, and X. Zhang. 2020. 'Do House Prices Affect Fertility Behavior in China? An Empirical Examination.' *International Regional Science Review* 43, no. 5: 423–49. doi.org/10.1177/0160017620922885.

Conley, T.G., C.B. Hansen, and P.E. Rossi. 2012. 'Plausibly Exogenous.' *The Review of Economics and Statistics* 94, no. 1: 260–72. doi.org/10.1162/REST_a_00139.

Deng, Y., J. Gyourko, and J. Wu. 2012. 'Land and Housing Price Measurement in China.' In *RBA Annual Conference Volume—2012*, 13–43. Sydney: Reserve Bank of Australia. www.rba.gov.au/publications/confs/2012/deng-gyourko-wu.html

Dettling, L.J., and M.S. Kearney. 2014. 'House Prices and Birth Rates: The Impact of the Real Estate Market on the Decision to Have a Baby.' *Journal of Public Economics* 110: 82–100. doi.org/10.1016/j.jpubeco.2013.09.009.

Eftimoski, M., and K. McLoughlin. 2019. 'Housing Policy and Economic Growth in China.' *Bulletin*, March. Sydney: Reserve Bank of Australia. www.rba.gov.au/publications/bulletin/2019/mar/housing-policy-and-economic-growth-in-china.html.

Fang, H., Q. Gu, W. Xiong, and L.-A. Zhou. 2015. *Demystifying the Chinese Housing Boom.* NBER Working Paper No. 21112, April. Cambridge, MA: National Bureau of Economic Research. doi.org/10.3386/w21112.

Fox, R., and R. Finlay. 2012. 'Dwelling Prices and Household Income.' *Bulletin*, December Quarter. Sydney: Reserve Bank of Australia. www.rba.gov.au/publications/bulletin/2012/dec/pdf/bu-1212-2.pdf.

Gabriel, M., K. Jacobs, K. Arthurson, T. Burke, and J. Yates. 2005. *Conceptualising and Measuring the Housing Affordability Problem.* National Research Venture 3: Housing Affordability for Lower Income Australians Research Paper 1, May. Melbourne: Australian Housing and Urban Research Institute. www.ahuri.edu.au/sites/default/files/migration/documents/NRV3_Research_Paper_1.pdf.

Gan, Q., and R.J. Hill. 2009. 'Measuring Housing Affordability: Looking beyond the Median.' *Journal of Housing Economics* 18, no. 2: 115–25. doi.org/10.1016/j.jhe.2009.04.003.

Glaeser, E., W. Huang, Y. Ma, and A. Shleifer. 2017. 'A Real Estate Boom with Chinese Characteristics.' *Journal of Economic Perspectives* 31, no. 1: 93–116. doi.org/10.1257/jep.31.1.93.

Götmark, F., and M. Andersson. 2020. 'Human Fertility in Relation to Education, Economy, Religion, Contraception, and Family Planning Programs.' *BMC Public Health* 20, no. 1: 1–17. doi.org/10.1186/s12889-020-8331-7.

Gyourko, J., C. Mayer, and T. Sinai. 2013. 'Superstar Cities.' *American Economic Journal: Economic Policy* 5, no. 4: 167–99. doi.org/10.1257/pol.5.4.167.

Huang, Y., S. He, and L. Gan. 2021. 'Introduction to Special Issue: Unpacking the Chinese Dream of Homeownership.' *Journal of Housing and the Built Environment* 36: 1–7. doi.org/10.1007/s10901-021-09827-y.

Jain, A.K. 1981. 'The Effect of Female Education on Fertility: A Simple Explanation.' *Demography* 18, no. 4: 577–95. doi.org/10.2307/2060948.

Kemp, J., A. Suthakar, and T. Williams. 2020. 'China's Residential Property Sector.' *Bulletin*, June. Sydney: Reserve Bank of Australia. www.rba.gov.au/publications/bulletin/2020/jun/chinas-residential-property-sector.html.

Kiviet, J. 2020. 'Testing the Impossible: Identifying Exclusion Restrictions.' *Journal of Econometrics* 218, no. 2: 294–316. doi.org/10.1016/j.jeconom.2020.04.018.

Kostelecký, T., and J. Vobecká. 2009. 'Housing Affordability in Czech Regions and Demographic Behaviour: Does Housing Affordability Impact Fertility?' *Czech Sociological Review* 45, no. 6: 1191–213. doi.org/10.13060/00380288.2009.45.6.02.

Kripfganz, S., and J. Kiviet. 2021. 'Kinkyreg: Instrument-Free Inference for Linear Regression Models with Endogenous Regressors.' *Stata Journal* 21, no. 3: 772–813. doi.org/10.1177/1536867X211045575.

Lee, D.S., McCrary, J., Moreira, M. J., and Porter, J. 2022. 'Valid T-Ratio Inference for IV'. *American Economic Review*, 112, no. 10: 3260–3290.

Lee, J., and Y. Zhu. 2006. 'Urban Governance, Neoliberalism and Housing Reform in China.' *The Pacific Review* 19, no. 1: 39–61. doi.org/10.1080/09512740500417657.

Li, A., Q. Mo, W. Li, and Y. Zhang. 2015. 'ELES-Model Based Housing Affordability Comparative Research of Urban Households in Beijing between 2004 and 2014.' *Annals of Data Science*, no. 2: 205–16. doi.org/10.1007/s40745-015-0043-y.

Li, K., Y. Qin, and J. Wu. 2020. 'Recent Housing Affordability in Urban China: A Comprehensive Overlook.' *China Economic Review* 59 (February): 101362. doi.org/10.1016/j.chieco.2019.101362.

Li, Y., A. Li, Z. Wang, and Q. Wu. 2018. 'Analysis on Housing Affordability of Urban Residents in Mainland China Based on Multiple Indexes: Taking 35 Cities as Examples.' *Annals of Data Science* 6, no. 2: 305–19. doi.org/10.1007/s40745-018-0168-x.

Li, Y., D. Zhu, J. Zhao, X. Zheng, and L. Zhang. 2020. 'Effect of the Housing Purchase Restriction Policy on the Real Estate Market: Evidence from a Typical Suburb of Beijing, China.' *Land Use Policy* 94 (May): 104528. doi.org/10.1016/j.landusepol.2020.104528.

Lin, X., T. Ren, H. Wu, and Y. Xiao. 2020. 'Housing Price, Talent Movement, and Innovation Output: Evidence from Chinese Cities.' *Review of Development Economics* 25: 76–103.

Liu, Q., R.-A. Fernando, and J. Han. 2020. *Is China's Low Fertility Rate Caused by the Population Control Policy?* Levy Economics Institute Working Paper No. 943, January. Annandale-On-Hudson, NY: Levy Economics Institute of Bard College. papers.ssrn.com/sol3/papers.cfm?abstract_id=3520031. doi.org/10.1111/rode.12705.

Man, J.Y. 2011. *China's Housing Reform and Outcomes.* Cambridge, MA: Lincoln Institute of Land Policy.

National Bureau of Statistics (NBS). 2012. *Chinese Urban Household Survey (UHS).* Beijing: National Bureau of Statistics of China. www.stats.gov.cn/sj/ndsj/2021/html/sm06.htm.

Nevo, A., and A.M. Rosen. 2012. 'Identification with Imperfect Instruments.' *The Review of Economics and Statistics* 94, no. 3: 659–71. doi.org/10.1162/REST_a_00171.

Pan, L., and J. Xu. 2013. 'Housing Price and Fertility Rate.' *China Economic Journal* 5, nos 2–3: 97–111. doi.org/10.1080/17538963.2013.764675.

Panopoulou, G., and P. Tsakloglou. 1999. 'Fertility and Economic Development: Theoretical Considerations and Cross-Country Evidence.' *Applied Economics* 31, no. 11: 1337–51. doi.org/10.1080/000368499323229.

People's Bank of China (PBC). 2015. 'Notice from a Meeting of the People's Bank of China, the Ministry of Housing and Urban–Rural Development, and the China Banking Regulatory Commission on Issues Related to the Personal Housing Loan Policies.' 30 March. Beijing: People's Bank of China. www.pbc.gov.cn/goutongjiaoliu/113456/113469/2811338/index.html.

Staiger, S., and J.H. Stock. 1997. 'Instrumental Variables Regression with Weak Instruments.' *Econometrica* 65, no. 3: 557–86. doi.org/10.2307/2171753.

Stone, E.M. 2010. 'What is Housing Affordability? The Case for the Residual Income Approach.' *Housing Policy Debate* 17, no. 1: 151–84. doi.org/10.1080/10511482.2006.9521564.

Waxman, A., Y. Liang, S. Li, P.J. Barwick, and M. Zhao. 2020. 'Tightening Belts to Buy a Home: Consumption Responses to Rising Housing Prices in Urban China.' *Journal of Urban Economics* 115 (January): 103190. doi.org/10.1016/j.jue.2019.103190.

Wu, F. 2015. 'Commodification and Housing Market Cycles in Chinese Cities.' *International Journal of Housing Policy* 15, no. 1: 6–26. doi.org/10.1080/14616718.2014.925255.

Xinhua. 2021. 'Decision of the CPC Central Committee and the State Council on Optimising Birth Policy to Promote Long-Term Balanced Development of Population.' 20 July. Beijing: General Office of the State Council of the People's Republic of China. www.gov.cn/zhengce/2021-07/20/content_5626190.htm.

Appendix 8.1

Table A8.1 Summary statistics of calculating a housing affordability index (RMB)

City	Per capita urban disposable income		Per capita urban consumption expenditure	
	Mean	SD	Mean	SD
Shanghai	51,471	13,930	34,664	9,177
Dongguan	43,701	6,183	30,700	3,338
Ürümqi	28,263	10,310	22,773	9,458
Foshan	40,283	8,801	29,222	5,085
Lanzhou	25,444	8,272	19,234	5,777
Beijing	51,627	13,791	34,929	7,281
Nanjing	45,283	11,806	26,882	5,939
Nanning	27,569	6,723	13,896	3,954
Nanchang	30,737	8,651	20,597	4,828
Xiamen	43,367	9,229	28,664	5,636
Hefei	31,607	8,406	20,498	4,125
Harbin	29,560	7,263	22,177	4,649
Dalian	34,148	8,313	24,524	4,803
Tianjin	34,191	7,235	25,393	6,154
Taiyuan	26,862	6,067	15,636	3,324
Ningbo	46,810	11,343	28,444	6,543
Guangzhou	46,626	11,180	35,227	6,396
Chengdu	33,090	7,930	22,212	4,371
Wuxi	44,110	11,074	27,892	6,634
Kunming	32,596	9,035	21,012	6,032
Hangzhou	47,119	11,863	32,186	8,205
Wuhan	35,334	10,258	23,683	6,335
Shenyang	33,909	9,031	25,144	5,895
Jinan	39,284	8,868	25,070	6,250
Haikou	27,752	7,187	20,124	4,988
Shenzhen	46,156	9,392	32,209	7,080
Zhuhai	39,237	9,555	29,076	6,653
Fuzhou	34,905	8,001	23,985	5,315
Suzhou	48,638	12,841	29,613	6,976
Xining	23,990	7,199	17,314	5,391
Xian	34,116	6,290	22,661	3,222
Guiyang	26,916	6,899	21,079	5,841
Zhengzhou	30,196	7,562	20,612	4,966
Chongqing	27,084	6,549	19,376	4,058

City	Per capita urban disposable income		Per capita urban consumption expenditure	
	Mean	SD	Mean	SD
Changchun	28,121	6,459	22,828	5,491
Changsha	38,625	10,602	27,498	8,310
Qingdao	39,473	9,637	25,646	6,012

SD = standard deviation
Note: The mean for each city is the average of the sample years.
Source: Author's own.

Table A8.2 Potential omitted variable

	(1)
Log of land price	0.03
	(0.03)
Years of urban female education	−0.00
	(0.01)
Log of urban population density	0.02
	(0.07)
Log of GDP per capita	−0.14
	(0.14)
Urban dependency ratio	0.00
	(0.00)
Composition of tertiary sector to GDP	−0.01
	(0.01)
Urban unemployment rate	−0.00
	(0.02)
Year fixed effects	Yes
City fixed effects	Yes
No.	140
R-squared (within)	0.19
No. of cities	70

Note: The dependent variable is the land area at city level.
Source: Author's own.

9

Chinese women in the workforce and free school lunches: A 'small' program with big implications

Ge Wang, Xinjie Shi and Jane Golley

Introduction

Over the past three decades, the participation rate of Chinese women in the workforce has fallen almost continuously, from 73 per cent in 1990 to just 59 per cent in 2020 (World Bank 2022). This overall trend is troubling for a country that is now experiencing negative population growth, along with a rapidly ageing population. With the Three-Child Policy delivering little in the way of expanding the population 'from below', maximising the labour force participation of all working-age people who are willing and able to work will be essential for sustaining China's GDP growth in the decades ahead. Raising the participation of women in the workforce seems like a straightforward way of contributing to this goal.

Of course, it is not that simple. Deciding whether to stay home and care for children or go out to work has long been a dilemma for women across the world, especially in developing countries (Conroy 2019). Traditionally, child care and other forms of domestic work have been considered the responsibility of women, with men taking on the responsibility of earning income for their households (Barber and Odean 2001). This continues to be the case in China, with mothers not only being the primary caregivers for about three-quarters of all children (SSWC 2021),[1] but also shouldering the responsibility for cooking, washing, helping with homework and picking up children during the standard working week (Gurley-Calvez et al. 2009; Debela et al. 2022). Even when employed outside the home, women spend an average of 154 minutes a day on

---

1   SSWC is the Survey on Social Status of Women in China, which is conducted every 10 years, with samples spread across China.

housework, compared with 78 minutes for men (SSWC 2021). In short, women often assume greater responsibility for raising children at home, sacrificing opportunities for paid work as a result.

It is well known that the lack of widespread access to government-subsidised child care and early education facilities is a significant constraint on Chinese women's work choices (Cao 2019). In 2022, the number of nurseries per 1,000 people was 2.57, with a nationwide enrolment rate of just 5.5 per cent, compared with enrolment rates in the Netherlands, South Korea and France of more than 60 per cent (NHC 2022). Even with the quantity of childcare facilities set to increase in the years ahead, their high cost, poor quality and uneven distribution between urban and rural areas will mean that many poor, rural Chinese women will continue to have no choice but to take on the burden of child care themselves (Huang and Li 2022; Landivar et al. 2022).

Childcare subsidies and access to early education facilities are not the only ways to advance the participation of mothers in the workforce. As Nobel Laureate Claudia Goldin (2021: 6) explains: 'The fundamental problem for women trying to attain the balance of a successful career and a joyful family are time conflicts.' For many rural Chinese mothers, a significant constraint stems from the fact that they often spend lots of time preparing lunch at home, with students rushing to and from school for lunch, either on foot or requiring lifts from their parents or grandparents (but usually their mothers). As one indicator of this, in an impact evaluation of the Preschool Nutrition Pilot we conducted in several counties in Hunan Province in 2021 (WFP 2022), we found that the primary caregiver (usually the mother, sometimes the grandmother, very occasionally the father or grandfather) spent about two hours each day preparing and delivering lunch to their children. This suggests that when schools provide free lunches, there are likely to be significant time savings on lunch preparation and commuting.

This chapter demonstrates how the introduction of the China Rural Nutrition Improvement Program (CRNIP),[2] through its provision of free lunches across hundreds of the most impoverished counties in China, has indeed freed up time for Chinese rural mothers, resulting in a significant and positive causal impact on their labour force participation (LFP). More specifically, using the 1 per cent samples of the 2010 and 2015 Chinese population censuses, we apply the widely used (see, for example, Baker et al. 2008; Lefebvre and Merrigan 2008; Cascio 2009; Nollenberger and Rodríguez-Planas 2015; Bettendorf et al. 2015) difference-in-differences (DD) method to investigate whether providing free lunches for students enrolled in compulsory education through the CRNIP increased maternal LFP. Established in March 2011 to combat childhood malnutrition in China's most impoverished rural areas, this program is backed by central government provision of subsidies for nutritious meals for students participating in compulsory education (grades one to nine) in pilot counties, and also offers special financial support for the construction of school canteens. Focusing on women aged 30–55 years with at least one child in compulsory education, we find that

---

2   Also known as the Student Nutrition Improvement Program (SNIP) or School Meal Reform (SMR).

the program led to a 4.25 percentage point increase in maternal LFP. We further show that the primary channel through which this operated was via the reduction in time spent on child care—estimated at 2.8 hours daily—which enabled mothers to pursue opportunities for local, informal off-farm work. Our results confirm that the labour force participation of rural fathers has not been impacted by the program.

The remainder of the chapter is structured as follows. The next section introduces the relevant literature that informs our expectations of the potential impacts of the CRNIP on maternal LFP. Following this, we present the data and method. The main empirical findings are then presented, including an exploration of the mechanisms linking free lunches and maternal LFP. Our conclusions offer policy recommendations that go beyond free lunches to consider the broader implications of reducing the household and childcare burdens of Chinese women in the context of a declining and ageing population.

The CRNIP and its potential impacts on maternal LFP

Theoretically, child care and labour force participation have been established as a trade-off for mothers. Mincer (1962) pointed out that caring for small children was one of the most difficult forms of housework for women to substitute away from, and Becker (1985) likewise suggested that child care was one of the most effort-intensive household activities, posing significant constraints on women's labour market performance. Low-cost or free public childcare services and subsidies for child care relieve mothers (and other primary caregivers) of the pressure of housework (Fitzpatrick 2012), providing opportunities for them to enter the labour market.

Empirically, the causal impact of expanding childcare services on increasing female labour force participation is well established in the international literature. In developed countries including the United States, Canada, Norway and the Netherlands, greater access to preschools and childcare subsidies have been shown to have positive impacts on maternal LFP, with the magnitude varying depending on which women are eligible and the nature and quantity of specific policies. For example, in the United States, greater access to preschools improved the LFP of women by approximately 10 percentage points, with stronger positive effects observed on single mothers with at least one child under the age of six (Fitzpatrick 2012).[3]

Less research has been done on developing countries, but there is evidence, for example, that after-school child care increased maternal LFP by 7 percentage points in Chile (Martínez and Perticará 2017). In China, the introduction of new childcare facilities has been found to increase maternal LFP by 5 percentage points (Du et al. 2018).

---

3   See also, for Canada, Lefebvre and Merrigan (2008); and, for the Netherlands and Norway, Bettendorf et al. (2015).

This is particularly true in rural areas, where the availability of childcare services including preschools has been linked to a whopping 56 per cent increase in the likelihood of female off-farm employment (Xiong and Li 2016).

Further to the specifics of the CRNIP, in late 2011, the central government identified 699 poor and remote counties that would receive funding to implement the program for students in compulsory education. Another 891 local government–selected pilot counties were added to the counties in the national pilot scheme,[4] making a total of 1,590 counties in 29 provinces that had implemented the program. According to the official document (GOSC 2011), central government finance provides each primary and junior high school student with RMB3 and RMB4 a day, respectively, with an additional RMB1 for boarding students. From the launch of the program through to 2017, the central government allocated RMB159.1 billion to the CRNIP, covering 134,000 schools and benefiting approximately 36 million students in pilot schemes (CDRF 2017). This chapter focuses on the impact of the program for the national pilot scheme.[5]

An important feature of the CRNIP is that school canteens are the primary mode of program delivery: by 2016, more than 76 per cent of schools in the program had adopted this mode (CDRF 2017). Therefore, the availability of a school canteen for lunches is a crucial factor in determining whether students eat lunch at school, and hence in determining the impact of those lunches on maternal LFP. We draw on this feature in our econometric analysis below.

After establishing a causal link between the introduction of the CRNIP and maternal LFP, we further investigate the mechanisms through which this link operates. While it is theoretically possible that the introduction of the CRNIP could impact maternal LFP via providing more time and more financial support for households with school-age children, we expect the direct effect of relaxing mothers' time constraints to be more significant than the indirect effect of relaxed financial constraints—particularly given a highest possible subsidy per student of RMB100 per month. Our background research for this chapter revealed this to be the case, so we focus only on the time issue here. Our analysis reveals that the additional time is not enough to enable rural mothers to migrate to cities for work, as we would expect given that other household and childcare commitments remain. Instead, we confirm that the CRNIP results in higher rates of maternal participation in local off-farm and informal employment. We also confirm that this is a distinctly gendered issue: the CRNIP has no impact on the labour force participation rates of fathers.

---

4   Beginning in March 2012, the central government encouraged local governments to initiate their own pilot programs, with funding responsibilities resting on the local authorities. Unlike the nationally selected pilot counties, the implementation of the local-level pilot programs varies widely between provinces.
5   This is because there are likely to be confounding factors for the local-level pilots, which make interpretation of the results difficult.

The data

Our empirical analysis uses the 1 per cent samples of the 2010 and 2015 Chinese population censuses and Chinese county statistical yearbooks. These data enable us to identify all those households with at least one child, along with the necessary information about the employment status, age and education levels of their mothers. The list of national pilot counties is sourced from the official website of the Ministry of Education.[6] Information about the program's implementation is obtained from the official website of the China Development Research Foundation (CDRF 2017). By comparing data from before and after the implementation of the program, we can assess its impact on maternal (and paternal) LFP.

To ensure consistency with the general regulation that students must be at least six years old to attend primary school, we restrict our sample to mothers with at least one child aged between 6 and 14 years in September 2010 and 2015 (with their age calculated to the month). We identify whether a child received free lunches based on their location at the time of the survey. Additionally, we limit the age range of mothers to 30–55 years to ensure that the sample falls within the labour force age range. We exclude households from Beijing, Tianjin and Shandong provinces due to their distinct nutrition improvement programs.[7] Ultimately, we retain a total of 181,851 individuals, from 22 provinces, 219 cities and 1,471 counties across the two time periods.

The key dependent variable for the baseline analysis is maternal LFP, which includes all mothers who are employed or actively seeking jobs.[8] The variable *employed* takes a value of one if the mother responds affirmatively or indicates 'on-the-job leave, study, temporary or seasonal closure' to the question 'Do you work for more than one hour for income?' Otherwise, it takes a value of zero. The *actively seeking job* variable takes a value of one if the mother responded positively to the question 'Have you looked for a job in the past three months?', which includes activities such as 'Applying for a job at an employment agency, seeking assistance from friends and relatives to find jobs, advertising, attending a job fair, preparing for self-employment, and other'. Otherwise, we define an individual as not participating in the labour force.

In the subsequent analysis of the mechanisms linking time savings to LFP based on the type of employment, we focus on those women who are *employed* as the dependent variable, further identifying those who are employed in farm and non-farm employment, as well as in formal and informal employment. Using the occupation codes of the

---

6   The list of national and local pilot counties is available from MOE (2019).
7   Official documents indicate that Beijing, Tianjin and Shandong have implemented different nutrition improvement programs, so we exclude them from our analysis.
8   This is based on the official definition by the World Bank that the labour force participation rate is the proportion of the population aged 15–64 who are economically active, encompassing all individuals who contribute labour to produce goods and services during a specified period. China calculates its LFP rate, which includes individuals who are unemployed but actively seeking employment, using the following formula: LFP rate = (people with jobs + people currently seeking work) / (people aged 16–64) * 100 per cent.

population censuses, we categorise farm workers as those involved in agriculture, forestry, animal husbandry and sub-fishery. All other occupations are classified as off-farm employment.[9] We also consider an alternative classification, divided into formal, informal and 'other'. Formal jobs include highly skilled professionals such as doctors, teachers and accountants, while informal jobs are characterised by low skill requirements and high mobility, such as farming, cleaning, babysitting, waiting tables, textile work, porter services and sales. Occupations that do not fit neatly into these two categories are classified as 'other'. It is worth noting that informal employment encompasses activities that include elements of 'farm' employment, such as agricultural growers and related sales services, as well as non-farm employment. We also identify mothers who migrate for work based on their responses to the question 'Whether they have left their registered household location within the past year?' Mothers who answered 'yes' to the question were categorised as migrant workers. Our analysis here focuses mainly on non-migrants because this is where the CRNIP's impacts lie.

The main independent variable of interest is whether the mother has any child in a national pilot county and therefore is a recipient of the CRNIP program. Other independent variables include a range of individual, household and county-level factors that we expect will influence women's LFP decisions. For individuals, this includes their education level, ethnicity (a dummy variable equal to one for non-Han and zero for Han), age, marital status (a dummy variable equal to one if married, zero if not) and whether the mother is responsible for caring for the family (a dummy variable equal to one if so). For households, we include the gender and grade of the youngest child and the number of children. County-level variables seek to control differences in the level of development, including GDP per capita, population density, the share of secondary employment in total employment and average household per capita savings.

The descriptive statistics for these variables are provided in Table 9.1, with some key features noted here. First, we confirm the general trend of declining labour force participation for Chinese women, with the percentage of surveyed mothers participating in the workforce falling from 81 per cent in 2010 to 76 per cent in 2015. The employment figures indicate that a significant proportion of these mothers were actively seeking work, with the gap between LFP and employment widening to 9 percentage points in 2015. Also noteworthy is the high proportion of rural non-migrant mothers engaged in informal employment, averaging 56 per cent across the two time periods. Most of these workers are engaged in off-farm employment, averaging 51 per cent of the workforce of non-migrant mothers. Of all the surveyed women participating in the workforce, 7.7 per cent identified as migrants, with most of these working in informal and off-farm employment.

---

9   This classification may not fully align with reality as there are, for example, service occupations within the agricultural sector that do not constitute farm work. However, this is the best breakdown we can provide given the limitations of the data.

Table 9.1 Summary statistics

Variables	Overall	2010	2015
Key dependent variables			
Labour force participation	0.78	0.81	0.76
Employment (%)	69.8	76.6	67.2
* Informal*	56.5	63.7	54.0
* Off-farm*	51.7	60.8	47.7
Non-migrant employment (%)			
* Informal*	56.9	64.4	54.3
* Off-farm*	50.6	60.3	46.0
Migrant mothers (% of total mothers)	7.7	9.0	7.2
Independent variables			
National_pilot_county	0.16	0.06	0.19
Individual controls			
Ethnic minority	0.07	0.03	0.09
Years of schooling	9.1	9.3	9.0
Age	41.3	37.3	42.9
Marriage	0.94	0.97	0.93
Domestic_care	0.21	0.18	0.22
Household controls			
Child_gender (of youngest child)	0.86	0.67	0.94
One_child	0.45	0.66	0.36
Primary_school	0.93	0.83	0.98
County controls			
Ln(GDP_perCapita)	12.9	12.4	13.1
Ln(Popu_density)	5.9	6.0	5.8
Ln(Empl_SecIndu)	8.0	7.0	8.4
Ln(Saving)	14.9	14.9	14.9
Observations	**181,851**	**51,064**	**130,787**

Note: All variables are as defined in the text.
Sources: 1 per cent samples of the 2010 and 2015 Chinese population censuses.

The descriptive statistics also reflect China's ageing population, with the average age of mothers rising by more than five years between 2010 and 2015. In 2015, 43 per cent of mothers were over the age of 45 years, whom we classify as older mothers, with the remaining 57 per cent classified as younger mothers. On average, the surveyed group has completed junior high school (nine years of schooling). When we explore differences in the education levels of mothers, we classify those who have finished at least senior high school as 'more educated' (10 per cent of the sample in 2015) with the remainder being 'less educated'. Finally, while we do not focus on gender differences in our analysis

195

below, it is rather striking that 94 per cent of all households in 2015 reported that their youngest child was male, with just 36 per cent of households reporting having one child only.

Method: Establishing a causal link between the CRNIP and LFP

To examine the impact of the CRNIP on maternal LFP, we employ a standard difference-in-differences (DD) model. This model compares the LFP status of mothers before and after the implementation of the CRNIP in counties that adopted the program with those that did not adopt it during the same period. The baseline DD estimation is specified as Equation 9.1.

Equation 9.1

$$LFP_{i,t,c} = \beta_0 + \beta_1 Treated_c \times Post_t + X\gamma + \theta_a + \varphi_c + \omega_t + \varepsilon_{i,t,c}$$

In Equation 9.1, i indicates the individual (mother), c and t indicate county and year, respectively, and $LFP_{i,t,c}$ represents the LFP status of the mother. $Treated_i$ takes a value of one if the mother i has any child who was in a national pilot county, and zero otherwise. $Post_t$ is a post-treatment indicator taking a value of one if t = 2015 and zero if t = 2010. X is a vector of individual, household and county-level factors that potentially affect maternal LFP. θ_a is the age fixed effects, capturing the difference in job opportunities due to age; φ_c is county-level fixed effects, controlling for all the time-invariant characteristics of the counties; ω_t is the year fixed effects; and $\varepsilon_{i,t,c}$ is the error term. To address potential serial correlation and heteroscedasticity, we follow Duan et al. (2024) in clustering the standard errors at the county–year level, because this is the level at which our primary variable of interest, the introduction of the CRNIP, is determined. We are primarily interested in β_1, which denotes the percentage point change in maternal LFP between 2010 and 2015, stemming from the implementation of the CRNIP.

The underlying assumption of the DD model is that, apart from the CRNIP, counties that adopted the program would otherwise have followed similar trends to those that did not. According to official statements (CDRF 2017), the national pilot counties were selected based on criteria such as being 'poor' and 'remote'. A primary concern is that the counties were therefore not randomly selected, which poses a potential threat to this assumption. To address this, we follow the approach of Gentzkow (2006) and Li et al. (2016) by controlling for the initial selection criteria to mitigate any pre-existing differences between the CRNIP and non-CRNIP counties.

To ensure balance between the treatment group and the control group, we take three further steps, as recommended by Agarwal and Qian (2014) and Li et al. (2016). First, we identify the key determinants for the selection of CRNIP counties, building on the criteria of poverty and remoteness, including whether they have been identified as a 'national poverty-stricken county'; dummy variables for county-level cities, country-boundary counties and autonomous counties;[10] as well as county land relief, county average land slope and the fiscal gap between expenditure and revenue (see descriptive statistics in Appendix Table A9.1).

Second, we conduct balancing checks between the treatment group and the control group to observe any selection differences, confirming that these selection criteria did indeed differ between the treatment and control groups. Panel A in Table 9.2 reports the separate regression results for the treatment and control groups (in columns [1] and [2], respectively), with column (3) revealing that six of the seven selection criteria significantly differ between the groups, with the exception being for country-boundary counties. For example, 5.5 per cent of the CRNIP counties are county-level cities, while the proportion is 18.9 per cent in the non-CRNIP counties. This demonstrates the importance of these selection criteria in determining the treatment status.

Third, we must verify whether controlling for these key determinants of CRNIP counties' selection alleviates the imbalances between the treatment and the control groups. Panel B in Table 9.2 compares group differences in the initial year (2010) for various other indicators of economic and social development, which we expect to be closely related to both the program and our outcome variable (LFP): population density, secondary industry employment, rural employed population, household savings deposits, night light, grain output and aged dependency ratio.[11] Again, columns (1)–(3) in Panel B show that there are significant differences between CRNIP and non-CRNIP counties along all of these dimensions. Fourth, we verify that controlling for these key determinants of CRNIP counties' selection eliminates the statistical differences in these other variables between the two groups. This is shown in the final column (4) with statistically insignificant coefficients on all these other indicators (except for grain output). Consequently, the crucial problem of identification is (largely) resolved as the treatment and control samples are (largely) balanced.

---

10 Both county-level cities and counties belong to county-level administrative units in China's administrative divisions, but there are significant differences in many aspects: county-level cities tend to be more densely populated, more urbanised and have higher fiscal autonomy than counties. Thus, we expect fewer of them to be selected for the CRNIP program.

11 *Population density* is calculated by dividing the resident population by the administrative area at the end of 2010. *Secondary industry employment* is the number of people employed in secondary industries per 10,000 people. *Rural employed population* represents the number of rural people employed per 10,000 people. *Household savings deposits* is the balance of household savings deposits (RMB10,000). Night-light data come from the US Defense Meteorological Satellite Program, which captures images of the Earth at night from 20.30 to 22.00 pm local time as an indicator of the level of development. *Grain output* is total grain output (10,000 tonnes). *Aged dependency ratio* is the proportion of the elderly (aged more than 60 years) in the labour force (aged 16–60 years).

Table 9.2 Balancing checks of treatment and control groups

Variable	Treatment group (1)	Control group (2)	Unconditional difference (3)	Conditional difference (4)
Panel A: Selection criteria				
County-level city (1 = Yes, 0 = No)	0.055	0.189	−0.134***	
	[0.228]	[0.391]	(0.022)	
National poverty-stricken county (1 = Yes, 0 = No)	0.606	0.036	0.569***	
	[0.489]	[0.187]	(0.033)	
Country-boundary county (1 = Yes, 0 = No)	0.017	0.015	0.002	
	[0.129]	[0.122]	(0.008)	
Autonomous county (1 = Yes, 0 = No)	0.092	0.011	0.081***	
	[0.288]	[0.103]	(0.016)	
Land relief (degree)	1.063	0.229	0.834***	
	[0.867]	[0.328]	(0.050)	
Land slope (degree)	7.907	2.617	5.290***	
	[4.402]	[2.686]	(0.319)	
Ratio of fiscal expenditure to fiscal revenue 2009	8.606	3.031	5.575***	
	[8.598]	[2.811]	(0.551)	
Panel B: Other characteristics				
Density of population, 2010 (person/sq km)	298.727	938.269	−642.542***	76.165
	[290.357]	[1258.748]	(52.248)	(59.149)
Employed population in secondary industry, 2010	2.362	12.028	−9.665***	−0.294
	[2.902]	[17.238]	(0.670)	(0.958)
Rural employed population, 2010	29.312	65.216	−35.904***	6.241
	[22.924]	[90.026]	(3.516)	(4.051)
Household per capita savings deposits, 2010	44.319	574.511	−530.192***	−18.446
	[77.475]	[1133.367]	(41.320)	(52.952)
Night light, 2010	1.379	14.709	−13.331***	−1.372
	[2.910]	[16.867]	(0.676)	(1.150)
Grain output, 2010	28.279	89.953	−61.674***	−12.821**
	[28.697]	[181.213]	(6.870)	(6.021)
Aged dependency ratio, 2010	12.292	12.745	−0.453***	0.485
	[1.616]	[1.892]	(0.098)	(0.357)

*** significant at 1 per cent
** at significant at 5 per cent
* significant at 10 per cent
Notes: Columns (1) and (2) show means and standard deviations in square brackets. Column (3) reports the unconditional difference between the treatment and the control groups. Column (4) reports the conditional difference of these characteristics of a regression on the treatment dummy controlling for the selection criteria. All the regressions are clustered at the county level. Standard errors in parentheses.
Sources: 1 per cent samples of the 2010 and 2015 Chinese population censuses and 2010 county statistical yearbooks.

Results: The impact of the CRNIP on maternal LFP

The baseline estimation results are presented in Table 9.3. In column (1), we report the impact of the CRNIP on maternal LFP, controlling only for individual and household characteristics. The results indicate that the program increased maternal LFP by 4.86 percentage points. County controls are added in column (2). In column (3), we include interactions of the seven key determinant variables with the treated variable. These regressions consistently reveal a significantly positive effect on maternal LFP, with our preferred specification in column (3) indicating an increase of 4.25 percentage points after the implementation of the CRNIP.

While this magnitude is small compared with those of other childcare subsidies and after-school services cited above, this is not surprising since the provision of school lunches does not eliminate care activities altogether. That said, it is a significant impact. In contrast, the final two columns of the table replace maternal LFP as the dependent variable with paternal LFP—first, for all fathers (in column [4]) and then for those fathers whose wives have migrated for work (who might be expected to be more involved in child care as a result, in column [5]). In neither case does the free lunch program impact on the LFP of fathers, confirming that this is a gender-specific issue—affecting only women's work choices.

Table 9.3 The impacts of the CRNIP on maternal LFP

	Maternal LFP			Paternal LFP	Paternal LFP (in households where mother has migrated to work)
	(1)	(2)	(3)	(4)	(5)
Treated*Post	0.0486***	0.0425***	0.0425***	−0.0017	0.0001
	(0.008)	(0.008)	(0.008)	(0.006)	(0.007)
Individual and household controls	YES	YES	YES	YES	YES
County controls		YES	YES	YES	YES
Selection criteria*treated			YES	YES	YES
County fixed effects	YES	YES	YES	YES	YES
Year fixed effects	YES	YES	YES	YES	YES
Age fixed effects	YES	YES	YES	YES	YES
No. of clusters	1,869	1,869	1,869	2,352	2,044
Observations	181,851	181,851	181,851	236,968	57,987
R-squared	0.632	0.632	0.632	0.155	0.216

*** significant at 1 per cent
** at significant at 5 per cent
* significant at 10 per cent
Note: Individual, household and county-level controls are as described in the text.
Sources: 1 per cent samples of the 2010 and 2015 Chinese population censuses.

Table 9.4 unpacks this baseline result by investigating differences across subcategories of mothers. In the first two columns, we identify mothers with one child and more than one child, with the results indicating that the program has a significant impact on both. We then identify younger and older mothers and find that only for younger mothers (in column [3]) is there a statistically significant impact of the CRNIP on their LFP, although it is only weakly significant and small in magnitude. Using the definition of 'more educated' as senior high school level and above, we find that the CRNIP impacts significantly and positively on both more and less-educated mothers (although we observe more heterogeneity when we unpack this finding further below). The final two columns confirm that the program only impacts significantly on those women who have not migrated for work; it is insignificant for those who have. This is not surprising, as free lunches do not alleviate all household responsibilities and, given the small magnitude of the financial subsidy they embody, they seem unlikely to either trigger a decision to migrate or affect the labour force choices of mothers who have already migrated. As such, our mechanism analysis below focuses only on those women who have not migrated for work (92.3 per cent of the total sample).

For robustness, we assess the potential impact of omitted variables on the results by conducting a placebo test that randomly assigns the counties adopting the CRNIP pilot (as in Chetty et al. 2009; La Ferrara et al. 2012; Li et al. 2016). Of the 699 national pilot counties initially identified by the government, only 339 match our database. To ensure comparability, we randomly selected 339 counties and assigned them the status of having adopted the CRNIP in 2015. We then used this false treatment status variable to conduct a placebo DD estimation using the specification in column (3) of Table 9.3. Given the random generation process of these data, the false CRNIP variable should yield a non-significant estimation close to zero. If it shows a significant estimation, it indicates a misspecification of the DD estimation. We repeat this randomised process 500 times to enhance the identification power of the placebo test and confirm no statistical significance, further validating our claim that the positive and significant effect of the CRNIP on maternal LFP is not driven by unobserved factors.[12]

---

12 Appendix Figure A9.1 displays the distribution of estimates from these 500 runs. It is evident that the distribution of estimates from random assignments is centred on zero, with a standard deviation of 0.008. This suggests that there is no effect associated with the randomly constructed CRNIP pilot counties. Moreover, the baseline estimate (from column [3] of Table 9.3), depicted by the red line in the figure, lies outside the entire distribution.

Table 9.4 Heterogeneity analysis of the impact of the CRNIP on LFP

	Maternal LFP							
	Only one child (1 = Yes)	Two or more children (1 = Yes)	Younger mothers (1 = mother's age ≤45)	Older mothers (1 = mother's age >45)	Less-educated mothers (1 = lower than senior high school)	More-educated mothers (1 = graduated at least senior high school)	Migrant mothers (1 = mothers who left the residence within the past year)	Non-migrant mothers (1 = mothers who have not left the residence within the past year)
	(1)	(2)	(3)	(4)	(5)	(6)	(7)	(8)
Treat*Post	0.0324***	0.0349***	0.0166**	0.0340	0.0446***	0.0597***	0.0044	0.0464***
	(0.010)	(0.011)	(0.006)	(0.021)	(0.008)	(0.021)	(0.011)	(0.009)
Control variables	YES	YES	YES	YES	YES	YES	YES	YES
County FE	YES	YES	YES	YES	YES	YES	YES	YES
Year FE	YES	YES	YES	YES	YES	YES	YES	YES
Age FE	YES	YES	YES	YES	YES	YES	YES	YES
No. of clusters	1,868	1,867	1,867	1,829	1,869	1,426	1,446	1,868
Obs.	81,497	100,353	127,482	54,358	166,349	15,337	13,774	167,930
R-squared	0.687	0.601	0.704	0.538	0.638	0.534	0.731	0.628

FE = fixed effects

*** significant at 1 per cent

** at significant at 5 per cent

* significant at 10 per cent

Note: Control variables are as described in the text.

Sources: 1 per cent samples of the 2010 and 2015 Chinese population censuses.

Mechanisms: More time for what kind of work?

To explore how the provision of school lunches frees up time for Chinese mothers, we utilise the China Education Panel Survey (CEPS),[13] which provides detailed information on time use for parents (while the census data do not). The CEPS is a national survey conducted by Renmin University of China, encompassing 28 counties, 112 schools, 428 classes and 20,000 junior high school students (in grades seven to nine). The first question that is useful for our analysis is 'Does the school provide free lunch?' The provision of free lunch at school does not necessarily indicate that the school is in a CRNIP pilot county, but it is a reasonable substitute, especially as we limit the sample to focus only on rural areas for the years 2013 and 2014 (that is, following the implementation of the program). The second crucial question is in the parents' questionnaire, regarding the average daily time spent directly with their children.

Using OLS to assess whether there is a causal relationship between free lunches and childcare time could result in biased estimates. Although reverse causality may not be an issue (as school-level lunch provision is unlikely to be affected by women's employment), omitted variables could compromise our estimation as this is a cross-sectional analysis with only one year of data. For example, the provision of free lunches in the past (which we are unable to observe) could affect both the current provision of lunches and women's employment. To overcome these issues, we use a two-stage least squares (2SLS) model, with canteens as the instrumental variable (IV). Using the canteen as an IV satisfies the assumptions of relevance and exclusivity. Specifically, as noted previously, the existence or construction of a canteen is basically a prerequisite for qualifying for the CRNIP, and for determining whether students eat lunch at school. Furthermore, the provision of free lunches serves as the primary means through which the canteen influences mothers' decisions to work. The data indicate that 86 per cent of schools have a canteen for students, while only 18 per cent have implemented a free lunch program (see the descriptive analysis of CEPS data in Appendix Table A9.2). This suggests that while the canteen is a necessary condition, it is not sufficient for the implementation of a free lunch program. Additionally, the first-stage regression indicates that canteens are strongly correlated with free lunches (column [1] in Table 9.5) and the weak instrument test and exogeneity test (column [3] in Table 9.5) confirm that the canteen is an effective instrumental variable. The estimation results in column (3) of Table 9.5 indicate that having a child eat lunch at school reduces childcare time by approximately 2.8 hours, which is consistent with the evidence we gathered during the impact evaluation of the Preschool Nutrition Pilot in Hunan Province in 2021.

---

13 CEPS is an open-access database. See: ceps.ruc.edu.cn/sjcg/yjcg.htm.

Table 9.5 Time savings from free lunches

	Free lunch	Time a primary caregiver spends on child	
	First stage	OLS	2SLS
	(1)	(2)	(3)
Canteen	0.149***		
	(0.009)		
Free lunch		−0.287***	−2.836***
		(0.090)	(0.782)
Control variables	YES	YES	YES
Weak instrument test			237.85***
Wald test of exogeneity			219.70***
Observations	9,564	9,564	9,564

*** significant at 1 per cent
Notes: Control variables are as described in the text. Standard errors are in parentheses.
Source: 2013–14 China Education Panel Survey (CEPS).

This result prompts questions about the type of work mothers pursue and how this will vary across different individual characteristics, including age, level of education and type of employment. For example, women in the most impoverished rural households often pursue off-farm employment to increase their income, in part due to their limited holdings of agricultural land (Rajkhowa and Qaim 2022). It has also been suggested that younger women may demonstrate a greater inclination than older women to seek off-farm work (Roosaar et al. 2019). Women who are constrained by the demands of child care also tend to have a higher demand for flexible jobs (Conroy 2019). Informal jobs are more likely to offer this flexibility, while also being characterised by temporary or shorter duration and lower skill requirements in comparison with permanent positions (Reichenberg and Berglund 2019). Given these attributes, informal work is likely to be favoured by less-educated mothers who have limited employment options and are more likely to accept informal employment despite formal employment bringing more benefits (Conover et al. 2022).

To explore these possibilities further, we now narrow our attention to those women who are actively employed (thereby excluding those who are seeking work in the LFP definition above) and who have not migrated for work. We begin by repeating the baseline analysis in Table 9.3 above, using the preferred specification shown in column (3), but with employed women now as the dependent variable. As shown in column (1) of Table 9.6, this indicates that the CRNIP raises mothers' total employment by 2.44 percentage points, with the comparison group being unemployed mothers. This figure seems intuitively reasonable set against the 4.25 percentage point increase in LFP revealed in Table 9.3, with the difference being attributable to women who may have begun actively seeking work after the introduction of the CRNIP but had not yet found work by 2015.

Table 9.6 Employment options

	Employment (1 = employed, 0 = unemployed)	Farm (1 = employed on farm, 0 = unemployed)	Off-farm (1 = employed off-farm, 0 = unemployed)	Informal (1 = informal employment, 0 = unemployed)	Formal (1 = formal employment, 0 = unemployed)
	(1)	(2)	(3)	(4)	(5)
Treated*Post	0.0244**	−0.0030	0.0454***	0.0297*	0.0205
	(0.012)	(0.015)	(0.015)	(0.015)	(0.013)
Control variables	YES	YES	YES	YES	YES
County FE	YES	YES	YES	YES	YES
Year FE	YES	YES	YES	YES	YES
Age FE	YES	YES	YES	YES	YES
No. of clusters	1,869	1,865	1,868	1,868	1,859
Observations	167,930	110,809	108,549	119,300	62,457
R-squared	0.671	0.668	0.638	0.670	0.477

FE = fixed effects
*** significant at 1 per cent
** at significant at 5 per cent
* significant at 10 per cent
Note: Control variables are as described in the text. Standard errors in parentheses.
Sources: 1 per cent samples of the 2010 and 2015 Chinese population censuses.

The remaining four columns identify a subcategory of employment that is assigned a value of one (for mothers engaged in farm, off-farm, formal and informal employment), with the corresponding comparison group being unemployed mothers, assigned a value of zero. The estimation results in column (2) show that there is no impact on employment in the farm sector, while the statistically significant results in column (3) indicate that the CRNIP increases employment in the non-farm sector by 4.54 percentage points. Similarly, column (4) indicates that there is no significant impact of the program on formal employment, while column (5) indicates an increase of 2.97 percentage points in the informal sector. Note that these percentages need not add up to the overall change in employment given the overlap between non-farm and informal employment explained above.

Given these findings, our final investigation focuses on off-farm and informal employment and explores heterogeneity across the different subcategories of mothers introduced above. Table 9.7 shows that, for off-farm employment, the impacts of the CRNIP are significant for mothers with only one child and for less-educated mothers, while Table 9.8 indicates a significant impact for mothers with more than one child and for less-educated mothers. In neither case does age seem to be an important factor. We cannot explain the different findings for the number of children, but one point seems to be consistently supported by the evidence provided here: the CRNIP benefits less-educated mothers the most, providing them with opportunities to shift from unemployment to employment in the off-farm and informal sectors.

Table 9.7 Heterogeneity analysis of the impact of the CRNIP on off-farm employment

	Off-farm employment (1 = off-farm employment, 0 = unemployed)					
	Only one child (1 = Yes)	Two or more children (1 = Yes)	Younger mothers (1 = mother's age ≤45)	Older mothers (1 = mother's age >45)	Less-educated mothers (1 = junior high school and below)	More-educated mothers (1 = graduated at least senior high school)
	(1)	(2)	(3)	(4)	(5)	(6)
Treat*Post	0.0403**	0.0277	0.0142	0.0456	0.0477***	0.0179
	(0.017)	(0.017)	(0.012)	(0.040)	(0.015)	(0.079)
Control variables	YES	YES	YES	YES	YES	YES
County fixed effects	YES	YES	YES	YES	YES	YES
Year fixed effects	YES	YES	YES	YES	YES	YES
Age fixed effects	YES	YES	YES	YES	YES	YES
No. of clusters	1,854	1,855	1,863	1,789	1,868	1,374
Observations	50,970	57,562	77,090	31,437	94,801	13,556
R-squared	0.688	0.599	0.704	0.497	0.637	0.547

*** significant at 1 per cent
** at significant at 5 per cent
Notes: Control variables are as described in the text. Standard errors in parentheses.
Sources: 1 per cent samples of the 2010 and 2015 Chinese population censuses.

Table 9.8 Heterogeneity analysis of the impact of the CRNIP on informal employment

	Informal employment (1 = informal employment, 0 = unemployed)					
	Only one child (1 = Yes)	Two or more children (1 = Yes)	Younger mothers (1 = mother's age ≤45)	Older mothers (1 = mother's age >45)	Less-educated mothers (1 = junior high school and below)	More-educated mothers (1 = graduated at least senior high school)
	(1)	(2)	(3)	(4)	(5)	(6)
Treat*Post	0.0066	0.0326*	–0.0043	0.0408	0.0302**	–0.1026
	(0.016)	(0.018)	(0.013)	(0.029)	(0.015)	(0.243)
Control variables	YES	YES	YES	YES	YES	YES
County fixed effects	YES	YES	YES	YES	YES	YES
Year fixed effects	YES	YES	YES	YES	YES	YES
Age fixed effects	YES	YES	YES	YES	YES	YES

	Informal employment (1 = informal employment, 0 = unemployed)					
	Only one child (1 = Yes)	Two or more children (1 = Yes)	Younger mothers (1 = mother's age ≤45)	Older mothers (1 = mother's age >45)	Less-educated mothers (1 = junior high school and below)	More-educated mothers (1 = graduated at least senior high school)
	(1)	(2)	(3)	(4)	(5)	(6)
No. of clusters	1,861	1,859	1,865	1,808	1,868	580
Observations	50,269	69,024	77,629	41,651	115,631	3,355
R-squared	0.698	0.661	0.721	0.626	0.674	0.502

** at significant at 5 per cent
* significant at 10 per cent
Notes: Control variables are as described in the text. Standard errors in parentheses.
Sources: 1 per cent samples of the 2010 and 2015 Chinese population censuses.

Conclusion

This chapter investigated the impact of the China Rural Nutrition Improvement Program on the labour force participation of rural Chinese mothers. Our key finding was that mothers whose children were the recipients of free lunches in national pilot counties increased their LFP by 4.25 percentage points following the introduction of the program, while there was no impact on the LFP of fathers. We confirmed that the program reduced the time primary caregivers (almost all women) spent on child care by about 2.8 hours. This additional time was particularly important for less-educated women, who were able to seek informal and off-farm work in their residential area. This represents a small step towards relieving some of China's most impoverished rural women from unpaid domestic responsibilities, playing a positive role in reducing intrahousehold and interhousehold inequalities in the process.

This research contributes to the international literature that highlights the important connection between childcare services and women's labour force participation. Compared with the empirical findings in this literature, the magnitude of the CRNIP's impact was relatively small—as expected given the very small size of the financial subsidy embodied in the program and the remaining constraints imposed by the limited childcare services available for families in rural China. However, the significance of these findings should not be underestimated. Claudia Goldin's identification of time conflicts as the 'fundamental problem' for women the world over seeking to balance a busy working life with family commitments is confirmed by the findings in this chapter. If something that seems as 'small' (to those who do not make and deliver children's lunches every day) as free school lunches can encourage more women into the workforce, we can confidently assume that expanding access to preschool and after-school care services, underpinned by childcare subsidies, would have substantial impacts on the participation of rural Chinese women in the labour force. This offers a promising area for future research and an essential focus for the Chinese Government as it seeks to mitigate the challenges posed by China's declining and rapidly ageing population.

References

Agarwal, Sumit, and Qian Wenlan. 2014. 'Consumption and Debt Response to Unanticipated Income Shocks: Evidence from a Natural Experiment in Singapore.' *American Economic Review* 104: 4205–30. doi.org/10.1257/aer.104.12.4205.

Baker, Michael, Jonathan Gruber, and Kevin Milligan. 2008. 'Universal Child Care, Maternal Labor Supply, and Family Well Being.' *Journal of Political Economy* 116, no. 4: 709–45. doi.org/10.1086/591908.

Barber, Brad M., and Terrance Odean. 2001. 'Boys Will Be Boys: Gender Overconfidence, and Common Stock Investment.' *Quarterly Journal of Economics* 116: 261–92. doi.org/10.1162/003355301556400.

Becker, Gary S. 1985. 'Human Capital, Effort, and the Sexual Division of Labor.' *Journal of Labor Economics* 3: S33–S58. doi.org/10.1086/298075.

Bettendorf, Leon, Egbert Jongen, and Paul Muller. 2015. 'Childcare Subsidies and Labor Supply: Evidence from a Large Dutch Reform.' *Labor Economics* 36: 112–23. doi.org/10.1016/j.labeco.2015.03.007.

Cao, Yuan. 2019. 'Fertility and Labor Supply: Evidence from the One-Child Policy in China.' *Applied Economics* 51: 889–910. doi.org/10.1080/00036846.2018.1502868.

Cascio, Elizabeth U. 2009. 'Maternal Labor Supply and the Introduction of Kindergartens into American Public Schools.' *Journal of Human Resources* 44: 140–70. doi.org/10.1353/jhr.2009.0034.

Chetty, Raj, Adam Looney, and Kory Kroft. 2009. 'Salience and Taxation: Theory and Evidence.' *American Economic Review* 99: 1145–77. doi.org/10.1257/aer.99.4.1145.

China Development Research Foundation (CDRF). 2017. *Progress in Improving the Nutrition of Rural Students in Poor Areas.* Flagship Report. Beijing: CDRF. www.cdrf.org.cn/2017ztythbjbg/4163.htm.

Conover, Emily, Melanie Khamis, and Sarah Pearlman. 2022. 'Job Quality and Labor Transitions: Evidence from Mexican Informal and Formal Workers.' *The Journal of Development Studies* 58: 1332–48. doi.org/10.1080/00220388.2022.2061851.

Conroy, Tessa. 2019. 'The Kids Are Alright: Working Women, Schedule Flexibility and Childcare.' *Regional Studies* 53, no. 2: 261–71. doi.org/10.1080/00343404.2018.1462478.

Debela, Bethelhem Legesse, Esther Gehrke, and Matin Qaim. 2022. 'Links between Maternal Employment and Child Nutrition in Rural Tanzania.' *American Journal of Agricultural Economics* 103, no. 3: 812–30. doi.org/10.1111/ajae.12113.

Du, Fenglian, Zhang Yinyu, and Dong Xiaoyuan. 2018. 'The Impact of Childcare Type on Female Labor Force Participation Rate in Urban China.' *World Economy Papers* 3: 1–19.

Duan, Xueyi, Yinhe Liang, and Xiaobo Peng. 2024. 'Free School Meals and Cognitive Ability: Evidence from China's Student Nutrition Improvement Plan.' *Health Economics* 33, no. 7: 1480–502. doi.org/10.1002/hec.4824.

Fitzpatrick, M. Maria. 2012. 'Revising Our Thinking about the Relationship between Maternal Labor Supply and Preschool.' *Journal of Human Resources* 47: 583–612. doi.org/10.1353/jhr.2012.0026.

General Office of the State Council. (GOSC). 2011. *Opinions on the Implementation of the Nutrition Improvement Plan for Rural Compulsory Education Students.* State Affairs and Development Bureau (2011) No. 54. Beijing: General Office of the State Council of the People's Republic of China.

Gentzkow, Matthew. 2006. 'Television and Voter Turnout.' *The Quarterly Journal of Economics* 121: 931–72. doi.org/10.1162/qjec.121.3.931.

Goldin, Claudia. 2021. *Career and Family: Women's Century-Long Journey toward Equity.* Princeton, NJ: Princeton University Press. doi.org/10.1515/9780691226736.

Gurley-Calvez, Tami, Amelia Biehl, and Katherine Harper. 2009. 'Time-Use Patterns and Women Entrepreneurs.' *American Economic Review* 99: 139–44. doi.org/10.1257/aer.99.2.139.

Huang, Chen, and Li Ling. 2022. 'School-Age Population and Resource Supply of Urban and Rural Childcare Services from 2022 to 2050 Under the "Three Child" Policy.' *Education Research* 43: 107–17.

La Ferrara, Eliana, Alberto Chong, and Suzanne Duryea. 2012. 'Soap Operas and Fertility: Evidence from Brazil.' *American Economic Journal: Applied Economics* 4: 1–31. doi.org/10.1257/app.4.4.1.

Landivar, L. Christin, Willian J. Scarborough, Caitlyn Collins, and Leah Ruppanner. 2022. 'Do High Childcare Costs and Low Access to Head Start and Childcare Subsidies Limit Mothers' Employment? A State-Level Analysis.' *Social Science Research* 102: 102627. doi.org/10.1016/j.ssresearch.2021.102627.

Lefebvre, Pierre, and Philip Merrigan. 2008. 'Child-Care Policy and the Labor Supply of Mothers with Young Children: A Natural Experiment from Canada.' *Journal of Labor Economics* 26: 519–48. doi.org/10.1086/587760.

Li, Pei, Lu Yi, and Wang Jin. 2016. 'Does Flattening Government Improve Economic Performance? Evidence from China.' *Journal of Development Economics* 123: 18–37. doi.org/10.1016/j.jdeveco.2016.07.002.

Martínez, A. Claudia, and Marcela Perticará. 2017. 'Childcare Effects on Maternal Employment: Evidence from Chile.' *Journal of Development Economics* 126: 127–37. doi.org/10.1016/j.jdeveco.2017.01.001.

Mincer, Jacob. 1962. 'Labor Force Participation of Married Women: A Study of Labor Supply.' In *Aspects of Labor Economics*, edited by Universities-National Bureau Committee for Economic Research, 63–105. Princeton, NJ: Princeton University Press.

Ministry of Education (MOE). 2019. 'List of National and Local Pilot Counties for the Rural Compulsory Education Student Nutrition Improvement Program.' 19 April. Beijing: Ministry of Education of the People's Republic of China. www.moe.gov.cn/jyb_xwfb/xw_zt/moe_357/s6211/s6329/s6371/201904/t20190419_378881.html.

National Health Commission (NHC). 2022. *Statistical Bulletin on the Development of Health Care in 2022*. Beijing: National Health Commission of the People's Republic of China. www.nhc.gov.cn/guihuaxxs/s3586s/202310/5d9a6423f2b74587ac9ca41ab0a75f66.shtml.

Nollenberger, Natalia, and Núria Rodríguez-Planas. 2015. 'Full-Time Universal Childcare in a Context of Low Maternal Employment: Quasi-Experimental Evidence from Spain.' *Labour Economics* 36: 124–36. doi.org/10.1016/j.labeco.2015.02.008.

Rajkhowa, Pallavi, and Matin Qaim. 2022. 'Mobile Phones, Off-Farm Employment and Household Income in Rural India.' *Journal of Agricultural Economics* 73: 789–805. doi.org/10.1111/1477-9552.12480.

Reichenberg, Olof, and Tomas Berglund. 2019. 'Stepping up or Stepping down? The Earnings Differences Associated with Swedish Temporary Workers' Employment Sequences.' *Social Science Research* 82: 126–36. doi.org/10.1016/j.ssresearch.2019.04.007.

Roosaar, Liis, Jaan Masso, and Urmas Varblane. 2019. 'Age-Related Productivity Decrease in High-Waged and Low-Waged Employees.' *International Journal of Manpower* 40: 1151–70. doi.org/10.1108/IJM-03-2018-0086.

Survey on Social Status of Women in China (SSWC). 2021. *Fourth Survey on Social Status of Women in China: Main Data*. 27 December. Beijing: All-China Women's Federation and National Bureau of Statistics of China. epaper.cnwomen.com.cn/images/2021-12/27/4/04BLM04Cc27_h.pdf.

World Bank. 2022. 'Female Labor Force Participation.' *Gender Data Portal*, 10 January. Washington, DC: World Bank Group. genderdata.worldbank.org/data-stories/flfp-data-story/.

World Food Programme (WFP). 2022. *China, Impact Evaluation of the Preschool Nutrition Pilot in Selected Counties of Xiangxi Prefecture, Hunan, PR China*. Decentralized Evaluation Report. Beijing: WFP China Office. www.wfp.org/publications/china-preschool-nutrition-pilot-selected-countries-china-feb-2018-jan-2021-evaluation-baseli.

Xiong, Ruixiang, and Li Huiwen. 2016. 'Childcare, Public Service and Chinese Rural Married Women's Non-Farm Labor Force Participation: Evidence from CFPS Data.' *China Economic Quarterly* 16: 394–413.

Appendix 9.1

Table A9.1 Descriptive analysis of initial selection criteria

Selection criteria	Definition	Mean	SD
County-level city	= 1 if the county was county-level city; 0 = otherwise	0.163	0.369
National poverty county	= 1 if the county was national-level poverty-stricken county; 0 = otherwise	0.122	0.328
National border county	= 1 if the county's boundary (at least part of it) overlaps with country's boundary; 0 = otherwise	0.015	0.121
Autonomous county	= 1 if the county was autonomous county; 0 = otherwise	0.023	0.150
Land relief	Relief degree of land surface (°)	0.366	0.555
Land slope	County average land slope (°)	3.439	3.569
Fiscal gap	Ratio of fiscal expenditure to fiscal revenue	3.833	4.637

Note: Selection criteria variables are all reported for 2010.
Sources: 1 per cent samples of the 2010 and 2015 Chinese population censuses and 2010 county statistical yearbooks.

Table A9.2 Descriptive analysis of data from CEPS

Variables	Definition	Mean (1)	Std dev. (2)	School with free lunch (3)	School without free lunch (4)	Diff. (5)
Key variables						
Mother's employment	= 1 if the student's mother is employed; = 0 otherwise	0.925	0.263	0.960	0.918	0.042***
Free lunch	= 1 if the students are provided free lunch; = 0 otherwise	0.170	0.375			
Canteen	= 1 if the school is equipped with canteen; = 0 otherwise	0.858	0.349	0.954	0.838	0.117***
Childcare time	The time primary caregiver spent in child care (hours)	3.087	3.281	2.850	3.135	−0.285***
Student's characteristics						
Boy	= 1 if the student is a boy; = 0 otherwise	0.494	0.500	0.483	0.96	0.013
Lives on campus	= 1 if the student lives on campus; = 0 otherwise	0.484	0.500	0.625	0.455	0.169***
Siblings	Number of siblings	0.948	0.808	0.956	0.946	−0.010
Age	Years	14.167	1.279	14.280	14.144	−0.136***
Scores	Average test scores in Chinese, maths and English	69.946	8.613	69.995	69.937	−0.059

Variables	Definition	Mean (1)	Std dev. (2)	School with free lunch (3)	School without free lunch (4)	Diff. (5)
Key variables						
Cohabit	= 1 if the child lives with mother; = 0 otherwise	0.831	0.375	0.810	0.835	0.0247**
Health status	Scale: very unhealthy = 1; very healthy = 5	4.013	0.893	3.888	4.038	−0.023***
Local *hukou*	= 1 if the child's *hukou* is locally registered; = 0 otherwise	0.812	0.391	0.880	0.798	−0.081***
Household characteristics						
Mother's education	= 1 if the mother graduated from at least junior high school; = 0 otherwise	0.667	0.471	0.639	0.673	−0.034***
Parents' expectations	Parents' expectations for children's education (scale: very low = 1; very high = 9)	6.483	1.738	6.514	6.477	−0.037
Family's economic status	Scale: very poor = 1; very rich = 5	2.713	0.637	2.618	2.732	0.114***
Class and school characteristics						
Class rank	The ordinal class ranking in academic records within the same grade (scale: worst = 1; best = 5)	3.364	0.958	3.444	3.348	−0.096***
Class size	Class size (number)	48.123	11.999	48.527	48.040	−0.487
School rank	Ordinal school ranking in academic records within the same county (scale: worst = 1; best = 5)	3.802	0.830	3.713	3.820	0.107***
Public school	= 1 if a public school; = 0 otherwise	0.913	0.282	1.000	0.895	−0.105***
Region	The type of district in which the school is located					
Central urban area	Reference group	0.211	0.408	0.121	0.229	0.109***
Urban–rural fringe		0.245	0.430	0.274	0.238	−0.036**
Town outside the city		0.262	0.440	0.252	0.264	0.012
Village		0.283	0.450	0.353	0.268	−0.084***
Observations			9,564	1,622	7,942	

*** significant at 1 per cent
** at significant at 5 per cent
* significant at 10 per cent
Source: 2013–14 China Education Panel Survey (CEPS).

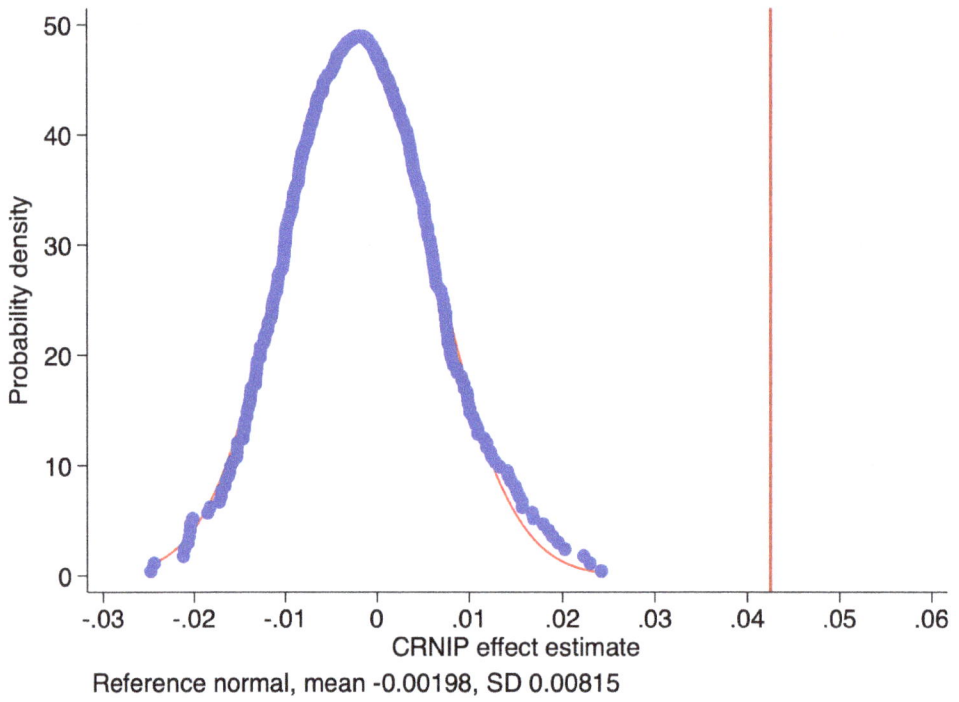

Figure A9.1 Placebo test

Sources: 1 per cent samples of the 2010 and 2015 Chinese population censuses.

10

Chips, subsidies and commercial competition between the United States and China

John Edwards[1]

The revolution in contemporary industrial and trade policy

In October 2022 the United States announced it would ban the sale of certain US-designed advanced semiconductors or 'chips' to China (BIS 2022).[2] At the same time, the United States sought the agreement of friends and allies to prevent them fabricating advanced semiconductors for Chinese clients or selling Chinese clients machinery to make advanced semiconductors. Explicitly intended to arrest China's progress in artificial intelligence (AI)—a technology of considerable significance—the US decision is among the most consequential and ambitious of recent years.

If the US policy succeeds in its intent, China will over time fall further and further behind the United States and its allies in the development of AI and its use in manufacturing, services and the military. Indeed, China will fall further and further behind in any process advanced chips facilitate. The consequences of a US failure are also considerable. If China can make its own versions of the products banned by the United States, the latter will have not only denied itself the biggest single export market for some advanced

---

1 This chapter is an extensively revised and updated version of a PowerPoint presentation given at the twenty-third China Update Conference in November 2023. The conference version was in turn an updated and reframed discussion based on my May 2023 Lowy Institute paper (Edwards 2023).
2 The release in part stated that: 'The export controls announced in the two rules today restrict the PRC's ability to obtain advanced computing chips, develop and maintain supercomputers, and manufacture advanced Semiconductors … [and] these rules make clear that foreign government actions that prevent BIS [Bureau of Industry and Security of the Department of Commerce] from making compliance determinations will impact a company's access to U.S. technology through addition to the Entity List.'

technology products but also markedly accelerated the creation of an advanced chip techno-sphere in China independent of the United States and its allies. In that outcome, the United States will have spurred the creation of a world market competitor in advanced technology products for which it now holds a substantial advantage.

Now second only to the United States in the research and development of AI, China is intent on applying advanced technology as widely as possible to its industries. There is no middle course for China. Denied both advanced chips and the means to make them, China must either make its own or resign itself to the gradual loss of industrial competitiveness.

Some years on from the October 2022 announcement, the result of the US policy innovation remains in the balance. Chinese businesses and authorities have demonstrated greater resilience, ingenuity and technical progress than US policymakers expected, but there is a long way for China to go before attaining a chip techno-sphere comparable with that of the United States and its allies. There are many risks to avert and technological challenges to overcome. Yet, in the view of one well-informed US analyst, the evidence so far suggests the export refusals by the United States are likely to 'founder on the rocks of reality' as China's businesses and authorities respond with very substantial investments (Evenett et al. 2024).

While the result remains in the balance, the episode already provides much material with which to survey the impact of the US chip denial and what it tells us about the future of global trading norms and the competition between China and the United States. In this respect, the chip competition is emblematic of the issues raised by new dimensions in trade and industry policy.

Behind the US decision was not only more than a decade of increasing political competition with China, but also a closely related decay of global disciplines to support free trade. Always closely connected, industry policy and trade policy have in important respects fused with a broad conception of national security. Contemporary government interventions described under any or all of these rubrics have initiated what are likely to be far-reaching changes in the global configuration of key industries. So, too, commercial and strategic considerations—formerly separate domains—now extensively overlap in the development and evolution of policy. Contemporary industrial subsidies and export controls thus raise new issues for global institutions and national governments.

One likely impact of this immense change in trade policy is to marginalise the customary focus on both regional and global trade agreements and to marginalise the World Trade Organization and national and international trade bureaucracies and the expertise they have accumulated over decades of recruitment, training and experience. The action is elsewhere and the players are changing.

Trade policy in the half-century after World War II was mostly about tariffs and mostly about cuts effected through global or regional agreements negotiated by trade officials. Contemporary trade policy, by contrast, is mostly about subsidies to support home production and state interventions to entrench national control of leading technologies. Rather than supporting declining industries against cheaper imports, as tariffs tended to do, contemporary subsidies often support research, development and production of advanced technology goods and services intended for world markets. Officials from national security agencies are as likely as trade officials to be framing these decisions.

Importantly, contemporary trade policies are more likely to be focused on supporting exports than hindering imports. As the trade rules monitor Global Trade Alert reported in 2021, the 'negative spill overs created by American, Chinese, and European subsidies to import-competing firms pale in comparison to those created by state incentives provided by these jurisdictions to their exporters' (Evenett and Fritz 2021: 35).

Much contemporary industry policy claims a broad national security rationale for government support of what are predominantly civilian technologies and commercial industries. And while, over decades, some international agreement has been reached to limit state subsidies, it is not at all clear what rules, if any, apply to this strategic competition.

Though the trend towards increased national support for 'strategic industries' has accelerated since the economic downturn following the 2008 GFC, it was not until April 2022 that the four most important world economic organisations produced their first joint report, *Subsidies, Trade, and International Cooperation*, on the growing extent of industry subsidies (IMF et al. 2022). Many of the data in this report by the IMF, the OECD, the World Bank and the WTO were drawn from a large global survey of industry subsidies by a private group, Global Trade Alert (GTA), published in October 2021. Subsequently, the US Center for Strategic and International Studies (CSIS) produced a report, sponsored by the US State Department, estimating industry subsidies in China and comparing them with other major economies (DiPippo et al. 2022).

The IMF has now introduced a database to track industry policies from calendar year 2023. In an associated paper, Simon Evenett et al. (2024) report that through 2023 alone the database recorded 2,500 new industry policy interventions, 71 per cent of which were 'trade distorting'. Over the same period, the term 'industry policy' occurred about 16,000 times in the major business press, compared with about half that number of mentions 10 years earlier. Just less than half of the interventions occurred in China, Europe and the United States. As Evenett and his colleagues report:

> The data show that the recent wave of new industrial policy activity is primarily driven by advanced economies, and that subsidies are the most employed instrument. Trade restrictions on imports and exports are more frequently used by emerging market and developing economies. Strategic competitiveness is the dominant motive governments give for these measures, but other objectives such as climate change, resilience and national security are on the rise. (Evenett et al. 2024: 2)

Corporate subsidies were the most common type of trade-distorting instrument and a common motive was 'strategic or geopolitical competition, for example to establish a first mover advantage in emerging technologies' (Evenett et al. 2024: 8).

Together with other work done by the IMF, OECD and WTO over recent years, these reports point to a considerable enlargement of industry subsidies since 2008—a portentous global phenomenon now deeply entangled with the wider competition between China and the United States.[3]

Different methodologies lead to very different estimates of the level of subsidies. While tentative and incomplete, the information collected thus far is nonetheless indicative of a major realignment of industry policy as a crucial tool of competition between nations.

The 2021 GTA report, for example, suggested that between 2008 and 2021, China, the United States and the European Union implemented more than 18,000 subsidy programs for their industries, with the number of identified programs split roughly equally between the three (Evenett and Fritz 2021). Together, China, the United States and the European Union account for more than half the number of total world subsidy interventions since 2008.

By 2019, the final pre-Covid year, total annual subsidies in the three major economies had reached more than US$361 billion—an amount greater than the annual GDP of four-fifths of the world's economies.[4] On some estimates, the total subsidies now paid are very much higher.

There is little doubt that these already huge government subsidies paid to their industries by the three economic superpowers are growing. According to the international institutions, the 'frequency and complexity' of 'distortive subsidies' are increasing and their 'growing use' changes trade and investment flows, undermines the rationale for tariff cuts and 'undercuts public support for open trade'. It is a pattern of vastly increased spending that the IMF, World Bank, WTO and OECD argue contributes to 'global trade tensions that are harming growth and living standards' (IMF et al. 2022: 3).

Even middle-ranking powers have difficulty matching the subsidies available in the major economies. Industry assistance through tax concessions and budgetary payments has been growing in Australia, for example—a trend evident in many other economies.[5] In April 2024 the Australian Government announced it intended to substantially

---

3   In addition to the reports cited, see also a recent piece that reaches similar findings using a novel methodology by Juhász et al. (2022).

4   In the 10 years from 2010 to 2019, the available data suggest that industry subsidies paid by governments in China, the United States and the European Union totalled more than US$3 trillion—an amount roughly twice the size of the total value of annual economic output in Australia. On some estimates, the total is considerably higher. See Evenett and Fritz (2021: Fig. 5, p. 15) for subsidies for the European Union and the United States drawn from IMF data and for reported subsidies to publicly listed Chinese firms (Table 5, p. 43).

5   The Australian subsidy total was US$11.3 billion (excluding economy-wide pandemic spending such as JobKeeper). See PC (2022).

increase subsidies in response to those provided by the major economic powers to their industries.[6] In international economic competition, however, the absolute size of subsidies matters far more than the relative size. EU subsidies in 2019 were 32 times bigger than Australian subsidies and US subsidies were nine times bigger. On one published estimate, Chinese subsidies were six times bigger; on others, a far higher multiple.[7] Against the big players, the smaller players and especially less-developed economies have trouble competing.[8] As the report of the four pre-eminent international economic organisations concludes, the 'renewed drive towards industrial policies to promote "strategic" sectors' distorts international competition, especially with smaller, poorer developing countries (IMF et al. 2022: 7).

The ability of the three economic superpowers—together accounting for more than half of global production—to out-subsidise most of the world's other economies is one important issue posed by the vast and increasing size of global industry subsidies. There is another. The new intensity of subsidisation—evident in the enhanced rivalry among the major economic powers—reflects changing forms of strategic competition that could impose unwelcome choices on the lesser powers.

Both China and the United States have focused recent industry policy on advanced-technology industries.[9] In a 2019 report, the OECD estimated total non-financial support to major aluminium producers in China was an average of US$2 billion a year over the period 2013–17 (OECD 2019a). In its report on semiconductors, the data suggest major producers in China receive subsidies in the order of four times more than those for aluminium (OECD 2019b). The IMF reported that total US industry subsidies across the entire economy were worth US$74 billion in 2019 (Evenett and Fritz 2021). Spending authorised under the 2022 *CHIPS and Science Act* alone is nearly four times bigger—and US subsidies to support green industries bigger still.

Much of the new spending is explicitly intended to gain decisive national advantage in the research and development of AI, supercomputing, big data, clean energy, biotechnology, electric vehicles and other frontier technologies.

---

6   The *Sydney Morning Herald* reported on 10 April 2024 that Prime Minister Anthony Albanese 'will point to massive subsidies and tax breaks in the United States, the European Union, Japan, Canada and South Korea to argue that Australia has to offer its own incentives or risk losing industries. "All these countries are investing in their industrial base, their manufacturing capability and their economic sovereignty," he says in the draft of a speech to be delivered to the Queensland Media Club in Brisbane on Thursday. "This is not old-fashioned protectionism or isolationism—it is the new competition"' (Crowe 2024).

7   See the appendix to my Lowy Institute paper (Edwards 2023) for a discussion of subsidy estimates, particularly for China.

8   There are few data on subsidies paid in the rest of the world but, by way of illustration, subsidies paid by G20 countries excluding India, China, Germany, France, the United Kingdom and the United States declined over the period 2009–19, according to the IMF. See Evenett and Fritz (2021: Fig. 5, p. 15).

9   The notion of 'strategic sectors' has shifted over the past 10 or so years. In the early years of this century, the industrial subsidy controversy was often about China's subsidies to its steel and aluminium industries, then rapidly increasing production and exports at the expense of European, Japanese and other producers. But while China remains a major producer in both industries, export volumes have declined.

While past industry policies diminished international trade by supporting import-competing industries, some contemporary industry policies could increase international trade by subsidising exports. Other subsidies could speed the transition towards cleaner energy by encouraging electric vehicle development, wind farms or solar energy installations. The US Congress, for example, authorised US$369 billion largely to subsidise green energy measures. While the impact of traditional subsidies on trade is the subject of agreed disciplines overseen by the WTO, the new subsidies are often not. Nor is the case for restricting them quite so clear.

Nor, indeed, is the value of these policies yet clear. Despite very large subsidies, China has yet to match the United States in the design of semiconductors, Taiwan and South Korea in the production of advanced semiconductors or the Netherlands in the production of machines to manufacture semiconductors. By contrast, its solar panel manufacturing industry has been an outstanding global success despite relatively little government support for the industry's creation (see Asia Society 2023; Nahm 2023). The US semiconductor industry—now to be subsidised—relied at first on military and other government support but its commanding world lead was built by mostly unsubsidised private business.

The strategic sector most prominent today is the design and production of advanced semiconductors—the tiny processors that now instruct everything from home appliances to passenger jets and from smartphones to supercomputers. In that sector, the competition is most intense between China and the United States, though that rivalry has several unusual characteristics. It is also a theatre of competition that is by far the most expensive to the subsidising nations.

The remainder of this chapter examines this most salient, costly and fraught example of great-power competition in trade and industry.

Background to the chip competition

Industry subsidies and export denials are entangled in the larger strategic competition between China and the United States. Industry policy is consequently entangled in national security policy.

The semiconductor competition between the United States and China is in several respects a new constellation of state intervention, subsidies and responses—one that does not easily fit into existing dispute categories or rules. In China, technology industry policy in recent years has taken the form of public–private partnerships, often but not always arranged by state entities. The forms of capital support can also (and deliberately) resemble Silicon Valley private equity consortiums and are similarly intended to provide a return to investors (Naughton 2021). Though lavish in scale and supported and often controlled by industry policy officials, much of the capital deployed is private. It is usually difficult to estimate the extent of government subsidy involved, not least because of disagreements about defining what constitutes a subsidy. There is no doubt, however, that the subsidies are considerable.

The United States has responded to China's declared technology ambitions with a combination of industry subsidies and export denials.[10]

The focus of competition began over what the industry describes as logic chips of the '7-nanometre processing node'—a term that once described the distance separating transistors and is now used more loosely to describe a chip generation. The 7 October 2022 announcement by the Biden administration of a ban on exports to China of advanced chips cited China's use of the chips (and supercomputing equipment, also included in the announcement) in military technologies and identification systems. As interpreted by reporters and Washington analysts, the broader purpose of the ban on advanced chip exports is to stop China's advances in AI—a field both the United States and China believe will shape technology development. The *Financial Times* (2022) reported, for example, that the United States introduced 'expansive chip export controls in an effort to slow China's progress in artificial intelligence and supercomputers and make it harder for the country to manufacture advanced semiconductors'. As CSIS analyst Greg Allen explains, with its chip export ban, the United States intends 'freezing the state of AI in the year 2022 for China. Soon, this will be very outdated technology' (quoted in Langer 2023).

A peculiarity is that, while the competition is between the United States and China, at the time of the October 2022 US announcement, *neither* country manufactured these advanced chips in commercial quantities. US or US-based firms may design advanced chips, but, by and large, they do not make them in the United States. Leading US manufacturer Intel does fabricate chips in the United States, but they are of older design. 'There's zero leading-edge production in the US', the head of the relevant branch in the US Department of Commerce told the *Wall Street Journal* in late 2023 (Fitch and Ip 2023).

China produces more chips than the United States, accounting for 16 per cent of the world's supply, against 14 per cent for the United States. But this does not apply to advanced chips. The United States relies on the Taiwan Semiconductor Manufacturing Company (TSMC) to produce its most advanced chips, in Taiwan. Taiwan accounts for 90 per cent of global advanced chip-making capacity and South Korea's Samsung for much of the remainder. Over the decades, TSMC has built up a prime position in the manufacture of leading-edge chips, the fabrication of which requires plants that could cost US$20 billion to construct and which may be superseded every couple of years by plants that fabricate yet more advanced chips. The initial costs and economies of scale

---

10 For an account of the October 2022 Biden administration's announcements on new export denials to China, see Kannan and Rizvi (2022).

in advanced chip fabrication are so vast that it is difficult to compete against the two leading manufacturers. The United States stopped trying a couple of decades ago. It has only recently resumed its efforts, and only with very big subsidies.

The chips sold by American technology company Nvidia that the United States refuses to export to China, for example, are made in Taiwan. Chinese businesses also contracted TSMC to make advanced chips. Under the US rules, TSMC cannot now make advanced chips for Chinese businesses.

Despite vast investments, China was until recently unable to make high-end chips at home. While that is changing, China appears to be still well short of the United States in chip design and behind TSMC in fabrication—at least in commercial quantities and with competitive production yields.

The United States now wants to resume fabricating more chips onshore, arguing that it is dangerous to be so reliant on shipments from Taiwan and South Korea for such a fundamental product. The US$39 billion in semiconductor manufacturing subsidies allocated in the CHIPS legislation is for foundries to replace imports from Taiwan, not China. In principle, the subsidies reflect the higher cost of setting up fabrication facilities in the United States. TSMC and Samsung have been pressed to produce advanced chips in the United States and, like Japanese auto firms half a century ago, they have complied. Intel is also planning to make advanced chips in the United States.

Yet, the new fabrication plants in the United States may not produce the most advanced chips (Miller 2022: 331, 334; see also Clark and Swanson 2023). Both TSMC and Samsung, supported by their governments, intend to keep the technology for, and production of, the most advanced chips in their home countries. By the time the new US foundries are built, TSMC will likely be producing more advanced chips in Taiwan than it will be in the United States (Ting-Fang 2023). While TSMC has now indicated it will fabricate in the United States more advanced chips that it had earlier promised, it argues that the most advanced chips must first be produced in Taiwan and with access to its central research facility on the island (Hille et al. 2024).

This onshore production aspect of the US program is justified as a necessary cost to minimise dependence on Taiwan, which may at some future point be either under China's control or a battlefield between China and the United States. While it is possible to build a chip foundry in the United States, it is not possible to source there (or in any other single country) all the materials and processes used in fabricating chips (see OECD 2019b). The United States thus ends up (at considerable cost) with US-based foundries that will produce contemporary though not leading-edge chips, but not independent of inputs from outside the United States. Indeed, China is now the predominant source of some of these materials, including neon gas and tungsten (Fitch and Ip 2023).

Successful implementation of this domestic production aspect of the US program will see advanced chips again made within its borders, at the expense of some production capacity that would otherwise have existed in South Korea and Taiwan. It is in principle like US policies in the 1980s to shift some motor vehicle production from Japan to the United States, with subsidies replacing threatened and real tariffs as the driver of change.

Export denials

Fabricating more chips in the United States is one arm of the current industry policy. The other and far more adversarial arm is to deny China the ability to use or make advanced chips. This is not an unprecedented tactic in international trade competition, but it is rare, and rarely successful. It is a tactic distinct from trade sanctions, which are generally applied in response to activity considered hostile by the initiating state, and which may be withdrawn if the hostile activity ceases. For example, many countries applied export sanctions on Iran to discourage its development of nuclear weapons, after agreement within the UN Security Council. The US routinely applies sanctions against states it considers hostile. China itself ceased exports of rare earths to Japan in 2010 during a dispute about the detention of the captain of a Chinese fishing trawler (Bradsher 2010). These are examples of sanctions imposed against specific behaviours, with at least a notional idea that the sanction could be lifted if the offending behaviour changed. Trade denials are also usual in war, such as the shipping embargoes imposed by the United Kingdom and other Allies on Germany through both world wars, and embargoes that Europe, the United States and their allies now place on certain materials for Russia. Another example is the oil embargo imposed by the United States and its Allies on Japan in 1941—a decision that left Japan with the choice of going to war with the United States to secure oil in the Dutch East Indies or complying with US demands that it withdraw from China. But it is less common in peacetime to permanently deny a product with the straightforward intention of preventing its use by a competing target country. There is no negotiation implied and no sense that the denial might be retracted if an offending conduct ceased. An earlier example is offered by Australia, which, to protect its wool industry, banned the export of merino rams from 1929 through to the late 1970s (de Silva 1988). Otherwise the tactic is rare, partly because it can only succeed in a very narrow class of products (see below).

The United States has long worked with its allies to refuse China access to the most advanced chips. This policy has now been enforced more rigorously and extended beyond what is at any time the latest chip generation. As US President Joe Biden's National Security Advisor Jake Sullivan (2022) framed it, the US objective is now to keep China as far behind as possible.

The US ambition is to arrest China's advance in AI by denying it access to the computing power the United States, Japan, South Korea, the United Kingdom, Western Europe, Singapore and Israel need to make their own advances in AI. Given the possible uses of AI over coming decades in commercial as well as military applications, the US ambition is very big indeed.

Since the United States does not in fact make the advanced chips it wishes to deny China, it must act through other countries to implement a successful ban. The United States must prevent TSMC and Samsung from making advanced chips on contract for Chinese firms. It must also do what it can to prevent China making advanced chips itself.

Yet, the machines necessary to fabricate advanced chips are not made in China or the United States, or in South Korea or Taiwan. They are made in the Netherlands, with most advanced chip fabrication depending on lithography machines manufactured by Dutch producer ASML. The United States must prevent ASML (or Japanese and Korean equipment makers, if they catch up with ASML) from selling advanced lithography machines to China. It is asking TSMC and ASML to lose revenue, which they are understandably reluctant to do. Since ASML machines and TSMC advanced chip fabrication incorporate some US designs and intellectual property, the United States asserts a right to refuse to allow the relevant licences to be used to export material to China.

The Biden administration's policy seeks not only to permanently stall China's progress in chip design and manufacture, but also to gradually degrade the capability it now has. As time goes by, and if it is unable to make the most advanced chips, China will fall further and further behind. The objective, it is widely agreed, is to disable China's advance in AI. As explained by the CSIS's Allen: 'The new American regulations say you cannot sell chips above a certain performance threshold to China anymore—the one that represents the current state of the art for training large AI models' (quoted in Langer 2023).

At the same time, the United States is banning the export to China of equipment to make advanced chips. As Allen says, the United States had permitted the sale to China of semiconductor manufacturing equipment 'that would allow China to advance, but with a certain technological distance. Now, there is active degradation of Chinese technological capabilities taking place.' Allen cites the example of semiconductor manufacturing facilities in China that can currently mass produce chips at the 14-nanometre process node. 'To those factories,' he says,

> you now can't even sell the old stuff anymore. And every semiconductor manufacturing facility on Earth is dependent upon US semiconductor manufacturing equipment. It's not just a one-time dependency—you need spare parts, software updates, etc. This policy is designed to put those advanced facilities out of business … Previously we tried to slow the pace of the advance. This is the first time we're actively trying to reverse technological progress.

As a result, 'slowly but surely, China's AI research is going to become less and less relevant to the state of the art as it exists in the United States, Europe, and Japan, for example' (quoted in Langer 2023).

China's response to the US export denial

As Allen says, the October 2022 announcement was a 'big, big change' in US policy. But will it permanently freeze China's semiconductor industry in 2022 or to chips no more advanced than the 14-nanometre process node (and over time also degrade that capacity), as Allen expected? This question bears on whether the export denial tactic will become more common and will be applied to a wider range of products for competitive advantage in international trade.

The rapidity of China's advance in AI surprised US officials and could have been a factor in the 2022 announcement. China is now at the world's technical frontier in AI, with scientific publications in the area equivalent in number to those of the United States. According to Allen, in AI, China has 'essentially achieved their first five-year goal, which was reaching and matching the state of the art'. China is on track 'to be the number-one publisher of some of the most highly cited AI research papers around the world', with 'a lot of companies who are generating a lot of revenue and are building really impressive stuff' and 'universities who are putting out a lot of impressive research in AI' (Allen, quoted in Schneider and Zhang 2023; see also Fitch 2019).

The Stanford University Global AI Index 2023 reinforces Allen's point (Stanford HAI 2024). Overall, in terms of research and development, China continued to lead the rest of the world in total AI journal, conference and repository publications. Ironically, again in terms of research and development in the field, the report found that the United States and China had the greatest number of cross-country collaborations in AI publications from 2010 to 2021, although the pace of collaboration has since slowed. It also found that the number of AI research collaborations between the United States and China had increased roughly four times since 2010 and was 2.5 times greater than the collaboration totals of the nearest country pair, the United Kingdom and China.

Remarkably, US sources estimate that China's AI workforce is not much smaller than that of the United States, and both are far ahead of any other economy. According to the MacroPolo *Global AI Talent Tracker* published in March 2024 and reported in the *MIT Technology Review*, in 2019, China had one-tenth of the 'most elite AI researchers' but, by 2022, it accounted for 26 per cent of this global AI community—just behind the United States at 28 per cent and making Chinese researchers 'the backbone of cutting-edge AI research' (MacroPolo 2024). The report also found that 80 per cent of graduates in this field from Chinese universities now stayed in China rather than seeking work in the United States. The United States continues to attract the most talent, though the gap between it and China in this respect has narrowed. In 2019, according to the report, almost three-fifths of top AI researchers worked in the United States, but three years later it was two-fifths.

China's AI shortcomings are not in research and development—areas where it matches the United States—but, most pertinently, in the computing power conferred by the most advanced chips.

The US export ban was certainly at least initially telling on China's capabilities to progress AI. According to a Taipei-based chip research service, China would need 30,000 of the banned Nvidia chips to commercialise a generative pretrained transformer (GPT) model comparable with that released by OpenAI as ChatGPT (Pan 2023). Covering an AI conference in China in January 2023, the *South China Morning Post* reported tech executives' views that China did not yet have in quantity chips comparable with those the United States now denies it (Zhang and Cao 2023).

Yet, there is plenty of evidence that China is now working around the US denials. One sign is that Chinese businesses appear to have already advanced well beyond 14-nanometre chips. Relatedly, Chinese businesses have produced at least 40 AI large language models, and in some reports many more.[11]

A Canadian tech news site reported in 2022 that the Chinese-owned Semiconductor Manufacturing International Corporation (SMIC) was producing 7-nanometre chips and had been for a while (Pan 2022a, 2022b). Widely read tech industry news site *Tom's Hardware* reported in September 2022 that SMIC was mass-producing at the 14-nanometre node and advancing to 7-nanometre and 5-nanometre nodes (Shilov 2022). The *Wall Street Journal* subsequently reported early in 2023 that 'many in Washington were blindsided' when they learned that SMIC, China's largest chip maker, was manufacturing the 7-nanometre chips—'a level of sophistication thought beyond its ability' (Fitch and Ip 2023).

While China's current fabrication abilities for advanced chips remain limited, there is little doubt Chinese businesses can now design very advanced chips. Chinese semiconductor companies have announced not only the successful design of 7-nanometre and 5-nanometre chips, but also a chip with equivalent functionality to the denied Nvidia chip (Fitch and Ip 2023). The BR100 from Shanghai start-up Biren Technology has 77 billion transistors and, according to one tech site, is designed for machine learning and comparable with the most advanced US chips designed for that purpose (Chips and Cheese 2022; see also WSJ 2023).

If Chinese companies can now design advanced chips, a constraint on China portrayed by Allen becomes the US ban on advanced chip-making equipment from ASML in the Netherlands. The most advanced machines made by ASML are extreme ultraviolet (EUV) lithography systems. Since 2019, the Dutch Government has denied ASML a licence to export these machines to China. In January 2023, the United States reached agreement with both the Netherlands and Japan to deny some advanced chip manufacturing machines to China—though it is not clear that either country has accepted all the controls sought by the United States (Hayashi and Salama 2023).[12]

---

11 'China has approved more than 40 artificial intelligence (AI) models for public use in the first six months since authorities began the approval process, as the country strives to catch up to the U.S. in AI development, according to Chinese media' (Ye 2024).
12 But see also a 2023 *X (Twitter)* thread by Paul Triolo: twitter.com/pstAsiatech/status/1642356571375280129 (2 April, 12.41 pm).

To beat the US ban, China must produce its own machines to make advanced chips or devise an alternative process it can assemble from materials to which it has access. China has plenty of chip-making equipment, importing US$150 billion of such machinery over the five years to and including 2022 (Slotta 2023). If it has managed to design and produce very advanced chips, advanced semiconductor manufacturing equipment is perhaps not beyond its range.

Nor does China require EUV lithography machines to make some versions of advanced chips. TSMC, for example, used older deep ultraviolet (DUV) lithography machines in the early stage of its 7-nanometre volume production (Wang 2022). ASML's former CEO Peter Wennink confirmed in 2023 that the company was still able to ship DUV machines to China (Gross 2023). More recently, Huawei filed a patent on a process using older lithography machines to fabricate very advanced chips.[13]

The United States began to restrict China's access to advanced chip manufacturing machines in 2016, and the ban on ASML selling EUV machines to China has been in place since 2019. Yet, Chinese businesses appear to have not only successfully designed versions of some advanced chips, but also managed to produce them.

It is also possible that there are not many more advances to be made in the size and power of chips. The CEO of Nvidia, for example, is sceptical that a great many more transistors can be lodged on a tiny piece of silicon (Kim 2022; see also Takahashi 2021). In the time it takes China to catch up to the frontier of today's chip technology, the United States, Taiwan, Japan and South Korea may not have been able to move as far forward in chip development as has been typical over the past 50 years.

ASML's Wennink told *Bloomberg* in January 2023 that China will sooner or later develop its own chip-making machines. 'If they cannot get those machines', he said, 'they will develop them themselves. That will take time, but ultimately, they will get there' (Koc 2023). Analysts at Georgetown University's Center for Security and Emerging Technology concede that China has the resources and the will, so catching up in semiconductor manufacturing equipment 'is not impossible' (Hunt et al. 2021). The Australian Strategic Policy Institute's Samantha Hoffman told the *ABC* in 2022 that, '[w]hile having a long way to go in its advanced chip manufacturing, China will likely close the technological gap' (Mann 2022).

Subsequent reporting and analysis have supported these early speculations. In February 2024 the *Financial Times* reported that SMIC was putting together production lines to make a 5-nanometre chip designed by Huawei and intended for use in its premium

---

13 Gao and Wu (2024) reported that 'Huawei Technologies Co. and a secretive chipmaking partner in China have filed patents for a low-tech but potentially effective way to make advanced semiconductors, raising the prospect that China could improve chip production techniques despite US efforts to halt its progress. The companies are developing technologies that involve self-aligned quadruple patterning, or SAQP, and should reduce their reliance on high-end lithography, according to patent filings to the Chinese intellectual property authority. That may allow them to produce advanced chips without ASML Holding NV's state-of-the-art extreme ultraviolet lithography equipment.'

smartphones (Financial Times 2024). The 5-nanometre chip is a generation behind the cutting-edge 3-nanometre chip made by TSMC, but nonetheless a considerable advance on the 7-nanometre chip the United States wanted to prevent Chinese businesses making. Huawei already deploys its 7-nanometre chip in premium smartphones. The *Financial Times* also reported that Huawei plans to make an AI processor, the Ascend 920. It is considered 'the most promising alternative' to Nvidia's graphics processing unit (GPU). SMIC charges 50 per cent more for its products from the 5-nanometre and 7-nanometre fabrication nodes than TSMC at the same nodes—perhaps partly a reflection of much lower yields of usable chips than TSMC has attained.

SMIC makes its product on foreign machines. Responding to these publicised advances, the United States has pressed Japan and the Netherlands to tighten restrictions on the export of chip-making equipment to China to include repair and servicing of machines already in use in China.[14] The United States has also pressed South Korea to join the denials of chip-making equipment, although the South Korean product is less sophisticated than the Japanese or Dutch machines.

A 2024 assessment by Paul Triolo, an American analyst affiliated with both the CSIS and the Albright Stonebridge Group, finds that Chinese businesses and particularly Huawei have made substantial progress in creating alternatives to the denied products. 'According to industry sources,' he writes,

> the advanced ASML DUV tools that SMIC and SMSC [Semiconductor Manufacturing South China Corporation] currently have could allow SMSC to add capacity of around fifty thousand wafers per month for a 7 nanometer process, though it is not yet clear whether this could cover all of China's advanced semiconductor requirements outside of cutting-edge smartphones. (Triolo 2024)

As well as its cooperation with SMIC and other fabricators, 'Huawei almost certainly has its own separate effort to build a domestic-only production process', with industry sources suggesting 'Huawei has already put together a 28-nanometer line and is now working toward a 14-nanometer capability'.

Working with SMIC and specifically SMSC, Huawei 'has achieved a breakthrough in getting back to near-cutting-edge design and manufacturing' with its 2023 Mate 60 phone. It

> represents a major milestone and a harbinger of the types of measures Chinese companies will take to engineer around U.S. technology restrictions. SMIC already had access to all the tools and well-known industry techniques—such as multi-patterning using ASML DUV tools, along with capable deposition and etch gear—to produce the Kirin 9000s system on a chip (SoC) at the heart of the Mate 60, and yields are likely to go up in 2024. (Triolo 2024)

---

14 *Financial Times*, [London], 7 March 2024.

Huawei, Triolo reports, has conducted R&D in critical areas, such as DUV and EUV lithography. Even so, 'Chinese lithography companies appear to be years behind industry leader ASML and Japanese firms such as Nikon and Canon in these areas, making lithography one of the critical technology bottlenecks'.

Adding to demand for the domestically produced substitutes in the chip supply chain, Chinese authorities are now requiring their use where feasible (Lin 2024).

How the US export denial and China's response could change the shape of the global technology industry

What might be the consequences of China's drive to replace the denied chips? Triolo argues that the US restrictions have touched off a revolution in chip technology in China. The revolution could produce a native Chinese counterpart of and rival to the US chip industry—a rival that would include the intermediate tools and processes required to made advanced chips. US suppliers in the chip supply chain will be squeezed out of the Chinese market.

Chinese companies (and authorities), Triolo (2024) writes, are not only concerned about existing restrictions, but

> are also worried about future controls, and will prioritize tool and material production lines free of Western inputs to reduce long-term risks. Hence, even if they can still acquire Western tools, virtually all leading Chinese foundries and memory companies are working methodically with domestic toolmakers to develop and validate equipment to eventually establish production processes largely free of Western equipment.

Thus, for semiconductors, 'what is happening in China will fundamentally change the industry over the next decade'.

Triolo adds that nothing will be guaranteed to succeed 'in the sense of producing end products comparable to those of the mainstream global semiconductor manufacturing process'. There will be winners and losers, 'with Western tool makers perhaps the biggest victims as they are gradually frozen out of what had been a huge, growing, and lucrative market that they dominated before October 7, 2022'.

For China's domestic industry, 'the most important impact of the controls was to massively incentivize designing U.S. technology out of the semiconductor space'. Before the October 2022 announcement, Triolo argues, 'Chinese technology firms acquired and used the most advanced equipment and services available, like their peers and competitors globally'. Chinese semiconductor firms 'largely ignored' the 2015 Made in China 2025 strategy, but that 'changed in 2023'.

One of the most important impacts of the October 2022 controls, Triolo writes, 'was to force the industry into boosting collaboration and innovation. This has happened quickly according to industry insiders, who note that there is now a high level of integration among the leading toolmakers and the foundries.'

As a result:

> Foreign toolmakers are expressing increasing concern that the improvement in the quality of the products of domestic toolmakers will also eventually enable them to compete outside of China, putting even more pressure on sales, revenue, and R&D budgets needed to maintain leading positions. (Triolo 2024)

Still, lithography remains a difficult challenge because 'even if SMIC and other foundries can leverage DUV gear for production at 7 nanometers, getting to more advanced nodes will require extreme ultraviolet (EUV) lithography systems, a niche where only ASML has been able to develop commercial systems'.

Triolo (2024) concludes:

> As of early 2024, the future of China's semiconductor industry remains hanging in the balance. Many technical hurdles must be overcome in order to build ecosystems that will allow high-end design firms such as Huawei, Alibaba, and others to design and manufacture advanced chips free of concerns around U.S. export controls. Given the number of different technology areas that are under intense development in China, it also remains to be seen when individual technologies or groups of key technologies will mature to the point of enabling scaled commercial production for a particular manufacturing-supply-chain element.

Huawei remains key:

> Especially if SMIC is able to get to some type of 5 nanometer process, it looks increasingly likely that Huawei will have a full lineup of largely domestically produced telecommunications, AI, server, computer desktop, smartpad, and smartphone semiconductors by 2025.

Chinese domestic toolmakers, Triolo writes, 'aim to put together commercial production lines at 28, 14, 7, and even 5 nanometers', still using existing DUV equipment. But these toolmakers will continue work on the more advanced EUV projects,

> including building up a cadre of engineers, managers, and supply-chain specialists to begin developing sustainable ecosystems for EUV systems development and deployment later in the decade. In the most optimistic scenario, according to some industry watchers, progress on EUV means that SMIC could get its hands on a prototype system to begin testing in 2025, but this scenario is much more optimistic than other industry assessments. (Triolo 2024)

Importantly, Chinese businesses have already attained the capacity to continue progress with AI models, which typically use a parallel graphics processing unit (GPU). 'For many applications, including 5G and training large language models', Triolo judges, 'the advanced DUV capability at SMIC and Hua Hong should be able to satisfy a growing portion of the domestic demand for advanced GPUs'.

Triolo concludes:

> Assuming Beijing's new semiconductor industry policy produces significant gains for technologies like DUV to keep China's design and manufacturing industry afloat, the advances made by domestic foundries and other key players in the Chinese semiconductor manufacturing supply chain will gradually produce two separate but linked manufacturing ecosystems: China domestic and global mainstream.

> At the end of the day, however, the U.S. approach to export controls—the belief that preventing Chinese firms from accessing key U.S. and allied-country technology will prevent Chinese companies from doing certain things—will founder on the rocks of reality. The underlying problem of U.S. export controls is that we are dealing with applied science, and there is no single path to achieving technological performance levels, only many different, albeit difficult paths. Chinese firms will find the paths that work well enough to continue to drive innovation.

> The impact of the U.S. approach to export controls in general, and on Huawei in particular, will likely mean that major U.S. and other foreign toolmakers are increasingly squeezed out of the Chinese market. (Triolo 2024)

AI and China's manufacturing industry

The counterpart or replacement chip techno-sphere under development in China will be more significant because AI development there is likely to be predominantly applied in manufacturing, where China already accounts for almost one-third of world output (World Bank 2022d). A China-developed advanced chip industry, and the AI and other applications that it would make possible, will likely be shaped by this intended end use. Publicly available sources point to a debate in China about priorities for spending on chip development and AI, with leaders in the area suggesting a higher priority for applications rather than basic research.[15]

In recent decades China has caught up with much of the advanced manufacturing of the United States, Germany, Japan and South Korea. China now accounts for more than half of global robot installations and, in 2022, installed very nearly twice as many robots as the combined total of Japan, South Korea, the United States and Germany (Richter 2023). Though the potential impact of AI in service industries is usually the

---

15 Post on www.chinatalk.media/ (22 March 2024).

centre of discussions in the United States and Europe, the impact of AI-enabled robots on China's manufacturing could be more consequential—for both China and the rest of the world.

Through its manufacturing sector applications, AI could make more difference to China's economy than to the United States'—and AI is only one of the multitude of technologies facilitated by advanced chips. Little wonder China's political leaders and businesses have given such high priority to and are investing so much in creating an alternative to the US-dominated advanced chip industry.

National security, commercial competition and the rest of the world

The ambition of the United States to freeze China's progress in making chips and particularly its progress in AI depends in large part on the continuing cooperation of other countries to enforce these denials. But while security allies may be willing to assist the United States in enforcing policies related to national security, they may not be so reliable if US motives are mostly about protecting the commercial leadership of its own industries or merely hindering China's economic growth. As EU official Thierry Breton told a Washington audience in late January 2023: 'You will always find Europe by your side when it comes to ensuring our common security in technology … [but] action should be limited to what is necessary from a security point of view' (in Hayashi and Salama 2023). Speaking in March 2023, European Commission President and former German defence minister Ursula von der Leyen moved closer to the US position (Fleming and Foy 2023). For Brussels, as for many capitals, determining what is necessary from a security point of view is yet unsettled.

Both China and the United States declare that technology leadership is a national security requirement. This is an argument for waiving WTO rules on subsidies and other forms of government industry support, though not one accepted by WTO members without detailed examination.[16]

The United States has claimed national security reasons for denying advanced chips and production technologies to China and for subsidising the fabrication of chips in the United States. (Existing military demand includes some advanced chips but is mostly

---

16 The Trump administration, for example, claimed a national security requirement to impose penalty tariffs on aluminium and steel imports from Europe, among other sources. In a recent finding, a WTO disputes panel decided that to be valid a national security exception could not just be claimed. It must be shown to be valid. In the case of aluminium and steel imports, it was not proved and the panel found against the United States. Not unexpectedly, the United States has rejected the WTO finding (Sherman and Josephs 2022).

for less advanced chips, of a kind that China now produces in considerable quantity. The major US military chip requirement is for 'legacy' chips—some now commercially obsolete.)[17]

There is no doubt AI has military and, more broadly, national security applications. These include facilitating cyberattacks and defending against them; improved battlefield surveillance; improved machine-guided weapons and weapons platforms such as military aviation and seacraft; and faster battlefield information collection, analysis and response. All are now in development among the major military powers—and many lesser powers—and have been for some time. Some Turkish armed drones now deployed in Ukraine, for example, are reportedly AI-capable (Manuel 2022).

There is also little doubt that the military applications of AI are a small sliver of the current and future uses of AI in commerce and economic transformation. As Washington analyst Paul Scharre (2023) points out, AI is a general-purpose enabling technology like electricity or computers. It is being developed by commercial firms for commercial markets, with the military in the United States, China and many other countries taking an interest in its possible applications.

The relationship between technology and the military has changed over the past few decades, at least in the United States. In the postwar decades, the US military and government institutions more broadly sponsored research that resulted in technologies that had military but also civilian applications (see Miller 2022: 29).

Today, the sequence has reversed, with commercial civilian technologies such as enhanced computer capabilities, advanced chips, high-speed computers and new communications capabilities sometimes also finding military uses. Once accounting for a very large share of total research and development spending in the United States, military R&D spending now accounts for very little of the total (Cheung 2022). Many contemporary technologies have some military applications, but most are developed for, paid for and applied to commercial use.

As a result, although both sides claim national security rationales for subsidising chip technologies and the United States claims it for denying China advanced chips, the technology 'war' is inevitably over products mostly commercial in their origin and purpose.

The products are mostly used for leisure, entertainment, convenience and health for ordinary people. The 'fourth industrial revolution', for example (the much-hyped expectation that AI, immense amounts of data and automation will revolutionise the production of goods and services while also creating new products and new markets), is primarily a story about cheaper products, speed and convenience—all directed

---

17 Most weapons produced in great numbers and deployed by the US or Chinese military use these older chip technologies. As the CEO of Lattice Semiconductor Corporation, a chipmaker for the defence industry, explained to the *Wall Street Journal*: 'Our products last for 15 or sometimes 20 years … So the risk of our products being obsolete is very low' (quoted in Fitch 2022).

at household consumers. So, too, the closely related Internet of Things, the market for computer games, electric self-driving vehicles, biotechnologies and much more. As the US Semiconductor Industry Association (2022) proudly proclaims: 'Global semiconductor sales are driven by products ultimately purchased by consumers.'

Under the Trump administration, technology competition with China was, for a significant faction within the executive, the spearpoint of a wider program to slow China's economic advance and stimulate US manufacturing. As former director for China in the National Security Council staff of the Obama administration Ryan Hass recounts in his 2021 book, *Stronger*, although the declared aim of the Trump administration's trade war on China was to compel China to amend its unfair trading practices,

> in the comfort of quiet conversations, US policymakers have readily acknowledged to me their underlying motivations to slow down China's rise and reinvigorate the US manufacturing sector. They saw trade activism against China as a means of pressuring companies to shift supply chains out of China, divest from China, and reinvest in the United States. (Hass 2021: 102)

The United States and China are using a very broad definition of national security in their competition over advanced chips. Each wishes to be independent in this crucial product. In most world capitals, this is understood and accepted as a fact of global politics—one impossible to change. The competition does not affect the legacy chips in common household, industrial and military use, and the competition in advanced chips comes at no great cost to third countries. But the US application of export denials that depend on the cooperation of its friends and allies poses somewhat different issues.

For US allies, the question is whether and to what extent they are willing to join the United States in arresting China's development of AI. For Australia, this could, for example, involve terminating research partnerships with Chinese academics in the AI field. There is already some evidence that China–Australia research collaborations have been scaled back (Pooley and Laurenceson 2023).

In the October 2022 announcement, the United States asserts a right to forbid technology exports to China from other countries if those products use US technology and fall within the scope of the US-controlled products lists. This could extend to, for example, Australia–China cooperation on supercomputing and other existing joint programs. According to Australia's Department of Foreign Affairs and Trade, 'Australian researchers rank 3rd for contribution to Chinese research publications, and vice versa … [and] there are literally thousands of partnerships' between Australian and Chinese researchers covering a wide range of science and technology fields, including agriculture, medicine and high-tech industries (Australian Embassy 2017).

The problems will be much more pressing if the United States moves ahead with wider export denials on technology to China, as Biden administration officials expected. As the Carnegie Endowment for International Peace reported in 2022, the new policy 'is unlikely to stay contained to semiconductors. Alan Estevez, the US undersecretary of commerce for industry and security, recently suggested the administration is also contemplating similar controls in areas like biotechnology' (Kannan and Rizvi 2022). Covering the speech by Estevez, the *New York Times* reported:

> When asked if the United States would consider further controls in quantum information science, biotechnology, artificial intelligence software or advanced algorithms, Mr Estevez said that he was meeting with his staff weekly to discuss such restrictions. 'Will we end up doing something in those areas? If I were a betting person, I would put down money on that.' (Swanson 2022)

The possible range of additional denials is very wide and would cover several areas in which Australia and China have established scientific and technical cooperation.

As Peterson Institute for International Economics president Adam Posen (2023) argued in *Foreign Policy* magazine, the 'US attempts to impose arbitrary export and investment restrictions on China that extend to other countries … [could] backfire'. For such restrictions to succeed, the United States 'would have to become a commercial police state on an unprecedented scale'.

Can the United States control China's technological development?

A broader issue raised by the US chip denial is whether the United States and its allies can successfully control China's technological development any more than China can control the technological development of the United States.

The technological competition between the two countries is so vigorous because the two contestants are so well matched. The United States is the bigger economy, with China's output four-fifths of America's measured in current exchange rates. It is not at all certain that China's output will surpass that of the United States before China's growth rate slows to America's likely growth rate (Rajah and Leng 2022). But China saves and invests more, with total investment each year 50 per cent higher than the United States (World Bank 2022b). China's manufacturing output is far bigger than that of the United States. In 2021, on World Bank numbers and measured in current US dollars, the US manufacturing sector was somewhat bigger than those of Germany and Japan combined. But it was only slightly more than half the size of China's manufacturing sector, which is comfortably bigger than the manufacturing sectors of Japan, Germany and the United States combined (World Bank 2022c). Once strong only in simple products such as clothes and shoes, China's manufacturing is now largely state of the art. In technological competition, China's much greater manufacturing output to some extent offsets its smaller economic size overall. Pertinent to the connection between manufacturing and technology, China dominates industrial robot installations.[18]

---

18 According to the Stanford *Artificial Intelligence Index Report 2024*, as early as 2013, 'China overtook Japan as the nation installing the most industrial robots. Since then, the gap between the total number of industrial robots installed by China and the next-nearest nation has widened. In 2021, China installed more industrial robots than the rest of the world combined' (Stanford HAI 2024).

Once well behind the United States and Europe in science and technology, China is rapidly catching up. Though the citation rates for Chinese research papers are lower than those for US papers, China and the United States now account for two-thirds of science papers published each year, split about equally between the two (Zwetsloot et al. 2021). China's top research institutions in science and technology are said to be lower in quality than comparable US institutions, but China produces each year many more graduates in science, technology, engineering and mathematics than the United States. The US Center for Security and Emerging Technology predicts that, by 2025, China will be producing nearly twice as many doctoral graduates in STEM (science, technology, engineering and mathematics) fields as the United States (and three times as many if non-American doctoral graduates from US universities and institutions are excluded from the US total) (Zwetsloot et al. 2021). Less than two-thirds of the US total 10 years ago, research and development spending in China is now about 85 per cent of the US total—and more than three times the total R&D spending of South Korea, Japan and Germany combined (OECD 2024). Though still catching up in many areas, China is at the forefront of some fields, including supercomputing. Reflecting their different economic structures, China favours some fields and the United States favours others.

If lagging the United States in science, China is closer in engineering. China operates hundreds of satellites, has launched numerous space probes and has begun building a permanently crewed space station (CSIS 2020).

For decades, the United States has pursued a policy of denying China the most recent chips and the most advanced machinery to design chips, either from US designers and fabricators or from allies such as Taiwan, South Korea, Japan and the European Union (Naughton 2021). For decades, China has attempted to build its own capability to design and fabricate chips, often with indifferent success. The United States remains ahead in design, though as we have noted, Chinese businesses have recently made gains (see, for example, Clay and Atkinson 2023). Despite the longstanding denials of the most recent chip generations, the most advanced of China's technology-based businesses evidently remain quite close to the global frontier.

In those same decades, the United States and its allies have maintained a ban on most weapons sales to China and on the sale of critical dual-use technologies. The US Department of Commerce has also not permitted the sale to China of a wide range of declared products and restricted others. US allies are expected to adhere to the US policy, and usually do. Yet, over the decades, China has independently developed nuclear weapons, modern intercontinental ballistic missiles and satellites—all despite strong US opposition.

In the military realm, US intelligence analysts expect China to continue to make technological advances. In a 2019 report on China's military capabilities, the US Defense Intelligence Agency concluded:

> In the coming years, the PLA [People's Liberation Army] is likely to grow even more technologically advanced, with equipment comparable to that of other modern militaries. The PLA will acquire advanced fighter aircraft, naval vessels, missile systems, and space and cyberspace assets as it organises and trains to address 21st century threats farther from China's shores. (DIA 2019)

In a world where basic scientific knowledge is available to anyone educated to understand it and where engineering skills are universally taught, preventing the spread of new technologies is hard. In past episodes, the United States failed in its objective of preventing China attaining capabilities that in important respects match its own.

The two big national economies remain entwined, even in technology. As the *Wall Street Journal* reported in March 2024, today China and the United States are 'simultaneously the other's biggest research partner and its biggest rival' (Hua 2024). In early 2024 the United States and China 'quietly' renewed their *Science and Technology Agreement*, first reached in 1979. There was no online statement. The renewal was for six months, signalling a difficult negotiation on its long-term status (Hua 2024).

Export denials and deglobalisation

Is the US chip denial merely one instance of a bigger trend to reverse China's integration into the global economy? Much depends on whether—as is sometimes eagerly supposed—a highly subsidised technology race is part of a wider 'deglobalisation' or 'onshoring' trend. So far, at least, there is little evidence of such a movement. Global trade has never been higher and cross-border investment has recovered from the Covid-19 downturn. Trade between the United States and China is strong, although the United States appears recently to be losing market share in China and China is losing market share in the United States (Bown and Wang 2023). Even so, in 2024 there was little sign that 'deglobalisation' had momentum. Trade in unfinished goods as a share of total goods trade is a rough indicator of the presence of global supply chains. Excluding fuels from the calculation, the WTO reports that in the fourth quarter of 2022 the ratio of unfinished goods to total goods in trade fell below 50 per cent and remained there through the first half of 2023. But, as the WTO adds: 'The shift is not dramatic: as measured by the average of exports and imports, the intermediate goods share has fallen to 48.5% in the first half of 2023, compared to an average of 51.0% over the previous three years.' It concludes that whether the

> decline is due to geopolitical tensions or the recent global economic slowdown is unclear. Whatever the reason, the data suggest that goods continue to be produced through complex supply chains, but that the extent of these chains may have reached their high-water mark. (WTO 2023)

Much the same may be said for world cross-border trade, which is another indicator of globalisation. On World Bank (2022a) numbers, global exports as a share of global GDP stood at 31.3 per cent in 2022, only marginally above the high of 31 per cent reached in 2008 but nonetheless the highest share ever. Trade as a share of GDP may have peaked, as of course someday it must. But it does not show any sign of deglobalisation. Nor, as reported by University of California at San Diego's Caroline Freund to an IMF conference in May 2023, is there 'consistent evidence of major changes that would be associated with reshoring or diversification' (Freund et al. 2023).

Evident rules for success in an export denial strategy

There are international rules against the kind of export denial the United States has imposed but 'national security' is an argument against their invocation. In any case, without an effective appeals process, WTO dispute findings are ineffective. But while international trade rules do not much constrain export denials as a competitive strategy, it is already evident that in practice a denial strategy must meet several tests to be effective. These revealed constraints limit export denials to a narrow class of goods and services.

The requirements are in some respect like those for run-of-the-mill sanctions imposed by one country or a coalition of countries for the explicit purpose of punishing conduct by the target country. Examples are US or UN Security Council sanctions against Iran or US, Western European and allies' sanctions against Russia. There are, however, important differences. Quite apart from the difference in purpose, the bar for success in ordinary sanctions is much lower. It is sufficient if they impede the target country or merely raise the cost of the behaviour to which the sanctioning states object. Sometimes it is sufficient for the initiating country to announce sanctions, however unlikely they are to be effective, simply to be seen to be doing something.

The following are some self-evident requirements for a successful export denial intended to prevent a competitor state from acquiring a capability it does not possess:

- The denied good or service must be highly sought after and valued by the target state:
  - preferably, the product is necessary in several high-value uses.
- The initiating state can impose and sustain a monopoly on the external provision of the good or service:
  - the initiating state does not need to make the denied product, but it must be able to control the supply.
- The targeted product cannot be produced by the target state or substituted by other products.
- The denial must disadvantage the target state (a lot) more than the initiating state.
- Possible reciprocity by the target state should not be greater than or equivalent in impact on the initiating state:
  - nor should a successful denial impose a considerable collateral cost on US allies.

- Preferably, the denial can be rationalised with some plausible justification—for example, national security, which defends the action against agreed global trade rules (WTO) or public expectations:
  - Awkward, for example, to deny lifesaving medicines.

These requirements leave only a small number of goods and services suitable for sustained and successful export denial. It is not nearly enough, for example, for the initiating state or its allies to make the product. The other requirements must also be fulfilled.

An additional consideration is that export denials or conventional sanctions are far more easily imposed on smaller states than bigger states, as the chip denial applied to China demonstrates. The closer a target state is to the capability of the initiating state— for example, in technological capacity, manufacturing or raw materials—the harder it will be to sustain an effective denial.

A successful export denial in such a key technology as advanced chips would likely encourage the more extended use of the weapon in competition between the major powers. A failure would discourage the tactic.

Technological competition and global rules

There are agreed global rules on government subsidies for industry, but none is likely to constrain this subsidised technological competition. Subsidies contingent on export performance are banned under long-established WTO rules. Beyond that prohibition, the rules are dependent on the effect of a subsidy on the welfare of other countries. Under the *Agreement on Subsidies and Countervailing Measures*, countries are entitled to take the counteraction of imposing higher tariffs if a trade partner pays certain kinds of subsidies to its industries (WTO 1994). To be an actionable infringement, the subsidy must be offered by a government body. The subsidy must significantly harm the trade of another country, which is then entitled to impose a duty equivalent to the subsidy. A subsidy available to all industries, even if provided by a public body, is not actionable. For example, a generally available tax concession for research and development spending is not actionable. As opposed to an export denial, it is difficult to fit technology subsidies into any actionable category. As for an export denial, that can be defended on national security grounds—as in the US case.

The only constraints on the trend towards increased industry subsidisation by the major powers, and to the closely linked trend towards non-commercial forms of competition in advanced technology, are commercial reality and budgetary imperatives.

From the point of view of middle powers such as Australia, some tendencies of this vastly expensive technological competition among the great powers are welcome, and some are not. It depends on the form the competition takes. While a problem for taxpayers in Europe, the United States and China, it is no problem for Australia and countries like it if great powers spend a lot on supporting advanced technologies. The rest of the world benefits from the products of the new technologies and may also acquire the technologies for use in their own products.

Yet, the widely expanded scope of product denials imposed by the United States on China poses new issues for third countries such as Australia. The interests of Australia and smaller economies like it lie in encouraging free commerce in technology and in discouraging tendencies to split the global economy into contending and restrictive technology domains. It has its proponents in the national security world, but a sharply divided global economy would be the least productive, the most unstable and the most alien to the freedom of global commerce on which the prosperity of Australia and countries like it has been built.

Furthermore, the competitors are well matched and a vigorous competition is more likely to produce favourable outcomes for the rest of the world than the domination of a technological field by one country. Lavish support for advanced technology also promises more rapid innovation and faster increases in productivity and living standards globally—even if they come at what may be considerable expense to major economies.

But the benefits of enhanced technology competition for the rest of the world can only be realised if the products of the new technologies are freely traded. If they are inaccessible to the rest of the world, the country possessing the monopoly may be able to advance its industries at the expense of other countries' industries.

This is true also if the products of new technologies and the technologies themselves are available only to some countries and not others. If Australia, for example, can acquire advanced products from the United States only at the cost of denying itself advanced products from China, its choices are restricted. It would also be participating in the creation of competing economic blocs that discourage trade and investment between them.

A final remark

The experience thus far of the US chip denial—intended as a lethal strike against China's AI development—is that its success is by no means assured. Indeed, the most likely result evident in 2024 is that the denial will be very inconvenient for China and could prove to be quite expensive as Chinese businesses work around the bans. But the ban has not crippled the development of AI or even specifically of large language models by Chinese businesses and researchers. It could result in the accelerated creation of an ecosphere competing with that of the United States and its allies.

In one of the few segments in which a denial strategy might have worked, it probably will not. The likely lack of success of the denial strategy, together with the lack of evidence of any substantial change in global supply chains or of China's dominance in manufacturing, is a remarkable reflection of the enduring force of a global economy driven by prices and comparative advantage.

References

Asia Society. 2023. *China's Industrial Policy: Roundtable Summary Report*. 24 January. New York: Asia Society Policy Institute in conjunction with Stanford Center on China's Economy and Institutions. asiasociety.org/policy-institute/chinas-industrial-policy.

Australian Embassy. 2017. 'History of Australia–China Science and Innovation.' *Innovation and Science*. [Online]. Beijing: Australian Embassy China. china.embassy.gov.au/bjng/20170119InnovationandScience.html.

Bown, Chad P., and Yilin Wang. 2023. 'Five Years into the Trade War, China Continues Its Slow Decoupling from US Exports.' *Realtime Economics Blog*, 16 March. Washington, DC: Peterson Institute for International Economics. www.piie.com/blogs/realtime-economics/five-years-trade-war-china-continues-its-slow-decoupling-us-exports.

Bradsher, Keith. 2010. 'Amid Tension, China Blocks Vital Exports to Japan.' *New York Times*, 22 September. www.nytimes.com/2010/09/23/business/global/23rare.html#:~:text=Industry%20officials%20said%20that%20mainland,Kong%2C%20Singapore%20and%20other%20destinations.

Bureau of Industry and Security (BIS). 2022. 'Commerce Implements New Export Controls on Advanced Computing and Semiconductor Manufacturing Items to the People's Republic of China (PRC).' News release, 7 October. Washington, DC: Office of Congressional and Public Affairs. www.bis.doc.gov/index.php/documents/about-bis/newsroom/press-releases/3158-2022-10-07-bis-press-release-advanced-computing-and-semiconductor-manufacturing-controls-final/file.

Center for Strategic and International Studies (CSIS). 2020. *How Is China Advancing Its Space Launch Capabilities?* China Power Project, 25 August. Washington, DC: CSIS. chinapower.csis.org/china-space-launch/.

Cheung, Tai Ming. 2022. *Innovate to Dominate: The Rise of the Chinese Techno-Security State*. Ithaca: Cornell University Press. doi.org/10.1515/9781501764356.

Chips and Cheese. 2022. 'Hot Chips 34—Biren's BR100: A Machine Learning GPU from China.' Post by clamchowder, *Chips and Cheese*, 4 October. chipsandcheese.com/2022/10/04/hot-chips-34-birens-br100-a-machine-learning-gpu-from-china/.

Clark, Don, and Ana Swanson. 2023. 'US Pours Money into Chips, but Even Soaring Spending Has Limits.' *New York Times*, 1 January. www.nytimes.com/2023/01/01/technology/us-chip-making-china-invest.html.

Clay, Ian, and Robert Atkinson. 2023. *Wake up, America: China Is Overtaking the United States in Innovation Capacity*. 23 January. Washington, DC: Hamilton Center on Industrial Strategy, Information Technology & Innovation Foundation. itif.org/publications/2023/01/23/wake-up-america-china-is-overtaking-the-united-states-in-innovation-capacity/.

Crowe, David. 2024. '"Make More Things Here": PM Pledges Mammoth Help for New Industries.' *Sydney Morning Herald*, 10 April. make-more-things-here-pm-pledges-mammoth-help-for-new-industries-20240410-p5fin5.html.

Defense Intelligence Agency (DIA). 2019. *China Military Power: Modernizing a Force to Fight and Win*. Washington, DC: Defense Intelligence Agency. www.dia.mil/Portals/110/Images/News/Military_Powers_Publications/China_Military_Power_FINAL_5MB_20190103.pdf.

de Silva, Janet. 1988. 'Embryo Export Raises Fears of Exploitation.' *Australian Financial Review*, 16 March. www.afr.com/companies/embryo-export-raises-fears-of-exploitation-19880316-k2p8f.

DiPippo, Gerard, Ilaria Mazzocco, Scott Kennedy, and Matthew Goodman. 2022. *Red Ink: Estimating Chinese Industrial Policy Spending in Comparative Perspective*. Washington, DC: Center for Strategic and International Studies. www.csis.org/analysis/red-ink-estimating-chinese-industrial-policy-spending-comparative-perspective.

Edwards, John. 2023. 'Chips, Subsidies, Security, and Great Power Competition.' *Analyses*, 28 May. Sydney: Lowy Institute. www.lowyinstitute.org/publications/chips-subsidies-security-great-power-competition.

Evenett, Simon J., and Johannes Fritz. 2021. *Subsidies and Market Access: Towards an Inventory of Corporate Subsidies by China, the European Union and the United States*. The 28th Global Trade Alert Report. London: CEPR Press. www.globaltradealert.org/reports/gta-28-report.

Evenett, Simon, Adam Jakubik, Fernando Martín, and Michele Ruta. 2024. *The Return of Industrial Policy in Data*. IMF Working Papers 24/1, January. Washington, DC: International Monetary Fund. www.imf.org/en/Publications/WP/Issues/2023/12/23/The-Return-of-Industrial-Policy-in-Data-542828. doi.org/10.5089/9798400260964.001.

Financial Times. 2022. 'How the US Chip Export Controls Have Turned the Screws on China.' *Financial Times*, [London], 22 October. www.ft.com/content/bbbdc7dc-0566-4a05-a7b3-27afd82580f3.

Financial Times. 2024. 'China on Cusp of Next-Generation Chip Production despite US Curbs.' *Financial Times*, [London], 6 February. www.ft.com/content/b5e0dba3-689f-4d0e-88f6-673ff4452977.

Fitch, Asa. 2019. 'China Gains on US in Highly Cited AI Research.' *Wall Street Journal*, 13 March. www.wsj.com/articles/china-gains-on-u-s-in-highly-cited-ai-research-11552485601.

Fitch, Asa. 2022. 'Chip Inventories Swell as Consumers Buy Fewer Gadgets.' *Wall Street Journal*, 27 December. www.wsj.com/articles/chip-inventories-swell-as-consumers-buy-fewer-gadgets-11672092605.

Fitch, Asa, and Greg Ip. 2023. 'Chips Are the New Oil and America Is Spending Billions to Safeguard Its Supply.' *Wall Street Journal*, 14 January. www.wsj.com/articles/chips-semiconductors-manufacturing-china-taiwan-11673650917.

Fleming, Sam, and Henry Foy. 2023. 'EU Strikes Back against China's "Divide and Conquer" Tactics.' *Financial Times*, [London], 30 March. www.ft.com/content/f814ff18-4c05-4589-9879-b0800ac3a4ed.

Freund, Caroline, Aaditya Mattoo, Alen Mulabdic, and Michele Ruta. 2023. 'Is US Trade Policy Reshaping Global Supply Chains?' Paper presented to IMF Conference on Geoeconomic Fragmentation, Washington, DC, 25 May. www.imf.org/-/media/Files/News/Seminars/2023/fragmentation-conference/session-5-paper-2-reconfiguration-of-global-value-chains.ashx. doi.org/10.2139/ssrn.4854859.

Gao, Yuan, and Debby Wu. 2024. 'Huawei Tests Brute-Force Method for Making More Advanced Chips.' *Bloomberg*, 22 March. www.bloomberg.com/news/articles/2024-03-22/huawei-tests-brute-force-method-for-making-more-advanced-chips.

Gross, Anna. 2023. 'ASML Chief Calls for "Sensible" Chip Export Controls from Dutch Government.' *Financial Times*, [London], 25 January. www.ft.com/content/efbf11d7-7d2a-4998-82fa-405c66ff127a.

Hass, Ryan. 2021. *Stronger: Adapting America's China Strategy in an Age of Competitive Interdependence*. New Haven: Yale University Press.

Hayashi, Yuka, and Vivian Salama. 2023. 'Japan, Netherlands Agree to Limit Exports of Chip-Making Equipment to China.' *Wall Street Journal*, 28 January. www.wsj.com/articles/japan-netherlands-agree-to-limit-exports-of-chip-making-equipment-to-china-11674952328?mod=djemalertNEWS.

Hille, Kathrin, Christian Davies, Song Jung-a, and Michael Acton. 2024. 'US Missing Pieces of AI Chip Puzzle Despite TSMC's $65bn Bet.' *Financial Times*, [London], 11 April. www.ft.com/content/10eadba6-f58d-4f88-8ac9-b5180550b7fc.

Hua, Sha. 2024. 'U.S. and China Extend Landmark Bilateral Deal, Very Quietly.' *Wall Street Journal*, 14 March: 1. www.wsj.com/world/china/u-s-and-china-extend-landmark-bilateral-deal-very-quietly-79fc2795?page=1.

Hunt, Will, Saif M. Khan, and Dahlia Peterson. 2021. *China's Progress in Semiconductor Manufacturing Equipment: Accelerants and Policy Implications*. CSET Policy Brief, March. Washington, DC: Center for Security and Emerging Technology, Georgetown University. cset.georgetown.edu/publication/chinas-progress-in-semiconductor-manufacturing-equipment. doi.org/10.51593/20190018.

International Monetary Fund (IMF), Organization for Economic Co-operation and Development, World Bank, and World Trade Organization. 2022. *Subsidies, Trade, and International Cooperation*. Joint Report, 2022/001. Washington, DC: International Monetary Fund. www.imf.org/en/Publications/analytical-notes/Issues/2022/04/22/Subsidies-Trade-and-International-Cooperation-516660

Juhász, Réka, Nathan Lane, Emily Oehlsen, and Verónica Pérez. 2022. 'The Who, What, When, and How of Industrial Policy: A Text-Based Approach.' *SocArXiv*, 25 August. steg.cepr.org/sites/default/files/2023-01/WP050%20JuhászLaneOehlsenPérez%20TheWhoWhatWhenAndHowOfIndustrialPolicy.pdf.

Kannan, Vishnu, and Mubashar Rizvi. 2022. 'What's in the Commerce Department's Recent Export Controls on Technology Bound for China?' *Lawfare Blog*, 23 November. Washington, DC: The Lawfare Institute. www.lawfareblog.com/whats-commerce-departments-recent-export-controls-technology-bound-china.

Kim, Tae. 2022. 'Nvidia CEO Says "Moore's Law Is Dead".' *Barron's*, [New York], 21 September. www.barrons.com/articles/nvidia-graphic-card-prices-moores-law-51663778838.

Koc, Cagan. 2023. 'ASML Says Chip Controls Will Push China to Create Own Technology.' *Bloomberg*, 26 January. www.bloomberg.com/news/articles/2023-01-25/asml-says-chip-controls-will-push-china-to-create-own-technology#xj4y7vzkg.

Langer, Marie-Astrid. 2023. 'Chip War between Washington and Beijing: "The US Is Freezing the State of AI in the Year 2022 for China."' *Neue Zürcher Zeitung*, [Zürich], 5 January. www.google.com/url?sa=t&source=web&rct=j&opi=89978449&url=https://www.nzz.ch/english/the-us-is-fighting-chinas-advances-in-ai-with-chip-export-bans-ld.1719557&ved=2ahUKEwi5_Z7l6LOFAxVXXWwGHXhADRsQFnoECBwQAQ&usg=AOvVaw3OpFUZWP5-NxQLhZDjaRwO.

Lin, Liza. 2024. 'China Tells Telecom Carriers to Phase Out Foreign Chips in Blow to Intel, AMD.' *Wall Street Journal*, [Updated 12 April]. www.wsj.com/tech/china-telecom-intel-amd-chips-99ae99a9?mod=hp_lista_pos3.

MacroPolo. 2024. *The Global AI Talent Tracker 2.0*. [Online]. Chicago: MacroPolo, Paulson Institute. macropolo.org/digital-projects/the-global-ai-talent-tracker/.

Mann, Toby. 2022. 'How the US Is Trying to Maintain Dominance of the Advanced Semiconductor Industry and Limit China's Ability to Develop Its Own.' *ABC News*, 25 September. www.abc.net.au/news/2022-09-25/us-microchip-ban-limit-china-technical-advances-semiconductor/101461042.

Manuel, Rojoef. 2022. 'Turkey Develops Tech Reducing Small Drones' Reliance on GPS.' *The Defense Post*, [Arlington, VA], 13 October. www.thedefensepost.com/2022/10/13/turkey-drones-gps-navigation/.

Miller, Chris. 2022. *Chip War: The Fight for the World's Most Critical Technology*. New York: Scribner.

Nahm, Jonas. 2023. 'How Solar Developed from the Bottom up in China.' *IGCC Blog*, 14 March. La Jolla, CA: University of California Institute on Global Conflict and Cooperation. ucigcc.org/blog/how-solar-developed-from-the-bottom-up-in-china/.

Naughton, Barry. 2021. *The Rise of China's Industrial Policy: 1978 to 2020*. Mexico City: Universidad Nacional Autónoma de México. ucigcc.org/publication/the-rise-of-chinas-industrial-policy-1978-to-2020/.

Organisation for Economic Co-operation and Development (OECD). 2019a. *Measuring Distortions in International Markets: The Aluminium Value Chain*. OECD Trade Policy Papers, No. 218. Paris: OECD Publishing. doi.org/10.1787/c82911ab-en.

Organisation for Economic Co-operation and Development (OECD). 2019b. *Measuring Distortions in International Markets: The Semiconductor Value Chain*. OECD Trade Policy Papers, No. 234. Paris: OECD Publishing. doi.org/10.1787/8fe4491d-en.

Organisation for Economic Co-operation and Development (OECD). 2024. 'Gross Domestic Spending on R&D, Total, % of GDP, 2000–2022.' *OECD iLibrary*. [Online]. Paris: OECD. www.oecd.org/en/data/indicators/gross-domestic-spending-on-r-d.html.

Pan, Che. 2022a. 'China's Top Chip Maker SMIC May Have Achieved Tech Breakthrough, Experts Say.' *South China Morning Post*, [Hong Kong], 26 July. www.scmp.com/tech/big-tech/article/3186672/chinas-top-chip-maker-smic-may-have-achieved-tech-breakthrough?module=inline&pgtype=article.

Pan, Che. 2022b. 'China's Top Chip Maker SMIC Achieves 7-nm Tech Breakthrough on Par with Intel, TSMC and Samsung, Analysts Say.' *South China Morning Post*, [Hong Kong], 29 August. www.scmp.com/tech/big-tech/article/3190590/chinas-top-chip-maker-smic-achieves-7-nm-tech-breakthrough-par-intel.

Pan, Che. 2023. 'Tech War: Chinese Chat GPT Ambitions Threatened by Lack of Advanced AI Chips Like Nvidia A100 GPU, Experts Say.' *South China Morning Post*, [Hong Kong], 2 March. www.scmp.com/tech/tech-war/article/3212128/tech-war-chinese-chatgpt-ambitions-threatened-lack-advanced-ai-chips-nvidia-a100-gpu-experts-say.

Pooley, Ethan, and James Laurenceson. 2023. *Australian Government Support for Research Collaboration with the PRC*. Working Paper, 17 July. Sydney: Australia–China Relations Institute, University of Technology Sydney. www.uts.edu.au/acri/research-and-opinion/analyses/australian-government-support-research-collaboration-prc.

Posen, Adam. 2023. 'America's Zero-Sum Economics Doesn't Add up.' *Foreign Policy*, [Washington, DC], 24 March. foreignpolicy.com/2023/03/24/economy-trade-united-states-china-industry-manufacturing-supply-chains-biden/.

Productivity Commission (PC). 2022. *Trade and Assistance Review 2020–21*. Canberra: Australian Government. www.pc.gov.au/research/ongoing/trade-assistance/2020-21/trade-assistance-review-2020-21.pdf.

Rajah, Roland, and Alyssa Leng. 2022. 'Revising down the Rise of China.' *Analyses*, 14 March. Sydney: Lowy Institute. www.lowyinstitute.org/publications/revising-down-rise-china.

Richter, Felix. 2023. 'China Leads Growth of Global Industrial Robot Stock.' *Statista*, 27 November. www.statista.com/chart/31337/new-installations-of-industrial-robots-by-country/.

Scharre, Paul. 2023. *Four Battlegrounds: Power in the Age of Artificial Intelligence*. New York: W.W. Norton & Company.

Schneider, Jordan, and Irene Zhang. 2023. 'China + AI = Military Advantage? Plus: DC Meetup!' *ChinaTalk*, 20 January. open.substack.com/pub/chinatalk/p/china-ai-military-advantage-plus?utm_campaign=post&utm_medium=web.

Semiconductor Industry Association. 2022. *Factbook*. Washington, DC: SIA. www.semiconductors.org/wp-content/uploads/2022/05/SIA-2022-Factbook_May-2022.pdf.

Sherman, Natalie, and Jonathan Josephs. 2022. 'WTO Says Trump's US Steel Tariffs Broke Global Trade Rules.' *BBC News*, 10 December. www.bbc.com/news/business-63920063.

Shilov, Anton. 2022. 'SMIC Mass Produces 14nm Nodes, Advances to 5nm, 7nm.' *Tom's Hardware*, [New York], 16 September. www.tomshardware.com/news/smic-mass-produces-14nm-nodes-advances-to-5nm-7nm.

Slotta, Daniel. 2023. 'Import Value of Machines for Manufacturing Semiconductors in China from 2012 to 2021 (in Million US Dollars).' *Statista*, 21 September. www.statista.com/statistics/1345297/china-import-value-of-semiconductor-equipment/#:~:text=Value%20of%20imported%20semiconductor%20machines%20in%20China%202012%2D2021&text=In%202021%2C%20China%20imported%20semiconductor,compared%20to%20the%20previous%20years.

Stanford Institute for Human-Centered Artificial Intelligence (Stanford HAI). 2024. *Artificial Intelligence Index Report 2024*. Stanford, CA: Stanford HAI. aiindex.stanford.edu/report/.

Sullivan, Jake. 2022. 'Remarks by National Security Advisor Jake Sullivan at the Special Competitive Studies Project Global Emerging Technologies Summit.' Speech, 16 September. Washington, DC: The White House. www.whitehouse.gov/briefing-room/speeches-remarks/2022/09/16/remarks-by-national-security-advisor-jake-sullivan-at-the-special-competitive-studies-project-global-emerging-technologies-summit/.

Swanson, Ana. 2022. 'The Biden Administration is Weighing Further Controls on Chinese Technology.' *New York Times*, 27 October. www.nytimes.com/2022/10/27/business/the-biden-administration-is-weighing-further-controls-on-chinese-technology.html.

Takahashi, Dean. 2021. 'Jensen Huang Gets Chip Industry's Highest Honor 28 Years after Founding Nvidia.' *Venture Beat*, 18 November. venturebeat.com/games/jensen-huang-gets-chip-industrys-highest-honor-38-years-after-founding-nvidia/.

Ting-Fang, Cheng. 2023. 'TSMC Reaffirms "Commitment to Taiwan" despite US Chip Push.' *Financial Times*, [London], 4 January. www.ft.com/content/6621d22b-b353-4504-a857-425e9fc8a92d.

Triolo, Paul. 2024. 'A New Era for the Chinese Semiconductor Industry: Beijing Responds to Export Controls.' *American Affairs* VIII, no. 1 (Spring). www.google.com/url?sa=t&source=web&rct=j&opi=89978449&url=https://americanaffairsjournal.org/2024/02/a-new-era-for-the-chinese-semiconductor-industry-beijing-responds-to-export-controls/&ved=2ahUKEwjxyPOc57OFAxUG7jgGHQIqD60QFnoECA8QAQ&usg=AOvVaw1W81bn7kc_9GKzCa4_BSBy.

Wall Street Journal (WSJ). 2023. 'Has Nvidia's A100 Chip Met Its Match with Biren's BR100 Processor?' *Wall Street Journal*, [*YouTube*], 12 January. www.youtube.com/watch?v=gPpAL_pG_Wc.

Wang, Che-Jen. 2022. 'China's Semiconductor Breakthrough.' *The Diplomat*, 20 August. thediplomat.com/2022/08/chinas-semiconductor-breakthrough/.

World Bank. 2022a. 'Exports of Goods and Services (% of GDP).' *Data*. Washington, DC: World Bank Group. data.worldbank.org/indicator/NE.EXP.GNFS.ZS.

World Bank. 2022b. 'Gross Fixed Capital Formation (Current US$)—China, United States, 1960–2021.' *Data*. Washington, DC: World Bank Group. data.worldbank.org/indicator/NE.GDI.FTOT.CD?locations=CN-US.

World Bank. 2022c. 'Manufacturing, Value Added (Current US$)—China, United States, 1971–2021.' *Data*. Washington, DC: World Bank Group. data.worldbank.org/indicator/NV.IND.MANF.CD?locations=CN-US.

World Bank. 2022d. 'Manufacturing, Value Added (Current US$)—China, World, United States.' *Data*. Washington, DC: World Bank Group. data.worldbank.org/indicator/NV.IND.MANF.CD?locations=CN-1W-US.

World Trade Organization (WTO). 1994. *Agreement on Subsidies and Countervailing Measures ('SCM Agreement')*. Washington, DC: WTO. www.wto.org/english/tratop_e/scm_e/subs_e.htm.

World Trade Organization (WTO). 2023. *Global Trade Outlook and Statistics. Update: October 2023*. Washington, DC: WTO. www.wto.org/english/res_e/booksp_e/gtos_updt_oct23_e.pdf.

Ye, Josh. 2024. 'China Approves over 40 AI Models for Public Use in Past Six Months.' *Reuters*, 29 January. www.reuters.com/technology/china-approves-over-40-ai-models-public-use-past-six-months-2024-01-29/.

Zhang, Lilian, and Ann Cao. 2023. 'China's ChatGPT Ambitions Must Overcome US Trade Restrictions on Advanced AI Chips, Experts Say.' *South China Morning Post*, [Hong Kong], 27 February. www.scmp.com/tech/tech-trends/article/3211684/chinas-chatgpt-ambitions-must-overcome-us-trade-restrictions-advanced-ai-chips-experts-say.

Zwetsloot, Remco, Jack Corrigan, Emily Weinstein, Dahlia Peterson, Diana Gehlhaus, and Ryan Fedasiuk. 2021. *China Is Fast Outpacing US STEM PhD Growth*. CSET Data Brief, August. Washington, DC: Center for Security and Emerging Technology, Georgetown University. cset.georgetown.edu/publication/china-is-fast-outpacing-u-s-stem-phd-growth/. doi.org/10.51593/20210018.

11

A policy analysis of the Belt and Road Initiative

Kunling Zhang[1]

Introduction

The year 2023 marked the tenth anniversary of China's Belt and Road Initiative (BRI). Aiming to transform and upgrade globalisation, promote global connectivity and realise shared prosperity for all countries, the BRI is considered a new model of international development cooperation (Chen et al. 2019; Zhang 2023). In the context of deglobalisation, the BRI has unique and vital significance for the economic development of China and the world at large. While the BRI has often been criticised by the West for its impacts on geopolitics, environmental protection, corruption, debt and so on, it has achieved fruitful outcomes over the past 10 years. More than 150 countries have signed BRI cooperation agreements; from 2013 to 2022, the total volume of imports and exports between China and Belt and Road countries (BRCs)[2] totalled US$19.1 trillion, with an average annual growth rate of 6.4 per cent; two-way investment between BRCs and China exceeded US$380 billion, of which China's outward direct investment exceeded US$240 billion; and the total value of newly signed contracts and the total turnover of China's contracted projects in BRCs have reached US$2 trillion and US$1.3 trillion, respectively (SCIO 2023).

Scholars have devoted considerable effort to understanding the policy effects of the BRI, especially on BRCs. Research examining the economic effects of the initiative has mostly shown positive results regarding trade gains, capital flows, poverty reduction and economic development (for example, de Soyres et al. 2019; Zhang 2023). Politically, the BRI is often accused of neglecting human rights and labour protections (Faiz 2019),

1   This research was funded by the Project of Philosophy and Social Sciences Planning of Guangdong (Grant No. GD23YYJ01); and the Major Project of the National Social Science Foundation of China (Grant No. 19VDL012).
2   BRCs are those that have signed a BRI cooperation agreement with China.

supporting authoritarian regimes (Sutherland et al. 2020), undermining Western efforts to promote good governance and creating corruption (Balding 2018). Therefore, there have been increasing concerns about and criticisms of the possibility of exporting the 'Chinese model' of development through the BRI (Fukuyama 2016; McGregor 2022), though most of those comments are more journalistic than academic in nature.

To improve international understanding of the BRI, in addition to the study of its policy effects, analysis of BRI policy itself is important, which is understudied in the current literature. Therefore, through a content analysis of key BRI policy papers and speeches, this chapter attempts to uncover the initiative's objectives, implementation instruments and supporting conditions according to the official discourse.

Analytical framework and policy text collection

The analysis of this structure must start from the content of BRI policy documents. This chapter mainly uses a qualitative policy analysis method—that is, content analysis. There are four steps of analysis: 1) construct an analytical framework; 2) systematically collect the relevant BRI policy documents; 3) identify the research scope of the policy documents to be analysed; and 4) use the constructed framework to analyse the policy texts within the research scope.

Three-dimensional policy analysis framework

Drawing on the policy analysis framework of Rothwell (1985), this chapter develops a three-dimensional framework of objective–instrument–condition (see Figure 11.1). *Policy objectives* are the desired outcomes of policy formulation and the goal of policy implementation. *Policy instruments* are the instruments and approaches used to achieve policy objectives. The extent to which the implementation of policy instruments can achieve the desired outcome depends largely on *policy conditions* to support and guarantee the implementation of policy instruments.

Scope of analysis

The system to be analysed here is the structure of China's major national policy documents on the BRI. This system is an organic combination of various BRI policies linked in a certain logical form. This requires us to analyse the content of the BRI policy documents and their internal logical connections and the kind of structure they embody. In addition, as Chinese President Xi Jinping stated in his speech at a 2016 symposium promoting the BRI, the initiative is the overarching plan for China's opening and international cooperation (SCIO 2023; Xi 2024). Therefore, the BRI policy system and China's opening policies are interrelated and both should be considered during analysis. However, since policies related to China's opening are relatively complex, the analysis here focuses on BRI policies, supplemented by policies on opening.

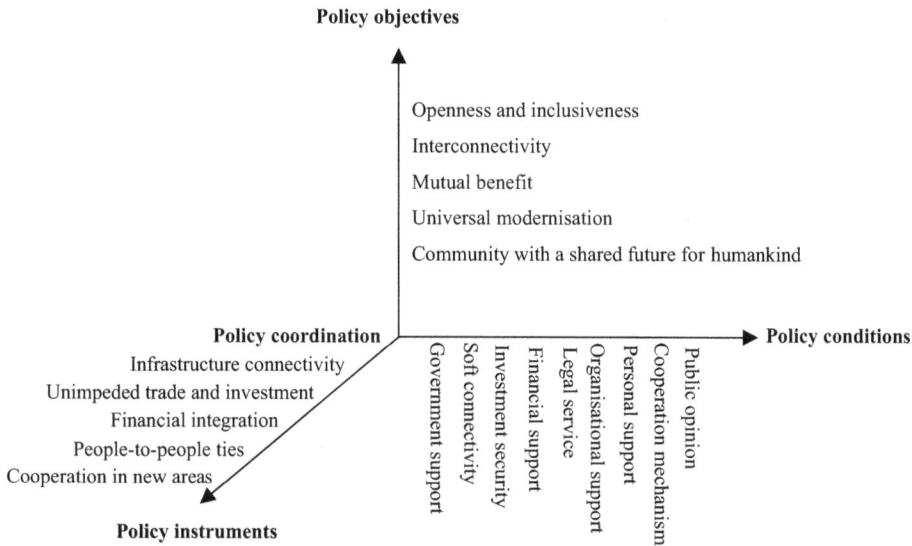

Figure 11.1 Analytical framework of the BRI policy system
Source: Author's own.

Policy document collection and descriptive statistics

The research samples in this chapter are BRI policies promulgated by state organs directly under the State Council and the Central Committee of the Communist Party of China from 2013 to 2023. The data come from the BRI Portal,[3] the Peking University law database (pkulaw.com)[4] and other official Chinese government websites. Among these documents, government reports that include only the progress of the BRI's development are excluded as they do not provide essential policy elements.[5] Important speeches by President Xi are included, particularly those at three symposiums on promoting the BRI and three Belt and Road Forums for International Cooperation. These texts, while not policy documents, are crucial to our understanding of the BRI policy system.

The data collection resulted in a corpus of 48 BRI policy documents: nine overarching policy texts (see Table 11.1) and 39 texts in specific fields. Figure 11.2 plots the time distribution of the BRI policy documents. It shows that the three years from 2015 to 2017 were a stage of rapid development of BRI policy. In 2017, 13 policy papers were issued. The rate has since levelled off.

3　The Belt and Road Portal is China's official BRI website. It is hosted by the State Information Centre under the guidance of the Office of the Leading Group for Promoting the Belt and Road Initiative and the NDRC: eng.yidaiyilu. gov.cn.

4　pkulaw.com is a well-known database of Chinese laws and regulations, hosted by Peking University Law School. The database contains Chinese laws and regulations, legal literature, judicial cases and other content, and is one of the important tools commonly used by legal practitioners and scholars.

5　Two notable documents include 'Building the Belt and Road Initiative: Concept, Practice and China's Contribution', issued by the Office of the Leading Group for Promoting the Belt and Road Initiative on 10 May 2017, and 'The Belt and Road Initiative: A Key Pillar of the Global Community of Shared Future' issued by the State Council Information Office on 10 October 2023 (SCIO 2023).

Table 11.1 Overarching policy documents on the BRI

Year	Title	Issuing entity/remarks
2015	'Vision and Actions on Jointly Building the Silk Road Economic Belt and the 21st-Century Maritime Silk Road'	National Development and Reform Commission, Ministry of Foreign Affairs, Ministry of Commerce (NDRC et al. 2015)
2016	'Let the BRI Benefit the People of All Countries along the Belt and Road'	Xi Jinping's speech at the first symposium on promoting the BRI (Xi 2024)
2017	'Work Together to Build the Belt and Road'	Xi Jinping's keynote speech at the first Belt and Road Forum for International Cooperation (Xi 2024)
2018	'Promote the BRI to be In-Depth and Practical to Benefit the People'	Xi Jinping's speech at the second symposium on promoting the BRI (Xi 2024)
2019	'Work Together to Create a Bright Future for the BRI'	Xi Jinping's keynote speech at the second Belt and Road Forum for International Cooperation (Xi 2024)
2019	'The Belt and Road Initiative: Progress, Contributions and Prospects'	Office of the Leading Group for Promoting the Belt and Road Initiative (2019)
2021	'Continue Promoting the High-Quality Development of the BRI'	Xi Jinping's speech at the third symposium on promoting the BRI (Xi 2024)
2023	'Vision and Actions to Unswervingly Promote Deepening and Solidifying the High-Quality Development of the BRI: The Development Prospects of the BRI in the Next Decade'	Office of the Leading Group for Promoting the Belt and Road Initiative (2023)
2023	'Build a World of Openness, Inclusiveness, Interconnection and Common Development'	Xi Jinping's keynote speech at the third Belt and Road Forum for International Cooperation (Xi 2024)

Source: Author's own summary.

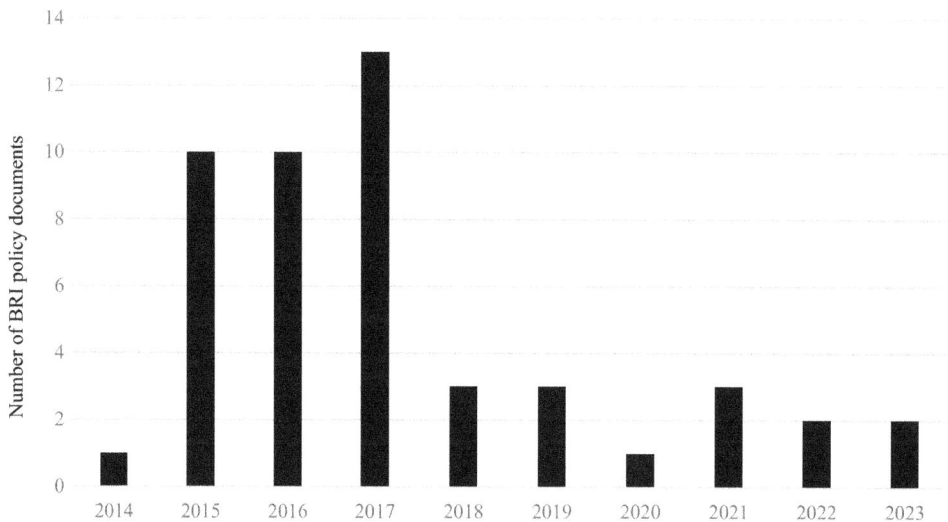

Figure 11.2 Distribution of BRI policy documents
Source: Author's own.

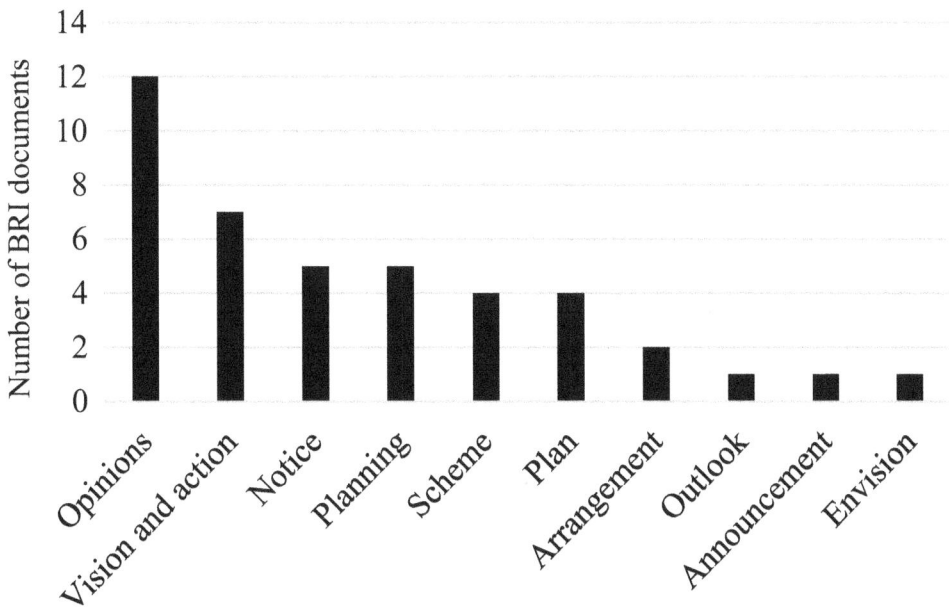

Figure 11.3 Promulgation form of the BRI policy documents
Source: Author's own.

The language adopted by Chinese policymakers when promulgating public policies is strictly arranged according to relevant laws and regulations and has certain policy implications. The language of BRI policy is most obvious in the form of 'opinions', 'visions and actions', 'notices', 'planning' and so on (see Figure 11.3). Among the 42 policy documents (excluding the six speeches by President Xi), 'opinions' dominate, with 12 such documents, followed by 'visions and actions'. It is worth noting that these are initiating documents and their enforceability is relatively weak. 'Notices' (five items), 'planning' (five items), 'plans' (four items), 'schemes' (four items), 'arrangements' (two items), 'announcement' (one item) and other genres are relatively specific, focusing on the operability and implementation of policies, and the efficacy is relatively high. Most BRI policy texts are guidance, initiative and planning documents, regulations, methods and rules. Specific rules to ensure the implementation of policies are, however, relatively lacking, indicating that the policy system is somewhat complete, but the policy supporting system must still be improved.

The issues relating to the BRI are complex and diverse and many official entities are involved in issuing policy documents. For example, the 'Opinions on Implementing the Belt and Road Initiative and Accelerating the Facilitation of International Road Transport' in 2016 were jointly issued by eight official entities—the most for any BRI policy document so far. As can be seen from Table 11.2, there are 30 policymaking entities in total, and seven departments have issued three or more BRI-related policies. Among them, the National Development and Reform Commission (NDRC) issued the largest number (12), all of which were jointly issued, followed by the Office of the

Leading Group for Promoting the Belt and Road Initiative,[6] the Ministry of Commerce, the Ministry of Foreign Affairs, the General Administration of Quality Supervision, Inspection and Quarantine, the Ministry of Ecology and Environment, the Supreme People's Court, the Ministry of Culture and Tourism and so on. These are the main institutions developing the BRI policy system.

Table 11.2 Entities issuing BRI policy documents

Entities	No. of individual promulgations	No. of joint promulgations	Total
National Development and Reform Commission	0	12	12
Office of the Leading Group for Promoting the Belt and Road Initiative	6	1	7
Ministry of Commerce	0	7	7
Ministry of Foreign Affairs	0	6	6
General Administration of Quality Supervision, Inspection and Quarantine	3	1	4
Ministry of Ecology and Environment	1	2	3
Supreme People's Court	3	0	3
Ministry of Culture and Tourism	2	1	3
Ministry of Industry and Information Technology	1	1	2
State Administration of Taxation	2	0	2
National Administration of Traditional Chinese Medicine	0	2	2
General Administration of Customs	1	1	2
Government of the Macau Special Administrative Region	0	1	1
State Administration of Science, Technology and Industry for National Defence	0	1	1
State Oceanic Administration[a]	0	1	1
China Development Bank	0	1	1
National Energy Administration	0	1	1
General Administration of Sport of China	0	1	1
General Office of National Health and Family Planning Commission[b]	1	0	1
State Post Bureau	1	0	1
Ministry of Education	1	0	1
Ministry of Science and Technology	0	1	1
Ministry of Agriculture and Rural Affairs	0	1	1

---

6   The Office of the Leading Group for Promoting the Belt and Road Initiative is under the NDRC, but in view of its importance, we distinguish them as different entities.

Entities	No. of individual promulgations	No. of joint promulgations	Total
China Insurance Regulatory Commission[c]	1	0	1
China Council for the Promotion of International Trade	0	1	1
National Certification and Accreditation Administration	1	0	1
Ministry of Public Security	0	1	1
Ministry of Finance	0	1	1
Supreme People's Procuratorate	1	0	1

[a] Now merged with the Ministry of Natural Resources.
[b] In 2018, the National Health Commission was established and the National Health and Family Planning Commission was disbanded.
[c] Currently under the National Financial Regulatory Administration.
Source: Author's own summary.

Content analysis of the BRI policy system

The analysis of the nine overarching policy documents mentioned above is the key to understanding the BRI policy system, on which the remaining 39 policy documents were formulated. Therefore, the policy analysis in this chapter is mainly based on the nine overarching policy documents, supplemented by the other 39 documents. This chapter also pays special attention to two documents, 'Vision and Actions on Jointly Building the Silk Road Economic Belt and the 21st Century Maritime Silk Road', jointly issued by the NDRC, the Ministry of Foreign Affairs and the Ministry of Commerce in March 2015 (hereinafter, 'Vision and Actions 2015') and 'Vision and Actions to Unswervingly Promote Deepening and Solidifying the High-Quality Development of the BRI: The Development Prospects of the BRI in the Next Decade', issued by the Office of the Leading Group for Promoting the Belt and Road Initiative in November 2023 (hereinafter, 'Vision and Actions 2023'). The former was the first official white paper on the BRI issued by the Chinese Government. It interprets the principles, framework, cooperation priorities and mechanisms and systematically proposes the policy direction and tasks of the BRI. The latter covers the improvements and developments of the BRI policy system over the past 10 years and is the overarching guide for promoting high-quality development of the initiative in the next 10 years. Analysis of these two documents, supplemented by other relevant policy content, will reveal the development of and changes to the BRI policy system to enhance our understanding of it. According to the previously established analysis framework of 'policy objectives, policy instruments and policy conditions', these three dimensions of the two policy documents were identified and analysed (as shown in Figures 11.4 and 11.5).

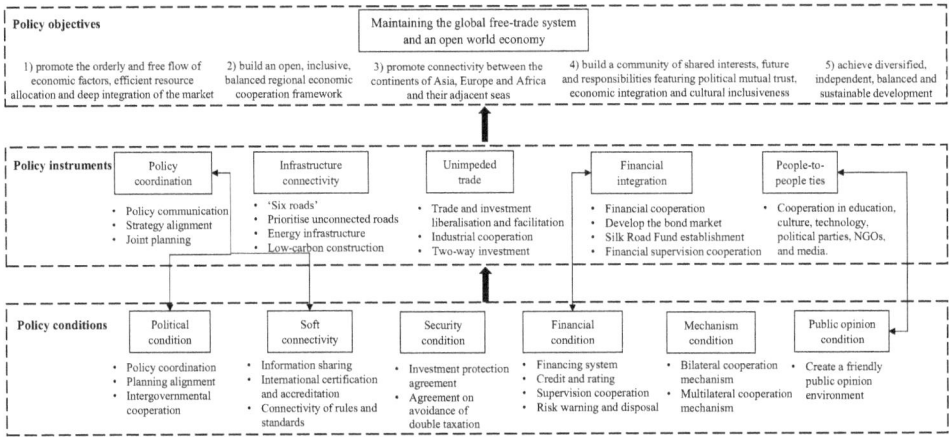

Figure 11.4 The framework of the BRI policy system in Vision and Actions 2015
Source: NDRC et al. (2015).

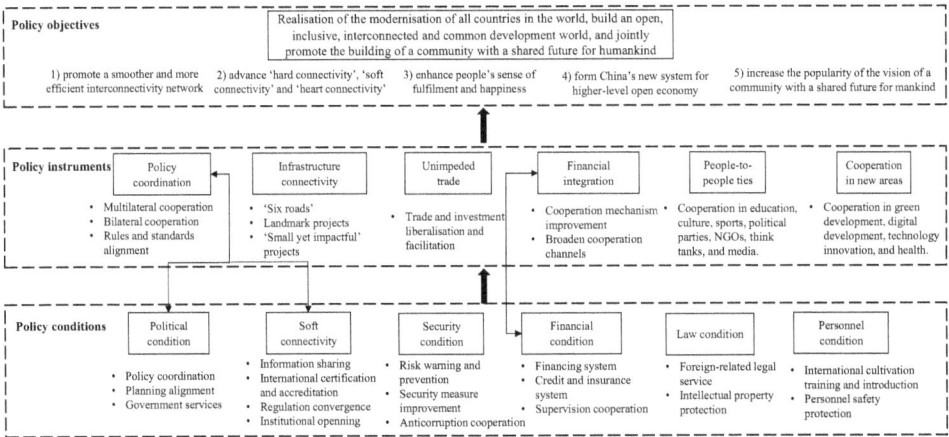

Figure 11.5 The framework of the BRI policy system in Vision and Actions 2023
Source: Office of the Leading Group for Promoting the Belt and Road Initiative (2023).

Policy objectives

In the Vision and Actions 2015, the overall policy objective of the BRI is set as 'maintaining the global free-trade system and an open world economy'. The document details at least five aspects: 1) promoting the orderly and free flow of economic factors, efficient resource allocation and deep market integration; 2) jointly building an open, inclusive and balanced regional economic cooperation framework; 3) promoting connectivity between Asia, Europe and Africa and their adjacent seas; 4) building a community of shared interests, a shared future and shared responsibilities featuring political trust, economic integration and cultural inclusiveness; and 5) achieving diversified, independent, balanced and sustainable development of countries along the Belt and Road. According to these objectives, the first goal of the BRI involves the 'world economy', indicating an economic rather than political focus. That means using only geopolitical thinking to understand the BRI could be misleading. Second, the BRI aims to 'maintain' a free and open global economic system rather than 'establish' a new one, indicating that the BRI is aiming to maintain the existing international economic system and framework, rather than breaking it and rebuilding. In addition, these objectives tend to be externally oriented—that is, the policy goals are internationally focused on economic ties between China and other countries, and there are fewer internally oriented goals focusing on domestic development.

Compared with Vision and Actions 2015, the policy objectives in Vision and Actions 2023 are more comprehensive and proactive and its overall goal is to 'promote realisation of the modernisation of all countries in the world, build an open, inclusive, interconnected and common development world, and jointly promote the building of a community with a shared future for humankind' (Office of the Leading Group for Promoting the Belt and Road Initiative 2023). It sets five goals: 1) promote a smoother and more efficient interconnected network and improve the systematic and tridimensional spatial framework of the 'six corridors, six roads and multiple countries and ports';[7] 2) promote enhanced practical cooperation, advance 'hard connectivity', 'soft connectivity' and 'heart connectivity'[8] and make new breakthroughs in building a healthy, green, digital and innovative Silk Road; 3) enhance a sense of fulfilment and happiness in the peoples of the BRCs, enrich the content and forms of people-to-people communication and cultural exchanges and continue to consolidate the foundation of public support and public opinion; 4) form China's new system for a higher-level open economy, steadily expand institutional opening based on rules, regulations, management and standards, continuously optimising the pattern of regional opening and injecting vitality into international cooperation; and 5) increase the popularity of the vision of a community with a shared future for humankind, demonstrating the international appeal of the BRI and making greater contributions to the building of an open, inclusive, clean and beautiful world that enjoys lasting peace, universal security and common prosperity.

The policy objectives in Vision and Actions 2023 are, first, more development oriented and therefore more comprehensive than the economically oriented statements in Vision and Actions 2015. Vision and Actions 2023 also contains a new proposition of 'the modernisation of all countries in the world'. Second, the use of phrases such as 'promote the realisation of' and 'promote the building of' show a more proactive attitude. Third, what is even more noteworthy is that four of the five major goals are externally oriented, while the fourth includes internally oriented content. This is in line with the instruction that 'BRI development should better service the building of

---

7   The 'six corridors' refer to six international economic cooperation corridors: the New Eurasian Land Bridge, the China–Mongolia–Russia Economic Corridor, China–Central Asia–West Asia Economic Corridor, China–Indochina Peninsula Economic Corridor, China–Pakistan Economic Corridor and Bangladesh–China–India–Myanmar Economic Corridor. The 'six roads' are railways, highways, shipping, aviation, pipelines and the information highway. 'Multiple countries' refer to a group of early BRI cooperation countries. 'Multiple ports' refer to several cooperative ports that ensure the safety and smooth running of major maritime transport routes.

8   'Hard connectivity', 'soft connectivity' and 'heart connectivity' refers to the connectivity of infrastructure, rules and standards, and people-to-people ties, respectively.

a new development paradigm'[9] emphasised by President Xi at the third symposium on promoting the BRI (Xi 2024). The aim of building a new system for a higher-level open economy is to help establish a 'dual circulation' development pattern through deeper and wider opening to the outside world and promote high-quality economic development and new opportunities for international cooperation and competition. This new system can also promote the high-quality development of the BRI.

Policy instruments

Since the BRI was proposed in 2013, its policy instruments have been clarified—namely, policy coordination, infrastructure connectivity, unimpeded trade, financial integration and people-to-people ties (referred to as the 'five connectivities'). The 'five connectivities' were first explained in detail in Vision and Actions 2015. Vision and Actions 2023 uses the same 'five connectivities' framework, but with some new developments. Vision and Actions 2023 contains a new policy instrument, 'cooperation in new fields', which includes content on international cooperation in green and digital development, technological innovation, health and other fields. Although the policy instrument is new, this content was covered in Vision and Actions 2015. For example, in terms of infrastructure connectivity, Vision and Actions 2015 emphasised the strengthening of 'green and low-carbon infrastructure construction and operation management, and taking into full account the impact on climate change'. In terms of unimpeded trade, it stressed 'the concept of an ecological civilisation in investment and trade, strengthening cooperation in fields of ecological environment, biodiversity and climate change response, and jointly building a green Silk Road'. For people-to-people ties, it stressed the strengthening of 'scientific and technological cooperation', joint construction of laboratories and centres for research, international technology transfers and maritime cooperation, promoting 'exchanges of scientific and technological personnel', cooperation in 'major scientific and technological research' and jointly enhancing 'scientific and technological innovation capabilities' (NDRC et al. 2015). However, given the continuous expansion of cooperation in green development, digitalisation, innovation, health and other fields under the BRI, listing 'cooperation in new fields' as a new policy instrument is in line with global developments.

It is worth mentioning that a progress report, *The Belt and Road Initiative: Progress, Contributions and Prospects*, issued by the Office of the Leading Group for Promoting the Belt and Road Initiative in 2019, lists 'industrial cooperation' in a single line alongside the 'five connectivities', and includes content on China's outward direct investment, international cooperation on production capacity, third-party market cooperation and building international cooperation parks. However, in Vision and Actions 2023, 'industrial cooperation' is not listed as a policy instrument and international cooperation on production capacity and international cooperation park construction are downplayed.

---

9   The new development paradigm refers to a 'dual circulation' development pattern in which the domestic economic cycle plays a leading role while the international economic cycle remains its extension and supplement.

In Vision and Actions 2023, the content of the 'five connectivities' has been developed. For example, in the infrastructure connectivity section, emphasis is placed on the promotion of landmark and 'small-scale yet impactful' projects.[10] It is required to

> coordinate the construction of a number of landmark projects, strengthen the connection with the national development strategy and market demand in BRCs, fully consider the interests and concerns of the government, locality and people of BRCs ... continuously 'polish' the 'golden signboard' of 'small-scale yet impactful' projects, focusing on key areas that are 'visible and tangible' for the people, and can easily improve people's sense of gain and happiness, including infrastructure construction, health, green ecology, agricultural cooperation, water conservancy, forest and grassland development, poverty alleviation and humanitarianism, education and training, etc., with the orientation of consolidating people's hearts, being 'down-to-earth', low-cost, and sustainable, deeply promote the construction of 'small-scale yet impactful' projects, and strive to create a number of new representative projects with demonstration effects. (Office of the Leading Group for Promoting the Belt and Road Initiative 2023)

This also reflects President Xi's keynote speech at the third Belt and Road Forum for International Cooperation, in which he said that 'China will coordinate the promotion of landmark projects and "small-scale yet impactful" projects related to people's livelihoods' (Xi 2024).

With the changes in the international development and cooperation situation, the policy instruments of the BRI have been adjusted, but the 'five connectivities' framework has remained relatively stable, although it has been developed. This shows that, to some extent, the 'five connectivities' framework has proven effective in practice.

Policy conditions

In some respects, policy instruments and conditions are interrelated and overlap; the distinction between the two is sometimes not clearcut. For example, the Vision and Actions for 2015 and 2023 both emphasise that 'enhancing policy coordination is an important guarantee for implementing the BRI'. This shows that policy coordination is not only a policy instrument, but also can provide conducive conditions for the BRI. Smooth policy coordination can provide a good political environment and better promote the connectivity of rules and standards between China and BRCs. The policy instrument of financial integration has the same properties—providing the right financial conditions for the BRI. The same is true of the policy instrument of people-to-people ties, which can contribute to positive public opinion and create a friendly environment for international cooperation under the BRI.

---

10 Notably emphasised in Xi Jinping's keynote speech at the third Belt and Road Forum for International Cooperation (Xi 2024).

By looking at both the 2015 and the 2023 Vision and Actions, we can see that the BRI policy conditions include politics, 'soft connectivity', investment security, finance, law, cooperation mechanisms, organisation and personnel. As high-quality development of the BRI enters a new stage, the establishment and improvement of the supporting policy system have become increasingly important. While Vision and Actions 2023 improves and develops the 2015 document, neither is sufficient for analysing the policy conditions of the BRI. Therefore, the analysis of policy conditions here also draws on seven other policy documents.

Political conditions

From an international cooperation perspective, political conditions involve strengthening international policy coordination and intergovernmental cooperation and aligning development strategies among the BRCs. At the same time, it requires BRCs to 'strengthen the building of a law-based and honest government, and establish a binding mechanism for implementing international agreements' (Xi 2024). Domestically, the political conditions of the BRI include improving policy services to strengthen support and the CPC's leadership in promoting the BRI (Xi 2024), which is not surprising since the Communist Party is the defining feature of Chinese socialism.

'Soft connectivity' conditions

Vision and Actions 2023 points out that the BRI considers the '"soft connectivity" of rules and standards as an important support'. 'Soft connectivity' refers mainly to the connectivity of rules and standards, including alignment with relevant international rules and standards and those in BRCs, the exchange of information in a broad sense and connectivity of laws, regulations, certification, accreditation and so on. It also emphasises institutional opening, which is a new policy to accelerate China's integration with international rules, standards and regulations.

Security conditions

This policy condition focuses on foreign investment and overseas infrastructure construction. The emphasis on risk and security in Vision and Actions 2023 is far greater than in the 2015 document. Vision and Actions 2015 only contained the policy condition of risk warning, response and disposal in the financial supervision section, and pointed out that it was necessary to 'improve the institutional arrangements for risk response and crisis disposal, build a regional financial risk early warning system, and form an exchange and cooperation mechanism for cross-border response and crisis disposal' (NDRC et al. 2015). Vision and Actions 2023 proposes to

> coordinate and strengthen risk prevention and control, establish and improve the … security system … guide enterprises to enhance the awareness and ability of risk prevention and control, effectively do a comprehensive risk assessment before 'going out', regulate overseas business behaviours, and strengthen risk source control.

Notably, it also emphasises policies on international anticorruption cooperation, to continuously promote the in-depth development of international anticorruption cooperation, insist that all international cooperation operates in a transparent way, launch the 'High-Level Principles for a Clean BRI', establish a … compliance evaluation system for the BRI corporations, and cooperate in research and training on a clean BRI, and work with all parties to build a clean Silk Road. (Office of the Leading Group for Promoting the Belt and Road Initiative 2023)

Financial conditions

The financial conditions are key to the sustainable development of the BRI. Policy conditions in the financial sector involve investment, financing, insurance, credit and related financial regulation and risk control systems, emphasising improvement of 'the financial cooperation mechanism' and expanding 'channels for investment and financing'.

Legal conditions

Vision and Actions 2023 proposes building an international legal service system for the BRI, which was not in the Vision and Actions 2015, including

> establishing an international commercial dispute settlement mechanism, promoting the construction of international commercial arbitration centres, participating in international rulemaking, strengthening the construction of foreign-related legal service institutions, promoting joint construction … of a legal database for BRCs, and strengthening international legal exchanges and cooperation. (Office of the Leading Group for Promoting the Belt and Road Initiative 2023)

Personnel conditions

Vision and Actions 2023 adds a call to 'strengthen the cultivation of international talent' to support the BRI, proposing the establishment of

> a scientific and effective mechanism for selecting and employing talent, strengthen the cultivation of talent in key areas of the BRI cooperation, build an international and interdisciplinary team of talent, improve the talent introduction system and the permanent residence system for foreigners, and create a good working and living environment to attract high-level overseas talent. (Office of the Leading Group 2023)

Organisational conditions

The Leading Group for Promoting the Belt and Road Initiative is at the core of the organisational conditions. At the 2018 symposium on the fifth anniversary of promoting the BRI, President Xi said:

> The Leading Group for Promoting the BRI should play a leading role in coordinating various regions and departments in accordance with the unified deployment of the Central Committee of the CPC. The group should clarify work priorities, refine work plans, decompose tasks at all levels, strengthen supervision and inspection, and promote the implementation of relevant deployments and measures one by one. (Xi 2024)

Cooperation mechanism conditions

With the deepening of the BRI, the establishment and improvement of all mechanisms are essential for the sustainable development of the initiative, including mechanisms for bilateral and multilateral cooperation, investment and financing, dispute settlement, risk early warning, prevention and control and emergency response.

Challenges ahead

While China has established a policy system for the BRI, the policies still face many challenges from geopolitics, participating countries and China itself.

Geopolitical challenges and competition

First, the global economic and political environments are becoming increasingly complex and uncertain, geopolitical games are deepening, ideological competition is becoming increasingly fierce, regional conflicts persist and the trend towards deglobalisation continues. The BRI includes several regions where great-power competition is most intense, such as the Indo-Pacific and Central Asia. The uncertainty of the geopolitical game has increased the complexity of global economic risks and international cooperation, which has brought serious challenges to the implementation of BRI policies. For example, in the context of the conflicts between Russia and Ukraine and Palestine and Israel, even if those states have signed cooperation agreements on the BRI, the wars have inevitably affected the advancement of the BRI in those countries. Second, the BRI has been criticised since it was first proposed in relation to the debt trap, economic dependence, exporting China's development model, corruption, environmental damage, lack of transparency and so on, though most criticisms lack solid scientific evidence. This has caused some countries to doubt China's intentions with the BRI and lowered their enthusiasm for cooperation, which hinder implementation of the initiative. Third, in the context of great-power competition, after the BRI was first proposed, major developed countries successively came up with similar plans, intending to compete with the BRI, including the 'Blue Dot Network' plan, a global infrastructure plan led by the United States, Japan and Australia, in 2019; the 'Build Back a Better World (B3W)' plan launched by the United States at the 2021 G7 summit to support infrastructure financing in developing countries; the 'Global Gateway' plan launched by the European Union in 2021; and the Indo-European Economic Corridor agreement, signed by the United States, India and other countries at the G20 summit in 2023. Since such plans focus on high-quality infrastructure construction and investment, they will inevitably (and intentionally) compete with the BRI, thereby weakening the international influence and policy attractiveness of the latter.[11]

---

11 Given alternative options are available, developing countries may to some extent benefit from the competition between the BRI and other international cooperation plans.

Challenges from participating countries

As most of the BRCs are developing countries,[12] they are in a period of political, economic and social transformation and development. There is great political uncertainty and often even social unrest. The institutional environment and the national governance capacity are relatively weak, and corruption is rife in some. Therefore, the implementation of the BRI in these countries faces greater challenges and uncertainties. There are more than 150 BRCs globally, with different levels of socioeconomic development and varying institutional environments, cultural backgrounds and histories. Research has shown that different institutional arrangements and cultural heritage carry different incentive effects, transaction costs and government effectiveness, which also increase the difficulty and complexity of international cooperation (Luo and Li 2023). For example, many countries have poor legal systems and low levels of free trade. There are still many trade and investment barriers between countries, including the implementation of relatively strict access licence systems, lack of harmonisation of customs procedures and inconsistent infrastructure construction standards and norms—all of which have hindered trade liberalisation and investment facilitation and brought huge challenges to the 'soft connectivity' of rules and standards under the BRI.

Challenges from the Chinese side

The BRI is a complex project and the construction of its policy system requires detailed planning. As the high-quality development of the BRI enters a new stage, construction of systematic mechanisms has become an endogenous demand (Li 2023). This includes mechanisms for demonstration before a project is launched, investment and financing at the beginning of a project, supervision during project operation, early warning and prevention of risks, dispute settlement, emergency response and so on, as well as coordination and connection between the various mechanisms to ensure sustainable development of the BRI.

Multilateral cooperation mechanisms must be promoted and deepened. Currently, dialogue and communication on the BRI rely mainly on bilateral mechanisms. Several multilateral cooperation platforms in professional fields have been established, including the Alliance of International Science Organizations, the Belt and Road International Lawyers Association, the BRI International Green Development Coalition, the Belt and Road Initiative Tax Administration Cooperation Mechanism and the Belt and Road Studies Network. The depth of cooperation and breadth of participation of these platforms, however, must be strengthened to advance the 'soft connectivity' of rules and standards. In this regard, Vision and Actions 2023 proposes to 'continue to build a complex international cooperation architecture led by the Belt and Road Forum

---

12 World Bank statistics show that nearly 80 per cent of the BRCs have economies below the middle-income level (Zhang 2023).

for International Cooperation and supported by bilateral, tripartite and multilateral cooperation mechanisms', indicating the role of the BRI forum will be strengthened in the future.

A financial policy system to support the BRI has not yet been formed and financial security must be strengthened. Although great achievements have been made in financial integration, the financial sustainability of the BRI faces a series of challenges, including limited financing channels, high costs of financial resources, stringent financing requirements, lack of a credit and insurance support system and lack of means for financial risk resolution.

The BRI has raised the demand for international legal services. However, China faces a lack of talent in this area, insufficient legal service institutions and a lack of integration with international standards. In addition, the BRCs are a diverse group with different legal systems, adding difficulties to international legal services in the BRI.

Talent is key to the development of the BRI. Infrastructure connectivity requires skilled craftspeople and international project management talent; free trade and financial integration require professional service talent such as in international economics and trade, law, finance, taxation and information consultancy. In terms of policy communication and people-to-people ties, strong and cross-cultural communication capabilities are much needed. The lack of relevant talent has led to problems such as imperfect international intermediary service organisations and professional service capabilities. The training of international talent and introduction of relevant supporting policies must be improved.

Discussion and implications

The analysis in this chapter shows that the BRI policy system is relatively complete. China is aiming to be more proactive and ambitious in its international cooperation under the BRI. The objective of the 'modernisation of all countries in the world' will be attractive to developing countries. The policy instrument of 'five connectivities' has become increasingly stable and the system of policy conditions has been continuously improved. The BRI policy system plays an increasingly important role in the high-quality development of the BRI although challenges remain.

Current BRI policies remain biased towards government guidance even though Vision and Actions 2023 emphasises coordinating the forces of government and markets to 'adhere to the principle of "enterprises as the mainstay, market operation, government guidance and international rules" to fully stimulate the enthusiasm of all parties to participate in the BRI'. Sustainable development of the BRI will ultimately depend on international cooperation under market mechanisms. Enterprises, especially in the private sector, should be given a greater role because they have a better understanding of market needs and can allocate resources more effectively than governments.

Therefore, the cultivation of market forces and encouraging market mechanisms to play a leading role will be an essential transformation for BRI policy development in the future.

References

Balding, C. 2018. 'Why Democracies Are Turning against Belt and Road.' *Foreign Affairs*, 24 October. www.foreignaffairs.com/articles/china/2018-10-24/why-democracies-are-turning-against-belt-and-road.

Chen, J., Y. Fei, P.T. Lee, and X. Tao. 2019. 'Overseas Port Investment Policy for China's Central and Local Governments in the Belt and Road Initiative.' *Journal of Contemporary China* 28, no. 116: 196–215. doi.org/10.1080/10670564.2018.1511392.

de Soyres, F., A. Mulabdic, S. Murray, N. Rocha, and M. Ruta. 2019. 'How Much Will the Belt and Road Initiative Reduce Trade Costs?' *International Economics* 159: 151–64. doi.org/10.1016/j.inteco.2019.07.003.

Faiz, A. 2019. 'Is China's Belt and Road Initiative Undermining Human Rights?' *The Diplomat*, 7 June. thediplomat.com/2019/06/is-chinas-belt-and-road-initiative-undermining-human-rights/.

Fukuyama, F. 2016. 'Exporting the Chinese Model.' *Project Syndicate*, 12 January. www.project-syndicate.org/magazines/china-one-belt-one-road-strategy-by-francis-fukuyama-2016-01.

Li, X. 2023. 'Path Selection for High-Quality Development of the Belt and Road: A Framework for Theoretical Analysis.' *Economic Perspectives* 10: 3–14.

Luo, Z., and Q. Li. 2023. 'Ten Years of the "Belt and Road Initiative" (BRI): Current Status of International Research and Prospects for Future Research.' *Economic Perspectives* 10: 15–23.

McGregor, R. 2022. 'Exporting the China Model.' *American Purpose*, 6 April. www.americanpurpose.com/articles/exporting-the-china-model/.

National Development and Reform Commission, Ministry of Foreign Affairs, and Ministry of Commerce. 2015. *Vision and Actions on Jointly Building the Silk Road Economic Belt and the 21st-Century Maritime Silk Road*. Beijing: National Development and Reform Commission, Ministry of Foreign Affairs, and Ministry of Commerce of the People's Republic of China. eng.yidaiyilu.gov.cn/p/1084.html.

Office of the Leading Group for Promoting the Belt and Road Initiative. 2019. *The Belt and Road Initiative: Progress, Contributions and Prospects*. Beijing: Foreign Language Press.

Office of the Leading Group for Promoting the Belt and Road Initiative. 2023. *Vision and Actions to Unswervingly Promote Deepening and Solidifying the High-Quality Development of the BRI: The Development Prospects of the BRI in the Next Decade*. Beijing: Office of the Leading Group for Promoting the Belt and Road Initiative. www.yidaiyilu.gov.cn/p/0F1IITOI.html.

Rothwell, R. 1985. 'Reindustrialization and Technology: Towards a National Policy Framework.' *Science and Public Policy* 12, no. 3: 113–30. doi.org/10.1093/spp/12.3.113.

State Council Information Office (SCIO). 2023. *The Belt and Road Initiative: A Key Pillar of the Global Community of Shared Future*. Beijing: State Council Information Office of the People's Republic of China. english.scio.gov.cn/whitepapers/2023-10/10/content_116735061.htm.

Sutherland, D., J. Anderson, N. Bailey, and I. Alon. 2020. 'Policy, Institutional Fragility, and Chinese Outward Foreign Direct Investment: An Empirical Examination of the Belt and Road Initiative.' *Journal of International Business Policy* 3, no. 3: 249–72. doi.org/10.1057/s42214-020-00056-8.

Xi, Jinping. 2024. *Xi Jinping on the Belt and Road Initiative*. Beijing: Central Party Literature Press.

Zhang, K. 2023. 'Can the Belt and Road Initiative Promote the Industrialization of Developing Countries?' *Global Journal of Emerging Market Economies* 15, no. 2: 215–33. doi.org/10.1177/09749101231167447.

12

Analysing the impact of China–Africa agricultural trade on rural transformation in Africa: An application of the gravity model

Siying Jia and Yu Sheng

Introduction

Agricultural exports have emerged as a pivotal driver of rural transformation in developing countries. By exporting primary agricultural products, developing countries obtain foreign exchange that not only allows imports and investments that stimulate economic growth, but also increases the possibility of boosting rural employment and incomes and reducing rural poverty (Dawson 2005; Valdes 1991; Maertens and Swinnen 2014). Consequently, agricultural exports from developing countries have seen a remarkable 199 per cent increase, reaching US$550 billion in value since 2004, surpassing the 135 per cent rise in exports from developed nations (Gillson et al. 2015). Moreover, developing countries at the forefront of agricultural exports, such as Brazil and Argentina in Latin America and China and India in Asia, have achieved significant accomplishments in rural transformation, confirming the pivotal role of agricultural exports in economic growth.

Over the past two decades, China and African countries have significantly strengthened bilateral cooperation in various fields, such as culture, economics and trade, contributing to the rapid growth of agricultural trade. Starting in the 1990s, the value of African agricultural exports to China surged from US$150 million to US$2.76 billion, in 2016, showcasing an impressive average annual growth rate of 12.4 per cent (UN Comtrade 2024). This substantial expansion of agricultural exports has been fostered by factors including increasing demand in China, complementarity in agricultural production between China and Africa, Africa's growing agricultural production capacity and the implementation of favourable trade policies (Sun et al. 2007; Zhang and Jie 2011; Gaogui 2014).

However, as the total volume continues to increase, the value added (net gain) of African agricultural exports to China has not shown significant change. The average value-added proportion of exports significantly declined, from 22.8 per cent in 1992 to 16.4 per cent in 2021 (World Bank 2023b), which was very different to the growth of export volumes. Few studies have examined African agricultural exports from the perspective of its value added, and most of those that have are focused on global value chain (GVC) theory. They suggest that the African agricultural sector's participation in GVCs is widely underestimated and significantly impacted by major trade drivers such as free-trade agreements and trade frictions (Balié et al. 2019; Fusacchia et al. 2022; Johnson and Noguera 2017). However, the existing literature does not examine whether and how African agricultural exports to China affect the value added and rural transformation they partly represent, and the specific role of China's demand, which can only be answered through in-depth analyses at the value-added level.

To fill the gaps in previous research, this chapter endeavours to unravel the impact of Chinese demand on African agricultural exports with a focus on its impact on the value added of those exports. We utilise data covering 41 African countries from 1992 to 2021, examining both aggregate and selected commodity-level data. The gravity model is employed as our empirical tool to, first, analyse agricultural exports from Africa to China and their determinants. We then decompose the change in value added of agricultural exports into two separate components, structural change and industrial upgrading change, to better understand the sources of the change in value added.

We find that, contrary to our general understanding, while Chinese demand promoted an increase in African agricultural export volumes, it did not help the growth of the value added of those exports. Further results after decomposition analysis show that China's increased food demand favoured relatively high-value commodities, leading to a positive composition effect. However, this is offset by the negative upgrading effects caused by constrained African agricultural production capacity. Bilateral trade policies also led to negative composition and positive upgrading effects.

The remainder of this chapter is organised as follows. Section two briefly discusses recent developments in China–Africa agricultural trade at both gross value and value-added levels, followed by a discussion of exports of selected commodities. Section three discusses the literature on the gravity model to be used and presents the model specification and estimation strategy. Section four presents a detailed description of the data source and variable definitions. Section five presents the main empirical results and their policy implications, while section six provides the conclusions.

Background for analysis

China–Africa agricultural trade and its value added

Although favourable relationships between China and African countries began to build in the 1960s, trade in agricultural products between the two did not show significant increases until 1990. Agricultural trade between China and Africa has since grown rapidly. The total volume of China–Africa agricultural trade increased from US$640 million in 1992 to US$7.68 billion in 2016, with an annual growth rate of 12.4 per cent. Specifically, agricultural exports from Africa to China increased significantly, from US$150 million in 1992 to US$2.76 billion in 2016 (UN Comtrade 2024) (Figure 12.1). Along with the increase in total exports, the product structure of Africa's agricultural exports to China has changed, with the proportion of high-value products gradually increasing. At the end of the twentieth century, Africa's main agricultural exports to China were lac (natural gum or resins) and raw unprocessed cotton. However, as we can see in Figure 12.2, the main exports have changed to high-value agricultural products such as oil seeds and tobacco, accounting for 34 per cent and 24 per cent, respectively, of total African exports.

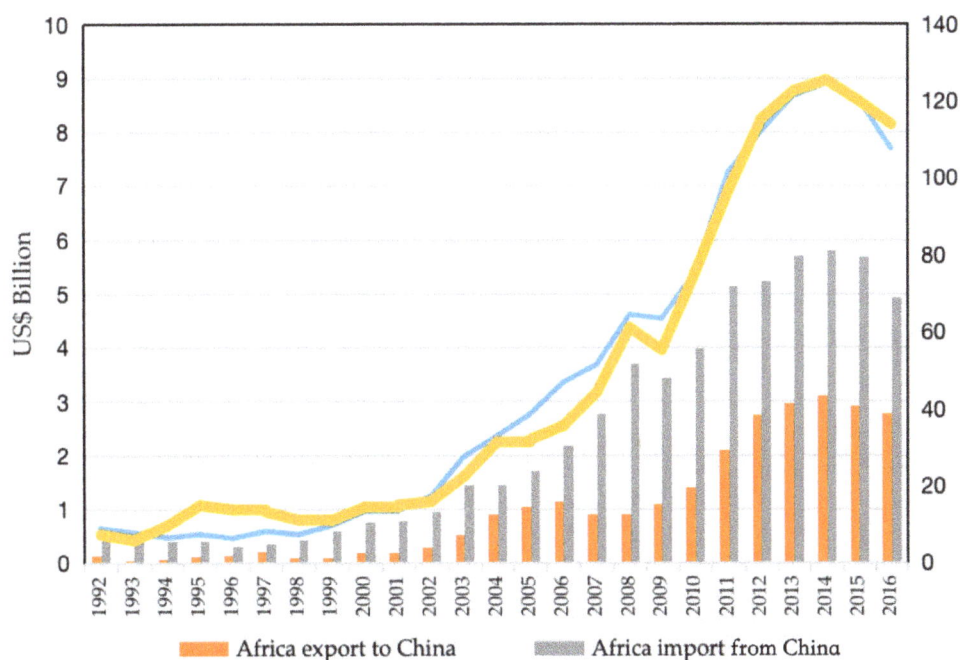

Figure 12.1 African agricultural exports to China (US$ billion, constant price)
Source: UN Comtrade (2024).

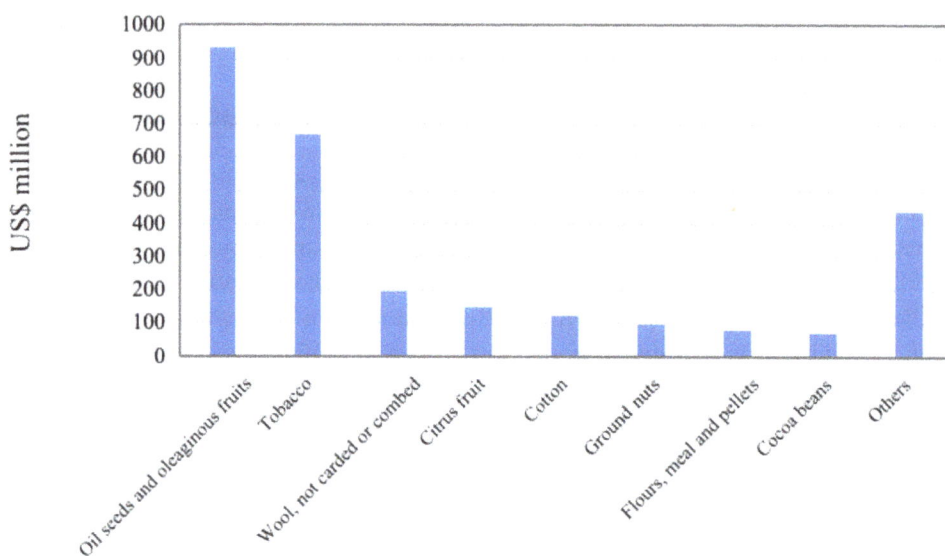

Figure 12.2 Exports of agricultural commodities from Africa to China, 2016 (US$ million)
Source: UN Comtrade (2024).

China's demand for agricultural products was an important driver of this rapid growth in exports. Since 1992, China's total agricultural imports have increased from US$7.43 billion to US$113.9 billion, with an annual growth rate of 443 per cent, providing a huge consumer market for African agricultural products. Moreover, the impact of Chinese demand on African agricultural exports is consistent with the comparative advantage of agricultural production between China and Africa. More specifically, Africa has a strong comparative advantage in cocoa, cotton lint, tea and tobacco compared with the rest of the world, which complements Chinese demand as it has gradually lost its comparative advantage in those commodities (Rao et al. 2020).

Moreover, variations in Chinese demand for different commodities shape the trajectory of African agricultural exports. High demand for cashew nuts in China demonstrates significant growth potential, impacting the livelihoods of smallholder farmers and industry workers in Tanzania (BFAP et al. 2017). Coffee, while experiencing remarkable growth, showcases the adaptability of smallholder farmers who navigate the complexities of the market through cooperatives and unions. Sesame, fuelled by the expansive Chinese market, not only contributes substantially to total export value but also positions African smallholder farmers to receive considerable benefits (UN Comtrade 2024). In contrast, the scenario for exports of cotton yarn is more nuanced, with a surge in export value until 2013, followed by a decline. While China's future demand for cotton yarn is anticipated to increase, the limited participation of smallholder farmers in its production poses challenges for achieving widespread benefits. The intricate interplay between small farms, demand dynamics and varied commodity outcomes underscores the complexities of African agricultural exports. Due to the differences in the value-added characteristics of each commodity, examination of the use of commodity-level data on African agricultural exports to China becomes crucial.

Although gross exports from Africa to China are on the rise, their value added has not significantly increased, particularly when examining the proportion of value added per unit of export. During the past 30 years, total agricultural value added increased from US$93.2 billion in 1992 to US$372.4 billion in 2021, achieving an average annual growth rate of 10 per cent (World Bank 2023b) (Figure 12.3). However, the average value-added share of GDP has seriously declined, from 22.8 per cent in 1992 to 16.4 per cent in 2021, and countries that once had a high value-added share have suffered from more severe decreases (for example, Burundi's value-added proportion has dropped from 59.3 per cent to 35.2 per cent and Ethiopia's from 66.0 per cent to 30.5 per cent) (Figure 12.4). In conclusion, while total exports have increased, there has been a decline in value added, which is crucial for future bilateral trade policymaking.

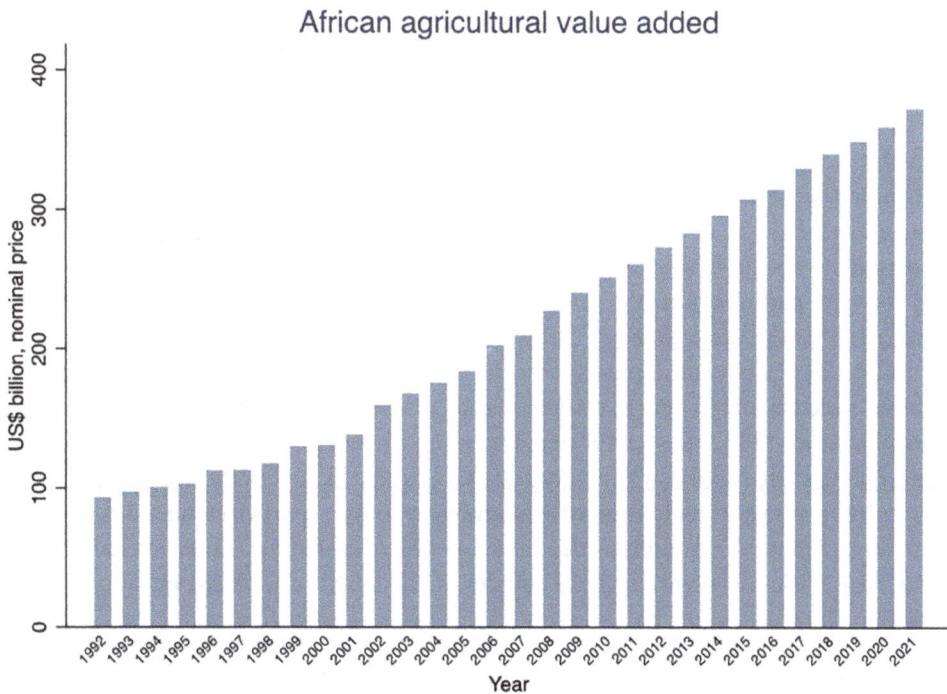

Figure 12.3 Value added of Africa–China agricultural exports, 1992–2021 (US$ billion, constant prices)

Source: World Bank (2023b).

African agricultural value added (share of GDP US$, 2015 prices)

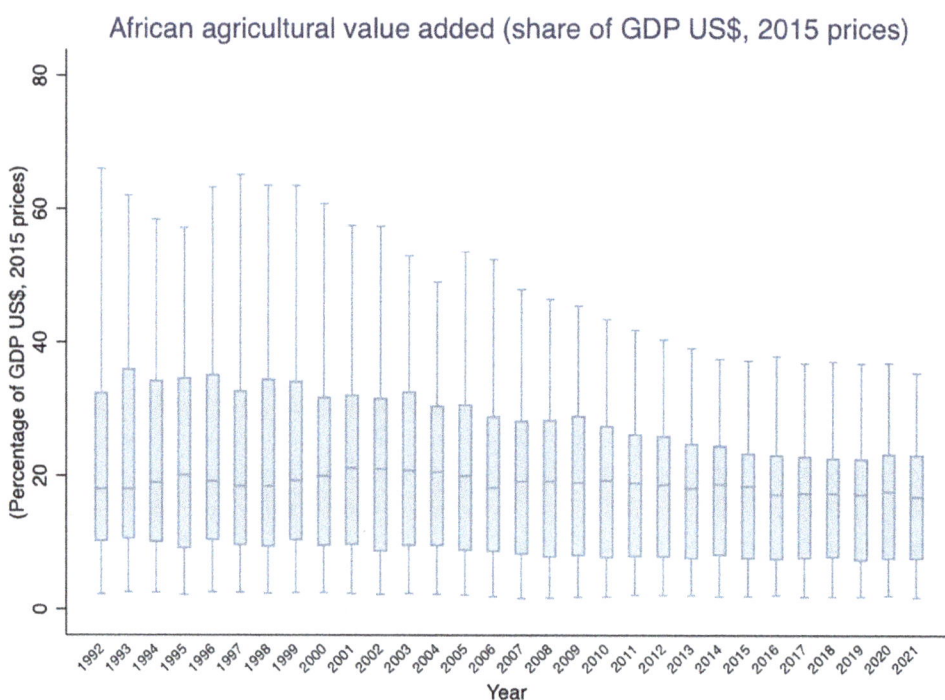

Figure 12.4 Value-added proportion of Africa–China agricultural exports (per cent)
Source: World Bank (2023b).

Few studies have examined the impact of bilateral agricultural trade on African agricultural value added. Balié et al. (2019) analysed the value added of African agricultural and food trade from the GVC perspective. Using value added to calculate the backward and forward participation of African agricultural and food sectors in GVCs, they concluded that the value added of African agricultural trade was widely underestimated by traditional trade measurements. In addition, by evaluating trade patterns in terms of value-added structure and extra-regional or intra-regional destinations, research by Fusacchia et al. (2022) suggested that free-trade agreements could have a significant impact on the value added of African agricultural trade. However, the existing literature did not fully answer the question of why the increase in exports to China did not also increase the value added and how this phenomenon is related to Chinese demand. This poses the question of identifying the sources of changing value added in exports from Africa to China.

In addition to growing demand in China, various other factors have driven the rapid development of agricultural trade between China and Africa. The first is the increase in Africa's agricultural production capacity. Total agricultural output in African countries (approximated by the real gross output value) has significantly increased, particularly after 2001 (Figure 12.5). Between 2001 and 2013, the average annual growth rate of agricultural output was 12 per cent a year (FAO 2019). The second factor is the improved political and economic bilateral relationships between China and Africa. Particularly since the Forum on China–Africa Cooperation (FOCAC) in 2000, China has encouraged imports from African countries. The Chinese Government has also encouraged its SOEs to make direct investments to establish factories in developing countries like Tanzania. Since most of these companies exported their products back to China, the growing access to cheap African labour and the Chinese Government's financial support have significantly reduced production costs, thereby promoting an increase in exports.

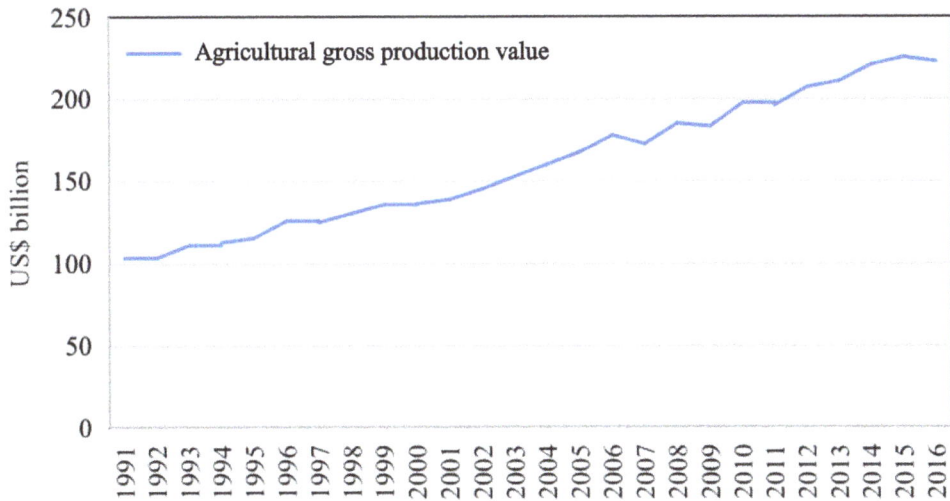

Figure 12.5 Real gross output value of African agricultural production, 1991–2016
Source: FAO (2019).

Gravity model and empirical specifications

The gravity model, originating in Newton's law of universal gravitation in physics, is not just a comprehensive set of economic theories, but also an important empirical tool in international trade. On the one hand, James E. Anderson (1979) published 'A Theoretical Foundation for Gravity Equation' that first established the theoretical principle of a gravity model. Subsequent theoretical contributions to the gravity model have been made to incorporate it into the system of classical economics (Anderson and van Wincoop 2003; Baldwin and Taglioni 2006; Helpman et al. 2008; Baier and Bergstrand 2009). On the other hand, in addition to original trade flows, the gravity model has been used in empirical studies to investigate increases in flows of migration, net assets, FDI and so on (Karemera et al. 2000; Okawa and van Wincoop 2012; Gopinath and Echeverria 2004). Multiple explanatory variables have been introduced into the empirical model, including population, per capita income, exchange rates, membership of economic organisations, common boundaries, common language and culture and so on (Linnemann 1996; Leamer 1974; Bergstrand 1985, 1989; Wei 1996).

As 'probably the most successful empirical trade device' (Anderson 1979: 106), the gravity model has been used as the main empirical tool for analysing determinants of value added in international trade. Balié et al. (2019) applied a structural gravity model to reveal the impact of trade policies on the participation of sub-Saharan Africa in agriculture and food GVCs. Based on a decomposition of the bilateral gross exports in terms of value-added content, they found import tariffs and regional trade agreements influenced not only the total amount of trade, but also the backward and forward participation of trade partners in GVCs. Johnson and Noguera (2017) used a multi-sector structural gravity model with input–output linkages to examine the decline in the ratio of value added to gross exports. They showed that changes in trade friction had a significant impact on both global and cross-regional value-added declines.

The basic empirical model specification in this chapter follows Linnemann (1996) and Anderson and van Wincoop (2003) (Equation 12.1).

Equation 12.1

$$\ln F_{ijt} = \alpha \ln M_{it} + \beta \ln M_{jt} + \gamma \ln D_{ij} + \delta \ln X_{ijt} + u_{ij} + v_{jt} + \varepsilon_{ijt}$$

In Equation 12.1, $\ln F_{ijt}$ is the natural logarithm of the value of country j's exports to country i at time t. This is the dependent variable to analyse the total amount and value added of agricultural exports from African countries to China. $\ln M_{it}$ and $\ln M_{jt}$ are the natural logarithms of time-varying importer-specific and exporter-specific variables, for which we use the income levels of exporting African countries and China. To examine the influence of Chinese demand on African agricultural exports, we also treat $\ln M_{it}$—a proxy for Chinese food consumption and demand—as our main independent variable. $\ln D_{ij}$ is the natural logarithm of distance between capitals or major ports in the two countries, i and j. X_{ijt} is a vector set that helps explain other variables in bilateral trade between two countries, including tariffs, exchange rates and trade costs between country i and country j. Both country-paired fixed effects (u_{ij}) and time fixed effects (v_{jt}) are controlled.

In addition to Chinese demand, we are interested in whether African agricultural production capacity and bilateral trade policy have any impact on agricultural exports to China. We therefore add two other independent variables: $\ln P_{jt}$, which represents the natural logarithm of the agricultural output of country j, and a dummy variable, T_{jt}, which takes a value of one if country j forms a bilateral preferential trade relationship with China in year t. Thus, our baseline model can be rewritten as Equation 12.2.

Equation 12.2

$$\ln F_{ijt} = \alpha \ln M_{it} + \beta \ln M_{jt} + \gamma \ln D_{ij} + \theta \ln P_{jt} + \mu T_{jt} + \delta \ln X_{ijt} + u_{ij} + v_{jt} + \varepsilon_{ijt}$$

In Equation 12.2, α, β, γ, θ, μ and δ are the parameters to be estimated and we are particularly interested in α, θ and μ; ε_{ijt} is the random error.

To analyse the role of Chinese demand, African domestic production capacity and favourable bilateral policies on both the total amount of and the value added to exports, and further identify the source and channel of those impacts, our baseline model Equation 12.2 contains three specification forms.

First, we examine the impacts of Chinese demand, African domestic production capacity and favourable bilateral policies on African agricultural exports to China. We focus on whether these three independent variables have played a different role in terms of the value added of exports. For these purposes, we estimate model specification one.

Specification 1: Examining the impact of Chinese demand on African agricultural exports and value added to exports (Equation 12.3).

Equation 12.3

$$\ln EX_{ijt} = \beta_0 + \beta_1 \ln D_{ij} + \beta_2 \ln CGDPPC_{it} + \beta_3 \ln GDPPC_{jt}$$
$$+ \beta_4 \ln GPV_{jt-1} + \beta_5 \ln REER_{jt} + \beta_6 FOCAC_{jt}$$
$$+ \beta_7 Port_{jt} + \beta_8 RD_{jt} + \beta_9 Tariff_{jt} + u_{ij} + v_{jt} + \varepsilon_{ijt}$$

In Equation 12.3, i represents China, j indicates major African countries that export selected agricultural commodities to China; t is the year (t = 1992, 1993, …, 2021); EX_{ijt} is the gross export value to China of country j at time t; D_{ij} is the distance between the capitals of China and country j; $CGDPPC_{it}$ is China's GDP per capita, which represents China's demand-side shock that we care about most; $GDPPC_{jt}$ is GDP per capita of country j at time t; GPV_{jgt-1} indicates gross agricultural output in year $t-1$ of country j, which represents African agricultural production capacity. $REER_{jt}$ is the real effective exchange rate of country j at time t; $FOCAC_{jt}$ is a dummy variable that means if country j at time t has joined FOCAC, the value of the data will be one, which means the country is a member of FOCAC at time t, otherwise it will be zero. RD_{jt} represents the length and density of operational railways in country j at time t; $Port_{jt}$ is a dummy variable that represents whether the country has a seaport at time t; and $Tariff_{jt}$ is the tariff charged by Chinese customs on agricultural export commodities.

To understand the role of the three major independent variables in terms of value added to exports, we modify Equation 12.3 into Equation 12.4 by changing the dependent variables into value added to exports.

Equation 12.4

$$\ln VA_{ijt} = \beta_0 + \beta_1 \ln D_{ij} + \beta_2 \ln CGDPPC_{it} + \beta_3 \ln GDPPC_{jt}$$
$$+ \beta_4 \ln GPV_{jt-1} + \beta_5 \ln REER_{jt} + \beta_6 FOCAC_{jt} + \beta_7 Port_{jt}$$
$$+ \beta_8 RD_{jt} + \beta_9 Tariff_{jt} + u_{ij} + v_{jt} + \varepsilon_{ijt}$$

In Equation 12.4, VA_{ijt} is agricultural value added.

Second, we analyse the impact of trade determinants on the proportion of value added to exports, as it can better reflect the structural changes of agricultural exports and we are interested in whether the impact differs from total exports and basic value added.

Specification 2: Examining the impact of Chinese demand on exports of agricultural commodities with different proportions of value added (Equation 12.5).

Equation 12.5

$$\ln VA\%_{ijt} = \beta_0 + \beta_1 \ln D_{ij} + \beta_2 \ln CGDPPC_{it} + \beta_3 \ln GDPPC_{jt}$$
$$+ \beta_4 \ln GPV_{jt-1} + \beta_5 \ln REER_{jt} + \beta_6 \ln FOCAC_{jt}$$
$$+ \beta_7 Port_{jt} + \beta_8 RD_{jt} + \beta_9 Tariff_{jt} + u_{ij} + v_{jt} + \varepsilon_{ijt}$$

In Equation 12.5, $VA\%_{ijt}$ is the proportion of value added in the total exports of country j at time t.

Last, by conducting the above empirical exercises, we can form a full picture of the impacts of Chinese demand, African production capacity and FOCAC trade policy on both export value and the level of value added. However, the results do not tell us how these impacts are generated. To get a better understanding of the sources of changing value added in exports, we decompose the impact into two separate channels. On the one hand, structural shifts in commodity exports would trigger a composition effect. Take Ethiopia's sesame seed industry as an example: when the share of sesame seeds (a relatively high-value product) in total agricultural exports to China increases, it promotes the total value added of Ethiopia's agricultural exports and causes a positive composition effect. On the other hand, within the same industry, changes in that commodity's value-added proportion would also produce an industrial upgrading (or degrading) effect. When Ethiopia's sesame farmers increase their productivity through timely planting and broadcasting, and more effective pest control protocols, or they gain increasing access to affordable credit, the value-added proportion of the industry's exports increases, leading to a positive industrial upgrading effect. The composition effect and upgrading effect interact and form the real effect of exports on value added—the one we can observe and measure in reality.

To measure both the composition effect and the upgrading effect, we should employ the export structure of all agricultural products from Africa to China and data on industrial upgrading. However, due to data constraints, we can only estimate the effect by adding a selected commodity-level exercise, which takes the form of model specification three (Equation 12.6).

Specification 3: Identify the sources of changing value added in exports by adding a selected commodity-level exercise.

Equation 12.6

$$\ln EX_{ijgt} = \beta_0 + \beta_1 \ln D_{ij} + \beta_2 \ln CGDPPC_{it} + \beta_3 \ln GDPPC_{jt}$$
$$+ \beta_4 \ln GPV_{jgt-1} + \beta_5 \ln REER_{jt} + \beta_6 \ln FOCAC_{jt} + \beta_7 Port_{jt}$$
$$+ \beta_8 RD_{jt} + \beta_9 Tariff_{jgt} + u_{ijg} + v_{jgt} + \varepsilon_{ijgt}$$

In Equation 12.6, g represents five selected commodities (sesame, cashew nuts, coffee, cotton yarn and lac); EX_{ijgt} represents the gross export value of commodity g to China by country j at time t; GPV_{jgt-1} represents the gross agricultural output of commodity g in year t–1 of country j; and $Tariff_{jgt}$ represents the tariffs charged by Chinese customs on commodity g.

Based on the estimated results of the commodity level in Equation 12.6, we can decompose the changes in value added of agricultural exports into two parts: the composition effect and the upgrading effect. First, the composition effect is calculated by a commodity-level aggregation of multiplying the impact of each trade determinant (Chinese demand, African production capacity and bilateral trade policy, which will be referred to as an external shock in Equation 12.7) on the value added of commodity k's exports by the export proportion of commodity k within the total exports of five selected commodities. Because we lack the value-added data at the commodity level, we estimate the impact by multiplying the impact of trade determinants on commodity k's export value (which is β_2 in Equation 12.6) by the value-added proportion of commodity k. The mathematical expression for the above calculation is Equation 12.7.

Equation 12.7

$$Composition\ Effect_{\_shock} = \sum_{k} \left(\beta_{\_shock\_k} * VA\_share_{\_k} * k\_share \right)$$

In Equation 12.7, $\beta_{\_shock\_k}$ represents the estimated effect of different *shocks* (Chinese demand, African production capacity and bilateral trade policy) on commodity k; $VA\_share_{\_k}$ represents the value-added share of commodity k; and k_share represents the export share of commodity k.

As we discussed earlier, the upgrading effect can be calculated using the overall effect minus the composition effect (Equation 12.8).

Equation 12.8

$$Upgrading\ Effect_{\_shock} = Real\left(Estimated\right)Effect_{\_shock} - Composition\ Effect_{\_shock}$$

Moreover, to estimate the model, we must cope with some potential econometric problems. For the 'zero' problems of the gravity model, we follow the traditional methods to replace the zero trade value with a minimal value of 0.00001. In addition, for the endogeneity problem that could occur when using an OLS regression, we employ a fixed-effects model with controls for both country-paired fixed effects and year fixed effects. However, given our approach is relatively simple, the regression results could still be affected by the aforementioned issues. Because we focus only on the positives and negatives of our estimation rather than the magnitude, the impact of those problems will not be too severe.

Data source and variables definition

This study uses unbalanced panel data on agricultural export flows, income, distance, geographical information and a few other group-specific measures. This dataset deliberately focuses on 41 of the 56 African nations[1] engaged in agricultural exports to China, collectively accounting for more than 70 per cent of Africa's total agricultural exports to China (UN Comtrade 2024), which can be considered representative to a certain extent. Covering the period 1992–2021, the data enable a comprehensive analysis of trends over nearly three decades.

Our primary dependent variables include export values (both aggregate and commodity level), value added and the proportion of agricultural value added. Export values from each country to China come from the UN Comtrade database, measured in US dollars and deflated using the US consumer price index for urban areas (1982 price). The value-added data for African countries are from World Bank (2023b) national accounts data, measured as their gross output value minus intermediate input value. Since agricultural export commodities account for most of the agricultural production sector in Africa (Valdes 1991), we use the aggregate agricultural value added instead of aggregating the value added of individual products, sourced from World Bank Open Data. Agricultural value added per unit of export is calculated by dividing the agricultural value added for each African country by its corresponding export values. Both the value added and its proportion are measured and deflated in the same way. Our independent variables include Chinese demand, African production capacity and bilateral trade policy. For Chinese demand, we use China's GDP per capita in 2023 US dollars from the *World Development Indicators* (World Bank 2023a). African countries' agricultural production capacity is indicated by their gross production value (constant 2004–06 US dollars) from the Food and Agriculture Organization database. Favourable trade policies are indicated by a FOCAC membership dummy variable from official FOCAC documents. The values of all variables are deflated in the same way.

For our commodity-level exercise, we select five key commodities—sesame, cashew nuts, coffee, cotton yarn and lac—based on their collective significance, as they constitute more than one-third of all agricultural exports from Africa to China. This selection ensures a complete representation of essential trading partners in Africa–China agricultural trade, contributing to a thorough understanding of the factors involved.

Other control variables come from data sources including the UN Comtrade database, *World Development Indicators* (World Bank 2023a), Infoplease (2019), *Bruegel Datasets* (Bruegel 2018), Google Maps, the UN Trade and Development *Trade Analysis*

---

1   Aggregate exports: Algeria, Angola, Benin, Botswana, Burkina Faso, Burundi, Cabo Verde, Cameroon, Central African Republic, Republic of Congo, Côte d'Ivoire, Egypt, Ethiopia, Gabon, Gambia, Ghana, Guinea, Kenya, Lesotho, Libya, Madagascar, Malawi, Mali, Mauritania, Mauritius, Morocco, Mozambique, Namibia, Niger, Nigeria, Rwanda, Senegal, Seychelles, South Africa, Togo, Tunisia, Uganda, Tanzania, Zambia, Zimbabwe. Cashew nuts: Benin, Republic of Congo, Côte d'Ivoire, Egypt, Mali, Nigeria, Togo, Tanzania. Coffee: Burundi, Democratic Republic of Congo, Ethiopia, Kenya, Malawi, Rwanda, South Africa, Uganda, Tanzania, Zambia. Sesame: Benin, Burkina Faso, Djibouti, Eritrea, Ethiopia, Kenya, Mali, Mozambique, Nigeria, Senegal, Somalia, Togo, Uganda, Tanzania. Lac: Chad, Republic of Congo, Djibouti, Egypt, Eritrea, Ethiopia, Ghana, Kenya, Madagascar, Mali, Niger, Nigeria, Somalia, Sudan, Togo, Tanzania, Zambia. Cotton yarn: Egypt, Ethiopia, Lesotho, Mozambique, South Africa, Uganda, Tanzania, Zimbabwe.

Information System (UNCTAD 2023), import and export tariffs for 1992–2021 (China Customs 2023) and Darvas (2012). The financial system is indicated by real effective exchange rates based on 2007 US dollars; infrastructure investment is represented by African countries' railway density and a dummy variable, *Port* (whether the African country has a seaport); and Chinese import tariffs on the commodity represent the tariff. Table A12.1 (Appendix) provides more details on the data and their sources.

Empirical results and analyses

Impacts on African agricultural exports and their value added

In this section, we use a gravity model to examine the impacts of Chinese demand, African production capacity and bilateral trade policy on African agricultural exports and value added. The estimation results based on the aggregate-level data are presented in Table 12.1. Columns (1)–(2), (3)–(4) and (5)–(6) of Table 12.1 present the estimation results of export value, value added and value-added proportion, respectively. Columns (1), (3) and (5) provide the OLS estimates, and the others present the fixed-effects estimates, where the country-paired fixed effects and time fixed effects are utilised to address potential bias.

We start by focusing on the impact of Chinese demand. We demonstrate that China's GDP per capita has a positive impact on African agricultural exports to China. After accounting for sample selection bias and heteroscedasticity, the coefficient remains at a positive and significant 2.599 under the fixed-effects model, which indicates that a 1 per cent increase in Chinese demand would trigger a 2.599 per cent increase in total exports. Our results are consistent with the existing literature. For instance, Li and Huang (2016) found that a 1 per cent increase in Chinese demand corresponds to a 2.02 per cent growth in African agricultural exports, aligning closely with our findings. The analysis using these models indicates that China's increasing demand played an essential role in increasing African agricultural exports.

In contrast, our analysis reveals that the increase in Chinese demand could have a negative impact on the growth of the value added of African agricultural exports. When applying the fixed-effects model, the estimated coefficient for China's GDP per capita turns negative and is not statistically significant. This suggests that, when considering sample selection bias and heteroscedasticity issues, Chinese demand appears to exert a negative influence on export value added, though the precision of the estimated impact is uncertain.

Moreover, this negative impact of Chinese demand can be further demonstrated by the estimation results on the value-added proportion of exports. As illustrated in column (6) of Table 12.1, the fixed-effects estimated coefficient for China's GDP per capita is –0.169 and turns statistically significant at the 1 per cent level. Our results, as Figure 12.6 shows, indicate that Chinese demand has significantly stimulated exports of agricultural products from Africa yet fails to promote the value-added growth behind export value—the reason for which is the major interest of our further analysis.

Table 12.1 Estimated determinants of Africa–China bilateral trade: Aggregate

	Aggregate					
	(1)	**(2)**	**(3)**	**(4)**	**(5)**	**(6)**
	EX	EX	VA_value	VA_value	VA_shr	VA_shr
	OLS	FE	OLS	FE	OLS	FE
lnD	−3.964***	-	−1.359***	-	−0.322***	
	(1.437)	-	(0.112)	-	(0.089)	
lnCGDPPC	1.879***	2.599***	0.005	−0.009	−0.002	−0.169***
	(0.693)	(0.854)	(0.057)	(0.051)	(0.045)	(0.034)
lnGPV_m	0.905***	0.239	0.649***	0.386***	0.020**	0.243***
	(0.146)	(0.936)	(0.014)	(0.097)	(0.010)	(0.085)
FOCAC	0.010	1.549*	−0.282***	0.036	−0.116***	−0.052
	(0.925)	(0.847)	(0.037)	(0.041)	(0.0342)	(0.043)
lnGDPPC	0.036	0.711	0.230***	0.322***	−0.713***	−0.053
	(0.245)	(1.469)	(0.020)	(0.116)	(0.0181)	(0.080)
lnREER	0.284	2.107	0.179**	−0.186	0.329***	-
	(0.916)	(1.599)	(0.075)	(0.128)	(0.0704)	-
Tariff	−12.65***	−0.555	−0.725	−0.054	−1.687***	−0.524*
	(4.574)	(6.400)	(0.443)	(0.303)	(0.323)	(0.268)
Port	0.842*	-	0.227***	-	0.268***	-
	(0.446)	-	(0.0384)	-	(0.0340)	-
RLD	0.966***	4.560*	−0.387***	0.174	−0.0846***	0.107
	(0.349)	(2.439)	(0.0406)	(0.119)	(0.0326)	(0.231)
_cons	25.95	−35.86***	8.974***	−2.055**	10.64***	4.175***
	(17.58)	(12.13)	(1.405)	(0.777)	(1.112)	(0.871)
No.	955	955	880	880	955	955
R²	0.448	0.512	0.851	0.738	0.786	0.399

FE = fixed effects
OLS = ordinary least squares
* $p < 0.1$
** $p < 0.05$
*** $p < 0.01$
Note: Standard errors in parentheses.
Source: Authors' own estimations.

As for African production capacity, the estimation results imply that, although its growth does not have a significant impact on total exports, it significantly increases both value added and its proportion of exports. The coefficients of columns (4) and (6) are 0.386 and 0.243, respectively, and all are significant under the fixed-effects model, which indicates that a 1 per cent increase in African agricultural production capacity would trigger a 0.386 per cent increase in total value added and a 0.243 per cent growth in the proportion of value added.

Estimated Effect on Gross Export and Value Added

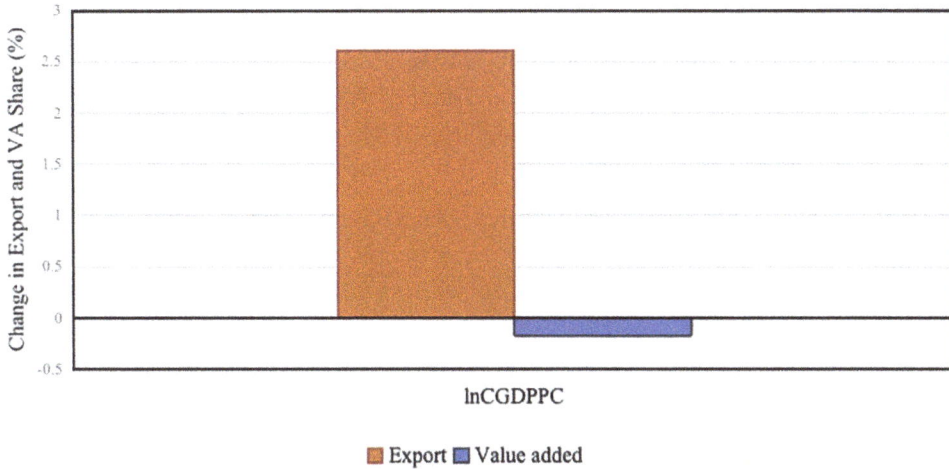

Figure 12.6 Impact of Chinese demand on African agricultural exports and value added to exports
Source: Authors' own estimations.

Last, the results show that FOCAC membership has a positive influence on the value of African agricultural exports. When it comes to value added, however, the impact is offset. The coefficients in columns (2), (4) and (6) are 1.549, 0.036 and –0.052, respectively, under the fixed-effects model, which indicate that FOCAC membership will trigger only a 1.549 per cent increase in total exports and has no significant impact on value added.

Combining the results, we argue that African production capacity not only positively influences the gross value of African agricultural exports to China, but also significantly stimulates the value-added proportion of those exports. However, although China's increasing demand plays an essential role as a trigger of African agricultural exports, it may have a negative impact on the growth of value added, which leaves a puzzle that needs further exploration. To determine the causes, we move to identifying the sources of change for the value-added proportion of African agricultural exports.

Change in value added to African agricultural exports to China and its decomposition

Following the decomposition method mentioned in the previous section, we combine the estimation results from that section with a commodity-level regression. This regression's results on export value are presented in Table 12.2. Columns (1)–(2), (3)–(4), (5)–(6), (7)–(8) and (9)–(10) of Table 12.2 present the estimation results for, respectively, sesame, cashew nuts, coffee, cotton yarn and lac. Columns (1), (3), (5), (7) and (9) of the table provide the OLS estimates and the others present the fixed-effects estimates, where the country-paired fixed effects and time fixed effects are utilised to address potential bias.

As shown in Table 12.2, the estimation results among different commodities are heterogeneous. For Chinese demand, positive impacts are observed for sesame, cashew nuts and lac; negative impacts are witnessed for coffee and cotton yarn. For African production capacity, positive impacts are witnessed for sesame and coffee; negative impacts are witnessed for cashew nuts and cotton yarn. For bilateral trade policy, positive impacts are witnessed for coffee and negative impacts are witnessed for sesame, cashew nuts, cotton yarn and lac.

Table 12.2 Estimated determinants of Africa–China bilateral trade: By selected commodity

	Five selected commodities									
	Sesame		Cashew nuts		Coffee		Cotton yarn		Lac	
	(1)	(2)	(3)	(4)	(5)	(6)	(7)	(8)	(9)	(10)
	OLS	FE	OLS	FE	OLS	FE	OLS	FE	OLS	FE
Dependent variable: Export value(ln)										
lnD	0.554		-35.790	-	-15.510	-	-43.400***	-	-16.780***	-
	(3.113)		(46.220)	-	(20.650)	-	(14.590)	-	(2.542)	-
lnCGDPPC	5.594***	4.291**	7.171***	8.009	1.3160	-27.370	-11.930***	18.060	6.176***	13.010
	(1.185)	(1.539)	(2.455)	(3.398)	(4.057)	(37.320)	(3.297)	(29.980)	(1.176)	(9.586)
lnGPV_m	1.646***	0.988	-0.448	-0.142	1.283	1.060	-4.396**	-3.313	-	-
	(0.291)	(0.835)	(0.911)	(0.388)	(0.990)	(0.825)	(1.480)	(2.194)	-	-
FOCAC	0.640	-0.287	-1.845	-6.430	3.338	89.56	-13.35**	-111.6	-5.124**	-37.38
	(1.491)	(1.691)	(5.156)	(10.02)	(5.534)	(122.4)	(5.685)	(76.95)	(2.202)	(29.07)
lnGDPPC	-1.574*	0.775	3.137	2.463	2.321	4.496	10.48***	15.62*	-2.080***	-0.778
	(0.934)	(1.647)	(3.085)	(2.446)	(1.531)	(3.171)	(2.598)	(4.953)	(0.495)	(1.433)
lnREER	-1.572	-3.047	0.993	0.756	1.378	-1.533	-2.535	-7.193	0.397	-0.314
	(1.385)	(3.437)	(1.163)	(0.607)	(2.435)	(4.571)	(3.398)	(7.128)	(0.775)	(1.257)
Tariff	-0.358		-	-	-5.994*	-	5.482	-	-3.545***	-
	(0.992)		-	-	(3.184)	-	(4.116)	-	(0.949)	-
Port	4.013**	-10.14	-2.937	-30.66*	2.351	-11.49	-11.74**	8.175*	4.855***	-8.167
	(1.775)	(10.83)	(4.640)	(10.36)	(1.614)	(27.56)	(4.813)	(3.269)	(1.242)	(6.042)
RLD	33.38**	16.46	17.03*	11.52	4.597	-1.513	-181.1***	-167.3	54.25***	-1.052
	(15.66)	(21.12)	(8.941)	(4.622)	(16.68)	(24.64)	(50.78)	(84.41)	(8.959)	(8.488)
_cons	-35.66	-18.74	278.9	-63.95***	116.4	162.0	521.8***	-131.9	128.4***	-76.11
	(30.78)	(22.52)	(450.1)	(5.111)	(215.0)	(225.0)	(170.3)	(222.3)	(23.68)	(64.16)
No.	258	258	78	78	129	129	102	102	358	358
R²	0.703	0.720	0.801	0.812	0.556	0.444	0.699	0.587	0.322	0.128

FE = fixed effects
OLS = ordinary least squares
* p < 0.1
** p < 0.05
*** p < 0.01
Note: Standard errors in parentheses.
Source: Authors' own estimations.

Then, following the method mentioned in the previous section, we begin to decompose the impact of Chinese demand on value added into the composition effect and the upgrading effect. In so doing, we first use the estimated coefficients of China's food demand on commodity k in Table 12.2, multiplying by k's export share of total selected commodities, to predict the structural change caused in agricultural exports. We then use the predicted export structure as a weight to aggregate the value-added proportion of each commodity to calculate the impact of China's food demand on average value added to agricultural exports through changing the commodity structure. Then, by isolating the composition effect from the overall impact, we unveil the industrial upgrading effect, which is difficult to observe directly in reality.

The decomposition results are presented in Figure 12.7. The red and the dark-blue bars represent the estimated effect (effects represented in Table 12.1) on total exports and on value added, respectively. The green and the light-blue bars represent the composition effect and the degrading effect, respectively, triggered by Chinese demand. On the one hand, Chinese demand contributes to a positive composition effect, which indicates that Chinese demand could favour high value-added commodities such as lac and cashew nuts. These results are also well supported by real-world data on Chinese demand (Table 12.3), as the exports triggered by this demand tend to lean more towards high-value-added products, while being less inclined towards exports of low-value-added products. On the other hand, demand also triggers a negative upgrading effect that offsets the positive composition effect caused by structural changes in export commodities, resulting in the significantly negative impact of Chinese demand on the value-added proportion of African agricultural exports to China.

Estimated composition and upgrading effect

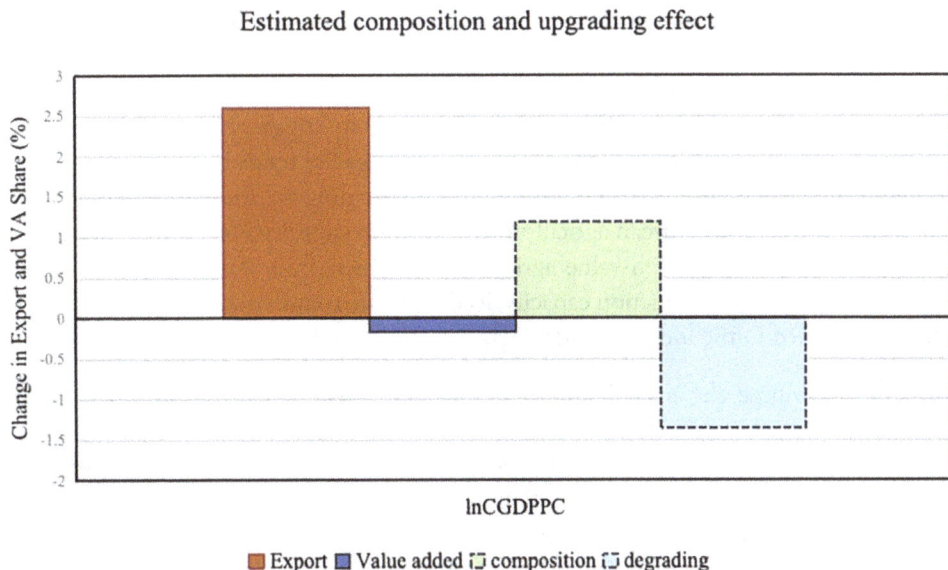

Figure 12.7 Change in value added of African agricultural exports to China and its composition

Source: Authors' own calculations.

Table 12.3 Export share and value-added share by commodity (per cent)

	Sesame		Cashew nuts		Coffee		Cotton yarn		Lac	
Year	Share	VA	Share	VA	Share	VA	Share	VA	Share	VA
1992	0	-	0	-	0	-	0	-	100.00	99.93
1995	0	-	0	-	0	-	0	-	100.00	99.93
1998	11.93	15.00	17.05	70.14	8.56	28.08	1.80	38.64	60.67	99.75
2001	10.15	15.49	10.38	70.68	4.11	28.91	22.29	40.24	53.06	99.76
2004	52.05	18.54	0.00	74.88	10.75	36.89	4.35	25.98	32.84	98.77
2007	95.77	18.21	0.65	73.85	0.39	37.24	0.81	28.88	2.37	99.77
2010	94.69	18.19	0.64	71.82	1.02	37.34	2.16	55.39	1.49	98.68
2013	94.67	16.12	0.71	71.99	0.83	34.00	2.87	54.47	0.92	99.11
2016	94.77	-	0.21	-	1.84	-	2.52	-	0.66	-
2019	88.02	-	1.18	-	5.63	-	1.40	-	3.78	-

VA = value added
Source: Authors' own estimations.

In summary, we discover that Chinese demand was causing a positive composition effect yet a negative upgrading effect on African agricultural exports. It is natural to wonder why the demand-side factor of Africa–China agricultural trade did not positively influence the growth of value added. We propose several possible explanations for this puzzle. First, our decomposition results are based on a partial equivalence gravity model, which means there could be other factors that we have not considered that are also affecting Africa's agricultural exports to China. More importantly, due to data constraints, there is no direct way of zooming in on the upgrading effect of exports, which is why we also include agricultural capacity to represent the supply-side impact and conduct a similar decomposition. The results are presented in Figure 12.8. We discover that, contrary to the Chinese demand-side impact, African production capacity triggers positive composition and upgrading effects, meaning that African supply capacity tends to trigger the export of high-value-added products and productivity upgrading of the entire agricultural industry. The results for African agricultural production capacity suggest that increasing demand from China for high-value agricultural products from Africa could, to some extent, surpass Africa's production capacity, leading to an overall decrease in productivity, which is reflected in the industry-wide degrading effect we have calculated.

We also decompose the overall impact of bilateral trade policy following the same method. The results are presented in Figure 12.8. We discover that membership of FOCAC, which indicates bilateral trade policies, turns the composition effect negative while the upgrading effect is positive. Following our previous interpretation, FOCAC trade policy tends to stimulate the increase in exports of low-value-added products. This indicates that, relative to market-driven forces on the demand side, trade policies are more inclined to encourage the export of products in which Africa has a comparative advantage, rather than those most in demand in China but with the greatest growth potential in African production.

Estimated composition and upgrading effect

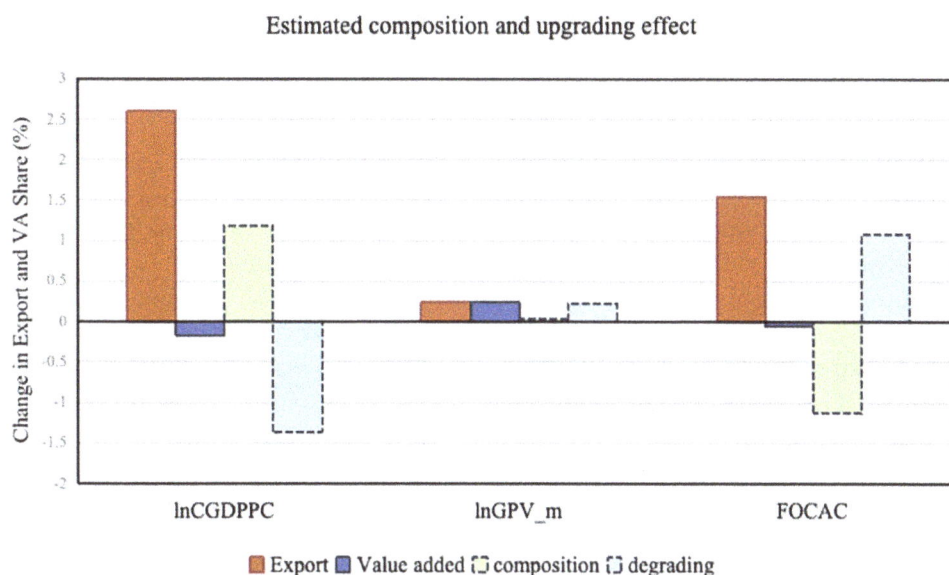

Figure 12.8 Various determinants: Composition and degrading effect
Source: Authors' own calculations.

Conclusions

This chapter aims to investigate the influence of China–Africa agricultural trade on rural transformation in Africa, with an emphasis on constructing the decomposition of the change in value added of agricultural exports based on commodity structure. The gravity model is used to analyse the factors influencing African agricultural exports, focusing especially on Chinese demand, African production capacity and bilateral trade policy through FOCAC. We then calculate the composition and upgrading effects based on the estimation results of the gravity model. To conduct the analysis, we utilised a country-trade paired panel dataset covering 41 African countries over the period 1992–2021.

We demonstrate that although increasing Chinese demand and FOCAC membership played essential roles as triggers for African agricultural exports, they could have a negative impact on the growth of value added to African agricultural exports. On the other hand, African production capacity not only positively influenced the gross value of African agricultural exports to China, but also significantly stimulated the value-added proportion of those exports. Moreover, our decomposition exercise indicates that the exports triggered by Chinese demand tend to lean more towards high-value-added products, causing a positive composition effect and a negative upgrading effect. A potential explanation we proposed is that the increasing demand from China for high-value agricultural products from Africa could, to some extent, surpass Africa's production capacity, leading to an overall decrease in productivity. The positive upgrading effect of increasing African production capacity to some extent supports that. In addition, the impact of trade policy is the opposite to that of Chinese demand, resulting in a negative structural composition effect and a positive industrial upgrading effect. These findings suggest that future trade policies should aim to enhance African agricultural production capacity to better align with Chinese demand. Only by doing so can we achieve more effective cooperation in agricultural trade, leading to mutually beneficial outcomes.

In summary, this study contributes to the understanding of Africa–China agricultural trade dynamics, shedding light on the multifaceted impacts of Chinese demand, African production capacity and bilateral trade policies. The findings pose intriguing questions for future research and policymaking, emphasising the need for a holistic approach that considers both demand-side and supply-side dynamics in shaping the trajectory of agricultural trade between Africa and China.

References

Anderson, James E. 1979. 'A Theoretical Foundation for Gravity Equation.' *The American Economic Review* 69, no. 1: 106–16.

Anderson, James E., and Eric van Wincoop. 2003. 'Gravity with Gravitas: A Solution to the Border Puzzle.' *American Economic Review* 93, no. 1: 170–92. doi.org/10.1257/000282803321455214.

Baier, Scott L., and Jeffrey H. Bergstrand. 2009. '*Bonus Vetus* OLS: A Simple Method for Approximating International Trade-Cost Effects Using the Gravity Equation.' *Journal of International Economics* 77, no. 1: 77–85. doi.org/10.1016/j.jinteco.2008.10.004.

Baldwin, Richard, and Daria Taglioni. 2006. *Gravity for Dummies and Dummies for Gravity Equations*. NBER Working Paper 12516, September. Cambridge: National Bureau of Economic Research. doi.org/10.3386/w12516.

Balié, Jean, Davide Del Prete, Emiliano Magrini, Pierluigi Montalbano, and Silvia Nenci. 2019. 'Does Trade Policy Impact Food and Agriculture Global Value Chain Participation of Sub-Saharan African Countries?' *American Journal of Agricultural Economics* 101, no. 3: 773–89. doi.org/10.1093/ajae/aay091.

Bergstrand, Jeffrey H. 1985. 'The Gravity Equation in International Trade: Some Microeconomic Foundations and Empirical Evidence.' *The Review of Economics and Statistics* 67, no. 3: 474–81. doi.org/10.2307/1925976.

Bergstrand, Jeffrey H. 1989. 'The Generalized Gravity Equation, Monopolistic Competition, and the Factor-Proportions Theory in International Trade.' *The Review of Economics and Statistics* 71, no. 1: 143–53. doi.org/10.2307/1928061.

Bruegel. 2018. *Bruegel Datasets*. Brussels: Bruegel. www.bruegel.org/datasets.

Bureau for Food and Agricultural Policy (BFAP), Sokoine University of Agriculture, and International Food Policy Research Institute (IFPRI). 2017. 'Prioritizing Policies for Driving Inclusive Ag Transformation: Tanzania Pilot Study Output 2: Value Chain Selection First Draft.'

Darvas, Zsolt. 2012. *Real Effective Exchange Rates for 178 Countries: A New Database*. Working Paper 2012/06. Brussels: Bruegel.

Dawson, P.J. 2005. 'Agricultural Exports and Economic Growth in Less Developed Countries.' *Agricultural Economics* 33, no. 2: 145–52. doi.org/10.1111/j.1574-0862.2005.00358.x.

Food and Agriculture Organization of the United Nations (FAO). 2019. *FAOSTAT: Food and Agriculture Data*. [Online]. Rome: FAO. www.fao.org/faostat/en/#home.

Forum on China–Africa Cooperation (FOCAC). 2004. *African Members of FOCAC*. [Online]. Beijing: FOCAC. www.focac.org/eng/ltjj_3/ltffcy/.

Fusacchia, I., J. Balié, and L. Salvatici. 2022. 'The AfCFTA Impact on Agricultural and Food Trade: A Value Added Perspective.' *European Review of Agricultural Economics* 49, no. 1: 237–84. doi.org/10.1093/erae/jbab046.

Gaogui, Xian, and Zhou Deyi. 2014. 'Analysis and Explanation of the Impact of Tariff-Free Policy on China–Africa Trade: Panel Data Analysis Based on Tariff-Free Agricultural Products.' *International Economic and Trade Exploration* 30, no. 4: 75–84.

General Administration of Customs of the People's Republic of China (China Customs). 2023. 'Customs Statistics.' *Data*. [Online]. Beijing: General Administration of Customs of the People's Republic of China. stats.customs.gov.cn.

Gillson, Ian John Douglas, and Amir Alexander Fouad. 2015. *Trade Policy and Food Security: Improving Access to Food in Developing Countries in the Wake of High World Prices (English)*. Washington, DC: World Bank Group. documents.worldbank.org/curated/en/203531468330023474/Trade-policy-and-food-security-improving-access-to-food-in-developing-countries-in-the-wake-of-high-World-prices. doi.org/10.1596/978-1-4648-0305-5.

Gopinath, M., and R. Echeverria. 2004. 'Does Economic Development Impact the Foreign Direct Investment–Trade Relationship? A Gravity-Model Approach.' *American Journal of Agricultural Economics* 86, no. 3: 782–87. doi.org/10.1111/j.0002-9092.2004.00625.x.

Helpman, Elhanan, Marc Melitz, and Yona Rubinstein. 2008. 'Estimating Trade Flows: Trading Partners and Trading Volumes.' *The Quarterly Journal of Economics* 123, no. 2: 441–87. doi.org/10.1162/qjec.2008.123.2.441.

InfoPlease. 2019. *Distance Calculator*. [Online]. Washington, DC: InfoPlease. www.infoplease.com/atlas/calculate-distance.html.

Johnson, R.C., and G. Noguera. 2017. 'A Portrait of Trade in Value-Added over Four Decades.' *Review of Economics and Statistics* 99, no. 5: 896–911. doi.org/10.1162/REST_a_00665.

Karemera, D., V.I. Oguledo, and B. Davis. 2000. 'A Gravity Model Analysis of International Migration to North America.' *Applied Economics* 32, no. 13: 1745–55. doi.org/10.1080/000368400421093.

Leamer, Edward E. 1974. 'The Commodity Composition of International Trade in Manufactures: An Empirical Analysis.' *Oxford Economic Papers* 26, no. 3: 350–74. doi.org/10.1093/oxfordjournals.oep.a041294.

Li, Hao, and Huang Jikun. 2016. 'China–Africa Agricultural Trade: Empirical Study on Development Status and Influencing Factors.' *Exploring Economic Issues*, no. 4: 142–49.

Linnemann, Hans. 1996. *Econometric Study of International Trade Flows*. Amsterdam: North-Holland Publishing Company.

Maertens, M., and J. Swinnen. 2015. *Agricultural Trade and Development: A Value Chain Perspective*. WTO Staff Working Paper, No. ERSD-2015-04. Geneva: World Trade Organization.

Okawa, Y., and E. van Wincoop. 2012. 'Gravity in International Finance.' *Journal of International Economics* 87, no. 2: 205–15. doi.org/10.1016/j.jinteco.2012.01.006.

Rao, S., X. Liu, and Y. Sheng. 2020. 'China's Agricultural Trade: A Global Comparative Advantage Perspective.' In *China's Challenges in Moving towards a High-income Economy*, edited by Ligang Song and Yixiao Zhou, 37–74. Canberra: ANU Press. doi.org/10.2307/j.ctv1zcm2t6.9.

Sun, Dongsheng, Liu Heguang, and Zhou Ailian. 2007. 'The Structure and Characteristics of China–Africa Agricultural Trade.' *China's Rural Economy*, no. 11: 15–25.

United Nations Commodity Trade Statistics Database (UN Comtrade). 2024. *UN Comtrade Database*. [Online]. comtradeplus.un.org/.

United Nations Trade and Development (UNCTAD). 2023. 'Data, Statistics and Trends in International Trade.' *UNCTAD Trade Analysis Information System (TRAINS)*. [Online]. Geneva: UNCTAD. unctad.org/topic/trade-analysis/data-statistics-and-trends.

Valdes, A. 1991. 'The Role of Agricultural Exports in Development.' In *Agriculture and the State: Growth, Employment and Poverty in Developing Countries*, edited by C. Peter Timmer, 84–115. Ithaca, NY: Cornell University Press. doi.org/10.7591/9781501737954-005.

Wei, S.J. 1996. *Intra-National Versus International Trade: How Stubborn Are Nations in Global Integration?* NBER Working Paper 5531. Cambridge: National Bureau of Economic Research. doi.org/10.3386/w5531.

World Bank. 2023a. *Databank: World Development Indicators*. [Online]. Washington, DC: World Bank Group. databank.worldbank.org/source/world-development-indicators.

World Bank. 2023b. 'Indicators.' *Data*. [Online]. Washington, DC: World Bank Group. data.worldbank.org/indicator.

Zhang, Haisen, and Xie Jie. 2011. 'Determinants and Potential of China–Africa Agricultural Trade: An Empirical Study Based on the Gravity Model.' *International Trade Issues*, no. 3: 45–51.

Appendix A

Table A12.1 Description of the main variables in this chapter

Variables	Indicator	Data resource
Trade flow value	Export value (US$)	UN Comtrade (2024)
Value added in export	Gross output value minus intermediate input value (US$)	World Bank (2023b)
Distance	Distance between capitals of two countries (kilometres)	InfoPlease (2019)
GDP per capita	GDP per capita (current US$)	World Bank (2023a)
Financial system	Real exchange rate (based on 2007 US$)	Bruegel (2018)
Infrastructure investment	Operational railway density (kilometres per 100 square kilometres)	World Bank (2023a)
Infrastructure investment	Seaport (whether the country has a seaport)	Google Maps
Tariff	Tariff	UNCTAD (2023); China Customs (2023)
FOCAC	Membership of FOCAC	FOCAC (2004)
Output value	Gross production value (constant 2004–06 US$)	FAO (2019)

Index

www.ingramcontent.com/pod-product-compliance
Lightning Source LLC
Chambersburg PA
CBHW080130270326
41926CB00021B/4414